Ireland, Germany and the Nazis

GW00587181

Ireland, Germany and the Nazis

Politics and Diplomacy, 1919–1939

MERVYN O'DRISCOLL

FOUR COURTS PRESS

This book was set in 10.5 on 12.5 pt Ehrhardt
by Mark Heslington, Scarborough, North Yorkshire for
FOUR COURTS PRESS LTD
7 Malpas Street, Dublin 8, Ireland
www.fourcourtspress.ie
and in the United States for
FOUR COURTS PRESS
c/o ISBS, 920 N.E. 58th Avenue, Suite 300, Portland, OR 97213.

A catalogue record for this title is available from the British Library.

ISBN 978-1-84682-657-3

First published 2004
Second edition 2017

Printed in Ireland
by SPRINT-Print, Dublin.

Contents

In loving memory of Muriel

Preface to the Second Edition

When Germany sneezes, Europe catches a cold. Europeans will appreciate this revision of a familiar adage, as it possesses some truth. German developments have reverberated even in the more distant Atlantic periphery, from the commencement of the twentieth century.

Ripening Great Power antagonisms before 1914, World War I, the interwar international order, and World War II all revolved around the 'German question'. They shaped the wider environment in which the Irish nation-state germinated and consolidated. Ireland was indelibly imprinted by these developments and changes. Its leaders and representatives had to take positions on the evolving German question and its impact on the European setting, and evaluate their implications for Ireland. The German question, in effect, defined Ireland to a degree that is neglected in Irish public and historical debates. It has been refracted through the lens of Anglo-Irish relations.

Irish public and historical discourses, of course, often rehearse or review a handful of selected Irish-German highlights. These include Roger Casement's ultimately failed and tragic efforts to secure German support for the Easter Rising (1916). Then it is frequently recalled that the initial passages of the Proclamation of the Irish Republic, read by Pádraig Pearse on the steps of the General Post Office on 24 April 1916, asserted that revolutionary Ireland was supported 'by gallant allies in Europe'. This was a reference to imperial Germany fighting Britain in the Great War. There is also some Irish recognition of the German part in the early efforts of the Irish state to industrialise, most memorably in the Siemens-Schuckert company's construction of the landmark Ardnacrusha hydroelectric power station in the 1920s. The epochal paintings of the construction of the facility by Seán Keating are forever associated with the enterprise. The unreceptive attitude of independent Ireland to Jews fleeing Nazi Europe is also remembered. Many are aware of Charles Bewley, the Irish representative in Berlin from 1933 to 1939, who was anti-Semitic and an apologist for the Nazi regime. The outlawed Irish Republican Army's (IRA) efforts to coordinate with German intelligence services during World War II against Britain are part of the national memory. Eamon de Valera's government interned IRA suspects and a number of German agents as an imminent danger to Irish neutrality. Public controversies still rage about the circumstances, import and connotations of de Valera's expression of condolences on the death of the German head of state, Adolf Hitler, to the German diplomatic representative in May 1945. Thus, when *Ireland, Germany and the*

Nazis was first published in 2004, there tended to be a limited appreciation of the wider and deeper state of Irish-German diplomatic and political relations.

The objective in 2004 was to provide a comprehensive historical account of the relationship as it progressed in time, within a broad international context. It was hoped it would appeal to Irish, German and international readers as not only a case study of Ireland's early foreign relations and of small-state diplomacy, but also an alternative perspective to the dominating Irish-British one of that period. This was the formative period for independent Ireland as it struggled to project an international identity in the undefined interwar world. No systematic scholarly account of Ireland's bilateral relationship with a mainland European state was available in English at that point. Horst Dickel, Jürgen Elvert and some others had laid some advantageous groundwork in the German language. However, their otherwise valuable work occurred before the opening up of the Irish state archives in the early 1990s. *Ireland, Germany and the Nazis* illuminated the budding diplomatic and political relationship by drawing heavily on government and other records in Ireland, and, to a lesser extent, in Germany. Apart from offering a diplomatic history of Irish-German relations, it also provided an account and analysis of the trading connections.

Although trained as a diplomatic and political historian, I discovered in the course of research that commercial calculations were eternally influential in contacts between states. Trade normally possesses political overtones, but trade diplomacy is often treated as the poor cousin, rather than the partner, of political diplomacy, in the field of international history. Commercial questions often take up the lion's share of diplomats' time. Trade and money, after all, are major sinews of power and independence. It was no different in the case of early Irish emissaries and diplomats stationed in Germany. Paradoxically, this hardly registered in the Irish accounts of interwar relations with Germany and other states, other than Britain. However, the historical record revealed that successive Irish administrations identified Germany as the potential European counterweight to Ireland's dependence on the British market.

Ireland's main trading interest in Germany was to export cattle. This predated the outbreak of the Anglo-Irish Economic War in 1932. Germany's need to re-establish itself as an exporter and earn foreign currency after World War I meant that it presented an attractive trading partner for Ireland. Pragmatism drove both the Irish and German sides of the commercial relationship. Ireland had the weaker hand; it needed Germany more than Germany needed Ireland, except in the early and mid-1920s, when Germany was seeking re-integration with, and rehabilitation by, the rest of the world.

In contrast to most works of Irish diplomatic and political history, *Ireland, Germany and the Nazis* also recognised the importance of socio-cultural links and shared historical memory. This was inescapable in light of Irish efforts to employ cultural connections and the diaspora to construct compelling arguments in support of Ireland's separatist claims and identity. The Celtic

Church's evangelisation in Europe during the Dark Ages, particularly in German-speaking regions, was evoked in diplomatic efforts to legitimise Ireland's claim to a special association or friendship with Germany. Indeed, some key early Irish diplomatic personnel were Celtic Studies scholars educated in Germany. The department of external affairs, and other ministries of the Irish government, were alive to the advantages of engaging in public diplomacy in Germany and other countries. Irish agents and diplomats exploited any historical and cultural connections they could draw on to build some influence in other states and societies. As a small state, Ireland relied heavily on what 'soft power' it possessed; it barely had a hard-power footprint.

In 2016, when the possibility of revising *Ireland, Germany and the Nazis* arose, I began to take stock of recent publications with a view to updating the text. In the period since the book's publication in 2004 there has been a vigorous output of material on Irish-German and German-Irish relations, generally. A notable quantity of this is the progeny of Dr Gisela Holfter and Dr Joachim Fischer, who instituted the Centre for Irish-German Studies at the University of Limerick and Maria Immaculata College, Limerick, in 1997. Their initiative has been fruitful. The centre has successfully drawn together a national and international network of scholars, especially in the areas of intercultural studies, literature, media analysis, business and economics. An impressive suite of publications has emerged from the centre's endeavours, and its annual conference sheds light on many aspects of Irish-German Studies across a broad time period. The centre has made a pronounced contribution in the field of literature, travellers' accounts and cultural connections. One of the centre's perennial aims has been the collection and publication of the personal histories, oral testimonies and biographies of German-speaking refugees and exiles who came to Ireland fleeing Nazi persecution after 1933. In this regard, the centre has performed an indispensable service in tracking down and personalising the human costs of Nazi totalitarianism and racialism. Its work collecting the life stories and experiences of the few individuals who managed to surmount Ireland's unwelcoming attitude – particularly towards Jews – after 1933 leads one to speculate that Ireland might have saved many more Jewish lives, and those of other minorities and opponents of Nazism, had it found the courage, will and humanity to do so. The hidden histories of exiles and refugees unearthed by the Centre for Irish-German Studies confirm the findings and conclusions of *Ireland, Germany and the Nazis*, as well as the seminal work of Dermot Keogh in the field of Ireland's Jewish-refugee policy.

The recent work of discovering and publishing life histories and biographies pertinent to *Ireland, Germany and the Nazis* ranges further though. Kevin McCarthy's *Robert Briscoe* exposes the noteworthy life and career of this Dublin republican, who played a key role in the IRA during the War of Independence, most notably in running arms from Germany to Ireland. He figures as a perennial personality in Irish-German relations after 1919. Briscoe became the sole

Jewish member of Dáil Éireann when he was elected a Fianna Fáil TD in 1927. He held a Dáil seat in south Dublin without a break until 1965, and had a close but complex relationship with Eamon de Valera. Briscoe became a supporter of the physical-force Zionist movement in 1938, once he began to appreciate the plight of the Jews in Nazi Germany. McCarthy's biography partially unveils how the Briscoe-de Valera relationship may have influenced de Valera and Ireland's policy on Jewish refugees.

There are several other recent biographies that illuminate the lives of people who appear in the pages of *Ireland, Germany and the Nazis*. Especially captivating is Gerry Mullins' *Dublin Nazi no. 1*. Mullins has produced a revealing account of the life and career of Adolf Mahr, which draws on official and publicly available sources. Notably, it benefits from privileged access to Mahr's offspring and some of the personal papers in their possession. Mahr was the Austrian archaeologist who became director of the National Museum of Ireland. He is sometimes referred to as the founder of modern (i.e., scientific) archaeology in Ireland. He has also acquired a degree of infamy, because he became the unrivalled senior Nazi in Ireland before 1939. Mullins' sympathetic account humanises Mahr. It reveals his traditional German nationalist motivations, as well as his complexity on matters such as Nazi policy towards Jews.

Another recent biography of interest is Tom Garvin's *The lives of Daniel Binchy*. It fills out our appreciation of the formation, outlook and academic career of perhaps the greatest Celtic Studies scholar of his generation. He spent a spell engaged in Irish diplomacy in Germany (1929 to 1932). Julius Pokorny was a fellow Celtic Studies scholar and philologist who also played a significant role in Irish-German relations after 1919. He educated some of the new generation of Celtic Studies scholars, supported Irish nationalist causes and eventually fell foul of the Nazis' anti-Semitic policies. He took over Kuno Meyer's chair of Celtic at the University of Berlin in 1920, but was later suspended and dismissed from his post by the Nazis. This impelled him to seek Dublin's assistance. Pól Ó Dochartaigh's fine biography of Pokorny combines intellectual history with life history and political history. David O'Donoghue's *The Devil's Deal* is also a useful accompaniment. It opens up the life of Jim O'Donovan, who was a crucial figure in organising the IRA's 'S' (sabotage) bombing campaign against Britain during 1939 and 1940. That brought the IRA to the attention of the Abwehr (German intelligence), leading to his appointment as the IRA's liaison with German intelligence in 1939. O'Donoghue's biography profited from extensive cooperation from Jim O'Donovan's offspring, including access to his notes and unpublished memoir. In sum, there are several recent works of biography that enrich our appreciation of some of the people involved in aspects of Irish-German relations after 1919. However, none of the new books or new evidence from personal papers fundamentally alters the narrative and conclusions of *Ireland, Germany and the Nazis*.

The contribution of one author, however, deserves particular acknowledgement. Christopher Sterzenbach's detailed exploration of German-Irish relations during the Weimar Republic is to a considerable degree complementary. His research is rigorous and methodical, but it is written mainly from the German, as opposed to the Irish, perspective. Sterzenbach draws on exhaustive research in the German archives. He does a magnificent job, but he doesn't shake my conclusions, and usually confirms them. For instance, Sterzenbach concludes that Binchy lacked instructions from Dublin, but he tried to influence Ireland's German policy and contributed to clarifying the rights of the self-governing dominions for the German public, and he succeeded in stimulating German interest in Ireland. The degree to which he was able to influence Weimar policy towards Ireland was limited, though. Sterzenbach also pays useful attention to the emergence of trade as an important factor in the relationship. However, he has approached the subject from Weimar's, rather than Saorstát Éireann's (the Irish Free State's), perspective.

Overall, *Ireland, Germany and the Nazis*, as a study of the interwar bilateral relationship from the Irish state perspective, has stood the test of time so far. No new bodies of evidence or alternative analyses have been forthcoming that challenge its narrative or its findings, even though several complementary works have appeared that enhance our wider understanding of some of the protagonists, and of the period.

I wish to thank those who have materially assisted or supported the publication of this edition. I am especially grateful to Sam Tranum and Four Courts Press for printing the book in paperback. I would also like to extend my thanks to Dr Donal Corcoran and Professor Matthew MacNamara for their care in helping to track down errors in the original text. My thanks also to Dr Michael Kennedy for identifying recent literature of relevance.

Preface

Independent Ireland may not have been in the cockpit of European power politics but it could not escape its repercussions. A reading of a standard Irish history textbook gives little impression of Irish involvement in major European, indeed global matters, in the first half of the twentieth century, except insofar as these directly related to the Irish national project. The average person might be forgiven for concluding that Irish governments lived in some hermetically sealed and introverted self-made Irish world and lacked any position on the central question preoccupying Europe after World War I, that is, Germany's place in the European order.

Undoubtedly, the acquisition of independent statehood and the process of nation-building (and state-building) was a major preoccupation of Irish government during the period between 1919 and 1939. Admittedly, the redefinition of the Irish relationship with Britain was the central lens through which Irish governments viewed international politics. Nonetheless, it had noteworthy relationships with many states other than Britain, members of the British empire-commonwealth and the USA, as a country of major Irish immigration. This book instead turns the focus towards Germany.

In undertaking postgraduate research on this general area in the early 1990s and in returning to the subject more recently, I have become indebted to many individuals and institutions who have offered me advice and support. Firstly, I thank my present colleagues at University College Cork (Professor Dermot Keogh, Dr Geoffrey Roberts, Dr Donal Ó Drisceoil, Dr Andrew Bielenberg, Dr Andrew McCarthy, Gabriel Doherty), and my former colleagues at the University of Wolverhampton (Gordon Niven, Michael Haynes) who all provided me with unstinting encouragement and vibrant intellectual debate. Many others also generously offered their time and expertise in tracking down references and facilitating debate. In particular Dr Mark Hull, Dr Michael Kennedy, the late Commandant Peter Young, Professor Eunan O'Halpin, Finín O'Drisceoil, Robert Patterson, Niall Keogh, Dr Joseph Skelly and Commandant Victor Laing.

Ms Celia Weston acted as an invaluable copyeditor and proofreader. Celia Weston's and Michelle O'Mahony's sharp eyes and incisive comments on several drafts of the text facilitated the reduction of the original manuscript into a readable and more concise form. Yann Kelly-Hoffman of Cover to Cover did a magnificent job in completing the index. Michael Adams, Martin Fanning, Anthony Tierney, Ronan Gallagher and all the staff of Four Courts Press

exuded good-natured patience in waiting for the final manuscript. Their professionalism and efficiency once they finally received the manuscript is much
appreciated. Ms Charlotte Holland, one of our irreplacable executive assistants
at the department of History, UCC, came to my rescue on innumerable occasions during the final stages of the preparation of this book.

During the researching of this book several libraries and archives made their
resources available to me. I wish to express my thanks to the staff of all of these
including those of the: Military Archives, Cathal Brugha Barracks, Dublin;
National Library of Ireland; Public Record Office, London; Political Archives,
Berlin; Irish National Archives, Dublin; Boole Library, Cork; Cambridge
University Library, Cambridge; University College Dublin Archives; and
Trinity College Dublin Archives. Without the professionalism and patience of
the staff of such institutions genuine historical research would be impossible.

I wish to acknowledge the vital financial assistance I received which made
completion of this research possible. First, the School of Languages and
European Studies, University of Wolverhampton provided me with a generous
grant to undertake archival research in Dublin. Second, the Faculty of Arts,
University College, Cork provided an invaluable grant aiding the completion of
the manuscript. Third, the Higher Education Authority's (HEA) Programme
for Research in Third Level Institutions (PRTLI) supplied valuable financial
aid to undertake archival research in Berlin. This was provided under the auspices of UCC History Department's PRTLI-funded research project, 'Culture,
contact, nation and state: Ireland in a comparative context'. Consequently, this
monograph was made possible by all of the aforementioned institutions, grant
awarding bodies and individuals.

NOTE ON NOMENCLATURE AND REFERENCING

Readers are advised that research for the first chapter was conducted prior to the
extensive cataloguing of papers relating to the foreign affairs of Dáil Éireann,
the Provisional Government and the first months of the Free State Government
(DE/PG/IFS). These were catalogued after 1992 as the Early Series (ES). As
some documents accessed before 1992 proved elusive in the post-1992 Early
Series, they still retain an older referencing system (DE/PG/IFS). Generally,
most of the documents relating to Irish relations with Germany for 1921, 1922
and 1923 are to be found in boxes 33 and 34 of the Early Series (ES).

In terms of nomenclature the phrases 'minister of external affairs' and
'department of external affairs' are employed throughout the text for consis-
tency and stylistic convenience. It was only after the Ministers and Secretaries
Act, 1924 that the minister of external affairs was redesignated minister for
external affairs. In 1971 the minister and his department were renamed 'minister for foreign affairs' and 'department of foreign affairs'.

Abbreviations and Glossary

AA	Auswärtiges Amt (German foreign office)
AO	Auslandsorganisation
BVP	Bayerische Volkspartei (Bavarian People's Party; Catholic)
CAB	Cabinet Office, Britain
CAUR	Committee of Action for the Universality of Rome
CCOG	Celtic Confederation of Occupational Guilds
CE	*Cork Examiner*
CRS	Confidential Report Series, Department of Foreign Affairs
CIF	Carriage, insurance and freight (included in the price quoted)
DAAD	Deutscher Akademischer Austauschdienst (German Academic Exchange Service)
DD	Dáil Debates
DDP	Deutsche Demokratische Partei (German Democratic Party; liberal)
DFA	Department of Foreign Affairs (Department of External Affairs before 1971)
DIC	Department of Industry & Commerce
DF	Department of Finance
DJ	Department of Justice
DBFP	Documents on British Foreign Policy
DGFP	Documents on German Foreign Policy
DIFP	Documents on Irish Foreign Policy
DNB	Deutsche Nachtrichten Büro (German News Bureau)
DNVP	Deutschnationale Volkspartei (German National People's Party; nationalist)
DVP	Deutsche Volkspartei (German People's Party; national liberal)
DO	Dominions Office, Britain
DT	Department of the Taoiseach
ESB	Electricity Supply Board
FO	Foreign Office, Britain
G2	Irish Military Intelligence
ICCR	Irish Coordinating Committee for Refugees
ICF	Irish Christian Front
IFS	Irish Free State

IHS	*Irish Historical Studies*
II	*Irish Independent*
IP	*Irish Press*
ISIA	*Irish Studies in International Affairs*
IT	*Irish Times*
KPD	Kommunistiche Partei Deutschlands (German Communist Party)
LN	League of Nations file series, Department of Foreign Affairs
MAI	Military Archives of Ireland, Dublin
MI5	British Military Intelligence or Security Service (domestic)
MI6	British Military Intelligence (foreign)
MIS	Military Intelligence Summaries
NAI	National Archives of Ireland, Dublin
NAI DE	National Archives of Ireland, Dáil Éireann
NAI DFA D/PG/IFS	National Archives of Ireland, Department of Foreign Affairs, Dáil/Provisional Government/Irish Free State series
NAI DFA ES	National Archives of Ireland, Department of Foreign Affairs, Early Series
NAI DFA LN	National Archives of Ireland, Department of Foreign Affairs, League of Nations series
NLI	National Library of Ireland, Dublin
NSDAP	Nationalsozialistische Deutsche Arbeiterpartei (National Socialist German Workers' Party; National Socialists; Nazi party)
PA	Political Archives, Berlin
PREM	Prime Minister's Office, Britain
PRO	Public Record Office, London
SA	Sturmabteilung (Nazi storm troopers)
SS	Schutzstaffel (protection unit) denoting the Nazi elite guards
SPD	Sozialdemokratische Partei Deutschlands (German Social Democratic Party; Social Democrats)
SOF	Secretary's Office Files, Department of Foreign Affairs
UCC	University College, Cork
UCD	University College, Dublin
UCDA	University College, Dublin, Archives Department
USFA	Under Secretary for Foreign Affairs

GLOSSARY

Abwehr	German foreign intelligence agency
Abwehr II	Sabotage division of the German foreign intelligence agency, which also dealt with the question of national minorities
Anschluss	German unification with Austria
Fichte Bund	A German overseas propaganda agency
Erfüllungspolitik	Policy of fulfilling the conditions of the Treaty of Versailles (1919)
Führer	Hitler's title as leader of the NSDAP from 1923; in 1934 on the death of President Hindenburg Hitler combined the offices of chancellor and president in his person and Führer became his official state title
Führerprinzip	The leadership system adopted by Hitler in the NSDAP and the Third Reich which insisted that all decisions should be made by the Führer and established an effective one-man dictatorship
Gleichschaltung	Nazi co-ordination or unification of the Reich to produce a centralized Nazi party-state
Grossdeutschland	'Greater' Germany and the derivative belief that all ethnic and German-speaking peoples should be united in one German nation-state including Austria and the Sudetenland
Hitlerjugend	Hitler Youth
Irland-Redaktion	Nazi Germany's propaganda wartime Irish service
Land	One of the fifteen states that made up the German federation or Reich
Landstag	The lower house of parliament of one of the fifteen states of the Reich
Lebensraum	Living space
Luftwaffe	The air forces of the Third Reich
Ortsgruppenleiter	Local group leader
Reichstag	The lower house of the federal German parliament
Reichswehr	The German army of 100,000 soldiers as allowed to the German Republic (Weimar) under the treaty of Versailles
Saorstát	Saorstát Éireann (meaning Irish Free State) was the official name, in Irish, of the independent Irish state between 1922 and 1937
Seekriegsleitung	German Naval Command
Winterhilfe	Help for the winter: a Nazi charity whereby the wealthier members of society contributed aid to their poorer racial brothers

Introduction

'Nations like men have their infancy'
(Henry St John, Lord Bolingbroke).

To paraphrase Lord Bolingbroke, states also experience infancy. In January 1919 the recently elected Sinn Féin deputies formed an unofficial revolutionary parliament (Dáil Éireann) instituting a new era in Irish politics. Although Irish independence was not granted until the signing of the Anglo-Irish Treaty in December 1921, the Dáil inaugurated an ambitious clandestine government with an embryonic department of external affairs that sought international recognition for the state. 1919 was similarly important in European politics. It was the year of the Versailles treaty. Twenty years later, the contexts of European and Irish international relations were metamorphosed by the German-Soviet invasion of Poland, and the declaration of an Irish policy of neutrality. The entire period was formative for Irish, German and European history. In Ireland, Fianna Fáil replaced Cumann na nGaedheal as the government party spearheading a more overtly revisionist policy in relation to Britain, leading to strained relations, the emergence of an autonomous foreign policy and the Anglo-Irish Economic War. In Germany, the period marked the transition from Weimar democracy to the charismatic dictatorship of Adolf Hitler. The Third Reich ultimately destabilized the international climate, as Hitler intensified his revisionist demands and adopted a coercive course. For German domestic policy this meant the suppression of democracy, the inauguration of a one-party state, state-organized persecution of the Jewish minority, and an apparent economic miracle. The two states, asymmetrical in power, size and population, underwent divergent transformations. Since the haphazard German involvement in the Easter Rising of 1916, Irish-German connections had continued to develop. But until now Irish-German relations have escaped detailed examination except for their impact on Irish wartime neutrality.

Literature on Irish-German relations is now plentiful after at least three decades of research by many individuals.[1] Many of these works, however, tend to deal with the pre-war relationship simply as an introduction to Irish-German

1 J.T. Carroll, *Ireland in the war years, 1939–1945* (Newton Abbot, 1975); C.J. Carter, *The shamrock and the swastika* (Palo Alto, California, 1977); H. Dickel, *Die deutsche Aussenpolitik und die Irische Frage von 1932 bis 1944* (Wiesbaden, 1983); J.P. Duggan, *Neutral Ireland and the Third Reich* (Dublin, 1989); R. Fisk, *In time of war: Ireland, Ulster and the price of*

relations during World War II, thereby neglecting questions about Irish attitudes to appeasement, Irish views of Germany and central Europe and the
general interwar turmoil.[2] Irish attitudes to anti-Semitism on the other hand
have become the subject of a burgeoning literature pioneered by Professor
Dermot Keogh.[3] Most of the established literature, however, has a propensity to
presume that Irish-German interwar relations were based on the premise that
another war was inevitable. In other words, our knowledge of World War II
colours the analysis of the prewar period. One event that persistently intrudes
upon any consideration of Irish-German relations is the controversial visit in
May 1945 of the taoiseach, Eamon de Valera, to the German minister to Éire to

---

neutrality, 1939–45 (London, 1983); S. O'Callaghan, *The jackboot in Ireland* (New York,
1958); E. Stephen, *Spies in Ireland* (London, 1965). Several articles have also been published
on Irish-German matters during World War II. A selection of the best of these includes: C.
Carter, 'The spy who brought his lunch', *Éire-Ireland*, 10: 1 (1975), pp 3–13; C. Cox, 'Wir
fahren gegen Irland', *An Cosantóir* (May 1974 and March 1975); C. Cox, 'Militar
Geograpahische Angaben über Irland', *An Cosantóir* (March 1975); J.P. Duggan, 'Celtic
cloaks and teutonic daggers', *An Cosantóir* (May 1978), pp 143–4; J.P. Duggan, 'The German
threat – myth or reality', *An Cosantóir* (September 1989), pp 6–12. 2 Much of the existing
work that considers the inter-war period tends to be centred on the careers and personalities
of diplomats. John P. Duggan, for instance, focuses on the period of Eduard Hempel's posting as German minister plenipotentiary to Ireland from 1937 until 1945 in his pioneering
Neutral Ireland and the Third Reich. Even Andreas Roth's diplomatic biography, *Mr Bewley
in Berlin: aspects of the career of an Irish diplomat, 1933–1939* (Dublin, 2000), devotes most of
its coverage to the wartime period, by which time Bewley had retired from the Irish foreign
service and chose to return to fascist Europe. Nonetheless Bewley's tenure as Irish minister
plenipotentiary to Nazi Germany between 1933 and 1939 is the one aspect of Irish-German
inter-war relations that has attracted sustained attention. This is not surprising in light of the
controversial Mr Bewley's pro-Nazi tendencies. Other work on Bewley includes: D. Keogh,
Ireland and Europe, 1919–1989: a diplomatic and political history (Cork & Dublin, 1990), pp
28–9, 46, 47, 55–7, 100–5, 112; C. Bewley (edited by W.J. McCormack), *Memoirs of a Wild
Goose* (Dublin, 1989); M. O'Driscoll, 'Irish–German diplomatic relations, 1922–1939: an
examination of Irish diplomats' performances in Berlin', unpublished MA thesis, UCC,
November 1992'; D. Keogh, *Ireland and the Vatican: the politics and diplomacy of church–state
relations, 1922–1960* (Cork, 1995), especially pp 44–5, 51–71, 79–82, 91 n.101, 99–109). More
recently, the debate about Charles Bewley has developed in a new direction: when did Bewley
become a 'fellow traveller' of Nazism? How and why was he converted into an admirer of
Nazism? For more on the process of Bewley's formation as a Nazi sympathiser see M.
Kennedy, 'Our men in Berlin: some thoughts on Irish diplomats in Berlin, 1929–39', *ISIA*,
10 (1999); M. O'Driscoll, 'Inter-war Irish–German diplomacy: continuity, ambiguity and
appeasement in Irish foreign policy', in M. Kennedy & J.M. Skelly (eds), *Irish foreign policy,
1919–1966: from independence to internationalism* (Dublin, 2000), especially pp 82–7; 93–4.
Although Bewley occupied a central role in Irish-German relations before the outbreak of
World War II an undue focus on the personality of this one diplomat can obscure the many
other facets of the inter-war Irish-German relationship. 3 D. Keogh, *Jews in twentieth-century Ireland: refugees, anti-Semitism and the Holocaust* (Cork, 1998). Professor D. Keogh has
also notably initiated a whole new generation of primary research into Irish foreign policy
with his seminal work *Ireland and Europe*.

offer his condolences on the death of Hitler. De Valera was a strict adherent to diplomatic protocol and Hitler was the German head of state. Additionally, de Valera wanted personally to console the German minister Dr Eduard Hempel, an old school German gentleman diplomat, on the defeat of Germany. The taoiseach respected Hempel's honourable conduct during 'the Emergency' which had permitted the maintenance of Irish neutrality in difficult circumstances. Although de Valera's rationale for his misguided act of condolence on Hitler's death was explicable in these terms, the international furore created by his action irreparably damaged independent Ireland's international reputation.[4]

The popular Allied myth that Éire was pro-fascist was given succour by de Valera's act and combined with existing unproven insinuations that Irish republicans succoured German U-boats on the west coast of Ireland. De Valera's unbending refusal to countenance Allied use of the former Irish 'Treaty ports' (Cobh, Lough Swilly and Berehaven) as a base for the Atlantic battle undoubtedly embittered Allied opinion. Sir Winston Churchill's slurs that Éire was a haven for German espionage proved enormously injurious and must be seen as a rhetorical displacement device for British propaganda during Britain's most dangerous hour. In fact, Churchill undoubtedly knew that British intelligence, MI5, was well pleased with Irish counterespionage efforts during World War II.[5] Any consideration of Irish-German relations in the inter-war period therefore has to critically assess Irish attitudes to Germany as events actually developed, since all participants lacked the wisdom of foresight. For them World War II was not inevitable; it was not the defining historical event in their historical consciousness. It was the Great War and its repercussions that informed interwar thinking and actions. For Irish nationalism it was the War of Irish Independence, the Irish Civil War and the expansion of independence that informed policymakers to a great extent. But the wider international environment could not be ignored and proved influential in Irish foreign policy considerations on many occasions. The international threat of Nazi Germany undisputedly assisted Anglo-Irish reconciliation after the mid-1930s.

This book aims to present a more comprehensive analysis of Irish relations with Germany than those previously published.[6] In so doing, a distinction –

---

4 D. Keogh, 'Eamon de Valera and Hitler: an analysis of international reaction to the visit to the German Minister, May 1945', ISIA, 3: 1 (1989), pp 69–92. 5 E. O'Halpin (ed.), *MI5 and Ireland, 1939–1945: the official history* (Dublin, 2002). 6 Horst Dickel has unquestionably produced the best account of Irish-German relations between 1932 and 1944 and, though it is unlikely that this will ever be equalled in terms of coverage and quality, the work has been greatly neglected because English-speaking scholars have rarely used it. In addition, since the work was produced before 1990 it did not benefit from access to all of the Irish government papers. Nonetheless it still serves as a valuable resource for any work undertaken in the area of Irish-German relations. See Dickel, *Deutsche Aussenpolitik*. Recently an encouraging trend has emerged which takes a broader approach to Irish-German relations than the previously established historical literature and this suggests an interesting line for future

perhaps an artificial but nevertheless pertinent one – must be drawn between inter-state relations and inter-state diplomacy. Diplomacy is particular, exclusive and best described as the formal relationship between two states that recognize each other's right to exist. It is subject to the normal diplomatic conventions and international legal nuances that govern relations between institutionalized foreign services. Inter-state relations, conversely, are more general and inclusive embracing cultural, economic, social and political interactions between non-state actors as well as between states which do not have a formal diplomatic relationship. Hence, this book makes a distinction between pre-1929 Irish-German 'relations' and post-1929 diplomacy, since Irish-Weimar relations were only upgraded from consular exchanges to full diplomatic recognition in 1929 and 1930. However, even after 1929 effort is expended to discuss general Irish-German relations.

This book has three main lines of enquiry. It is firstly and primarily an investigation of Irish diplomatic relations with Germany, from the Irish perspective, during the interwar period, or the '20 years crisis'. This is necessary to gain an insight into the Irish perspective on the central international problems of the era. To this end, the southern Irish nationalist interpretation of historical questions surrounding interwar Germany is analyzed. Briefly these include: German treatment at the hands of the victors of the Great War; the Versailles treaty; the instability of the Weimar Republic; reparations; disarmament; the collapse of the Weimar Republic; the rise of Nazism; the nature of the Nazi state; and the origins of World War II.

A second motivation for investigating Irish-German relations concerns the perceptual gap in the historiography of Irish foreign policy. To date, Irish bilateral relations with continental European states have largely been ignored reflecting the Anglocentric nature of Irish historiography – caused by the understandable factors of historical and geographical proximity. The 'orthodox' nationalist tradition was promulgated by earlier chroniclers who were disadvantaged by lack of access to the archives of the Irish department of foreign affairs. They believed that Anglo-Irish relations shaped Irish foreign policy after Irish independence in 1922.[7] That perspective imputes southern Ireland's lack of interest in the European mainland was 'also a consequence of Ireland's lack of involvement in most of the specific issues arising out of the post-war settlement, such as the status of Germany, questions of reparations and of economic reconstruction'.[8] This 'traditional' interpretation of Ireland's post-independence

development as well. In particular see: J. Fischer, *Das Deutschlandbild der Iren, 1890–1939: Geschichte-Form-Funktion* (2 vols, TCD, Dublin, 1996); J. Fischer & J. Dillon (eds.), *The correspondence of Myles Dillon, 1922–1925: Irish-German relations and Celtic Studies* (Dublin, 1999).   7 P. Keatinge, *Formulation of Irish foreign policy* (Dublin, 1973).   8 Ibid., p. 16.

external relations has been substantially challenged by new scholarship based on Irish government archives, in particular by J.J. Lee and Dermot Keogh. The release of Irish government records under the 30-year rule from 1 January 1990 overcame the previous dearth of empirical material. Now a new generation of scholars has expanded on this line of investigation. Cumulatively their work demonstrates that independent Ireland had a more 'multidimensional' foreign policy than hitherto assumed by the 'orthodox' historiography.[9] For instance, Michael Kennedy has demonstrated that the League of Nations offered Saorstát Éireann (Irish Free State; hereafter Saorstát) a multilateral setting in which to project an image of independent Ireland as a radical revisionist British dominion that was European in its focus. Though such questions as reparations and the position of Germany were not destined to be a central preoccupation of Ireland, nonetheless Irish foreign policy did have to take account of these matters and adopt a position on them as we shall see.

However, the 'multidimensional' nature of Irish foreign policy in the '20 years' crisis' is liable to overstatement. Extending Irish autonomy within the Commonwealth and the League of Nations during the first decade of independence (1922–32) was an essential precursor to establishing a wider diplomatic network. The Saorstát had to demonstrate its genuine sovereignty within the Commonwealth. It played an influential role in the evolution of the British empire into a genuine commonwealth of nations, a more permissive political community necessitating the development of an Irish foreign service. The state did this from inside and outside the Commonwealth in a symbiotic, interwoven and dualist policy having the objective of maximizing Irish autonomy within the rules of the Anglo-Irish Treaty.

This stealthy Irish process had proven fruitful on all fronts by the end of the Cumann na nGaedheal decade (1932). The establishment of the Commonwealth precedent permitting dominions to initiate bilateral relations with the US and European continental powers was essential for upgrading the Free State's international status in the late 1920s. As T.P. Coogan says, 'the Cosgrave administration had been quietly striking off the imperial shackles in international relationships'. But this process was too low-profile, incremental and cumulative for many Irish nationalists.[10] De Valera's Fianna Fáil governments after 1932 benefited from increased Irish international autonomy. Cumann na nGaedheal's foreign policies in the 1920s contrived the necessary freedom of manoeuvre for de Valera to create an Irish republic (Éire) 'in all but name' in the 1937 constitution. Even de Valera was later to admit privately that the 'Free

---

9 A commendable effort to collate the efforts of many diverse historians actively producing this new and more sophisticated history of Irish foreign policy has been made in: Kennedy & Skelly, *Irish foreign policy*. 10 T.P. Coogan, *De Valera: long fellow, long shadow* (London, 1993), p. 422.

Staters' 'did a magnificent job'.[11] Therefore it was only in the early 1930s, firstly under Cumann na nGaedheal and later under de Valera's Fianna Fáil administrations, that the Saorstát had the liberty to develop a deeper 'multi-dimensional' foreign policy. By 1932 the Irish state had the extensive bilateral and multilateral diplomatic and commercial relations of a truly sovereign international actor. It developed a distinctive small power perspective in favour of international reconciliation and collective security. Irish-German relations reflect this gradual maturation in Ireland's external relations.

A third theme of this analysis is the institutionalization and professionalization of the Irish foreign service. Foreign services, to once again paraphrase Lord Bolingbroke, are a mirror of the infancy of states, to which the experience of the Irish foreign service in Berlin is a vivid testament. The professionalization of the service is necessarily a key theme in any study of the pre-1945 Irish foreign service. This has a strong bearing on Irish-German interwar relations, not least because of the difficulties the Saorstát encountered in establishing a Berlin legation and then in finding and retaining suitable career diplomats to represent it. The analysis here will focus on the professional quality and performance of the three men who were the main Irish representatives accredited to Berlin during the '20 years' crisis'. To make such an appraisal of diplomatic performance requires a multifaceted approach. This includes critically examining aspects of each diplomat's career, notably his diplomatic credentials, skills, social and political networks in Berlin; the accuracy of his diplomatic reporting; his reputation among his peers; and the importance attached to his contribution by senior officials in Dublin.

The three Irish representatives in Berlin who are subjected to this analysis are: John (or Jean) Chartres, the unofficial Irish representative to Weimar Germany from 1921 to 1922; Daniel A. Binchy, who represented the Irish Free State in Berlin from 1929 to 1932; and Charles Bewley, the Irish minister in Berlin from 1933 to 1939. Their role was crucial in terms of the impression they created in Germany of themselves and Ireland, and of their potential to influence the development of Irish-German relations. The confidential reports produced by Binchy and Bewley for the department of external affairs in Dublin are particularly significant in assessing their performances as diplomats. The reports are a measure of their familiarity with the situation in Germany, and provide both a contemporary external impression of Germany, and valuable insights into the quality of the diplomats producing them.

Bewley's calibre as a diplomat is a particular focus because he was present in Nazi Germany during most of its peacetime existence in the 1930s. Such an examination of Bewley is necessarily contentious because he has attracted sig-

11 Ibid., p. 426.

nificant negative comment already. He is alleged to have held anti-Semitic views, to have been Anglophobic and to have had a poor relationship with Eamon de Valera as minister of external affairs. An assessment of the veracity and accuracy of Bewley's own account in his *Memoirs of a Wild Goose*[12] is also indispensable. It has been claimed that his memoirs are merely an apologia, sanitising the author's career in the Irish foreign service to make it more acceptable to post-war public opinion. It has also been claimed that Bewley was 'an unreconstructed supporter of National Socialism' until he died in 1969.[13] Although his memoirs' usefulness as a historical source is dubious, it nevertheless provides a useful comparator for the attitudes and perceptions revealed in Bewley's confidential reports.

However, Irish-German relations during the inter-war crisis were about more than the work of individuals such as Bewley or Binchy or German diplomats. International relations, trade, migration and cultural exchange policies permeated the entire relationship. The threat of expansionist and aggressive Nazism eventually led to a certain meeting of moderate democratic minds between Ireland and Britain because of, or perhaps in spite of, the emergence of Irish neutrality as Éire's preferred policy in the latter 1930s. Although the Irish 'friendly neutrality' posture failed to meet all of Britain's defence needs, it did succeed in satisfying all sides' vital national security interests sufficiently (including Nazi Germany's) to avoid confrontation. Irish nationalism overwhelmingly refused to exploit Britain's difficulties and actively suppressed republican extremists who sought to do so.

12 Bewley, *Memoirs*; IT, 9 Dec. 1989.   13 IT, 9 Dec. 1989.

False starts, 1919–23

'The only foreign policy of the present government is to pacify the Allies.'[1]

'I do not know if Mr Bewley has ever called on Mr Chartres, but [the] friction between them, whoever be to blame is becoming ridiculous ... It is time for him and Mr Chartres to have a thorough understanding and a truce to the constant bickering ...'[2]

'Our former relations with England have given the impression to the German people that Ireland was to all intents and purposes nothing more than a province of Great Britain ... It will take some time before Germany comes to realise that Ireland has really come out of the corner. It is our duty to make our status clear to the German people and not the duty of the German people to go and look for the facts.'[3]

Berlin was not a primary political objective of Irish efforts to secure diplomatic representation during the Irish War of Independence, 1919–21. The European continent was largely ignored as preference was given to the largest global concentration of the Irish diaspora – the United States.[4] However, as the Irish War of Independence progressed Irish interest in continental Europe grew. Nevertheless, Berlin remained of marginal importance compared with the Irish fixation on the Vatican, Paris and the League of Nations. As the capital of the defeated Germany, it was far less significant for the clandestine Irish state than Paris which, in effect, became the headquarters of the Irish diplomatic offensive in western Europe[5] and became the centre from which Sinn Féin agents operated throughout Europe. The failure of Dáil envoy Seán T. O'Kelly's mission to the Paris peace conference (he was seeking recognition of Irish independence) and de Valera's endeavours to enlist American support (which aimed at winning international recognition of the covert Irish government by the victors of the Great War)[6] led to a more concerted diplomatic offensive to secure bilateral relations in other major European capitals. It was not until 1921 that consistent Irish efforts were made in Berlin. This chapter traces the gradual growth of Sinn

1 NAI, DFA, ES, Box 14, File 96, Bisonkind's memo, 19 Sept. 1921. 2 Ibid., Box 33, File 238, Walshe–Blythe, 27 Mar. 1922. 3 NAI, DFA ES, Box 34, File 240, Duane – industry and commerce, 19 Oct. 1923. 4 Keogh, *Ireland and Europe*, p. 7. 5 Ibid., p. 8. 6 D. Keogh, 'Origins of Irish diplomacy in Europe, 1919–1921', *Études Irlandaises*, 7 (1983), p. 150.

Féin's interest in Germany as an outpost for its representatives after 1919. It seeks to answer a series of questions: How did Irish republican interest in Germany originate? What were the motives for establishing an Irish representation in Berlin? What were German reactions to the Irish overtures? Dáil Éireann's incipient German policy is placed in the context not only of Anglo-Irish relations, but also of the broader tapestry of European relations after the Great War.

By late 1921 a sizeable Irish representation was present in Berlin but it encountered a difficult operational environment both in Ireland and Germany. After the Anglo-Irish Treaty was signed in December 1921 the German internal situation was still largely ignored as the splintered Irish republican movement moved towards a 'shooting war' between the pro-Treaty regulars of the provisional government and the anti-Treaty irregulars. In August 1922, Arthur Griffith, president and founder of Sinn Féin and delegation leader to the Anglo-Irish Treaty talks, died, and Michael Collins was assassinated. Extrajudicial killings, judicial killings and reprisals became commonplace in the guerrilla war that dragged on until 1923.[7] The coherence of the Berlin mission was badly affected at the very time when the opportunities to win international recognition appeared greatest. But Irish political fragmentation was not the only obstacle. Weimar Germany, too, was beset by the problems of civil strife and international confrontation.

EARLY LINKS

Deepening cultural and economic interaction between Ireland and Germany since the middle of the nineteenth century laid the foundations for early Irish attempts to establish a diplomatic base in the German capital, Berlin, in 1921. Several German universities had established Celtic Studies programmes and participated in the Irish cultural renaissance at the end of the nineteenth century.[8] Professor Heinrich Zimmer of Berlin University played an active role in pioneering German interest in the language. In 1903 the future first president of Éire, Douglas Hyde, persuaded Kuno Meyer – a German scholar and staunch supporter of the Irish language – to become the first director of the School of Irish Learning in Dublin. Meyer acceded to the chair of Celtic in Berlin in 1911 and was a firm supporter of Irish nationalism.[9] Since German academics led in the fields of philology and linguistics, they pioneered research into the Irish language. The interest of leading German scholars in Gaelic culture nurtured contacts with Irish nationalism.[10] Cultural exchanges created a

7 Ibid., pp 1–18.   8 See M. Elsasser, *Germany and Ireland: 1000 years of shared history* (Dublin, 1997).   9 Ibid., pp 26–9.   10 P. O'Connor, 'France and the Free State: Franco-

community of Irish and German linguists, indirectly fostering political and economic co-operation.

Although Irish nationalists' geopolitical calculations and natural religious affinities lay with Catholic and republican continental powers, the emergence of a united Germany after 1870 transformed the European balance of power. Irish physical force nationalism sought a sponsor for Irish independence. The ripening Anglo-German antagonism and the formation of the two rival alliance systems (Germany's Central Powers and the Anglo-French-Russian Triple Entente) presented Irish republicans with an opportunity to seek aid from imperial Germany rather than from French republicanism.[11]

The service of Major John MacBride's Irish brigade with imperial Germany against Britain during the Boer War preceded Irish nationalist advocate Roger Casement's efforts to enlist German support for the republican cause during World War I. Agatha Grabisch (née Bullitt), a journalist from the southern United States who was married to a German and was secretary of the German-Irish Society in 1921, said the Germans 'have always been interested in Ireland to a certain extent and they were even more interested because of being at war with the British'.[12] Casement, a former member of the British colonial services, attempted to exploit the German connection by establishing an Irish brigade in Germany during World War I and to land German armaments for the Easter 1916 rebellion. His efforts cost him his life.

St John Gaffney, an Irish-American who retired from his position as US consul at Dresden and Munich out of sympathy for the Easter Rising of 1916, played a role in these war years. He assisted Casement's efforts to establish the Irish brigade.[13] Together with Dr George Chatterton Hill, a former professor at Geneva University, Gaffney contributed to the foundation of the Berlin branch of the Friends of Irish Freedom. This was closely linked with the mother organization, founded in the US in 1916. German wartime sympathy for the Irish cause was further evinced by the foundation of the German-Irish Society after the Easter Rising. Chatterton Hill and Gaffney were major players in the society, which counted among its membership numerous German dignitaries. Kaiser Wilhelm II even sent official messages to the society supporting its fight for Irish independence.[14] However, German military defeat and the death in October 1919 of Professor Kuno Meyer, the society's president,[15] instituted a

Irish diplomacy, 1922–1931' (unpublished MA thesis, St Patrick's College, Maynooth, 1991), pp 98–9. **11** Ibid., p. 40. **12** Bewley, *Memoirs*, p. 79. **13** Elsasser, *Germany*, p. 38. **14** Ibid., p. 38. B.P. Murphy, *John Chartres: mystery man of the treaty* (Dublin, 1995), pp 31–2. Elsasser dates the foundation of the society to 13 February 1916 (Elsasser, *Germany*, p. 38). Murphy's account that is largely reliant on St John Gaffney's biography, *Breaking the silence*, places its birth a year later. Elsasser appears to confuse the establishment of the branch of the Friends of Irish Freedom in Berlin with the German-Irish Society one year later. **15** Murphy, *Chartres*, p. 32.

period of dormancy. The society largely proved ineffective though Agatha Grabisch remained as its nominal representative.[16] Viennese Professor Julius Pokorny was destined to be its only member to remain a figure in Irish-German affairs throughout the entire inter-war period. Born in Prague in the former Austro–Hungarian empire in 1887, he received a doctorate for his thesis on early Irish texts before World War I.[17] He succeeded to the chair of Celtic at the University of Berlin on the death of Kuno Meyer. His contributions to Celtic Studies included a '*Concise Old Irish Grammar*, the edition of several old Irish texts, a book on Irish lyrical poetry, the editorship – also in succession to Kuno Meyer – of the review *Zeitschrift für Celtische Philologie*'.[18] A regular visitor to the Gaeltacht, he was a fluent Irish speaker, actively supported the revival of the Irish language, and had lobbied for the inclusion of Irish as a matriculation subject for all students seeking to enter the National University of Ireland. He had supported Irish moves towards self-determination and, in 1916 at the time of the Easter Rising, published a history of Ireland in German entitled simply *Irland*. It was subsequently translated into English in 1933.[19]

Between 1918 and 1921 this ragtag group of Hiberno-enthusiasts continued on their lonely crusade on behalf of Irish nationalism and received little attention from Dublin. They operated largely in a freelance capacity and indigenous Irish republicans were unimpressed by the calibre of most members of the German-Irish Society in Berlin. Pokorny was the exception.[20] During the period 1919–21 several Irish agents visited Germany including Gerald Hamilton (alias 'The Traveller'), who recommended the appointment of a permanent representative from the putative Irish republic. There were also proposals for a Hamburg–Cork shipping route funded by Irish, German, and American sources; Hamburg's port being a particular focus for Irish activity during this period as a centre of IRA gunrunning operations.[21]

Meanwhile during the early 1920s a number of Irish Celtic Studies students spent time in Germany and Berlin completing their postgraduate studies including D.A. Binchy, Myles Dillon, M.A. O'Brien, and Nancy Wyse Power; and they were destined to establish what Dáithí Ó Cróinín terms 'a new generation of Celtic Studies' in Ireland when they returned.[22] Some of these played

---

16 Bewley, *Memoirs*, pp 78–9. 17 S. Ó Lúing, *Celtic Studies in Europe and other essays* (Dublin, 2000), pp 33–4. 18 See J.M. Hone's 'Foreword' to J. Pokorny (translated from the German by S.D. King), *A history of Ireland* (London, 1933), p. i. 19 Ó Lúing, *Celtic Studies*, p. 34. 20 NAI, DFA, ES, Box 2, File 1, Duffy letter, 5 Sept. 1919; ibid., Box 3, File 1, 18 Sept. 1919; ibid., Box 4, File 1, Duffy letter, 8 Feb. 1920; ibid., Box 5, File 1, memo from D. to L., 10 Dec. 1920; DIFP, vol. 1, Docs. 15 & 17; Murphy, *Chartres*, p. 35. 21 See Murphy, *Chartres*, pp 30–3. An Irish-American, John T. Ryan (alias 'Bisonkind' or Professor Jetter or Professor J.) on the run from the US for 'aiding and assisting German spies' during WWI was also in Germany in late 1920. He worked as an arms dealer for Joe McGarrity's Clann na Gael which was trying to supply the IRA. 22 See D. Ó Cróinín, review of Fischer & Dillon, *The correspondence of Myles Dillon* in *Peritia*, 12 (1998), p. 428.

a role beyond the academic realm in Irish-German relations. Nancy Wyse Power, a member of Cumann na mBan, and a graduate of Kuno Meyer's School of Irish Learning, had returned to Germany in November 1921 to complete her war-interrupted doctoral studies in Bonn. George Gavan Duffy, Sinn Féin's roving European envoy based in Rome, asked her to recover Irish funds from a Hamburg shipping agent, Jürgens, who had not delivered to the IRA the arms for which he had been paid. She failed but was destined, along with Jurgens and the missing Irish money, to become a focal point for Irish activities later.[23]

INITIAL ATTITUDES

As late as January 1921 Ireland's associate minister for foreign affairs, Count George Plunkett, remarked: 'The position of affairs on the continent of Europe is, as regards Ireland, naturally affected very seriously by the uncertain political and industrial conditions in each country.'[24] Germany, in particular, was in a state of disarray. To representatives of the Irish republican movement, therefore, Germany was not a suitable target for propaganda. In November 1918, with defeat in the Great War imminent, a provisional government led by the Social Democrats took over Germany. Kaiser Wilhelm II abdicated and the Weimar Republic was declared. The assembly that wrote the new German constitution met in Weimar in Thuringia in an effort to break with the militaristic and autocratic heritage of Berlin.

From the very beginning the Weimar Republic was beset by serious internal and external difficulties. In November 1918, workers and soldiers disillusioned with the war staged a revolt which failed but fed the subsequent right-wing nationalist myth that Socialists, Communists and Jews had stabbed Germany in the back. The Nazis and the extreme-right later argued that the Second Reich had been defeated by traitorous elements, conveniently ignoring the military defeat in 1918. The nationalist 'stab in the back' (*Dolchstoßlegende*) myth gained popular currency when the Weimar government accepted the harsh and humiliating conditions of the Versailles peace treaty. The first ever fully democratic German regime was not consulted during the treaty negotiations. Not only did it have to live with clause 231, under which the new government accepted that Germany was guilty of causing the war, it also had to cede large amounts of territory (Alsace-Lorraine, Schleswig, Pomerania, West Prussia, Posen, Upper Silesia, and all of the colonies) and 10 per cent of its population. Military-industrial potential was stymied by strict disarmament clauses, the demilitarization of the Rhineland and the placing of the Saarland under League of Nations control. In addition, Germany was required to pay large but inde-

---

23 Murphy, *Chartres*, pp 33–4; M. O'Neill, *From Parnell to de Valera: a biography of Jennie Wyse Power, 1858–1941* (Dublin, 1991), p. 126.   24 DIFP, vol. 1, Doc. no. 55.

terminate reparations to its former enemies. Admittedly the treaty could have been far harsher, but Britain and the US constrained the *revanchisme* of the French premier, Georges Clemençeau.[25]

Meanwhile the powers of the old right-wing imperial institutions remained intact, though dormant. The new democratic governments of Weimar were from the beginning dependent on the co-operation of the old order to govern. The civil service and the German army's officer corps remained. Indeed, in the first years of the new state's existence the democratic forces within the Weimar Republic used the forces of the old order to crush the extreme left-wing threats to the new state. Weimar was born unpropitiously as a semi-occupied, militarily defeated state with unreconciled internal socio-political cleavages. Its existence was fragile.

Irish republicanism, too, operated in an adverse climate. Not only was the outcome of the War of Independence uncertain, but also Britain was recognized internationally as the lawful government of Ireland. Although there was considerable sympathy for Irish republicans in countries such as Germany, gaining official support from foreign governments was contingent upon Irish nationalists securing a domestic military victory and on winning recognition in an environment in which Britain, as a victor of the Great War, controlled the balance of power on the continent. Realpolitik forced both the victors and the vanquished to defer to Britain.

In 1919 Irish republicans concentrated their diplomatic efforts on the Versailles peace conference. The first Dáil's 'Message to the Free Nations of the World'[26] on 21 January 1919 was drafted with the Versailles conference in mind. After US President Woodrow Wilson's 'Fourteen Points for a just peace', Eamon de Valera and Dáil Éireann had high expectations that the newly-proposed League of Nations would recognize an Irish nation-state under Wilson's principle of national self-determination. It soon became evident that this was not possible.[27] There was only a 'mere chance' that the Irish case for independence would receive a fair hearing amidst the Great Power wrangles over the future of Germany. This was confirmed by Sinn Féin's roving envoy George Gavan Duffy[28] who recognized that the French prime minister Georges Clemençeau held a dim view of Irish nationalism because he was determined to remain on good terms with Britain to defend France from future German aggression.[29] Furthermore Irish nationalism had a poor reputation in France because British propaganda had successfully portrayed Sinn Féin 'as friends of Germany and enemies of France'. An independent Ireland was likely 'to be the complacent tool of an aggressive Germany'.[30] So Ireland's attempt to gain international recognition from the League of Nations in 1919 was scuttled by Great

---

25 William Carr, *A history of Germany, 1815–1945* (London, 1969), pp 298–300.   26 DIFP, vol. 1, Doc. no. 2.   27 Ibid., Doc. no. 5.   28 Ibid., Doc. no. 8.   29 Ibid., Doc. no. 16. 30 Ibid., Doc. no. 50.

Power politics, Irish-German dalliances during the Great War, and Britain's pivotal role in international relations

In October 1919, in an attempt to neutralize Britain's influence, the Dáil
Committee on Foreign Affairs considered the appointment of consuls and representatives to countries in which no appointments had yet been made.[31] A
concerted effort to expand the representation of the Irish nationalist cause in
Europe began in mid-1920. Even then Berlin failed to attract Sinn Féin's attention and when it did perceptions were predominantly negative.[32] For instance,
when Duffy lobbied for Paris as the ideal site to establish a foreign press bureau
in August 1920, he discounted Germany: 'Central Europe is too unsettled and
desperate to trouble much about remote affairs, while the tendencies in
Germany are now in general quite openly pro-English and for reasons both
commercial and political seem likely to become more so ...'[33] At this stage the
siting of the headquarters of the League of Nations at Geneva meant
Switzerland emerged as the favoured base for Dáil propaganda operations in
central Europe.[34] After failing to achieve multilateral recognition from the
League of Nations, the putative Irish republic courted Catholic, Latin
European countries because they were judged likely to take an increasing interest in an independent Ireland as a bulwark of religion in a godless world.

In 1920 during his US tour, de Valera encountered talk of a general entente
of southern Europe, led by France, against the northern countries of Britain,
Germany and Russia. He instructed Duffy to discover if there was any truth in
it.[35] Duffy embarked on a Europe-wide tour to assess the rumours and, although
initially attracted to the idea of an Irish association with a pan-Latin movement
led by France, he finally concluded such a combination was impractical not least
because of French hostility to Irish nationalism. Instead Duffy favoured Irish
support for an American-German-Soviet economic alliance, 'to exploit Russia
with German brains and American dollars, an alliance which incidentally will
put Berlin on its feet financially and enable it much sooner than it would otherwise could to resist the aggression and refuse to submit to the exaction of the
Entente'. He also noted that 'the Germans are the only foreigners at home in
Russia', and that the Social Democratic government of Weimar was sympathetic
to Russia 'no matter what her form of government' as long as the Bolsheviks
undertook no communist propaganda in Germany. Duffy's grand tour transformed his previously sceptical interpretation of Germany's importance for
Irish foreign policy.[36] He became convinced that German resurgence was
inevitable and emphasized the importance of Irish representation in Germany.

Duffy hoped the Irish and German immigrant communities in the US would
co-operate in lobbying the US government to improve the international for-

---

31 Ibid.   32 DIFP, vol. 1, Doc. no. 37.   33 Ibid., Doc. no. 45.   34 Ibid., Doc. nos. 26, 37.
35 Ibid., Doc. no. 54.   36 NAI, DFA, ES, Box 33, File 232, Duffy–Brennan, 11 Mar. 1921.

tunes of their respective nations. In Germany Duffy received an enthusiastic response from businessmen and the general public. He was:

> tremendously impressed by the spirit and determination of the people and by the anti-Ally feeling generally prevalent despite official efforts at a pro-English policy. I have not in any of the War countries come across anything like the cool confidence and assurance with which the Germans view the future and many of their leading men are willing to be pro-Irish because England is our enemy ...[37]

In Hamburg, the shipping company responsible for fortnightly voyages to Dublin concluded that since 'Germany's sympathies are decidedly with Ireland' the two countries should boost their trade and economies by linking Ireland with Hamburg permanently 'to knock out England our common enemy'.[38] Of course Jürgens, the Hamburg shipping agency, had good commercial reasons to promote Irish-German relations since it had Irish shipping and trading links and was involved in gunrunning for the IRA.

Meanwhile Chatterton Hill from the German-Irish Society lobbied to establish an Irish press and information bureau in Berlin arguing that it was detrimental to Irish interests to permit the German public to be fed with news only from British sources.[39] Duffy, therefore, proposed the appointment of an Irish representative to Berlin[40] considering that the German attitude to Britain complemented Ireland's. He recognized, however, that before Germany could become an ally Ireland needed to win the War of Independence.

Duffy's support for a German-American–Soviet combination dovetailed with newly emergent Irish republican priorities. Despite the communist and anti-religious nature of the Bolshevik government in Russia, the Dáil was already flirting with that similarly embattled recognition-hungry putative state.[41] After the Anglo-French military intervention in the Russian civil war against the Red Army, the Bolsheviks faced the same foe – Britain – as Ireland. Initially, too, there had been strong populist and socialist tendencies in the Irish War of Independence so there appeared to be similarities between the Irish and Russian causes.[42]

---

37 Ibid., File 233, SEO–external affairs, 10 Feb. 1921. 38 Ibid., File 233, copy from Jürgens & Co. Hamburg (Marked D. D.), n.d. 39 Ibid., File 233(2), Chatterton Hill–Duffy, 6 Feb. 1921. 40 Ibid., File 233, SEO–DFA, 10 Feb. 1921. 41 DIFP, Vol. 1, Doc. 37. 42 Ibid., Docs. 33 & 34.

In January 1921 de Valera, recently returned from his US tour, asserted control over external relations with the aim of organizing Ireland's foreign affairs effectively for the first time.[43] He supported Duffy's recommendation to found a Berlin mission as part of an Irish association with a German-Soviet-American coalition of powers. On 9 March 1921, de Valera informed the clandestine Dáil's director of publicity, Erskine Childers, of his decision to open a propaganda bureau in Berlin, 'camouflaged perhaps under a trade title'.[44]

Influenced by Duffy, de Valera envisaged Berlin as the future centre of Irish operations in central Europe and as a key to winning Irish alignment with a speculative American-Soviet-German coalition. De Valera favoured appointing John Chartres, a former London *Times* journalist and staunch republican, as head of the bureau.[45] Married to the Italian novelist Annie Vivanti, also an advocate of Ireland in Italy and Switzerland, Chartres was a convert to the Irish cause, had spent time as a student in a German university, and was well connected to two of the key leaders of the Irish republican movement, Michael Collins and Arthur Griffith.[46] Chartres' republican credentials, his knowledge of Germany and journalistic skills were seen as major assets. But he was unable to go to Berlin immediately; when he arrived in Paris on 6 April 1921, he caught cold and was confined to bed.[47] As a stopgap measure, Nancy Wyse Power was sent to Berlin to set up the publicity bureau on the understanding that Chartres would relieve her later.[48]

Power left Dublin on 11 April 1921 and the Dáil hoped that before Chartres' arrival she could organize the fractious German-Irish Society to start producing the *Irish Bulletin*, to promote Irish independence to a German audience and counteract British accounts of the Anglo-Irish war.[49] This proved to be a difficult assignment. Her initial instructions were to assess the situation, to organize publication of the *Bulletin* and to remain in control for a few weeks until the project was viable.[50] Power quickly established contact with members of the divided German-Irish Society,[51] to galvanize them into producing the *Bulletin* but the omens were inauspicious. Previous reports from Berlin had highlighted:

43 Ibid., Doc. 59. 44 Ibid., Doc. 64. 45 NAI, DFA, ES, Box 14, File 96(11), de Valera–Duffy, 24 Mar. 1921. 46 Bewley, *Memoirs*, pp 76–7. 47 NAI, DFA, ES, Box 14, File 96(11), extract from O'Ceallaigh, n.d. 48 Ibid., de Valera–Duffy, 24 Mar. 1921. 49 NAI, DFA, ES, Box 33, File 238(3), Power note, 3 Mar. 1922. 50 NAI, DE, Box 8/1, Brennan–Collins, 6 April 1921; NAI, DFA, ES, Box 33, File 233, Brennan–de Valera, 29 Apr. 1921. 51 NAI, DFA, ES, Box 33, File 232, Nancy–Mother, 18 Apr. 1921.

almost everybody in Germany who purports to be working for Ireland's interest is more concerned in blackening the character of everybody else than in doing any useful work. The result is that no-one of those who have been working in Germany would be suitable as a representative there if it were decided to have one in that country.[52]

Power's experiences with members of the German-Irish Society in mid-1921 confirmed Dublin's worst suspicions. The society was riven by infighting and Power concluded that none of its members were suitable to edit the *Bulletin*. For instance, she recounted that although Chatterton Hill had a certain amount of journalistic ability and experience he did not have a good grasp of the Irish situation, needed to be supervised, and 'was not a person at all likely to accept any role but the main one ...'[53] She advised Dublin 'to have someone from home on the spot to prevent the locals eating one another up'.[54]

Power was scheduled to take up a position in University College, Dublin on 1 June.[55] At this crisis point prospective permanent candidates other than Chartres, who was still in Paris, were considered for the post and alternative duties for the highly-thought-of Chartres were discussed. Chartres advised that Switzerland would be a better centre for Irish propaganda activities in central Europe because an 'active man in Switzerland would antagonize France less than the same in Germany and could perhaps at the present moment do enough work into Germany'.[56] Hence Chartres' commitment to taking a post in Germany was questionable.

St John Gaffney, a former US consul to Germany, was contacted in the US and urged to go to Berlin to take charge.[57] But Nancy Power determined that the bureau be staffed by people who were not tainted by association with past Irish initiatives in the period 1916–20. She told de Valera that 'Mr G is described on all sides here – where unanimity is otherwise rare – as a person of appalling indiscretion ... He does not know one word of the language of the country, although he lived in it so long.'[58]

By the time Dublin received Power's warning, Gaffney had already embarked on his transatlantic voyage to Berlin via Paris. Nevertheless, acting on Power's advice,[59] the decision to appoint him to Berlin was rescinded and Chartres, following discussions in Dublin, was in late May confirmed as Irish envoy to Berlin instead.[60] An unhappy Gaffney was redirected to Switzerland, but refused to go because of his negative experiences when he had worked there for eighteen

---

52 NAI, DFA, ES, London 1919–21, Box 5, File 1, Memo from D. to L., 10 Dec. 1920. **53** Ibid., Power–Mother, 22 Apr. 1921. **54** Ibid., Box 33, File 239, Nancy–Mother, 18 Apr. 1921. **55** NAI, DE, 2/526, Power–de Valera, 11 May 1921. **56** NAI, DFA, ES, Box 14, File 96, extract from O'Ceallaigh, n.d. **57** Ibid., Clune (alias for Gaffney)–de Valera, 26 May 1921. **58** NAI, DE, 2/526, Power–de Valera, 11 May 1921. **59** NAI, DFA, ES, Box 14, File 97, to President, 28 May 1921. **60** Ibid., File 96, letter to Brennan, 21 May 1921.

months after the armistice. He had been repeatedly questioned by the Swiss police about his activities and finally refused re-entry into the country, precipitating his return to the US.[61]

Meanwhile during April and May, Nancy Power became discouraged about the advisability of establishing a Berlin bureau. Her arrival in Berlin coincided with the height of Weimar's political crisis over payment of reparations. The Versailles treaty had not specified the amount of war reparations to be paid and had given that task to the Inter-Allied Reparations Commission in consultation with the new German regime. As the final deadline for deciding the sum approached during May 1921, the Weimar regime's reluctance to pay became clearer.

Nancy Power noted that the Allied reparation demands, predicated on Germany's guilt for the war, had 'an extraordinary effect in hardening national opinion'.[62] Weimar sought a drastic reduction in Allied reparation claims, an end to the Allied occupation of the Rhineland, and the retention of Upper Silesia. The Allies retaliated in March 1921 by occupying Ruhr towns,[63] in response to which the German government protested and resigned.

A left-of-centre government under Joseph Wirth, formed in late May 1921, redirected Weimar towards a policy of fulfilment (*Erfüllungspolitik*) of the Versailles treaty. Acceding to Allied pressures Wirth commenced payment by instalments of the 132 billion Deutschmarks demanded by the reparations commission, anticipating that the Allies would eventually recognize the exorbitance of the payments and reduce them in accordance with Weimar's ability to pay. As Nancy Power observed, the time for starting a propaganda offensive for Ireland in Germany was 'ill-chosen'.[64]

The Weimar Republic was in a parlous state. Government was dependent upon unstable party coalitions of the Centre Party (*Zentrumspartei*), the Socialists (*Sozialdemokratische Partie Deutschlands*, SPD), the Democrats (*Deutsche Demokratische Partie*, DDP) and the German People's Party (*Deutsche Volkspartei*, DVP). Nine administrations rose and fell between February 1919 and the end of 1923.[65] These often minority governments were unpopular in a society that had unresolved structural problems and authoritarian leanings. Indeed Nancy Power believed the centrist parties and governments were 'not of

61 Ibid., Clune (alias for Gaffney)–de Valera, 26 May 1921. 62 Ibid., Box 33, File 232, Power, 29 Mar. 1921. 63 Carr, *History of Germany*, pp 311–12; Graham Ross, *The great powers and the decline of the European states system, 1914–1945* (London, 1983), p. 46. 64 NAI, DE, 2/526, Power–de Valera, 11 May 1921. 65 John Hiden, *The Weimar Republic* (London, 1996, 2nd ed.), pp 15–6.

much use to us', since the 'the aristocratic, "Militarist" elements are the anti-English ones'.[66]

One of the few opportunities for Irish-German collaboration in this period arose in May 1921 following the appointment of Irishman Séamus O'Connor to the German legal team defending a group of German soldiers against war crimes charges. In preparing a defence O'Connor contacted the Dáil seeking information about the British Army's excesses during the Anglo-Irish War.[67] The Dáil arranged to provide O'Connor with evidence of bad treatment of Irish prisoners by Britain. The publicity department in Ireland was anxious to maximize the propaganda value of the enterprise.[68] However, this indirect German contact with the unrecognized Irish government, although indicative of some German empathy, did not constitute official recognition.

Despite Power's doubts and de Valera's strictures about the linguistic ability of the permanent postholder in Berlin, Chartres was appointed. His grasp of German was allegedly limited[69] and he was often absent for long periods on government business elsewhere.[70] These shortcomings were to a certain degree compensated for by Nancy Wyse Power's decision to remain in Berlin as his assistant.

The Berlin mission's main function was to collect and distribute information, which it gathered from British and Irish newspapers and periodicals, categorized and distributed to influential people such as journalists, professors and the German Catholic hierarchy. The information was also used in the twice-weekly *Bulletin* of which 1,200 copies were issued. As minister of external affairs de Valera was kept abreast of the attitude of the German press towards developments in Ireland and German political developments as were likely to have international consequences.[71] The priority was to counter British propaganda in Germany where the newspapers were reliant on material from the London-based Press Association. To confront the unobtrusive British propaganda, the German inclination towards Britain and the better behaviour of British occupation forces, Power proposed that 'anti-English, as distinct from pro-Irish, propaganda would be of value'. Britain's contribution to the origins and waging of the Great War and its role in the Versailles treaty should be emphasized.[72]

---

66 NAI, DFA, ES, Box 33, File 232, Power, 29 Mar. 1921. 67 Ibid., Box 9, File 61, extract of letter to Brennan, 17 May 1921 & Brennan–publicity department, 14 June 1921. 68 Ibid., publicity–external affairs, 11 July 1921. 69 Bewley, *Memoirs*, pp 76–7. 70 Between September 1921 and August 1922 he was absent for nearly six months. On 5 November 1921 he attended the Anglo-Irish negotiations in London as secretary to the Irish delegation. In March 1922 he was transferred temporarily to Paris to take charge there. 71 NAI, DFA, D/PG/IFS Berlin 1922–24 (1922 Berlin Office), Chartres' memo: Berlin legation, note on staff and work, n.d. 72 NAI, DFA, ES, Box 33, File 232, Power memo, 29 Apr. 1921.

The *Bulletin* was best received in Bavaria, the predominantly Catholic south-ern part of Germany[73] and the Catholic Centre Party's news agency was 'at the disposal' of Chartres for the distribution of material of Catholic interest 'at least once a week'.[74] By April 1922 the *Bulletin* had published its 100th issue, having appeared twice weekly for a year.[75] Professor Julius Pokorny, the only member of the former German-Irish Society whom Power and Chartres held in esteem, had been appointed as editor and Chartres reported that both his advice and his translation of relevant articles into German for the *Bulletin* were invaluable.[76] Initially, the press bureau was located in the suburbs near Pokorny's house but, when he retired as editor, it was moved into rooms at the Eden Hotel in Berlin's city centre.[77] In spring 1922 an assistant to Chartres was appointed because the Berlin bureau's small staff faced an increasing workload.[78]

Meanwhile consolidation of diplomatic efforts had been achieved the previ-ous year when on 12 October 1921 Charles Bewley (1888–1969) was appointed from Dublin as consul to Berlin.[79] Bewley was destined to play a significant part in inter-war Irish-German relations and appeared suitably qualified. He was the eldest son of Dr Henry Bewley, a descendant of an old Quaker colonial family traditionally involved in Dublin commerce.[80] At the age of ten he had been sent to Park House, an English boarding school. In 1901 he won a scholarship and entered Winchester. Another scholarship took him to New College, Oxford,[81] and in 1910 he won the prestigious Newdigate Prize for English verse with his poem 'Atlantis', the first Irishman to do so since Oscar Wilde. Having graduated from Oxford with an honours degree in moderations and literary humanities,[82] he entered the legal profession and was called to the Irish bar in 1914, building up a successful practice on the Connacht circuit. For a time he was also acting professor of law at University College, Galway.[83]

At Oxford he converted to Catholicism, influenced by the charismatic Fr Martindale, SJ and his own doubts about the validity of his inherited Quaker beliefs.[84] He subsequently wrote prolifically for British and American Catholic newspapers.[85] Challenging his middle-class Protestant unionist background, he became a supporter of Sinn Féin and defended arrested IRA members during the Anglo-Irish War.[86] Having been an unsuccessful Sinn Féin election candi-date,[87] Bewley was also the first barrister in the republican courts of law.[88] He

---

73 Ibid., Box 34, File 239(1), report by Power, 8 May 1922.   74 NAI, DFA, ES, Box 34, File 239, Chartres memo: Berlin legation – note on work and staff, 21 Sept. 1922.   75 NAI, DFA, ES, Box 34, File 239, Power–Duffy, 8 May 1922.   76 Ibid., Box 33, File 232, E. S. memo, 4 July 1922.   77 Ibid., File 239, E. S, memo, 5 Sept. 1922.   78 NAI, DFA, D/PG/IFS Berlin 1922–24 (1922 Berlin Office), Chartres–Duffy, 1 Mar. 1922.   79 NAI, DFA, ES, Box 34, File 239, minister of external affairs–minister of finance, 17 Oct. 1921. 80 IT, 3 Feb. 1969. 81 Bewley, *Memoirs*, pp 13–24. 82 McCormack, 'Afterword: camp literature', in Bewley, *Memoirs*, pp 289–90. 83 IT, 3 Feb. 1969. 84 Bewley, *Memoirs*, pp ix, 32. 85 IT, 3 Feb. 1969. 86 Bewley, *Memoirs*, pp 54–67. 87 Ibid. 88 Bewley, *Memoirs*, p. 67.

was judged to be 'intelligent, articulate, a good linguist, and very widely read'[89] and to have a talent for foreign languages notably Latin, Italian and German.[90]

Bewley's main responsibility, from a rented office in Berlin,[91] was to promote trade and support the development of Germany as an export market for Irish raw materials and foodstuffs.[92] Seven months after his arrival and following the signing of the Anglo-Irish Treaty, minister of trade Ernest Blythe appointed Cornelius Duane as Bewley's assistant on 22 May 1922, hoping that a revival of trade with Germany would mean increased activity and require someone to assist Bewley in routine work enquiries.[93] Duane held a BA from the National University of Ireland, was a business student who, unfortunately, had only a very limited knowledge of German[94] but received language tuition after he arrived.[95] Finally, after years of neglect, Berlin had become part of the foreign affairs agenda and a rudimentary mission operated there prior to Ireland achieving statehood.

RECOGNITION-SEEKING AND GUN-RUNNING

But the Weimar Republic still refused to extend diplomatic recognition to the Irish mission.[96] As John Chartres, newly-appointed director of Ireland's publicity-cum-diplomatic bureau, remarked in July 1921: 'the Germans have always had that form of snobbery which admires foreign ways ... There is a sort of feeling that what is English is best.'[97] To retain Britain's favour, the Auswärtiges Amt (AA) or German foreign office was unwilling to recognize the Irish mission and Chartres was forced to adopt a low profile. He found it anomalous that Irish envoys in Allied capitals were able to announce themselves without restraint, while in an enemy capital the envoy was obliged to remain almost incognito.[98] In July 1921 his precarious situation was emphasized when he was granted only a temporary visa to reside in Berlin.[99] In the event of a British protest, the AA would simply not renew his short-term visa.[1]

The Anglo-Irish truce (11 July 1921) ushered in the tantalising prospect of improved Irish-German understanding. The subsequent Anglo-Irish negotiations were apparently greeted with genuine admiration in Germany and led to

89 Keogh, *Ireland & Europe*, p. 28. 90 McCormack, 'Afterword', pp 290–1. 91 NAI, DFA, ES, Box 34 File 239, Bewley memo, 10 Dec. 1921. 92 IT, 15 Mar. 1922. 93 NAI, DFA, ES, Box 34, File 239(6), Blythe–Bewley, 22 May 1922. 94 Ibid. 95 NAI, DFA, D/PG/IFS Berlin 1922–24, Blythe–Bewley, 22 May 1922; ibid., Bewley–department of trade, 9 June 1922. 96 NAI, DFA, ES, Box 33, File 232, Chartres–Brennan, 5 Sept. 1921. 97 Ibid., E. S. memo, 4 July 1921. 98 Ibid., Chartres–Brennan, 5 Sept. 1921. 99 Ibid. 1 Ibid., Chartres–Brennan, 4 July 1921; NAI, DFA, ES, Box 14, File 96, Brennan–de Valera, 25 July 1921.

Ireland being a much more prominent topic in the newspapers.[2] The Berlin mission reported:

> The success in forcing England to open up negotiations and the steady, undeviating adherence to principle in the President's communications seem wonderful to the Germans, who contrast them with the actions of the German government towards the same enemy. Both in the Reichstag and in the press there have been many eulogies ... In private conversation one constantly hears it said, 'Germany had much to learn from Ireland.'[3]

Nonetheless, the Berlin mission retained its irregular status awaiting the outcome of the Anglo-Irish negotiations. Chartres summed up the situation thus: 'Their [the AA] one aim, partly through policy as a measure against the French and partly through sheer fear of the consequences of a more independent attitude, is to stand as well with the English as possible.'[4] Chartres, therefore, remained reluctant to announce himself openly as the envoy of the Irish government because if a British protest were made, the Weimar government 'would give way at once and do whatever was required of it'.[5] Chartres' fears were realized in October and November 1921.

By this stage Chartres had already been temporarily recalled from Berlin to act as second secretary to the Irish plenipotentiaries sent to London to negotiate with British prime minister David Lloyd George.[6] John T. Ryan and a group of IRA operatives – Robert Briscoe, Seán MacBride and Charles McGuinness – remained active in Berlin.[7] Just prior to Chartres arrival in Berlin in June 1921, Ryan had been allegedly accepted as Ireland's representative by the AA in Berlin using signed credentials.[8] De Valera considered Ryan's secret work should not clash with Chartres' open work at all,[9] and wished the same system could be developed in other countries; that was an open diplomatic mission and a covert intelligence service running in parallel.[10] However, it was not that simple. Chartres was directly accountable to the putative department of external affairs, but his mission also had associations with Michael Collins' operatives in Berlin and he had communications with Collins.[11] His receipt of £80 from Michael Collins on 3 January 1922 signified some unspecified involvement in covert military activities as well as in publicity-cum-diplomatic matters.[12]

The link between the military and the propaganda projects did jeopardize the standing of the Irish overt mission in Germany. Robert Briscoe, a Dublin-born Jew of Lithuanian origin,[13] was running guns on the orders of Michael Collins.

2 NAI, DFA, ES, Box 33, File 232, Chartres–Brennan, 5 Sept. 1921.   3 Ibid.   4 Ibid. 5 Ibid.   6 Murphy, *Chartres*, p. 51.   7 Ibid., pp 48–9. NAI, DFA, ES, Box 23, File 140, memorandum, 6 Mar. 1922.   8 NAI, DFA, ES, Box 14, File 96, USFA–de Valera, 1 June 1921.   9 Ibid.   10 Ibid.   11 Murphy, *Chartres*, p. 49.   12 Ibid., p. 91.   13 Ibid.

A trawler, the *Anita*, and its cargo of arms was discovered and impounded in Hamburg and its crew arrested on 6 October in compliance with Weimar's disarmament undertakings under the treaty of Versailles.[14] The news of Irish gunrunning in Berlin coincided with the British discovering another IRA gunrunning plot in Cardiff. Uproar ensued in the British press, producing an uncomfortable meeting for the Irish with Lloyd George during the sixth plenary session of the Anglo-Irish negotiations in October.[15]

Simultaneously, Weimar came under intense pressure in the German press to explain its contacts with London concerning the Hamburg gunrunning affair. Lloyd George reportedly said that the German government had warned him of the impending importation of arms into Ireland. Right-wing newspapers in particular were outraged by Weimar's alleged collaboration with the British, forcing the German government to deny that it had officially communicated with London, claiming that official circles had no idea of the manner in which the British government had been notified.[16] German assistance to the Irish would be more forthcoming in the subsequent Hamburg gunrunning trial.

The hostility of demobbed German army officers towards the British was invaluable in the IRA's search for arms. Indeed, Briscoe was instructed by his lawyer to pose as the Irish republican consul in Hamburg to help free his accomplice, Captain Charles McGuinness of the *Anita* because the Germans were rather sympathetic to their cause, and would not ask many questions.[17] Briscoe discovered the German officials were positively deferential. McGuinness and the ship were released after paying a fine of only a few pounds, despite admitting loading the *Anita* with arms for the IRA. Under the Versailles treaty, the arms should have been destroyed, but the sympathetic authorities surreptitiously diverted them from destruction to the backdoor of Briscoe's warehouse. Briscoe concluded that the Germans did not like the British at all.[18]

German feeling was even more bitter towards France as a result of her aggressive interpretation of the Versailles treaty and this steered Weimar's foreign policy towards Anglo-German friendship.[19] So British pressure on the AA during the Hamburg crisis threatened the very existence of the Berlin press bureau. Nancy Power was forced to leave Berlin briefly in early November and took the opportunity to again argue that Chartres should be posted in Berlin permanently. She wrote about the haphazard nature of the Berlin bureau: 'It is

---

14 R. Briscoe (with A. Hatch), *For the life of me* (Boston & Toronto, 1958), p. 99. 15 Coogan, *De Valera*, p. 258. 16 DFA, ES, Box 33, File 233, Chartres–USFA, 26 Nov. 1921. 17 Briscoe, *For the life of me*, p. 100. 18 Ibid., pp 100–1. For additional discussion and background see: A. Roth, 'Gun running from Germany to Ireland in the early 1920s', *Irish Sword*, 22: 88 (2000), pp 209–10. 19 NAI, DFA, ES, Box 233, SEO–external affairs, 10 Feb. 1921.

quite impossible for any man to keep in touch with the political feeling of a foreign country if he is to spend four weeks in London, one week in Berlin and
then another four in London.'[20]

Despite Weimar realpolitik and the semi-nomadic existence of the unrecognized
Irish representatives in Berlin, many Germans were privately sympathetic to the
Irish cause. Reaction to the signing of the Anglo-Irish Treaty in the German
press expressed the general friendliness of Germany[21] and the Treaty received
voluminous coverage eulogising the Irish spirit and its achievement, often under
headlines such as 'Ireland's Victory'.[22] The Weimar government also welcomed
the Anglo-Irish Treaty but on the basis of self-interest because it considered the
treaty would allow Britain to combat more effectively French designs on
Germany. There was even some speculation that France had fuelled the Irish
Civil War to distract Britain from continental considerations.[23]

The drift towards civil war confounded Irish efforts to gain official diplomatic recognition. Michael Collins and Eamon de Valera took until May to
agree to an election in June 1922[24] and German doubts about Irish internal stability grew.[25] In any case, as the reports sent by Chartres and Power show, the
fragile and controversy-ridden Weimar Republic was too preoccupied with its
own survival to give much consideration to Irish affairs. The democratic regime
was barely surviving and staggered through successive grave crises in early
1922.[26] In such confused and unpredictable domestic and international circumstances, further complicated by the difficulty of interpreting the treaty and the
Saorstát's dominion status, Weimar persisted in its circumspect policy towards
the Irish representatives. As late as June 1922 Bewley warned that Weimar
would not and could not afford to take even the slightest step which might risk
offending British susceptibilities.[27]

Although the Irish presence in Berlin increased following the signing of the
Anglo-Irish Treaty, the Irish delegation remained preoccupied with basic publicity and press functions, while the trade representative was simply a travelling
salesman. The Treaty failed to advance Irish-German diplomatic relations. The
attitude of the Weimar regime was typified by their reluctance in mid-1922 to

20 Ibid., Box 33, File 233, Power–de Valera, 5 Nov. 1921. 21 Ibid., Box 34, File 239(3),
J.C. minute, 4 Feb. 1922. 22 Ibid. 23 NAI, DT, S 2305, Bewley–department, 8 Aug.
1922. 24 F.S.L. Lyons, *Ireland since the famine*, (London, 1973, 2nd ed.), pp 457–8.
25 Ibid., p. 455. 26 NAI, DFA, ES, Box 33, File 236, Chartres–Duffy, 4 Feb. 1922; ibid.,
File 239, Power–Duffy, 31 Mar. 1922. 27 NAI, DFA, ES, Box 34, File 239, Bewley–department, 1 June 1922.

appoint as German consul J.C. Foley FAA, Director of Dowdall & Co., shipping agents, Cork.[28] The German authorities wanted a guarantee that the appointment would not create difficulties in their relationship with Britain.[29] The AA's written refusal to consider the matter was pointedly addressed to Bewley as an individual, leading him to observe 'that the German Foreign Office does not wish to recognize representatives of the Irish Free State even unofficially'.[30]

By September 1922, as normality slowly returned to Ireland, Irish businesses also lobbied for a German consul in Ireland[31] and on 20 November Bewley finally recorded success: a German consul general would be appointed to Dublin in the New Year, and then the German consul would investigate the proposal for a vice-consul in Cork. Nevertheless, he recommended that it would:

> be better not at present to publish anything in the Irish papers on the subject as the German officials admit frankly that they are very anxious not to do anything which could be construed as an attempt to undermine English interests, and they are still very doubtful about the attitude of the new Conservative Government in England.[32]

When Bewley made another effort to gain at least tacit recognition of the Irish delegation in Berlin,[33] Weimar still refused to recognize his credentials.

INTERNECINE SQUABBLING

Despite some positive signs from German Catholic and intellectual supporters, the Irish delegation remained fractured by personal and political disputes, problems dating back to the start of the Anglo-Irish negotiations and Bewley's arrival in Berlin.[34] Consuls functioned under the auspices of the nascent department of trade and commerce, while political agents, diplomats, and publicists were under the jurisdiction of the department of external affairs. Problems of co-ordination, overlap and division of duties arose between the two.[35] Bewley dealt with commercial treaties and recommended that this work should properly be done by a commercial attaché of the delegation and be under the supervision of the political head, as was the case in other countries.[36]

---

28 NAI, DFA, D/PG/Saorstát Berlin 1922–24 (untitled folder), DFA to Messrs. Dowdall & Co., 6 June 1922. 29 NAI, DFA, ES, Box 34, File 239, Bewley–department, 1 June 1922. 30 Ibid., Box 36, File 255, Bewley–department, 21 Sept. 1922. 31 NAI, DFA, D/PG/Saorstát Berlin 1922–4 (unnamed folder), secretary of department of trade and commerce–Bewley, n.d. 32 NAI, DFA, ES, Box 33, File 238, Bewley–department, 25 Nov. 1922. 33 Ibid. 34 Ibid., File 239(6), minister of external affairs–minister of finance, 17 Oct. 1921. 35 Ibid., File 234, Bewley–Ó hAodha, 2 Sept. 1922. 36 Ibid., File 234, Bewley minute, 21 Mar. 1922.

Bewley had sought originally the post of political envoy in Berlin but had to settle for that of consul.[37] Nonetheless he hankered after the political post held by Chartres and persisted in seeking it whenever an opportunity presented itself.[38] Personal and professional relationships among the Irish in Berlin were at a nadir, particularly after an encounter between Bewley and gunrunner Robert Briscoe in January 1922. They had previously met on a number of occasions, often at a Jewish-owned music hall called the Tauenzien Palast. Subsequently Briscoe received a complaint from the owner about Bewley's conduct on the night of 19 January. Briscoe, a Jew, a future TD and lord mayor of Dublin, reported that Bewley had arrived in the evening in a rather advanced state of intoxication, and 'on my name being mentioned burst forth into a string of most abusive and filthy language. His chief point of argument as an excuse for this attitude was my faith'.[39] Briscoe further alleged that Bewley had made extremely derogatory remarks about Jews in general, and had to be forcibly ejected from the premises.[40] When later confronted by Briscoe and his colleague, ship's captain Charles McGuiness, Bewley admitted his impropriety and apologized. Briscoe chastised Bewley for associating with Jürgens, the Hamburg shipping agent who had reneged on a promise to supply the IRA with guns and ammunition despite taking a deposit of £20,000.[41] Briscoe and his associates had been forced to recover the deposit through physical intimidation and reprimanded Bewley for dealing with such an 'embezzler'.[42] Briscoe lodged an official complaint with Chartres citing Bewley's ostensible anti-Semitism as grounds for his removal.[43] Chartres recommended Bewley be transferred elsewhere because:

> such behaviour in a public place by a gentleman known to represent officially a department of the Irish government reflects injuriously upon our country's reputation here. Moreover, an anti-Semitic outburst by an Irish official in a country where Jews are very numerous and very influential was an extraordinary indiscretion from the point of view of Irish material interests.[44]

In his defence Bewley argued that Briscoe masqueraded as an accredited consul for Ireland. On the evening of 19 January he claimed one of the staff of the Tauenzien Palast music hall had asked him whether Briscoe was an Irish consul:

---

37 Bewley, *Memoirs*, p. 76. 38 NAI, DFA, ES, Box 33, File 234, Bewley, 21 Mar. 1922. See NAI, DFA, ES, Box 33, File 234, Aire–Bewley, 31 Mar. 1922; NAI, DFA, ES, Box 33, File 234, Bewley–Ó hAodha, 2 Sept. 1922. 39 Ibid., Box 34, File 239, Briscoe–Chartres, 21 Jan. 1922. 40 Briscoe, *For the life of me*, p. 259. 41 NAI, DFA, ES, Box 34, File 239, Briscoe–Chartres, 21 Jan. 1922. 42 Briscoe, *For the life of me*, pp 92–3. 43 NAI, DFA, ES, Box 34, File 239, Briscoe–Chartres, 21 Jan. 1922. 44 Ibid., Chartres–Duffy, 30 Jan. 1922.

I said that he was not, and added that it was not likely that a Jew of this type would be appointed. (The conversation was in German.) I regret having made the latter remark and have already expressed my regret to Mr Briscoe. At that moment, a German Jew who was sitting near said that I had insulted his race and after a further short conversation I left the café.[45]

Chartres countered that occasionally circumstances might require Briscoe to impersonate a properly accredited representative of Ireland.[46] Briscoe insisted he had credentials to act on behalf of Ireland (probably from Michael Collins). Bewley also alleged that Briscoe's dislike of Jürgens was based not on the failed arms deal, but on Jurgens' establishment of a rival shipping line to compete on the Hamburg-to-Ireland route, since Briscoe had purchased a steamer, *City of Dortmund*, in mid-1921 to run between Hamburg, Bremen, Belfast and Dublin. It had an all IRA crew and its purpose was to train men for the smuggling business, to smuggle men into and out of Ireland, and to import the ingredients for explosives into Ireland. The steamer had begun to operate in the winter of 1921.[47] Bewley further suggested that Briscoe was an anti-Treaty profiteer who used his position falsely to present himself as an Irish consul for personal gain. He said Briscoe and McGuinness did not recognize what they termed the 'so-called Free State' and had been heard to disparagingly refer to 'Michael Collins and his dupes'.[48] Blythe, the minister for trade, concluded that Briscoe was 'a decidedly shady character'.[49] He told George Gavan Duffy towards the end of March there was no proof that the music hall incident had occurred other than Briscoe's statement. 'You are aware of the character which this gentleman bears and I need scarcely point out to you that little weight should be attached to any statement made by him'.[50] Duffy later admitted he knew Bewley was 'mad on the Jewish question and the incident ... was inexcusable' but Briscoe was nevertheless 'an undesirable person'.[51]

CONSULAR DIFFICULTIES

By March, Chartres was claiming Bewley had instigated 'a unilateral interruption of official relations' between the two of them.[52] In April 1922, he declared Bewley was 'unfamiliar with the canons of conduct to be observed by public men entrusted with the representation of Irish national interests abroad' and he

---

45 Ibid., memo handed to Chartres on 28 Jan. 1922 (presumably Bewley's). **46** Ibid. **47** Briscoe, *For the life of me*, pp 105–7. **48** NAI, DFA, ES, Box 34, File 239, unsigned memorandum entitled 're-Briscoe', (*c.*early Feb. 1922). **49** Ibid., Blythe–Duffy, 16 Feb. 1922. **50** Ibid., Bewley–Duffy, 25 Mar. 1922. **51** Ibid., Box 33, File 234, Duffy–Chartres, 29 Mar. 1922. **52** Ibid., Box 34, File 239, Chartres–Duffy, 5 Apr. 1922.

allowed his words and actions 'to be influenced by personal feelings without regard to the limitations placed on them by his official position'. Chartres recommended that in the national interest Bewley should be given a fresh start elsewhere.[53]

The hostilities spilled over into the daily operation of the mission requiring Dublin to intervene. Disputes arose between Chartres and Bewley on such matters as the repatriation of the remaining members of Casement's international brigade and the granting of visas to German nationals seeking to visit Ireland.[54] The Chartres–Bewley dispute impinged, too, on the delicate Anglo-Irish issue of who had the right to grant entry to the Saorstát. The provisional Irish government and London officials had agreed a procedure for granting permits to former enemy aliens (Germans and Austrians) wishing to travel through Britain to the Saorstát. The government arranged to consult the British authorities if German or Austrian citizens sought to enter the Saorstát via England.[55] The provisional government also promised London that in cases of direct entrance by former enemy aliens:

> no persons will be allowed to land ... except in cases where strong evidence is adduced to show that they are desirable immigrants. The greatest care will be taken to exclude all persons in whose cases grounds exist for suspicion that their real object is to reach Great Britain.[56]

The Berlin mission was to investigate carefully the references given by persons wanting to travel by that route and to endorse their passports.[57] To ease the dispute between Bewley and Chartres, Bewley was made responsible for non-Germans wishing to enter Ireland, while Chartres vetted German applicants.[58]

The Weimar Republic meanwhile continued to deny the mission official recognition. In addition, the spiral towards civil conflict in Ireland in 1922 alerted Weimar to the danger of any premature recognition of the Provisional government. It was unclear whether the Provisional government, which was succeeded by the first Saorstát government, could maintain control in the face of anti-Treaty hostility. Bickering inside the Berlin mission detracted from the business of recognition-seeking as the trade and publicity missions squabbled over jurisdiction.[59] Bewley's enduring failure to communicate with Chartres in the diplomatic office, combined with intensifying personal acrimony, fuelled a destructive dynamic. By July 1922 Duffy was anxious that Chartres should

53 Ibid., Box 33, File 234, Chartres–Duffy, 5 Apr. 1922. 54 Ibid., Box 33, File 238, Chartres–department, 28 Feb. 1922 & Box 33, File 238, Chartres–Duffy, 3 Mar. 1922. 55 NAI, DFA, ES, Box 18, File 118. 56 Ibid., Irish home office to HM chief inspector, aliens branch, home office, May 1922. 57 Ibid. 58 NAI, DFA, ES, Box 34, File 239, Duffy–Blythe, 29 Mar. 1922. 59 For example, see NAI, DFA, ES, Box 34, File 239.

attempt to establish official diplomatic relations with Germany. Chartres replied:

> my hands are tied until Mr Bewley has left Germany. The démarches which I have in contemplation and for which preliminaries have been settled, have specific purposes; other persons and influences will be drawn in; and there is a point at which contact with Mr Bewley would be inevitable. An influential friend, who has provided me with access to the Ministers, assures me that such contact would be prejudicial.[60]

The outbreak of the Irish Civil War exacerbated the animosity between Bewley and Chartres.

TREATY SPLIT

The Irish split over acceptance of the Treaty undermined the cohesiveness of the infant Irish foreign service and heightened tensions in Berlin. On 16 January 1922, Blythe instructed Bewley not to intervene in the looming 'political controversy'[61] about the Treaty. Blythe, as minister for trade and commerce, told Bewley that the Dáil had approved the Anglo-Irish Treaty and that he was an officer of the legal government of Ireland despite the breakaway of an anti-Treaty party.[62] Duffy meanwhile occupied an incongruous position: he was now external minister but he was not a member of the Provisional government. Nor was he part of the emerging anti-Treaty group although he believed that too many concessions had been granted to the British.[63] Chartres, left in limbo, was embarrassed by the lack of instructions from Duffy at a time of considerable political confusion.[64]

Bewley, by comparison, was closely supervised by his superior, Blythe, who was avowedly pro-Treaty. On 29 June, the day following the commencement of the siege on the Four Courts in Dublin, Blythe told Bewley:

> that the present is not a conflict between the two opposing political parties but a necessary measure taken by the Government to protect the fundamental rights of the people of the country against a section of the community who have avowed their determination to oppose the will of the country by force of arms and who, on their own admission, aim at bringing about a condition of things which would impel England to attempt a reconquest of the country.[65]

---

60 NAI, DFA, ES, Box 33, File 234, Chartres–Duffy, 23 July 1923. **61** NAI, DFA, ES, Box 34, File 239, Blythe–Bewley, 16 Jan. 1922. **62** Ibid. **63** Keogh, *Ireland & Europe*, pp 14–15. **64** NAI, DFA, ES, Box 34, File 239, Duffy–Chartres, 19 June 1922. **65** NAI,

Bewley believed the Anglo-Irish Treaty granted wide powers of self-government to the Irish Free State;[66] there was nothing that could not be altered once
the executive power was in their hands.[67] He assiduously implemented his
instructions and complained that no steps had been taken by Chartres to present
the Irish Provisional government's views to the German public. Following a tip-
off from Professor Pokorny, Bewley alleged that the Chartres-produced
Bulletins of 8 and 10 July contravened Blythe's instructions to avoid treating the
Irish unrest as 'a conflict between two opposing parties'.[68] The *Bulletin* printed
only 42 lines of personal details about the two heads of the Irish government,
Collins and Griffith, whereas 92 lines were devoted to people who had taken
part in the conflict in Dublin against the existing government, and who
belonged to a party which believed that open war should be waged against
England until Ireland's unrestricted freedom had been won. Arguing that twice
as much space had been devoted to the Irregulars as to the government heads,[69]
Bewley suggested, '[t]he general tone may be judged by the sentence: "Liam
Mellows [an anti-Treatyite] has always been a fighter for freedom".'[70] Germans
interested in Ireland were surprised that the *Bulletin* 'should take up a neutral,
if not a hostile attitude towards' the Irish government, he said.[71] As Pokorny
wrote: 'Such fine talk might be all right in Ireland, but since when does foreign
propaganda consist in glorifying the deadly enemies of a lawful government of
one's country?'[72]

Blythe viewed Chartres' assessment of the key Irish personalities as biased
and disloyal[73] and concluded that Chartres was not a proper person to represent
Ireland in Germany.[74] He advised Duffy that Chartres should be dismissed,[75]
provoking Duffy to chastise Chartres for extolling de Valera and his friends (the
anti-Treaty side) when they were wrecking the country.[76] Chartres countered
that the only expressions of appreciation that had appeared in the *Bulletin* were
for Collins and Griffith, and the remainder was a bare chronological recital of
facts. He did admit, however, the disputed *Bulletin*'s irregular coverage coincided inconveniently with the outbreak of the Civil War. But he claimed the issue
of 8 July appeared when those in Germany had no news of any outbreak or
expectation of an extended civil war. Everyone had expected the riots to be over
immediately. Indeed, his view was that to harp on Irish differences would have

DT, S 2105, Bewley–Blythe, 15 July 1922.   66 Bewley, *Memoirs*, p. 76.   67 Ibid., p. 86.
68 NAI, DT, S 2305, Bewley–Blythe, 17 July 1922.   69 Ibid.   70 NAI, DFA, ES, Box 33,
File 234, Bewley–Blythe, 11 July 1922.   71 Ibid.   72 NAI, DFA, D/PG/IFS, Berlin 1921,
1922, 1923 (addenda), Pokorny–Bewley, 14 July 1922.   73 NAI, DFA, ES, Box 33, File 234,
Blythe–Duffy, 21 July 1922.   74 Ibid., Blythe–each member of the ministry, 27 July 1922.
75 Ibid., Blythe–Duffy, 21 July 1922.   76 Ibid., Duffy–Chartres, 21 July 1922.

prejudiced the prospects of his special task of seeking formal diplomatic recognition.[77]

Michael Collins, in contrast to Blythe, Bewley and Duffy, was more cautious and balanced in his assessment of Chartres' alleged disloyalty:

> I am inclined to agree with Mr Bewley that it is not strictly playing the game, but I think that the matter is so cleverly done that you would be rather in a unique position to take disciplinary action. I think you can only note it and note similar future things and then deal with the accumulative effect.[78]

Chartres appealed to Griffith, resenting Duffy's accusation that he was using his position to turn German public opinion against the government.[79] But Chartres was further undermined when Joseph Walshe, the acting secretary at the department of external affairs, told Chartres that his explanation of events was merely evasive and explained nothing, while the so-called chronological facts Chartres had printed in the *Bulletin* were tantamount to approval of the anti-Treaty side.[80] Bewley, in the meantime, had extended his criticisms to argue that the *Bulletin*'s anti-British propaganda was counterproductive in predominantly Anglophile Germany.[81]

One anonymous, but well-connected, member of the Provisional government or its administration defended Chartres, arguing that it was remarkable that Bewley, as an official of the department of trade and commerce, should criticize the work of an official of the department of external affairs. He believed that Bewley's complaint about the treatment of Anglo-Irish relations in the *Bulletin* was trivial. This anonymous critic of Chartres' dismissal proceedings pinpointed that Bewley's allegations against Chartres were based on uncorroborated hearsay and vested interests. For example, Bewley's main informant, Professor Pokorny, was anxious to resume the work of translating the *Bulletin* into German that he had given up in the summer of 1921. Chartres' anonymous defender revealingly advised the minister of external affairs that

> it appears quite plain to me that the present Govt. arrangements in Berlin cannot continue with advantage, & your proposed interview with the Envoy [Chartres], may lead to more suitable arrangements being made. Judging from the questions you asked me today re Mr C's [Chartres] connection [*sic*] with Barton, Masonry etc – it strikes me there is a campaign to push him out of your service. Before that culminates I would like to

---

77 Ibid., Chartres–Duffy, 27 July 1922. 78 NAI, DFA, ES, Box 34, File 234, Collins–Blythe, 28 July 1922. 79 Ibid., Chartres–president, 27 July 1922. 80 Ibid., Walshe–Chartres, 8 Aug. 1922. 81 NAI, DT, S 2105, Bewley–department of trade, 11 Aug. 1923.

impress upon you the confidence that A.G. [Arthur Griffiths] & Mick [Michael Collins] reposed in him.[82]

But the impetus behind Chartres' enforced exit from the foreign service was unstoppable and it set in motion the disintegration of the Berlin mission.

DISMEMBERMENT

The impetus to dismiss Chartres grew during July and August as the threat of the anti-Treatyites to the Provisional government. On 25 July, George Gavan Duffy resigned in protest against the spirit of narrowness and intolerance in the cabinet.[83] Arthur Griffith replaced him but died on 12 August and Michael Collins was killed at Béal na mBláth, West Cork, on 22 August. In September, Desmond FitzGerald was appointed minister of external affairs.

The department of external affairs had already ordered the *Bulletin* to halt production for the remainder of August and September.[84] Both Power and Chartres were recalled to Dublin for discussions and an investigation into the alleged anti-Treatyite misdemeanours of the mission in Berlin. In October 1922 Power was formally transferred back to Dublin.[85] Ironically, the presumption of the anti-Treatyites was that Nancy Power was a government supporter. In December her premises in Camden Street were destroyed in one of a series of arson attacks against pro-Treatyites.[86] Such was the tragedy of civil war that individuals who failed to identify openly with either side became the targets of both sides.

The withdrawal of Chartres from Berlin proved to be controversial and pro-tracted. In September, FitzGerald decided to transfer Chartres to work in the department of trade and commerce in Dublin.[87] Chartres maintained that new accusations made by Bewley that he and Nancy Power had caused grave scandal by living in the same hotel in Berlin were instrumental in the termination of his Berlin posting.[88] Chartres presumed Bewley's denunciation was an extension of the personal hostility towards himself, which had originated with Chartres' report on Bewley's conduct in the Taunzien Palast music hall.[89] A furious Chartres was reassigned. But the matter did not end there. His conduct of finances as Irish envoy in Berlin was investigated by the comptroller and auditor general in the spring of 1923.[90] Chartres was required to reimburse a relatively

---

82 NAI, DT, S.2305, anonymous memo, n.d.   83 Keogh, *Ireland & Europe*, p. 15. 84 NAI, DFA, D/PG/IFS Berlin 1921–3, 'Berlin office', Walshe–Chartres, 8 Aug. 1922. 85 NAI, DFA, ES, Box 34, File 239, Walshe–Power, 2 Oct. 1922.   86 Keogh, *Twentieth-century Ireland*, p. 16.   87 NAI, DFA, ES, Box 33, File 234, Chartres–president, 28 Oct. 1922.   88 Ibid., Chartres–President, 12 Oct. 1922.   89 Ibid.   90 See NAI, DFA, ES, Box 19, File 121.

minor sum related to travel and clothing expenses even though the investigation was discontinued for want of documentary evidence. However, Chartres' refused to pay the trivial sum and challenged the legitimacy of the department of finance's demands, which he considered a grievous slight on his reputation and a contributing factor in his removal from Berlin. Ernest Blythe as minister of finance (from 1923) played a significant role in pursuing Chartres for payment of the travel and clothing expenses up until 1926 and unrelentingly questioned Chartres' financial competency during his Berlin posting.[91]

The whole episode of Chartres' dismissal was indicative of a politically-motivated purge of the embryonic civil service during the Civil War years. George Gavan Duffy's resignation from his position as minister of external affairs in July 1922 and his alienation from the Provisional/Free State governments, for instance, proved to be a major disruption to the young Irish foreign service.

Meanwhile, on 2 September, Bewley, presumably in another effort to secure the post of political envoy in Berlin, informed Blythe that he intended to retire on 1 October,[92] and inquired whether the government would appoint political representatives to other German-speaking capitals.[93] He, in turn, was summoned to Dublin to discuss the mission's future as all commercial agents were being brought under the authority of the department of external affairs.[94] Bewley's bluff had been called but he did not retire immediately and returned to Berlin to continue his commercial work.[95] His eventual resignation in early 1923 was not only a result of his dissatisfaction with the post of trade representative but was ostensibly linked to his displeasure at the evolving Anglo-Irish relationship. In late 1922 passport and visa protocols were largely taken over by the British consul in Berlin, and visas were granted in consultation with the British authorities.[96] Bewley became frustrated by what he conceived as undue Irish deference to Britain.[97] Ironically Bewley resigned in February for much the same reasons as he had criticized Chartres. He had earlier complained that Chartres was excessively anti-British, but now he believed that the Saorstát's policies were overly Anglophile and servile. In fact, Leopold Kerney, an anti-Treatyite who had been removed from the Irish foreign service, congratulated Bewley for resigning. On 17 March 1923 Kerney telegrammed Bewley: '[I]f rumour respecting your attitude [is] correct accept my congratulations'[98] although Bewley denied such suggestions that he was disloyal to the Saorstát government.[99]

91 NAI, DFA, ES, Box 19, File 121, MacGrath–Walshe, 24 Jan. 1923 & Chartres–Blythe, 25 Apr. 1923 & MacGrath–Brennan, 28 July 1925. **92** NAI, DFA, ES, Box 33, File 238(1), Bewley–Blythe, 2 Sept. 1922. **93** Ibid. **94** Ibid., Walshe–Bewley, 30 Sept. 1922. **95** Ibid., Bewley–department, 10 Feb. 1923. **96** Ibid., Gearóid Ó Lochlainn's report on Brussels and Berlin (Nov.–Dec. 1922); Bewley, *Memoirs*, p. 88. **97** NAI, DFA, ES, Box 34, File 241, Bewley to ministry of foreign affairs, 6 Feb. 1923. **98** Ibid., Kerney–Bewley, 17 Mar. 1923. **99** Ibid., File 241, Bewley–Kerney, telegram, 24 Mar. 1923.

Conor Duane succeeded Bewley as Irish trade representative in March 1923,[1] but the outlook for Irish-German relations was discouraging and there had been suggestions that he should have been appointed to Denmark instead because elements of the civil service in Dublin viewed the German political and economic environment as commercially unfavourable.

Unsettled conditions in both Ireland and Germany had wreaked havoc with the possibilities for increasing Irish-German trade. Bewley early in his appointment to Berlin in April 1922 had summed up the issues inimical to greater commercial interaction between Ireland and Germany[2] and to normalcy in Irish-German diplomacy. The disturbed state in Ireland deterred German businessmen (and the Weimar government). Only a return to security or peace in Ireland would improve trade. However, the War of Independence was followed by the Civil War going on into 1923. Bewley suggested, too, the formation of Irish importer organisations to place sizeable orders with German firms and to expedite delivery.[3]

One example of how the Civil War disrupted Irish-German trade was the Free State's detention of Briscoe's *City of Dortmund* on suspicion of anti-Treatyite activities in August 1922. The Hamburg steamer was prevented from landing her cargo in Cork and was diverted to Dublin and impounded. This led to a delay in the distribution of German products to clients in Cork and the fact that the Irish army, rather than trained stevedores, landed the goods caused considerable damage.[4] Furthermore, the prolonged detention of the merchant ship prevented the resumption of normal trade between Hamburg and Cork.[5] It took until November 1925 for the German exporters to be compensated for their increased costs and losses relating to the impounding of the *City of Dortmund* in 1922, disrupting trade relationships.[6]

Bewley's second argument put forward in 1922 was that unstable economic and political conditions in Germany had a deleterious impact on the development of Irish-German links. German prices were uncompetitive despite depreciation of the German mark and the cost of German manufactures being quoted in sterling. Bewley discovered that under the treaty of Versailles German payment of reparations in kind, for example, coal effectively subsidized German industrial competitors and forced some German firms to import raw materials.[7] Bewley concluded correctly that there was little likelihood of balanced Irish-German trade because, despite a German export drive to earn foreign currency, the state of the German economy and German restrictions on

---

1 Ibid., File 240, O'Duffy's memorandum, n.d.   2 NAI, DFA, ES, Box 19, File 124, Bewley–department, 28 Apr. 1922.   3 Ibid.   4 NAI, DFA, GR 149, O'Brien–Walshe, 25 Aug. 1922.   5 Ibid.   6 Ibid., Walshe–Dehn, 11 Nov. 1925.   7 Ibid.

imports severely limited opportunities for Irish exporters.[8] In addition, the Weimar Republic experienced catastrophic hyperinflation during 1922 and 1923. The Weimar governments used the hyperinflation they created through their cheap money policy – printing reichsmarks – as an argument for the reduction of reparations.[9]

In February 1923, therefore, Bewley's resignation led the secretaries of the departments of external affairs and trade and commerce to suggest that an Irish trade representative would be of greater utility in Denmark than in Germany.[10] However, Desmond FitzGerald, minister of external affairs, maintained that a Berlin office was needed on general political grounds[11] and, as he told the Dáil in June 1923, the Berlin mission was doing useful work.[12] The mission thus received a stay of execution but it was clear that many Dáil deputies regarded political envoys as financial liabilities of uncertain use, forcing FitzGerald to tell the Dáil that Irish foreign representatives were temporary until made permanent and their survival depended on the 'value for money' they represented.[13]

When he took over in March 1923 Duane nonetheless was anxious to improve Irish-German trade relations and set about his task which included compiling lists of German importers of Irish goods and reporting on German economic conditions.[14] He believed much good could be derived to the immediate advantage of Ireland[15] and that German capital and technical skills could be used to develop the deficient Irish economy.[16] Duane also thought more attention should be paid to positive propaganda, highlighting the distinction between Irish and British people as many Germans perceived Irish people to be a derivation of the British race.[17] Unfortunately just as, in Duane's words, the Saorstát was 'turning the corner' by defeating the anti-Treatyites, the Weimar Republic sunk to new depths during the Ruhr crisis of 1923, precipitated by France's occupation of the area.

The Wirth government's *Erfüllungspolitik* had failed to secure any rapid downward revision of Germany's reparations bill. The Allies were alarmed about the Rapallo Agreement between Soviet Russia and Weimar Germany on 16 April 1922 which cancelled out each other's reparations claims. France used postponement by Germany of timber reparations shipments and a German request for a three- or four-year moratorium as a justification to occupy the Ruhr in the winter of 1922–3. In concert with Belgium, France isolated the Ruhr and the Rhineland from Weimar as an economic unit and proceeded to

---

8 Ibid.; IT and *Dublin Evening Telegraph*, 10 May 1922. 9 D.J.K. Peukert, *The Weimar Republic: the crisis of classic modernity* (London, 1991), pp 52–66. 10 NAI, DFA, ES, Box 34, File 240(2), Walshe–DIC, 15.2.1923 & DIC–Walshe, n.d. 11 Ibid., File 241, secretary of trade and commerce to Walshe, 19 Feb. 1923. 12 *Dáil Debates*, vol. 3, 25 June 1923, col. 2394. 13 Ibid., cols. 2394–97. 14 NAI, DFA ES, Box 34, File 240, Duane–industry and commerce, 19 Oct. 1923, n.d. 15 Ibid. 16 Ibid. 17 Ibid.

extract resources. The Germans responded with a general strike and passive resistance which completely devalued the German mark and led to escalating inflation throughout Germany.[18] The catastrophic nature of that hyperinflation is highlighted by the fact that in January 1923 the wholesale price index in Germany was 2,783 times higher than in 1913. By December 1923 that index was 1,261 thousand million times higher.[19]

One result was that the cost of living in Berlin inflated to such an extent that Duane's salary was worthless. On 13 November 1923, facing financial embarrassment and looming hunger,[20] he asked for immediate recall. A salary increase would not alter his decision: 'because money is no reward for the physical strain to which one is at present subject in this city'.[21] The Weimar Republic appeared to be under serious threat from political extremists of the right and left: separatist risings had occurred in the Rhineland and in October Communist uprisings took place in Saxony and Hamburg. In November, Adolf Hitler with his ill-planned Nazi Beer Hall putsch in Munich, backed by the war hero General Erich Ludendorff, attempted to take over Bavaria to launch a national revolution.

After successive difficulties, it was the German inflationary winter of 1923–4 that finally terminated Irish representation at Berlin. The Irish would not return for another five years. Duane ended his appointment to Berlin reporting pessimistically that, '[t]he political structure of Germany has been shattered and the economy has been in agony since 1918. The very obvious signs of hunger and want moving side by side with luxury cannot but create a despondent feeling'.[22] While commenting on the uprisings he noted astutely:

> Generally speaking such universal unrest does not contribute anything in the nature of economic or industrial progress but it cannot last indefinitely and a distracted Europe must make up its mind to secure order as a preliminary to progress.[23]

In spite of nearly three years of efforts by Dáil, provisional government and Saorstát representatives in Berlin, Ireland's diplomatic enterprise collapsed ignominiously.[24] Government circles regarded the closure of the Berlin mission as temporary and prompted by Duane's resignation. But the *Evening Post* newspaper insinuated that a re-opening was unlikely, citing lively criticism in the Dáil about the cost of maintaining representatives abroad.[25] Fighting the financially regressive line of government backbenchers, Richard Mulcahy, the minister of defence, advocated the earliest possible re-opening of the Berlin mission and even that Chartres return. Closure was a distinct loss and would incur the unnecessary cost of reconstructing an Irish presence at a later date, he said.[26]

---

18 Ross, *Great powers*, pp 47–8. 19 Peukert, *Weimar*, p. 64. 20 NAI, DFA, ES, Box 34, File 240, Duane–external affairs, 13 Nov. 1923. 21 Ibid. 22 Ibid. 23 Ibid. 24 IT, 3 Jan. 1924. 25 *Evening Post*, 4 Dec. 1923. 26 NAI, DT, S.2305, Mulcahy–Cosgrave, 5

BALANCE SHEET OF A FAILURE

The Irish mission in Berlin from 1921 to 1923 offers intriguing insights into two initial phases of Irish diplomacy. It began as the republican movement's propaganda enterprise to gain international support for its goals and aims. Then, after the Anglo-Irish Treaty, the activities of the Berlin mission epitomized the difficulty of transforming a propaganda mission into a recognized legation with a full range of diplomatic and consular functions. In both phases the venture operated in the highly adverse international climate that characterizes many nations' initial steps towards statehood. But the Irish international position was, in addition, acutely affected by the unstable postwar conditions. Not only were Irish nationalists seeking independence from a metropolitan power that had emerged victorious in war but one which also held the balance of power between France and Germany. The US retreat into diplomatic isolationism assured Britain's elevation in European affairs and hampered an unprejudiced hearing of the Irish nationalist case. This was exacerbated as the frail Weimar Republic and France vied for British support. It was impossible under such circumstances for the Berlin mission to gain German recognition. While the official position of the Weimar Republic on recognition of Irish diplomatic independence was unhelpful, to safeguard its own strategic interests, this belied widespread unofficial government sympathy for the Irish before and after the Anglo-Irish Treaty. The strongly pro-Irish trend in German public opinion compelled the Weimar Republic to give Irish revolutionary nationalism preferential treatment on at least one occasion – the Hamburg gunrunning incident during which the perpetrators escaped serious punishment with smuggled armaments in contravention of the treaty of Versailles. Furthermore Weimar did not suppress the unrecognized Irish trade and publicity mission.

Unfortunately, the adverse conditions encountered by the Berlin mission were worsened by its own conduct. Association with gunrunning from Hamburg and other covert operations was potentially harmful to diplomatic, publicity and commercial representation. In addition, and from its very formation, the hapless Irish mission was beset by internecine disputes and rivalries dating from its origins in the querulous Irish-German Society. This was followed by the unseemly disputes between Bewley, the trade representative, and Chartres and Power in the publicity section. The *ad hoc* nature of the representation was understandable, but the irreconcilable personality differences were the root of the problem which the divisions of the Irish Civil War simply amplified. The department of external affairs had appeared satisfied with the

Jan. 1924; Mulcahy–Cosgrave, 15 Jan. 1924. Mulcahy (in charge of defeating the 'irregulars' during the civil war) clearly had no doubts about Chartres' political reliability notwithstanding the inflammatory allegations concerning Chartres' allegiances.

Bulletin's editorial policy and content until the critical period of July and August 1922. Until then, too, Chartres was highly thought of by Collins and Griffith. It could credibly be argued that the Berlin mission's case for survival after 1923 would have been strong except for the Bewley-Chartres antagonism.

The key question is: was John Chartres an anti-Treatyite and disloyal to the provisional government in mid-1922? The evidence points in the direction of a rehabilitation of Chartres. Although the situation is highly ambiguous, the written record indicates that Bewley was instrumental in levelling allegations that Chartres' editorial policy at the *Bulletin* was anti-Treatyite and, secondly, in prosecuting a slander campaign against both Chartres and Power. Yet Chartres agreed with the Free State constitution, so on the constitutional question he was pro-Treaty. The timing of the final allegations about Chartres and Power having an illicit affair is crucial. Until then it appeared that Chartres was likely to continue in his post in Berlin after discussions with the new minister of external affairs, Desmond FitzGerald. Chartres concluded that these new allegations led to his formal removal from Berlin. Chartres went on to work for the department of industry and trade for the remainder of his career and was apparently a loyal citizen of the new Free State, despite the vendetta waged against him. The Bewley-Chartres-Blythe tangle generates a distinctively unsalubrious picture.

Another peculiarity of the Berlin mission was that the Irish representatives generally paid little attention to reporting the domestic turmoil that characterized Weimar 1921 to 1924.[27] Most surprisingly there was no sustained analysis of German reparations resistance or European foreign policy generally. France's and Great Britain's divergent policies towards the implementation of the treaty of Versailles were ignored. The precarious situation of Germany was not analyzed by the Berlin mission.

This neglect of Germany's central role in European affairs is all the more remarkable because the very foundation of the mission was based on George Gavan Duffy's optimistic forecast of a new powerful German-American-Soviet coalition of powers, although such a trilateral arrangement did not occur. Weimar instead developed bilateral relationships with the two ideological opponents, the US and the USSR. Instead of the US providing the capital to modernize the USSR as Duffy had proposed, it provided Germany with the credit to meet its reparation repayments and to reconstruct its economy in the mid-1920s under the 1923 Dawes Plan and later the 1929 Young Plan. The 1920s also witnessed the two European outcasts, the Weimar Republic and the Soviet Union, forming a tentative and secret alliance of convenience to overcome their international predicaments. Weimar's new 'eastern orientation'[28] was exemplified by the Weimar–Soviet Rapallo treaty of April 1922, which was in turn strengthened by the 1926 treaty of Berlin.[29] The Weimar–Soviet alliance,

---

27 Cf. Murphy, *Chartres*, p. 124.   28 Peukert, *Weimar*, p. 59.   29 Carr, *History of Germany*,

more provocative and rhetorical than real, commenced the normalization of the Soviet Union's international status. In addition the Reichswehr (German army) leadership used the Soviets to circumvent the treaty of Versailles secretly to produce, develop and test new military equipment (e.g., tanks) in the Soviet Union.[30]

But 1923 was the *année terrible* for the Weimar Republic that finally terminated the remnants of Irish representation in Berlin. In one sense the Berlin mission originated with Duffy's positive report in early 1921 and its disintegration began after his resignation in July 1922. Its core period of operation was brief – June 1921 to July 1922 – and even this was subject to significant endogenous and exogenous constraints. Fortunately this Irish diplomatic failure did not prevent improved Irish-German links in the mid-1920s.

p. 330. **30** J. Hiden, *Germany and Europe, 1919–1939* (London, 1977), pp 90–3.

2

Resurrection, 1923–32

'Aujourd'hui on peut dire sans exagération que l'Etat Libre tend à devenir une sorte de province de l'Allemagne et comme son bastion avancé dans le système anglo-saxon.'[1]

'[T]he Foreign Office is not really interested in us any more than it is in any small unimportant state situated a considerable distance from its frontiers. It thinks of us in precisely the same terms as it thinks, say, of Bulgaria or a small central American republic. It is concerned to maintain the most friendly relations possible with us, but it apparently has no appreciation whatever of our importance as a member of the British Commonwealth ... Indeed, the whole policy of the Foreign Office seems to be to treat us as if we were a republic in name as well as in fact.'[2]

Ireland largely neglected formal diplomatic relations with European countries in the mid-1920s. Redefining Commonwealth and dominion status was the major preoccupation of the Saorstát, but it also began to develop a distinctive role in the League of Nations. The department of external affairs' personnel pool and organization was decimated by the Civil War, the results of which were epitomized by the abandonment of the Berlin mission in 1923. The gradual reconstruction of the foreign service thereafter, to create an effective career service, proved problematic. Many viewed a diplomatic service as an unaffordable luxury. The British preference for the absorption of external affairs into the department of the president was given concrete expression in the department of finance's demands to rationalize departments.[3]

The Cumann na nGaedheal government's foreign policy after 1922 aimed to reinterpret Commonwealth ties in terms consonant with Irish nationalism and in accordance with Irish interests and aspirations.[4] It was determined to prove that acceptance of the Anglo-Irish Treaty (1921) had been justified.[5] The newly independent state gradually redefined its relationship with the old metropolitan power as it emerged into the international arena and encountered unfamiliar problems. It defined its independence *vis-à-vis* the former ruling power and tried, at the same time, to extend and assert its new found independence. The

1 Quai d'Orsay, Europe 1918–1940, vol. 15, Blanche–Herriot, 4 April 1925, pp 146–52.
2 NAI, DFA, EA 231/4B, Binchy memo, 27 May 1930. 3 Keogh, *Ireland & Europe*, pp 18–19. 4 N. Mansergh, 'Ireland: external relations, 1926–1939', in F. MacManus (ed.), *The years of the great test* (Cork, 1967), p. 127. 5 Keatinge, *Formulation*, p. 16.

re-emergence of Irish diplomatic representation in Berlin in 1929 and 1930 was part of this.

Once reciprocal bilateral representation was finally established with Germany and the Commonwealth repercussions dealt with, Daniel A. Binchy MA, PhD, BL, the first official Irish diplomatic representative to Germany, was able to concentrate on his new role. He proved to be an able diplomat. He gained access to many of the key political, social and economic actors in the late Weimar Republic during the limited period before his premature retirement from the Irish foreign service in 1932. In retrospect, his threat assessment of the Nazis and the durability of the Weimar Republic was flawed, but he nevertheless was one of the more accomplished of the first generation of Irish diplomats.

WEIMAR'S TRANSFORMATION

The German economic and political situation had stabilized since Conor Duane's enforced retreat from Berlin in late 1923. 1923 and 1924 represented Weimar's *Stunde Null*, or 'zero hour'. Hyperinflation destroyed the wealth and savings of the middle classes. Embittered nationalism was rampant and extremism burgeoned. Foreign policy was a failure and passive resistance to the provocative occupation of the Ruhr by France and Belgium was dropped. In the May 1924 national elections the DNVP won 19.5 per cent of the vote and the National Socialists won 6.5 per cent, their largest vote so far. Meanwhile the Communists (KPD) also made massive gains winning 12.6 per cent of the vote. The parties of the centre-left Weimar coalition that had ensured the survival of the troubled Republic until 1923, especially the Social Democrats, lost ground to the extremists and the coalition collapsed.[6] This threat to Weimar and the stability of post-war Europe forced a return to political realism and compromise by the moderates and centrists. After the summer of 1924 several factors contributed to European stability.

Gustav Stresemann, German foreign minister from November 1923 until his death in October 1929, emerged as Weimar's primary statesman. He pursued the policy of *Erfüllungspolitik* or fulfillment of the Versailles treaty's stipulations, and steered the DVP party towards constructive arbitration and coalition building to create a series of centre-right coalitions to tackle Weimar's problems. Under his influence the political elites of Weimar finally appeared to accept coalition-building, negotiation and compromise as a necessary political basis for a stable currency, low inflation and a return to economic normality.[7] The

6 Peukert, *Weimar*, pp 70–5, 193.   7 C.S. Maier, *Recasting bourgeois Europe: stabilization in France, Germany, and Italy in the decade after World War I* (Princeton, 1975), pp 483–94,

election in 1925 of the establishment nationalist icon General Paul von Hindenburg as federal president, together with the far-right DNVP's support of the centre-right cabinet, pointed to at least a limited reconciliation of imperialist-nationalist forces with the regime.[8]

The fragile stability of Weimar was underwritten by US dollars. In November 1923, US leaders were fearful that continued Franco–German wrangling would prevent European post-war recovery, lead to global depression and assist the advance of Bolshevism. The US brokered a reparations agreement, the Dawes Plan, to reduce Germany's annual payment of reparations in line with German economic performance, thus providing the economic breathing space of reduced payments between 1924 and 1929. The Plan smoothed the way for US banks to extend short-term credit and to stabilize the new reichsmark which was tied to the Gold Standard.[9] The provision of US credit converted German industrialists and landlords to a policy of co-operation with the Weimar governments.[10] The Dawes Plan was only an interim settlement and, in 1929, Stresemann achieved the crowning glory of his fulfillment policy, the Young Plan, a revised reparation schedule which ended foreign control over German reparations. This reduced the total reparations bill to 37,000 million marks (£1,850 million) from the 132,000 million marks (£6,600 million) that the Allies had originally demanded in 1921.[11]

The domestic stabilization of Weimar and the reparations settlement aided the international rehabilitation of Weimar. Stresemann led the way to a normalization of Weimar's role in international relations by agreeing to the Dawes Plan. His *Erfüllungspolitik*, his acceptance of the European balance of power and his dedication to rapprochement with his western neighbours increased international trust in the Weimar regime. The settlement of the reparations issue under the Dawes Plan facilitated France's withdrawal from the Ruhr in 1925. In addition, Stresemann's policy of rapprochement led to the multilateral Locarno pacts in 1925 under which Germany guaranteed not to seek to alter its western borders. Weimar's signature of the Locarno pacts eased the way for Germany's admission to the League of Nations in 1926, to become part of the collective security system. Then in 1928 Weimar, as a signatory of the Kellogg–Briand pact, symbolically renounced the use of force to settle foreign policy disputes. By the end of 1929 all British, French and Belgian troops had left the occupation zones in the Rhineland. Germany was, once again, one of the world's great industrial nations in which domestic conflict had abated.[12] In parallel with the

---

508–615.   8 Ibid., p. 489.   9 J.M. Carroll, 'Owen D. Young and German reparations: the diplomacy of an enlightened businessman', in K.P. Jones & A. DeConde (eds), *U.S. diplomats in Europe, 1919–1941* (Oxford, 1981), pp 46–51; Peukert, *Weimar*, pp 60–1, 64. 10 Maier, *Recasting*, p. 488.   11 Carr, *History of Germany*, p. 332.   12 Ibid., p. 333; C.S. Maier, 'Recasting bourgeois Europe', in C. Emsley, A. Marwick & W. Simpson (eds), *War, peace and social change in twentieth-century Europe* (Milton Keynes, 1989), p. 141.

return to relative Germany stability, its bilateral contacts with the Saorstát developed.

IRISH–GERMAN EXCHANGES

An analysis of the records reveals that even before 1930 there were significant Irish-German exchanges. Despite the dearth of formal diplomatic bilateral relations between 1924 and 1929, Irish-German contacts flourished at the multilateral, trade and cultural levels. Irish-German cultural relations were strengthened after the end of the Irish Civil War, drawing on German scholarship's interest in Gaelic culture. The National University of Ireland (NUI), the Royal Irish Academy and the Saorstát government encouraged and sponsored Irish-German academic exchanges. NUI summer schools attracted large numbers of German philologists. Meanwhile the German presence extended to other areas of Irish life with the employment of many talented Germans in the service of the Saorstát: in 1923 General Richard Mulcahy recruited Colonel Wilhelm Fritz Brase, the music instructor to the First Regiment of the German Grenadier Guards and the former head of the Royal School of Music in Prussia, and his assistant Captain Sauerzweig, to found the successful Irish Army School of Music;[13] Aloys Fleischmann was responsible for the success of the music department at University College, Cork; Walter Bremen, who died in 1927, was director of the National Museum of Ireland; and Dr Adolf Mahr, an Austrian and a pre-historian, was appointed keeper of antiquities at Ireland's National Museum in September 1927 and in 1934 became director of the museum.[14] The small but not insignificant number of Germans who emigrated to the Saorstát in the 1920s included several hundred German workers employed at the Ardnacrusha hydroelectric power station construction site. Although they were only temporary residents there was an increase in Irish-German marriages.

In the political arena, by contrast, Irish-German interaction was more problematic. The Irish republican cause was promoted widely in Weimar Germany by the author Francis Stuart and by members of the IRA's left wing, Seán MacBride, Peadar O'Donnell and Donal O'Donoghue. De Valera, in his new role as leader of Fianna Fáil, the recently founded moderate Irish republican party, visited Berlin in 1928 as a member of the Inter-Parliamentary Union.[15] Undoubtedly, these republican activities discomfited the Cumann na nGaedheal government.

Government-to-government relations, however, were extremely cordial. Irish involvement in the League of Nations led to a detectable Europeanization

13 Elsasser, *Germany*, p. 45; Keogh, *Jews*, p. 106; O'Connor, 'France', p. 104. 14 Ibid.; D. O'Donoghue, *Hitler's Irish voices: the story of German radio's wartime Irish service* (Belfast, 1998), pp 4–7. 15 Elsasser, *Germany*, pp 41–2.

of Irish foreign policy whereby the Saorstát developed its small power diplomacy. The Saorstát adhered to the progressive view that, '[i]t was essential that Germany be brought into the international community'.[16]

In the winter of 1924 and early 1925 Georg von Dehn-Schmidt, the German consul general in Dublin and former consul in Liverpool, submitted two reports to Ireland's minister of external affairs, Desmond FitzGerald, concerning the potential implications of League membership for German defence.[17] German foreign minister Stresemann was preparing the ground for German membership of the League of Nations and the Free State was canvassed as a potential supporter. Weimar kept FitzGerald apprized of its grievances about French occupation of the Rhineland and the failure of other European states to disarm.[18] The Free State was an active League member and a revisionist small power (in the sense of favouring revision of the Versailles treaty's requirements) in favour of equality of rights for all nations. Its view was that continued British jurisdiction over the Treaty ports in Ireland (the three strategic ports of Lough Swilly, Castletown-Berehaven and Queenstown or Cobh) was equivalent to Allied occupation of the Rhineland.

The Saorstát's stance in the League of Nations' Assembly was broadly similar to that of the Weimar Republic and of the Soviet Union. It saw the Versailles system as unjust and dominated by the victors of the Great War. French security concerns led to the enforced disarmament of Weimar Germany, as a forerunner to general European disarmament.[19] But universal arms reduction did not take place because France and Britain disagreed about how to implement disarmament. France wanted 'security before disarmament',[20] but Britain was a maritime power and was effectively disarmed as a land power anyway.[21] The Weimar Republic felt victimized. As an official Weimar statement to FitzGerald pointed out, 'Germany has disarmed to such an extent that she is at the mercy of her neighbours, who are all armed to the teeth. On the other hand, Germany's adversaries have not even begun the disarmaments they promised in the treaty of Versailles, but on the contrary are endeavouring to organize the economical forces of their nations for war purposes'. Germany had only an ill-equipped, 100,000-strong, ageing army dwarfed by the 7 million-strong armies of its neighbours France, Poland, Czechoslovakia and Belgium.[22] FitzGerald

---

16 M. Kennedy, *Ireland and the League of Nations, 1919–1946: international relations, diplomacy and politics* (Dublin, 1996), p. 73.   17 NAI, DFA, LN 37, Dehn-Schmidt–FitzGerald, 1 Jan. 1925 & Dehn-Schmidt–FitzGerald, 7 Mar. 1925.   18 Ibid., FitzGerald–Dehn-Schmidt, 3 Jan. 1925.   19 Hiden, *Germany and Europe*, pp 15–16; M. Vaïsse, 'Security and disarmament: problems in the development of the disarmament debates, 1919–1934', in R. Ahmann, A. M. Birke & M. Howard (eds), *The quest for stability: problems of Western European security, 1918–1957* (Oxford, 1995), pp 173–200.   20 K. Hovi, 'Security before disarmament, or hegemony? The French alliance policy, 1917–1927', in Ahman et al. (eds), *Quest for security*, pp 115–26; P. Towle, 'British security and disarmament policy in Europe in the 1920s', pp 127–54.   21 Towle, 'British security', pp 127, 130.   22 NAI, DFA, LN 37,

promised Dehn-Schmidt that he would use the German information to lobby for an alleviation of Germany's situation.[23]

Germany formally applied for League membership in February 1926 on condition that it gained a permanent seat on the League Council in recognition of its equality as a Great Power.[24] An extraordinary assembly of the League of Nations in March 1926 was convened to consider Germany's application. That assembly's political commission, of which FitzGerald was a member, recommended Germany's admission unanimously but subsequent arguments concerning the composition of the League Council resulted in the postponement of the German application question until later in the year.[25] Weimar was subsequently admitted to the League and gained an exemption from the collective security clause (Article 16) by arguing that, 'a country like Germany which is in a central position and completely disarmed' would bear an unbearably high risk of destruction in a League War.[26] Weimar's admittance to the League inferred a gradual international rehabilitation, but it was more cosmetic than real.

Like Germany and the Soviet Union[27] the Saorstát called for a general disarmament conference to be held and backed the aspirational 1928 Kellogg–Briand pact; a 'pietistic agreement to renounce war' that lacked enforcement rules.[28] Nevertheless as Ernest Blythe, Ireland's minister of finance, said the pact was 'a great and impressive effort to save humanity from a possible renewal of the horrors of war ... a new summons to the nations to bestir themselves in solving their greatest problems'.[29] He believed a general disarmament conference had been 'postponed too long ... There can be no approach to the certainty of peace until a serious beginning has been made with disarmament.'[30]

When the long-awaited conference was convened in February 1932 it was too late. The League by that stage had proved incapable of putting into operation its collective security ideals to prevent the Japanese invasion of Manchuria after September 1931.[31] But this corrosion of international peace was not yet apparent in the late 1920s.

untitled and unsigned memorandum, *c*.December 1924/January 1925. **23** Ibid., FitzGerald–Dehn-Schmidt, 3 Jan. 1925. **24** M. Kennedy, 'The Irish Free State and the League of Nations, 1922–1932' (PhD thesis, NUI, UCD, 1993), p. 122. **25** NAI, DFA, DT, S 8176, report of the delegate of Saorstát Éireann–the Extraordinary Assembly of the League of Nations (March, 1926); NAI, DFA, LN 37, MacWhite–FitzGerald, 13 Feb. 1926. **26** NAI, DFA, LN 37, Dehn-Schmidt–FitzGerald, 1 Jan. 1924. **27** Kennedy, *Ireland*, p. 122. **28** Z. Steiner, 'The League of Nations and the quest for security', in Ahmann et al., *Quest for stability*, p. 51. **29** UCDA, P24/203. **30** NAI, DT, S. 8179. **31** Steiner, 'League of Nations', pp 68, 58–9.

TRADE PROMOTION

Irish-German relations continued to progress during this period, particularly in the commercial, the consular and, finally, the diplomatic areas. In April 1923 the symbolic renunciation by the Saorstát of the British 26 per cent reparations tax on all German imports had conveyed its sympathy with Germany's treatment at the hands of the Great War victors.[32] The renunciation of the reparations tax presented German exporters with a comparative export advantage to the Saorstát compared with the rest of the Commonwealth. Increasing Irish-German trade led in 1925 to an upgrading of the German consulate in Dublin to a consulate general.[33] German industry benefited from both Dehn-Schmidt's good standing and his strong representation of Weimar Germany. German merchant shipping companies began to operate regular services from Hamburg to Cobh and Galway. German passenger liners regularly docked in Irish ports.[34]

The Saorstát's limited economic modernization and industrialization were advantageous for German-Irish trade. German expertise in electrics, chemicals, steel structures and plant machinery gave Weimar a significant advantage in winning contracts from government and semi-state bodies such as the Electricity Supply Board.[35] In 1925 the German company Siemens-Schuckert was awarded the contract to build the Shannon hydroelectric plant at Ardnacrusha.[36] Dublin corporation and the Tramway Company of Dublin also granted German firms large contracts to supply cheap housing, electrical cables and lead piping. As a result, German imports to the Saorstát grew quickly, peaking in 1926 during the construction of Ardnacrusha power station, decreasing thereafter, but remaining stable at twice 1924 levels (see table on p. 61).[37]

The Saorstát and the Weimar Republic began negotiating a bilateral commercial treaty in 1925 to place trade on a more formal footing. Until then foreign trade treaties concluded by Britain before Irish independence had regulated Irish trade relations. New bilateral commercial treaties were seen as reinforcing Irish sovereignty and international status, giving the trade negotiations a distinct political dimension.[38]

However, the negotiations proved to be more complicated and demanding

---

32 O'Connor, 'France', pp 104–5.   33 Elsasser, *Germany*, p. 45.   34 O'Connor, 'France', p. 116.   35 Ibid, p. 106.   36 For a recent informative and multidimensional investigation of the Ardnacrusha project see A. Bielenberg (ed.), *The Shannon scheme and the electrification of the Irish Free State: an inspirational milestone* (Dublin, 2002), in particular G. O'Beirne and M. O'Connor, 'Siemens-Schuckert and the electrification of the Irish Free State', pp 73–99 therein. The collection as a whole indicates the powerful impact that the construction of the Ardnacrusha scheme had on Irish culture, art, politics and economics, and the role that it played in ensconcing Siemens-Schuckert in the Irish market. The wider social influence of many hundreds of German workers and experts who spent an extended period working on the project is also usefully considered.   37 Ibid., pp 104–7.   38 NAI, DFA, 314/88, memo on commercial treaties, 6 Mar. 1928.

than the Saorstát had initially envisaged. Irish-German commercial negotiations began in 1925 with the minister of external affairs assuring the Germans that Ireland did not intend to seize the property of German nationals as was its right under the Versailles treaty.[39] The trade bargaining, conducted primarily by officials of the department of industry and commerce between 1925 and 1930, became deadlocked in mid-1929 with the realization that Ireland's inherited British system of commercial treaty making conflicted with the German system. Under the Irish system when a country entered a trading agreement with the Saorstát it was assigned 'most favoured nation status' whereby tariffs were applied at the same level on the goods from all countries, outside the British Commonwealth, with which it had a formal treaty.[40] The Germans sought 'reciprocal national treatment' for individuals, associations, companies and shipping, effectively abolishing the commonwealth preference. Ireland was only prepared to offer 'most favoured nation status' to Germany because 'if it accorded [reciprocal] national treatment to one, this meant the grant of it to all'.[41] Fortunately, in December 1929, Dehn-Schmidt and Otto Sarnow, of the German ministry of finance, suggested a compromise which became the basis of an agreement. The Saorstát would extend national treatment to German citizens, companies and navigation and, in return, would maintain its imperial preferences but extend 'most favoured nation status' to Germany for customs duties.[42] The Irish negotiators believed the German proposal to break the stalemate was prompted by the anxiety felt by Weimar about the future of German firms, 'of which Siemens-Schuckert may be taken as an example, engaging in business in the Saorstát under conditions in which they may expect strong competition from British firms'.[43]

The Irish negotiators submitted a unanimous report recommending that the Saorstát accept this German proposal which conceded much of what the Saorstát had demanded. Ireland had effectively secured 'most-favoured-nation treatment' for German exports to the Irish market, while maintaining open access to the German market for firms such as Ford and Jacobs, as well as for agricultural and industrial exports. The negotiators argued that British rather than German firms posed a threat of 'economic penetration' of the Free State's markets. German imports could be controlled because the Germans recognized the Saorstát's right to impose preferential duties in favour of Britain and the Commonwealth.[44] The Saorstát signed a treaty of commerce and navigation with Germany on 12 May 1930,[45] representing an important watershed in Irish

39 NAI, DFA, DT, S. 4825, Walshe–secretary of executive council, 8 Apr. 1928. 40 NAI, DFA, 314/88, department of industry and commerce memo, *c*.May 1928. 41 NAI, DT, S.4825, negotiations for a commercial treaty with Germany, *c*.Dec. 1929. 42 Ibid.; NAI, DT, S.4825, memo by Dehn-Schmidt, *c*.Dec. 1929. 43 NAI, DT, S. 4825, negotiations for a commercial treaty with Germany, report of the Saorstát representatives, *c*.Dec. 1929. 44 Ibid. 45 Treaty of Commerce and Navigation between the Irish Free State and Germany

commercial relations. It was the first ever such treaty negotiated successfully by the Saorstát. Germany became the Saorstát's second largest trading partner after Britain.

This expansion in Irish-German trade was only a qualified and relative success. Britain remained the Saorstát's predominant trading partner in the 1920s and the 1930s accounting for more than 90 per cent of Irish foreign trade.[46] It was to the Saorstát's advantage to diversify into new foreign markets and, while limited success was registered in commercial relations with Germany, Ireland never actively provided substantial incentives. A significant increase in Irish-German trade might have occurred with a more pro-active Irish policy.[47]

Fiscal continuity and economic conservatism dominated the Cumann na nGaedheal government's trade and industry policies in the 1920s. The Saorstát eschewed the economic nationalism of past dead leaders, Arthur Griffith and James Connolly, concentrating instead on a return to economic normalcy.[48] Unfortunately, partition underlined the predominantly pre-industrial, agricultural and rural nature of southern Ireland's economy. The government's view was that the upheaval caused by protectionism would have increased the suffering of the Irish population after the civil strife. Furthermore the socio-economic groups who tended to support the Cumann na nGaedheal party – the export-led large-scale cattle farmers, the Anglocentric financial sector, professionals and export-oriented food and drink processing firms such as Guinness, Jacobs, Ford, Carroll etc. – relied on the maintenance of free trade with Britain for their affluence.[49] So the Saorstát followed a *laissez faire*, non-interventionist and export-oriented economic (that is, an agriculture-based) policy, thus limiting the role of the state in industrialization and reinforcing pre-independence trade patterns. The new state involved itself in industrial matters only to prevent the formation of private monopolies in strategic sectors such as electricity generation, cement production, sugar refining and radio broadcasting. Ironically, it was state intervention in those sectors that stimulated German imports into Ireland from the mid-1920s with Ireland experiencing a severe trade deficit with Germany throughout much of the interwar period[50] which proved impossible to rectify in the short- or medium-term.

In the 1920s reciprocity in Irish-German trade was hampered by a multitude of factors. First, Weimar Germany's trade policy was export-oriented to earn foreign currency to finance foreign loans and reparations. In particular it was sterling-hungry and opportunities for large Irish export contracts were correspondingly limited. It seems, too, that the Anglocentric nature of Irish trade,

(Dublin, Paper No. 223, 1930). **46** K.A. Kennedy, T. Giblin & D. McHugh, *The economic development of Ireland in the twentieth century* (London, 1988), pp 182–3. **47** Ibid., p. 35. **48** J. Meenan, 'From free trade', in MacManus (ed.), *Great test*, p. 70. **49** Kennedy et al., *Economic development*, pp 34–6; M.E. Daly, *Industrial development and Irish national identity, 1922–1939* (Syracuse, 1992), pp 8, 20. **50** Elsasser, *Germany*, p. 44.

the language barrier, and a lack of Irish entrepreneurial acumen meant the German market was not seen as a lucrative possibility. Secondly, Irish exports of livestock were of little interest to the German market, while products such as butter, meat, and eggs were highly perishable and considered to be of a low standard. Moreover, in spite of its industrialized status, Germany had its own large, domestic agricultural sector and ready access to the export-oriented Danish agricultural producers, as well as the predominantly peasant economies of eastern Europe. Transportation difficulties were compounded by the large price gap between the mainly primary products the Free State sought to export and the more expensive manufactured products and plant machinery it wanted to import to be able to modernize. This gap between import and export prices was attenuated by the slump in agricultural prices in the 1920s.[51] But as Irish–German trade was minuscule by comparison with Anglo-Irish trade this adverse trade imbalance was ignored in the 1920s.

Saorstát imports (valued in £sterling) from Britain,
Germany and France, 1924–30

Year	United Kingdom	Germany	France
1924	45,601,452	733,642	414,691
1925	43,858,645	888,481	387,872
1926	39,880,161	2,300,153	520,515
1927	40,613,300	1,496,090	423,847
1928	40,495,346	1,841,516	445,706
1929	41,762,536	1,549,856	445,706
1930	39,635,077	1,329,931	445,444

Source: O'Connor, 'France', p. 106

DIPLOMATIC REACTIVATION

The department of external affairs' survival as a separate entity in the Irish civil service during the first decade of its history was a significant accomplishment given the state's focus on domestic concerns, financial retrenchment, London's resistance to separate dominion diplomatic representation, and the predominantly Anglocentric Irish agenda. The department's persistence owed a lot to the tenacious rearguard action by 'the father of modern Irish diplomacy',[52] Joseph P. Walshe, who was acting secretary for most of the 1920s.[53]

51 Kennedy et al., *Economic development*, p. 37. **52** Coogan, *De Valera*, p. 423. **53** D. Keogh, 'Profile of Joseph Walshe, secretary, department of foreign affairs, 1922–46', ISIA, 3: 2 (1990), pp 65–6.

The turning point for the institutionalization of foreign relations was 1927 when Professor T.A. Smiddy was appointed as minister plenipotentiary to the newly-founded Irish legation in Washington DC, and a US legation was sited in Dublin.[54] Diplomatic recognition and reciprocity with the US immediately raised the international status of the Saorstát and provided a precedent for diplomatic representation in non-Commonwealth capitals. The appointment of the forceful Kevin O'Higgins as minister of external affairs on 23 June 1927, and later the 'talented' and 'intelligent' Patrick McGilligan on 12 October 1927, signalled the increasing prominence accorded to external affairs in the executive council, as the Irish cabinet was known.[55] Walshe had been promoted from acting secretary to secretary on 8 August 1927,[56] making subversion of the autonomy of the department impossible.

The Irish continued their quest to expand diplomatic independence within the elastic but constraining limits of dominion status. The inauguration of the Berlin legation in 1929 was a groundbreaking development in the establishment of the diplomatic independence of the dominions. In 1928 external affairs minister McGilligan convinced his executive council colleagues of the need to expand and modernize the skeletal department's overseas structure.[57] The plan was prompted by the foundation of Canadian legations in Tokyo and Paris.[58] Ireland had rediscovered the significance of relations with central Europe six years after George Gavan Duffy identified Berlin as an advantageous Irish diplomatic base.[59] The proposal to open Irish legations in Paris, Rome, and Berlin provoked a high level of intra-Commonwealth argument about the co-equal status of the dominions with Britain and the unity of the Commonwealth. The respective functions of Britain's ambassador and the dominion minister, and the relationship of the two diplomats in the foreign capital to which they were both accredited, was another source of intra-Commonwealth controversy.[60] But the Irish were determined to express their autonomy on the international stage[61] because 'the appointment of ministers to one of the great European powers would very clearly establish the fact which is not at the moment appreciated, that the Saorstát must be regarded as a unit in international affairs in no way subservient to Great Britain'.[62] The Saorstát wanted to demonstrate formally to non-Commonwealth states that dominions had separate and independent foreign policies to Britain.[63]

---

54 Keogh, *Ireland & Europe*, p. 23. **55** Ibid., pp 24–5. **56** Keogh, 'Profile of Joseph Walshe', p. 66. **57** Keogh, *Ireland & Europe*, p. 26. **58** NAI, DT, S. 5736A, Saorstát representatives abroad, 11 June 1928. **59** Keogh, *Ireland & Europe*, pp 14–15, 18. **60** See: NAI, DT, S. 5736A & NAI, DT, S. 2011A. **61** NAI, DT, S. 2011A, prime minister (Pretoria)–McGilligan, 22 May 1929. **62** NAI, DT, S. 5736A, Saorstát representatives abroad, 11 June 1928. **63** NAI, DT, S. 2011A, prime minister (Pretoria)–McGilligan, 22 May 1929.

On 31 July 1928 Ireland's executive council authorized the creation of a legation in Berlin.[64] McGilligan consistently demanded that all matters relating to the Saorstát should be dealt with by an Irish minister in a foreign capital in accordance with the principle of equal status agreed at the 1926 Imperial Conference.[65] Britain's adherence to the principle of imperial diplomatic unity[66] had to be reconciled with the Irish demand that, in foreign capitals, dominions' relations with each other and with Britain should be on virtually the same basis as relations with unassociated countries. Sustained Irish pressure, in concert with South Africa, succeeded in implementing the 1926 Balfour Declaration. This had declared that Britain and its dominions were 'autonomous communities within the British Empire, in no way subordinate one to another in any aspect of their domestic or external affairs, although united by a common allegiance to the Crown and freely associated as members of the British Commonwealth of Nations'.[67] The Irish legation in Berlin was, therefore, both an important precedent in the development of the Commonwealth and another step in Ireland's evolving autonomy. A full German legation in Dublin would symbolize German acceptance of Irish autonomy and co-equality within the Commonwealth.

Weimar consented to the Irish proposal to open diplomatic relations on 22 November 1928.[68] The German government intended to 'seek the consent of the Reichstag for the conversion of the consulate general in Dublin into a legation'.[69] On 8 January 1929 the Irish cabinet decided to appoint Daniel A. Binchy as minister plenipotentiary and envoy extraordinary at Berlin.[70] But there were problems. Charles Bewley lobbied actively for the Berlin posting, but was instead assigned to the Vatican.[71] Meanwhile Binchy was reluctant to accept the post because he reputedly disliked Germans.[72] This convinced the cabinet that Berlin was perfect for Binchy because McGilligan and Marcus O'Sullivan (minister of education) were loathe to appoint Bewley to Berlin as his open German proclivities could have been an embarrassment and upset the British.[73] Binchy, on the other hand, could be relied on for 'mannerly discretion', objective reporting, and not offending the British. Binchy had extensive knowledge of, and contacts in, Germany as he had studied at Munich university in the early 1920s. He had also studied in Paris, The Hague and Geneva giving him wide exposure to continental life, in addition to his impressive legal and academic credentials. He was considered to be a good linguist and was professional.[74] Unfortunately,

64 NAI, DT, S. 5736A, executive council minutes, 31 July 1928. **65** Ibid., Murphy–Harding, 17 Sept. 1928. **66** NAI, D/T, S. 2011A, Amery–all dominions, circular B no. 136, 21 Dec. 1928. **67** Lyons, *Ireland since the famine*, p. 508. **68** NAI, DT, S. 5736A, Rumbold–Cushendum, 23 Nov. 1928. **69** Ibid., Amery–McGilligan, 22 Nov. 1928. **70** Ibid., decision of the executive council, item no. 5, 8 Jan. 1929. **71** Duggan, *Neutral Ireland*, p. 28. **72** Ibid., pp 26–7. **73** Ibid., p. 27. **74** Keogh, *Ireland and Europe*, pp 29–30.

his initial contact with the Auswärtiges Amt (AA) or German foreign office was problematic.

The local foreign ministry is the main point of contact for a minister in their host country.[75] The welcome a diplomat receives initially is important to establish the level of respect the host nation has for his home country. The official welcome Binchy received in 1929 from the AA was inauspicious. Binchy recorded that, 'their attitude throughout ... was one of complete unconcern mixed with a great deal of prevarication'.[76] Establishing an Irish legation in Berlin and a German legation in Dublin were psychologically significant for the Saorstát, but not for Weimar. Irish impatience with German delays permeated the entire period from July 1929 to September 1930, when the official accreditation procedures were eventually completed in Dublin and Berlin. The Irish had a sense of urgency but were faced with German inertia.[77]

One factor that had contributed to the Saorstát's decision to include a Berlin legation in its foreign affairs expansion plan of 1928–9 was persistent lobbying by the German consul general in Dublin, Georg von Dehn-Schmidt. He had emphasized to the department of external affairs the great interest which German official circles took in the new Saorstát, and the eagerness with which they looked forward to the arrival of an Irish minister in Berlin. Binchy, *in situ* in Berlin, concluded that Dehn-Schmidt had 'considerably overestimated the interest' which the AA took in Ireland. When Binchy arrived in Berlin in July 1929 the AA officials were apologetic and relieved that the Saorstát would not be offended by the temporary postponement of Binchy's reception. Binchy left Berlin for Dublin temporarily, returning to Berlin again in October 1929. The situation had not improved. It was 'only with considerable difficulty' that arrangements for his presentation of credentials to President Hindenburg were made for 26 October.[78] The mitigating circumstances for the seemingly casual German treatment of the Saorstát were that, although the prospects for Germany had been positive in 1928, by 1929 and into 1930 the Weimar Republic was in crisis. In retrospect, the Irish diplomatic offensive in 1929–30 occurred at a singularly unfavourable moment because 1929 was 'wahrhaftig eine année terrible' (truly a terrible year) for Germany.[79]

The apparent return to stability in Germany and Europe after 1923 has retrospectively been described by various commentators as 'relative',[80]

75 See E. Clark, *Corps diplomatiques* (London, 1973). 76 NAI, DFA, 18/10, Binchy–Walshe, 12 Aug. 1930. 77 See NAI, DFA, E.A. 231/4B. 78 NAI, DFA, E.A. 231/4B, Binchy memorandum, 27 May 1930. 79 Maier, *Recasting*, p. 141. 80 Carroll, 'Owen D. Young', p. 53.

'deceptive',[81] and an 'illusion'.[82] Gustav Stresemann, architect of Weimar's mid-decade recovery, died on 3 October 1929, a few days before Binchy returned. Stresemann was succeeded by Julius Curtius, who was unfamiliar with his new position and lacked the political acumen of Stresemann. But it was not Stresemann's premature death that caused the catastrophic implosion of the Weimar. It is more accurate to say that the foreign, domestic and economic policies Stresemann introduced were fragile, not least because of the severe constraints of the Versailles treaty, the French-led 'anti-revisionist bloc', and German nationalist resentment.[83] On the one hand, Stresemann encountered domestic hostility from the right for accepting effective disarmament, territorial shrinkage, reparations and the war-guilt clause. On the other hand, he had to accept these unpalatable external impositions as part of his *Erfüllungspolitik* to gain international credibility and equality for Germany. Once achieved, he could use Anglo-American sympathy to secure the piecemeal revision of Versailles and reparations. Concurrently, France and Poland remained suspicious of the Weimar Republic's intentions towards revising its Versailles-imposed truncated eastern borders. But Stresemann, a revisionist by stealth, failed to meet the immediate demands of his domestic critics. Five years of diplomacy had failed to pacify unrealistic domestic expectations and foreign 'revanchism'. Stresemann was the victim of irreconcilable demands and Weimar was powerless to compel a solution in line with its ideals.

This underlying problem in 1929 was similar to that of 1923. The sole difference was that an external appearance of relative mid-decade stability was sustained by US credit which lay at the heart of a new global financial system as a precursor to the post-1945 Bretton-Woods order. Historian John Hiden points out that, 'between 1924 and 1930 some 25.5 billion marks flowed into Germany in the form of loans and investment whereas Germany paid, ultimately, a total of some 22.9 billion marks in reparations ...'[84] German reparations were inseparable from, although not explicitly linked to, the repayment of European (particularly British and French) war debts to the US. The US was not, however, prepared to countenance a complete writing-off of Allied war debts primarily for domestic reasons.[85] Thus Europe's mid-decade stability survived and the corporatist solutions pioneered during this period were a model for western Europe's post-World War II prosperity. But as a trenchant critic of the global financial system, Eric Hobsbawm, says: 'The entire House of Cards of reparations collapsed' in October 1929 with the Wall Street Crash.[86]

---

81 Peukert, *Weimar*, p. 191.　82 Carr, *History of Germany*, p. 335.　83 P. Kennedy, *The rise and fall of the great powers: economic change and military conflict from 1500 to 1700* (London, 1989), p. 358.　84 Hiden, *Weimar*, p. 33.　85 Maier, 'Recasting bourgeois Europe', p. 148. 86 E. Hobsbawm, *Age of extremes: the short twentieth century, 1914–1919* (London, 1994), p. 99. See also: Carr, *History of Germany*; A.J. Nicholls, *Weimar and the rise of Hitler* (London, 1974); V.R. Berghahn, *Modern Germany: society, economy and politics in the*

The Saorstát was understandably annoyed about German tardiness on diplomatic reciprocity. Although Binchy presented his credentials as envoy extraordinary and minister plenipotentiary to President Hindenburg on 26 October 1929, the governor-general in Dublin only received Dehn-Schmidt's equivalent credentials as German minister to the Saorstát on 2 September 1930. The German finance minister had objected to the immediate creation of a legation in Dublin, arguing 'that it should be created in the ordinary way after the next budget'.[87] So the Dublin legation had to await that budget in April 1930.[88] As an *ad hoc* measure, Dehn-Schmidt was appointed chargé d'affaires in Dublin, with diplomatic powers equivalent to those of Binchy.[89] But the fall of the 'Grand Coalition' in Weimar with the resignation of the Müller cabinet on 27 March 1930 caused further delays. The foreign affairs budget estimates were submitted to the Reichstag which wanted cutbacks, ensuring a 'long and tedious' passage.[90]

The new, non-party minority government under Heinrich Brüning was essentially the old Müller line-up but without the Social Democrats. Initially the Social Democrats tolerated Brüning and his policies, but the outlook remained bleak. The interests of working-class supporters of the Social Democrats were to be sacrificed to satisfy surviving Wilhelmine interests of the Reichswehr, Junkers and big business. The political situation was precarious,[91] and certainly not ideal for a small young state, ambiguously linked to the British Commonwealth, seeking to upgrade its diplomatic connections with Weimar. The Cumann na nGaedheal government was now worried about critical public opinion: 'If action is much further delayed people will begin to wonder whether the British are not taking a hand in the game'.[92] By 27 May 1930, a disenchanted Binchy suggested that he be instructed 'to enter a very sharp protest'. He said he had fallen

> into the error of overestimating German interest in us ... Apparently the Foreign Office thinks that it has salved its conscience by appointing a Chargé d'Affaires ad interim and that the question of a full Legation can be conveniently shelved until more important matters have been dealt with.[93]

The situation was a stark reminder of the low priority accorded to Ireland on the German agenda. If the Weimar political situation had been more stable, the

twentieth century (Cambridge, 1987, 2nd edition); K.D. Bracher, *The German dictatorship: the origins, structure, and consequences of national socialism*, (London, 1973); M. Laffan (ed.), *The burden of German history, 1919–1945* (London, 1988). **87** NAI, DFA, 18/10, Binchy–Walshe, 11 Dec. 1929. **88** Ibid. **89** NAI, DFA, EA 231/4B, Binchy memorandum, 27 May 1930. **90** NAI, DFA, 18/10, Binchy–secretary, 8 Apr. 1930. **91** Carr, *History of Germany*, p. 343. **92** NAI, DFA, 18/10, Walshe–Binchy, 14 May 1930. **93** NAI, DFA, EA 231/4B, Binchy memorandum, 27 May 1930.

matter of diplomatic reciprocity would undoubtedly have proceeded uncontroversially. But, the German domestic environment continued to worsen.

In June the German foreign affairs budget had a very difficult passage through its committee phase as attempts to save money were made.[94] On 16 July 1930, the Reichstag rejected Brüning's overall budget proposals after the Socialists refused to co-operate, forcing President Hindenburg to dissolve the Reichstag. Brüning governed with the support of presidential decrees, until a new Reichstag could be elected in September.[95] Provision for financing the Dublin legation was given force of law by presidential decree.[96] So, the legislation that founded the German legation in Dublin had the dubious honour of being one of the first acts of the new presidential government, a government which later facilitated Germany's transition to fascist dictatorship.

APPOINTING A GERMAN MINISTER

The choice of a German minister to Dublin was another problem. The Saorstát assumed that Dehn-Schmidt would be promoted from chargé to minister. The Irish government was extremely satisfied with his overall performance as consul general (1924–30) and chargé d'affaires (1930) because he had done much to promote Irish–German relations[97] and had facilitated Irish–German arrangements for Siemens-Schuckert to lead the construction of the Ardnacrusha hydroelectric power station on the Shannon.[98] But on 19 June 1930, an AA official mentioned that objections had been raised to Dehn-Schmidt's promotion. Binchy assured him that from the point of view of the Irish government and the Irish general public Dehn-Schmidt was the most suitable candidate.[99] Baron von Ow-Wachendorf, an official in the Commonwealth section of the AA who was well known to the Irish in Berlin and a member of the German Catholic Centre Party, was being pushed energetically for the post by the Centre party.[1] At this stage Ow-Wachendorf was considered favourite in Brüning's circle. Indeed, Ow-Wachendorf 'had been definitely nominated for the post and had been called to see the chancellor, Brüning, who discussed the relations between Germany and Ireland in detail with him', Binchy reported.[2]

Ignorant of the lobbying on behalf of Ow-Wachendorf, Binchy made 'strong representations' to the AA on Dehn-Schmidt's behalf. His intervention was decisive in securing Dehn-Schmidt's appointment, thus disappointing the Centre party and damaging Binchy's relations with what, from an Irish point of

94 NAI, DFA, 18/10, Binchy–Walshe, 6 June 1930. 95 Berghahn, *Modern Germany*, p. 94. 96 NAI, DFA, 18/10, MacCauley–Walshe, 31 July 1930. 97 Ibid., McGilligan–Curtius, 1 Jan. 1930. 98 IT, 3 Sept. 1930. 99 NAI, DFA, 18/10, Binchy–Walshe, 20 June 1930. 1 NAI, DFA, EA 231/4B, Binchy–Walshe, 21 Aug. 1930. 2 NAI, DFA, CRS 19/10, Binchy–Walshe, 14 Mar. 1931.

view, should have been the most co-operative German political party. The Irish legation normally worked with Ow-Wachendorf in the AA, but after Binchy's intervention Ow-Wachendorf avoided him and delegated one of his juniors to deal with the Irish legation over the telephone.[3]

Binchy's handling of the situation did ultimately lead to a reconciliation with Ow-Wachendorf but in any case the problem became moot when the baron was posted to Luxembourg on 9 March 1931.[4] Binchy personally preferred Ow-Wachendorf to Dehn-Schmidt[5] but realized that he was, as a typical upper-class German, an Anglophile who might cause problems in Dublin.[6] By comparison, Dehn-Schmidt could be counted upon as a balanced, career diplomat well acquainted with Irish politics.

DIPLOMATIC TRIANGLES

From the outset Binchy was concerned about the AA's attitude to Ireland.[7] He was agitated by what he saw as their attempts to ignore Irish membership of the Commonwealth and their treatment of the Saorstát as 'a small completely isolated state'. Binchy certainly believed 'our international position and our significance in German eyes would be infinitely stronger if our independent position and status within the British Commonwealth was clearly recognised'.[8] The Saorstát's influence on the Commonwealth and the formulation of its common foreign policy potentially increased Ireland's international profile. This view was partly confirmed in February 1931 when Brüning asked Binchy questions about the position of the dominions within the Commonwealth leading Binchy to surmise that, 'he was chiefly anxious to know whether we were in a position to influence the policy of the British Commonwealth as a whole and of Great Britain in particular towards Germany'. Binchy concluded that, 'our chief significance in German eyes is whatever influence we can exert on the policy of the Commonwealth as a whole'.[9]

If Brüning was so apparently alert to Ireland's potential, why did the AA, at least initially, treat the Saorstát as any other small, insignificant distant state? Binchy reasoned it was because Britain would 'gain most by this policy'.[10] The British embassy treated the Irish legation in exactly the same way, as separate despite the Commonwealth link. The similarity between AA and British embassy policies was uncanny. Considering the British embassy's position of power in German politics, and the Anglophile character of the AA, the British

3 Ibid.   4 Ibid.   5 NAI, DFA, 231/4B, Binchy–Walshe, 21 Aug. 1930.   6 Ibid., Binchy memo, 27 May 1930.   7 Ibid.   8 Ibid.; NAI, DFA, EA 231/4, Walshe–Binchy, 16 June 1930. Walshe and McGilligan agreed with Binchy.   9 NAI, DFA, CRS 19/10, Binchy–Walshe, 2 Mar. 1931.   10 NAI, DFA, EA 231/4B, Binchy memo, 27 May 1930, p. 8.

embassy had the means and contacts to influence the AA's attitude towards the Saorstát legation.[11] Binchy's paraphrase of the British embassy's rationale was:

> Now that an Irish Legation has come to stay in Berlin, the only thing to be done from the 'Imperial' point of view is to circumscribe and localise its activities as much as possible, and to secure that, while dealing with all questions exclusively connected with Germany and Ireland, it should be carefully kept out of discussions of all important general matters which, as hitherto, should be settled between the Foreign Office and H.M. Embassy.[12]

He believed that this British policy of isolating the Saorstát legation was intended 'to convey the impression that the Irish legation is only competent to deal with exclusively Irish matters, and that matters involving the Commonwealth as a whole are still the inviolable preserve of the British Embassy'.[13] Ironically, the British imperialists and the Irish republicans were in agreement.

Binchy persevered in trying to cultivate good relations with the British embassy but his overtures were not always reciprocated. Binchy then believed he had found a British vulnerability, a way to assert Irish membership of the Commonwealth and to demonstrate Irish co-equality. But popular opinion at home, especially republican opinion, would have been outraged had it become known what this course involved. Binchy sought and received permission to fly the British flag over the Irish legation for the king's birthday on 3 June 1930. The pretext he offered was that while this was not normal procedure in the Saorstát, the people this would irritate most would be the British. He sought revenge through an ostentatious display of tactical royalism. As he wrote:

> I am inclined to think that it would be a useful purpose, in opening people's eyes to the real nature of the Commonwealth and the separate personality of the crown in each State. I should say that the only people likely to be shocked here by our flagging would be the members of the British Embassy, who, as I describe in my detailed reports are most anxious to keep the King entirely and exclusively for themselves.[14]

Conversely, he overlooked the potential embarrassment for the Saorstát government, if flying the Union Jack was reported in Ireland.

Binchy, nevertheless, felt the British embassy members were personally agreeable and easy to work with and that the embassy's approach was to maintain good personal relations.[15] 'The rule seems to be that all political matters are tabu in conversation unless I introduce them, and then they are to be treated

---

11 Ibid., p. 8. 12 Ibid., p. 8. 13 Ibid., p. 19. 14 NAI, DFA, EA 231/4, Binchy–Walshe, 26 May 1930. 15 NAI, DFA, EA 231/4B, Binchy memo, 27 May 1930.

with polite reserve'.[16] Eventually the Irish legation seemed to receive the recognition it deserved from the British.[17] Nonetheless, an undercurrent of friction remained which was provocatively alluded to when Binchy met the British prime minister, Ramsay MacDonald, and the foreign secretary, Arthur Henderson, at a dinner in the British embassy on 28 July 1931. Binchy reported: 'The Prime Minister was pleased to be humorous: he asked me if I was returning home for the Horse Show and on my replying that I had no leave to spare, suggested laughingly that I should ask leave from him and thereby precipitate a constitutional crisis!'[18]

BINCHY'S 'CLUBABILITY'

In the initial months of his appointment Binchy's account of his posting creates an image of an enthusiastic minister plenipotentiary who enjoyed making contacts in Berlin. He overcame the initial difficulties with the AA and the British ambassador, cultivated other members of the diplomatic corps in Berlin and made the most of his opportunities to educate influential people about Ireland.

Binchy and Leo T. McCauley, the legation secretary, sought particularly to advance themselves with the US embassy and the US chamber of commerce.[19] According to Binchy's May 1930 report he was particularly successful with the US chamber of commerce.[20] He also reported contact with the successive US ambassadors Schurman and Sackett, the French ambassador de Margerie, successive papal nuncios, and the British ambassador Sir Horace Rumbold. He was also allegedly 'well acquainted' with the diplomats representing many European states: Austria, Hungary, Poland, Czechoslovakia, Belgium, the Netherlands, Norway, Denmark, Spain, Sweden, and Turkey. In the cases of the Spanish and Belgian representatives he had an initial advantage. Both had had Irish governesses and the Belgian minister spoke 'English just like a Dublin man'.[21] Binchy also had an *entrée* with the papal nuncio to Weimar who was the doyen of the diplomatic corps, Monsignor Eugene Pacelli. Binchy had met Pacelli, who became Pope Pius XII in 1939, when he was a student in Munich in the early 1920s.[22]

However, Binchy's support for Dehn-Schmidt as German minister to Ireland, in preference to the Centre party candidate Ow-Wachendorf, strained Binchy's relationship and created inauspicious circumstances for cultivating a close connection with that party.[23] It was a political party which fascinated the

---

16 Ibid., p. 18.   17 Keogh, *Ireland & Europe*, p. 31.   18 NAI, DFA, CRS 19/10, Binchy–Walshe, 29 July 1931.   19 NAI, DFA, EA 231/4B. Both Binchy and Schurman were academics who had studied similar subjects, and mixed in the same academic circles. 20 Ibid., p. 30.   21 Ibid., pp 19, 28–31.   22 Ibid., p. 18.   23 NAI, DFA, EA 231/4B, Binchy–Walshe, 21 Aug. 1930.

largely conservative Catholic nationalist party governing the Saorstát, Cumann na nGaedheal, immersed as it was in Catholic culture and seeking to maintain traditional Catholic values.[24] Close Irish diplomatic links with German Catholicism and with the Centre party were necessary because of the party's role as the parliamentary fulcrum in Weimar politics, demonstrated by its presence in the cabinets of 19 of the 21 governments of Weimar. Binchy appeared to have more success with other sections of the German political and bureaucratic elites. For instance, he established a rapport with the two successive AA Staatssekretars von Schubert and von Bülow, and with de Haas, the AA chief of the section dealing with the British Commonwealth.[25] He knew the new foreign minister, Julius Curtius, sufficiently well by May 1930 to write an assessment of him.[26]

But how did he achieve such access so quickly? First, the opening of the Irish legation in Berlin attracted considerable curiosity and Binchy received numerous invitations to events. Second, he was an impressive academic who communicated easily with other intellectuals and had the necessary credentials and sophistication to socialize effortlessly in diplomatic and political circles.[27] Perceiving that his role was to make an impact on the AA and larger embassies, he avoided dissipating time and energy in attending endless receptions and 'dull social functions' arranged by the 'smaller and more distant powers'. There was no advantage in courting their favour and he instead concentrated on the major powers and the German elites.[28]

Binchy recognized the necessity of projecting a positive image of the Saorstát in a Germany which displayed considerable ignorance about matters Irish. He considered that his primary objective was to enlighten the Germans. Unfortunately, he discovered that circumstances had not altered significantly from those encountered by Sinn Féin representatives in the early 1920s. The German upper classes indulged in 'a cult of English ways and English fashions which amounts almost to a religion' and thought Ireland was the 'next best thing' to Britain, only for its imitative qualities. Nonetheless, the popular German attitude towards Ireland was one of 'uninformed sympathy', according to Binchy, because the 'average German, while sharing to a certain extent the respect of his "betters" for England, is exceedingly friendly to Ireland, although he knows little or nothing about us' so he decided to initiate 'a steady campaign of publicity'.[29]

Using the initial media attention his appointment to Berlin attracted, Binchy emphasized the autonomy of the Saorstát as a dominion within the British Commonwealth to counter the prevalent German perception that Ireland was a

24 J.H. Whyte, *Church and state in modern Ireland, 1923–1979* (Dublin, 1980, 2nd ed.), pp 24–39. 25 NAI, DFA 231/4B, pp 10–11. 26 Ibid., p. 9. 27 NAI, DFA CRS 19/10, Binchy–Walshe, 2 Mar. 1931. 28 NAI, DFA 231/4B, Binchy minute, 27 May 1930, p. 28. 29 NAI, DFA 231/4B, Binchy minute, 27 May 1930.

province or colony of Britain. Once initial media interest waned, Binchy wrote
follow-up articles for German newspapers, magazines and journals and delivered numerous lectures to various organizations including the US chamber of
commerce, the League of Nations Society of Berlin University, the Society for
the Study of Foreign Affairs (Aussenpolitisches Kommittee), the Deutsche
Herrenclub, and the Juristiche Gesellschaft. His lectures focused on Irish political affairs, especially Ireland's 'constitutional and international status'.[30]
Binchy knew that his lectures appealed only to a limited public but it was an
important public: the educated and influential in university, diplomatic, legal
and government circles.[31] Distinguished German journals such as the *Zeitschrift
für Politik* and the *Diplomaten Zeitung* also ran articles by him on the matter of
Irish statehood.[32] He was encouraged to discover that many educated Germans
evinced a serious interest in Irish literary activities and Irish language revival
and his occasional lectures on Irish language and culture received particularly
wide newspaper coverage.[33]

Binchy's initial propaganda work on behalf of the Saorstát was appreciated
at home[34] with external affairs minister McGilligan and departmental secretary
Walshe 'particularly pleased with the way in which you attacked our fundamental enemy in every country, namely, the idea that we are a sort of bastard English
nation with no distinctive ancestry or civilization of our own'. Binchy was congratulated for 'securing the goodwill and esteem of the German people for the
Saorstát'. The cabinet was also in 'the fullest agreement with the line of policy
you have followed concerning our position in the Commonwealth'.

But Binchy's best intentions and efforts could not influence every German's
opinion of the Saorstát. The newspaper *Welt am Abend* in Berlin ran a series of
four articles entitled 'In the German Island' written by Max Taum which, to
Binchy's considerable displeasure, portrayed the Saorstát as one of the poorest
countries in the world, experiencing mass emigration and high unemployment.[35] The Saorstát was also sensitive to the German media's attitude to Irish
republicans and Irish political affairs generally. Following the defeat and re-
election of the Cumann na nGaedheal government in 1930, Binchy reported
German newspapers took the view that de Valera was a democrat seeking the
best for Ireland – not the undesirable republican revolutionary that Cumann na
nGaedheal would have liked them to believe.[36] Then in April 1930 an 'obscure

30 NAI, DFA, 231/4, Binchy–Walshe, 8 Feb. 1930; *Berliner Tageblatt*, 9 Feb. 1930.
31 NAI, DFA, 231/4B, Binchy minute, 27 May 1930. 32 NAI, DFA, 231/4, Binchy–
Walshe, 8 Apr. 1930 & Walshe–Binchy, 24 Apr. 1930. 33 Ibid. 34 Irish government members' perceptions of Germany and the German race were influenced by traditional
stereotypes of Germans as hardworking, dedicated, progressive, and technologically developed. See President Cosgrave in *Deutsche Allgemeine Zeitung*, 31 Oct. 1929. 35 *Welt am
Abend*, 21 Dec. 1929; NAI, DFA 231/4, Binchy–Walshe, 30 Jan. 1930. 36 NAI, DFA, EA
231/4B, Binchy–Walshe, 9 Apr. 1930; *Dresdener Anzeiger*, 12 Nov. 1929; *Berliner
Börsenkourier*, 27 Nov. 1929.

Berlin morning paper' called *Der Reichsbote* portrayed the Irish government as oppressive, an enemy of the people and as collaborators with the British to implement London's orders. Binchy, upset by such 'an obvious tissue of lies', duly protested to the AA.[37]

REPORTING GERMAN POLITICAL DEVELOPMENTS

Another important diplomatic function is to report economic, political, social and cultural developments and events in host countries. Usually diplomats devote themselves to interpreting publicly available material. Accurate, concise information assessment is dependent on a diplomat's knowledge of the host country, its political system and its people, predicated on a diplomat's contacts with government members, opposition leaders and civil servants. An effective diplomat must, therefore, maintain an extensive range of professional and personal contacts to be able to comment on events, remaining familiar not only with developments in the host country, but also with events at home.[38] Binchy, however, knew that it would be difficult with a staff of only two in the legation to remain in touch with all the information on Ireland in German newspapers. While there were only three or four dailies in Berlin, there were more than 300 daily newspapers throughout Germany.[39]

An insight into Binchy's analysis of German politics can be gained from articles he published on three figures central to Germany's transition from parliamentary democracy to fascist dictatorship: Chancellor Brüning, President Hindenburg and NSDAP leader Adolf Hitler. Although published in *Studies* between late 1932 and 1937 after his term as Irish minister in Germany, it is noteworthy that Binchy's assessment of the German political situation was similar[40] in thinking to his reports written from Berlin between 1929 and 1932. Of course, having left the diplomatic service in mid-1932 he had time to reflect and also knew the outcome of developments he had reported on a day-to-day basis when Irish minister to Germany.

GERMAN POLITICS

Binchy was posted to Weimar during a crucial period. The political and financial stability of the state Weimar were in doubt after the October 1929 death of foreign minister Stresemann who was a considerable loss to the young German

---

37 Ibid. **38** Clarke, *Corps*, pp 61–78. **39** NAI, DF, S. 71/4/30, Walshe–secretary of finance, 24 July 1930. **40** B.V. Burke, *Ambassador Frederic Sackett & the collapse of the Weimar Republic, 1930–1933: the United States & Hitler's rise to power* (Cambridge, 1994).

democracy.[41] The *Irish Times* complacently reported that, 'in its essentials his work was done' and that, 'Stresemann was able to make most of his countrymen take a more realist view' and follow a policy of fulfillment or *Erfüllungspolitik*.[42] In reality the façade of German democracy, economic prosperity, and stability collapsed.[43] The Stresemann era proved to be a temporary truce between democrats and anti-republican forces. Economic crises exacerbated the difficulties of forming stable government coalitions and nourished long-term unresolved German class and sectional conflicts. The candidate list system of proportional representation, which promoted fragmentation, bitter elections and divisive sectional cleavages, did not help either.[44] Meanwhile the bureaucracy, the judicial system, and the army or Reichswehr remained resentful and disdainful of parliamentarianism.[45] Political apathy was widespread and the political parties were incapable of preventing a dangerous drift from democracy.[46] As early as 1926 in the midst of apparent stability, State Secretary Otto Meissner was developing the alternative concept of a minority 'government of personalities' supported by the extensive use of presidential decrees under Article 48 of the Weimar constitution.[47] In effect, the parliamentary system was weakened from within by that loophole in the constitution and by an anti-democratic minded bureaucracy.

Binchy's presence in Weimar from October 1929 allowed him to witness the emergence of presidential government as the norm. He arrived during the final period of Hermann Müller's Social Democrat-dependent coalition government (which fell in March 1930 as the Great Depression began to affect Germany), and he left just before the resignation of Brüning as chancellor in May 1932. Following the collapse of Müller's government in March 1930 on the issue of financial retrenchment, Hindenburg appointed Brüning as chancellor. Brüning publicized his willingness to pursue the retrograde step of using presidential decrees to implement his programme of financial retrenchment if he failed to gain the necessary majorities in the Reichstag. When his financial proposals were rejected by the Reichstag on 16 July 1930 Hindenburg sanctioned them using a presidential decree under Article 48 of the constitution. Brüning then called a general election for 14 September 1930, after a majority of the Reichstag abrogated that legislation. In the intervening period Brüning ruled by presidential decree and during his succeeding years in the chancellery, whenever he lacked a majority in the Reichstag, he made regular recourse to the use of presidential decrees. Democracy survived during the Brüning era, but in spirit it perished while political intrigues flourished.

The rise of Nazism was not the cause but one consequence of Weimar's

41 IT, 4 Oct. 1929; Berghahn, *Modern Germany*, pp 90, 100–1. 42 IT, 4 Oct. 1939. 43 Nicholls, *Weimar*, p. 94. 44 H. Mommsen, 'The failure of the Weimar Republic & the rise of Hitler', in Laffan, *The burden of German history*, pp 116–30. 45 Ibid. 46 Carr, *History of Germany*, p. 337. 47 Berghahn, *Modern Germany*, pp 92–3.

structural crisis. Motivated by a fanatical sense of mission, blessed with orator-
ical skill, supported by a party converted to the *Führerprinzip* and expert in the
art of propaganda, Hitler exploited the turmoil in Weimar during Binchy's
posting. Organized labour lost its bargaining power in a period of mass unemployment and labour interests were gradually excluded from political
consideration. The radicalized unemployed joined the KPD. Extremism of both
the left and right gained popularity. But what did Binchy observe in particular?
Was he aware of the dangerous direction Weimar politics was taking?

Six months after he arrived he made an assessment of Curtius, the foreign
minister who took office after the death of Stresemann in late 1929. Curtius was
not particularly well suited to the portfolio since he was an economist by profession and 'formerly party expert and subsequently Minister for Industry and
Commerce'. A firm supporter of the policy of fulfillment from the outset 'it was
inevitable, for party and formal reasons' that Curtius should succeed
Stresemann, but Binchy added shrewdly:

> Stresemann was, in one sense, 'felix opportunitate mortis', because many
> of the real difficulties involved in his policy did not materialise until the
> period immediately following his decease. It must be said for Curtius that
> he has met and faced these difficulties with great courage and considerable
> ability in the domestic area.[48]

Curtius faced the unenviable task of turning back the rising tide of extremism.
Although the 1929 Young Plan had ensured better terms for the payment of
reparations, the extreme nationalists remained fundamentally opposed because
it admitted German culpability for causing the Great War under the 'war guilt'
clause of the Versailles treaty.[49] They succeeded in gaining 10 per cent of the
electorate's signatures to trigger a protest referendum.[50] Binchy highlighted
Curtius' lack of initiative in the area of foreign policy, but correctly noted that
Curtius would continue to pursue Stresemann's policy of fulfilment
tenaciously.[51]

Binchy's commentary on the run-up to the critical September 1930 federal
election was astute. He favoured efforts to amalgamate centrist parties because
of 'the bewildering number of parties (11) with which the electorate [...]
faced'.[52] He remarked: 'It is little wonder that the average German citizen is
dismayed with parliamentary institutions, and that they are driven to listen to

---

48 NAI, DFA, EA 231/4B, Binchy minute, 27 May 1930. Binchy was alluding to the campaign against the Young Plan by the conservative nationalist coalition of the DNVP,
Pan-German League, Stahlhelm and NSDAP. 49 Mommsen, 'The breakthrough of the
National Socialists', p. 94. 50 Ibid. In the protest referendum 5.8 million Germans (13.8%
of the electorate) voted against the Young Plan. 51 NAI, DFA, EA 231/4B, Binchy memo,
27 May 1930. 52 NAI, DFA, EA 231/4B, Binchy–Walshe, 15 Aug. 1930.

the crazy counsels of Hitler and his followers, who are clamouring for a dictator'.[53] His pro-democracy credentials and natural dislike of political violence meant he was appalled by the rise of the Nazis and Hitler.[54] Binchy had experienced the NSDAP soon after its foundation in the early 1920s. In November 1921, a German friend persuaded him to attend a meeting when he was a student at Munich University. Despite Hitler's 'insignificant exterior', Binchy discovered at this early stage that Hitler was 'a born natural orator' who seemed to 'take fire' as he launched into his address.[55] The content of Hitler's speech, he recalled, was extremely repetitive and conspiratorial, attacking Marxists, the October criminals, and Jews. But as Binchy's companion commented: 'No lunatic with the gift of oratory is harmless.'[56] Significantly, Binchy recognized nine years later in 1930 that Hitler's message remained 'substantially the same'.[57] By this time, however, the Nazis were on the brink of a national political breakthrough. Of the 'bible' of National Socialism,[58] Binchy sarcastically noted, 'anyone who has even attempted the task [of reading *Mein Kampf*] will readily understand why Hitler exalts the spoken over the written word'.[59]

In general, Binchy was dismayed at the way in which elections were run: 'defamation of one's opponents is regarded as a branch of political science'.[60] He was also critical of the left's accusation that the government's use of presidential decrees under Article 48 of the constitution was unconstitutional: 'it is difficult to see how one can violate a constitution by merely putting one of its articles in practice'.[61] He expected the Great Depression and the resultant high levels of unemployment to 'undoubtedly lead to a big increase of strength for the extreme Radicals on both sides, the Communists and the National Socialists ... Whether, the elections will result in a majority for the Moderate Parties is very doubtful.'[62]

On 14 September 1930 the Nazis won 107 seats in the Reichstag, having held only 12 seats in the previous parliament, transforming it into the second largest party after the Socialists. The Communists also increased their representation from 54 to 77 seats. All other parties lost seats apart from the two Catholic parties (Zentrum and BVP), which maintained their pivotal role in the Reichstag.[63] Binchy noted that the 'Centre Party, true to its traditions, is willing to ally either with the Socialists or the Moderate Conservatives, but will insist on certain guarantees as regards education, marriage and religion as a condition precedent to any alliance'.[64]

---

53 Ibid.   54 D.A. Binchy, 'Adolf Hitler', *Studies*, 22 (1933), pp 29–47.   55 Ibid., p. 29.
56 Ibid., p. 30.   57 Ibid.   58 Ibid., p. 31.   59 Ibid., pp 31–2.   60 D.A. Binchy, 'Paul Von Hindenburg, 1847–1934', *Studies* (June 1937), p. 232.   61 NAI, DFA EA 231/4B, Binchy–Walshe, 15 Aug. 1930.   62 Ibid.   63 Berghahn, *Modern Germany*, Table 18, p. 284. German unemployment figures, it should be noted, increased from 1.899 million people (or 8.5% of the total German workforce) in 1929 to 3.076 million people (or 14.0%) in 1930. 64 NAI, DFA, EA 231/4B, Binchy–Walshe, 15 Aug. 1930.

Binchy diagnosed Germany's electoral system as the main cause of political stagnation:

> The chief difficulty in the way of a satisfactory solution to Germany's political troubles lies in the electoral system at present in force. As you know, this is the so-called 'list system' of Proportional Representation. I only know of one other system which is more unsatisfactory and more conducive to the creation of small groups than it, and that is our system.[65]

More democratically-minded German politicians were surprised that Ireland engineered a comparatively stable two-party system on the basis of proportional representation and the single transferable vote. The former Socialist chancellor, Hermann Müller, begged Binchy in August 1930 to submit an article on this issue to a German political review (the Socialists were still in favour of PR). But Binchy tactfully refused reporting to Dublin that, '[n]aturally his idea was to make propaganda in favour of PR by holding up Ireland as an example of a country where it had not led to the creation of any undue number of parties'.[66] Binchy could not intervene in such a deeply divisive German political issue. Besides Müller had overlooked the fact that the Irish two-party system owed its existence to a civil war which had irreparably polarized political opinion.[67]

Despite Brüning's declining popular support, Binchy admired his willingness to have 'the courage to be unpopular'[68] and to tackle the 'heavy responsibility' placed on him by economic crises and political stalemate.[69] Binchy, however, failed to acknowledge the high costs of Brüning's constitutional dictatorship, especially the rise of extremism fuelled by the chancellor's domestic policies, exacerbating the political and economic crises.[70]

Brüning's methods of government and financially regressive policies were responsible for some of the increased support for radicals. He was labelled the 'Hunger Chancellor' as a result of his financial austerity. Binchy neglected to consider that Brüning was not able 'to offer the German people very much positive encouragement'.[71] By 1932, 29.9 per cent (or 5.603 million people) of the total German workforce was unemployed.[72] Brüning's austerity had only one advantage: it allowed Germany to plead insolvency in response to Allied demands for reparations, satisfying the German right – or so Brüning believed.[73] However, the resulting Hoover moratorium on reparations payments from 1 July 1931 did not appease those on the right who wanted a total renunciation of the Allied imposed German liability for reparations. The September 1930 federal election served notice on the Weimar Republic. By 31 July 1932, the

---

65 Ibid. 66 Ibid. 67 Ibid., Binchy–Walshe, 9 Apr. 1930. 68 D.A. Binchy, 'Heinrich Brüning', *Studies*, 21 (1932), p. 392. 69 Ibid., p. 393. 70 Burke, *Sackett*, p. 76. 71 Nicholls, *Weimar*, p. 110. 72 Berghahn, *Modern Germany*, Table 18, p. 284. 73 Ibid., p. 116.

Nazis had grown to become the largest Reichstag party commanding 230 seats, while the Communists (KPD) had increased their holding to 89 seats.[74]

Binchy, writing for *Studies* in September 1932, saw that Brüning did have faults. He believed, for example, that Brüning had delayed too long in confronting the Nazi challenge.[75] Nonetheless Binchy even then eulogized Brüning's 'iron will allied to a kind of spiritual serenity', his asceticism, his statesmanship, and his utter indifference to popularity'.[76] He compared Brüning to Kevin O'Higgins, the assassinated Cumann na nGaedheal home affairs minister who had been strong on law and order: 'He speaks coldly, but at times very vividly, marshalling his facts with deadly precision, appealing exclusively to the reason of his audience: listening to him in the Reichstag, I was invariably reminded of Kevin O'Higgins.'[77] Like Sackett, the US ambassador at the time, Binchy avoided any critical analysis of the authoritarian nature of Brüning's government. As with many other diplomats and commentators, he 'was never truly cognizant that Brüning's final goal was the restoration of the Hohenzollern dynasty'.[78] In retrospect Binchy's assessment of Brüning was too uncritical, but it reflected contemporary international and diplomatic opinion which viewed Brüning favourably as a European statesman preventing either the Nazis or the Bolsheviks from threatening the stability of central Europe.[79]

There are also parallels between Brüning and William T. Cosgrave, the president of the executive council of the Irish Free State (1922–32). Both lost power in their respective jurisdictions within the space of two and a half months for similar reasons. Cosgrave's socially conservative government reflected the interests of Cumann na nGaedheal's electoral base – the larger farmers and established business. In practice this resulted in financial retrenchment, cutting benefits to the elderly and blind, while dealing with the economic slump. Unemployment remained persistently high and Cosgrave's government was ideologically averse to any form of socialism or substantial state intervention in the economy.[80] These domestic policies which signalled an increasingly right-wing political approach had electoral consequences, and Cosgrave's brand of Catholic conservatism led to the use of 'red scare' tactics in 1931 and 1932.[81]

Binchy also revealed almost unqualified admiration for President Hindenburg. He told Walshe in January 1932:

74 Ibid., Table 42, p. 301.   75 Binchy, 'Brüning', p. 401. Here Binchy is alluding to Brüning's suppression of Hitler's SA or 'Brownshirts'.   76 Ibid., pp 401–2.   77 Binchy, 'Brüning', p. 403. Certainly Kevin O'Higgins and Heinrich von Brüning's cold rational public speaking style was different from Adolf Hitler's feverish emotionalism and simple message repetition which appealed to people's lowest instincts.   78 Burke, *Sackett*, p. 62.   79 Ibid., passim.   80 Lee, *Ireland, 1912–1985*, pp 124–6.   81 Keogh, *Twentieth–century Ireland*, pp 52–9; D. Keogh, 'De Valera, the Catholic Church and the "red scare", 1931–32', in J.P. O'Carroll and J.A. Murphy (eds), *De Valera and his times* (Cork, 1983), pp 134–59.

Hindenburg's future biographer will undoubtedly claim that at no period of his long life did he ever show such real greatness as during his tenure of the presidency. Since he swore allegiance to the Constitution of the Republic he has had to do many things which must have gone sorely against the grain for him ... Yet he has done well without flinching.[82]

Hindenburg was presented as sacrificing his peaceful retirement and curbing his monarchist and authoritarian faith to observe his 'constitutional duties' after 1925.[83] Of course, Binchy had not yet witnessed Hindenburg's dismissal of Brüning and his subsequent agreement to appoint Hitler as chancellor.[84]

ASSESSMENT

Irish-German contacts did increase somewhat in the mid-1920s. That Ireland drew parallels between Irish and German circumstances led to the expression of considerable empathy from the Irish for Germany's treatment under the treaty of Versailles. Even in this first decade of Irish independence the Saorstát evolved its own distinctive idealist small power view of international relations that placed a high value on collective security, universal disarmament, international dialogue and national self-determination. This idealism was, of necessity, constrained by the Anglo-Irish relationship and the commonwealth link, but it afforded the Saorstát a unique perspective on Weimar's postwar predicament.

Increased trade, European stability and cultural interchange paved the way for diplomatic discussions between the Saorstát and Weimar in 1928 and 1929. Unfortunately, the commencement of formal Irish-German diplomatic relations coincided with the re-emergence of regime-endangering instability in Weimar. In his first year Binchy generally achieved a high standard of reporting, sending home informative, relevant and analytical reports with information that would not otherwise have been be available to the department of external affairs. Irish newspapers, for instance, were heavily dependent on international news agencies (especially Reuters) and British newspaper sources (*The Times*).[85] As an effective diplomat Binchy could help an attentive government to assess its policies, to examine what was practical and to stimulate interest in new areas and new policies, or in reassessing extant policies. Following Binchy's report on 15 August 1930 concerning the 'position of the German parties in view of the approaching elections', Walshe responded that McGilligan would be very 'glad to have a general report on the position after the election has taken place. The

---

82 NAI, DFA CRS 19/10A, p. 2. Binchy–Walshe, 29 Jan. 1932. 83 Ibid. 84 This retrospective wisdom altered Binchy's assessment of Hindenburg as president considerably though he would always retain a very high personal regard for the old Prussian general. See Binchy, 'Hindenburg', passim. 85 See IT, November 1929, for example.

repercussions on foreign policy and the power of the Catholic Church in Germany would be of particular interest.'[86]

The department of external affairs lost the services of Binchy when he resigned on 23 March 1932.[87] Although he was well regarded in Berlin's diplomatic, intellectual and social circles and apparently valued in Dublin, he decided to return to his academic interests. Binchy was concerned that his reports on Weimar were not treated with due seriousness in Dublin.[88] He did not wish to be simply a symbol of Irish independence. He wanted to make a constructive contribution to the Irish state's interests, materially and politically, through his presence in Berlin. Unfortunately, Germany was not a high priority in Irish foreign policy although the legation was an important symbol of the Free State's internationalist ambitions. Nor could the Free State do much to alleviate the German imbroglio due to its relative international powerlessness. Duggan's suggestion that Binchy's reputed Germanoscepticism[89] played a role in his decision is a possible contributory factor. Elsasser's view that Binchy 'did not feel at ease' in his diplomatic role is worth considering.[90] His implicit suggestion that Binchy was a disorganized academic don requires evidential collaboration other than the anecdotal hearsay that on the occasion of his accreditation by President Hindenburg, Binchy had inadvertently forgotten his accreditation documents and had to hurriedly retrieve them before the ceremony.[91] It is discernible, however, from a reading his reports to Dublin that he was initially enthusiastic but he produced fewer diplomatic reports as his tenure in Berlin continued although Weimar's political crisis deepened.

Perhaps a better indication of why Binchy resigned can be obtained by looking at the timing of his decision. He resigned immediately after the announcement that de Valera's Fianna Fáil party had gained the most seats in the Irish general election of 16 February 1932, and had agreed a pact with the Labour party to form a government on 9 March 1932.[92] Binchy left the service later that month. Like many who were strongly identified with the Cumann na nGaedheal government and the department of external affairs at the time,[93] he was not alone in feeling antipathy towards those he believed had tried to 'wreck' the nascent Irish Free State during the Civil War, and feared reprisals for implementing repressive policies against Irish republicans.[94] The timing of Binchy's decision to re-enter academia was as likely to be politically motivated as a response to limited job satisfaction. Whatever the personal reasons for Binchy's departure from the foreign service, by March 1932 the Irish-German diplomatic relationship was finally well established.

---

86 NAI, DFA, EA 231/4B, Walshe–Binchy, 18 Aug. 1930.   87 NAI, DT, S. 5736A, Walshe–secretary of the executive council, 2 Mar. 1932.   88 Keogh, *Ireland & Europe*, p. 33.   89 Duggan, *Neutral Ireland*, p. 27, 34.   90 Elsasser, *Germany*, p. 46.   91 Ibid. 92 Keogh, *Twentieth-century Ireland*, pp 61–2.   93 Duggan, *Neutral Ireland*, p. 26. 94 Keogh, *Ireland & Europe*, pp 34–5.

3

Towards the Third Reich,
April 1932–August 1933

'The military spirit of Germany has been revived in all its glory by Hitler and his Storm Divisions' (McCauley).[1]

The secretary of the Berlin legation, Leo T. McCauley, was appointed chargé d'affaires after Binchy's resignation.[2] McCauley did not envisage filling the post for longer than two or three months[3] but his tenure was extended and he stayed from April 1932 to July 1933. McCauley witnessed firsthand the final months of the Weimar Republic and the first months of Hitler's rule. He observed Hindenburg's re-election as president on 10 April 1932, the fall of Brüning and the abortive authoritarian conspiracies of Franz von Papen and General Kurt von Schleicher. He also witnessed the initial transition phase to the Hitler state, including Hitler's appointment as chancellor (30 January 1933), the burning of the Reichstag (27 February 1933), and the passage of the Enabling Bill (23 March 1933) which transformed Hitler into a *de facto* dictator in a legal revolution.

McCauley proved to be a percipient, if sometimes ambivalent, commentator on German developments. He fulfilled his functions superbly bearing in mind that he was heavily burdened by the detailed work of intense Irish-German trade negotiations. The development of the Anglo-Irish Economic War after July 1932 highlighted the importance for the Irish government of the recent Irish-German Treaty of Commerce and Navigation (1930). Additionally, the first months of the Hitler government confronted McCauley and his superiors with the direct repercussions of its evolving anti-Semitic policies, not least the increased demand for immigration to the Free State.

The rapid changes in Germany presented problems for McCauley and the Irish government as they sought to protect Irish national interests, gain a foothold in the German market, understand the nature of the emerging dictatorship, and respond to the state-sponsored persecution of German Jews. At the same time, the Saorstát experienced dramatic changes. De Valera launched his constitutional revolution to destroy the Anglo-Irish settlement of 1921, leading to a dramatic deterioration in Anglo-Irish relations; a phase that was to last until

1 NAI, DFA17/18, McCauley–Walshe, 15 Mar. 1933.   2 NAI, DFA 17/18, Dublin–Berlin, 29 Mar. 1932.   3 Ibid., Walshe–secretary, department of finance, 24 Mar. 1933.

1938. Combined with the worldwide depression, the Economic War decimated Ireland's rural economy and fuelled the emergence and growth of a pseudo-fascist movement during 1933. The association of Eoin O'Duffy's Blueshirts with the Cumann na nGaedheal opposition embittered the political life of the country and potentially threatened democratic life and the rule of law. This direct experience of an internal threat to democratic government from a pseudo-fascist organisation is likely to have coloured de Valera's perceptions of the Nazi regime negatively although he did not apparently allow this to influence official state policy.

OPERATIONAL CONSTRAINTS

To begin to understand the obstacles McCauley encountered in 1932, the conditions of his appointment need to be considered. There had been fears, not realized, that de Valera's accession to power in 1932 would trigger a political purification of the civil service and in particular the department of external affairs. But the department continued to run smoothly without any enforced change in personnel.[4] Indeed, the new external affairs minister, de Valera, made McCauley's appointment as chargé.

The expectation was that an Irish minister plenipotentiary would soon be appointed to Berlin, but the recruitment of a suitable successor to Binchy proved difficult. The lack of an experienced pool of Irish diplomats with the necessary linguistic abilities for continental postings was a crucial problem in this early period of development for the Irish foreign service. McCauley's tenure as chargé was repeatedly extended until a suitable candidate for the Berlin legation could be found. He was hindered in his work by the false assumption in Dublin that his term of office would be brief.[5] That general attitude could explain McCauley's initial complaint that he received no policy guidelines, forcing him to solicit advice and instructions on matters which, he felt, the department should have given to him automatically.[6]

The culture of financial austerity imposed by Dublin's department of finance, combined with the expectation that he would be replaced imminently and disputes about his remuneration, caused McCauley additional aggravation. He felt obliged to minimise his use of hired transport and even missed functions when trams were not convenient or when he felt he could not justify the expense of taking a taxi. In June 1932 he reported that he had become 'highly expert in cadging for lifts from other diplomats'.[7] The department reacted promptly,

---

4 Keogh, *Ireland & Europe*, pp 34–5.   5 NAI, DFA 17/18, Walshe–secretary, department of finance, 24 Apr. 1933.   6 Ibid., McCauley–Walshe, 31 Mar. 1932.   7 Ibid., McCauley–Walshe, 18 June 1932.

almost shamefacedly, by granting a car hire allowance to McCauley while he remained as chargé.[8]

THE NAZI CHALLENGE TO BRÜNING

How useful was McCauley's assessment of German political developments? McCauley had to contend with the fluid and confusing circumstances of Germany's transition from nominal constitutional democracy to Nazi dictatorship. His lucid reports revealed how Hitler gradually confounded bourgeois complacency during these months, showing that the Irish chargé read the unfolding political situation almost flawlessly. From the outset, he grasped that Hitler was simply waiting for an appropriate opportunity to seize power.

The re-election of the ageing and ailing Hindenburg as president in April 1932 was never in doubt, but McCauley saw the election as an act of desperation by Chancellor Brüning to keep Hitler out of the presidency. Becoming Weimar president in 1932 would have been the optimum solution for Hitler, as he would then have had the power to rule by presidential decree. Hindenburg won a majority of the votes in the election of 13 March 1932, but Hitler's share of the vote prevented Hindenburg from gaining an overall majority, forcing a second round election run-off between Hindenburg, Hitler, and the Communist candidate, Ernst Thälmann. While Hindenburg's victory in the second round was a 'foregone conclusion', McCauley astutely observed that the transfer of votes from one of the failed first-round presidential hopefuls, Düsterberg of the German National Party, would be 'a strong indication of the probably future trend of events in Germany ...' The ex-crown prince's recent withdrawal of support from the German National Party in favour of Hitler's NSDAP was portentous.[9] McCauley duly recorded Hindenburg's expected victory on 10 April, but he also noted that Hitler added substantially more to his original vote than did Hindenburg. Hitler's support increased by 2 million votes and Hindenburg's by only 700,000 votes.[10]

McCauley believed that Hitler had to wait 'for the time when Hindenburg will no longer be his rival,'[11] or gain control of the Reichstag. McCauley highlighted the polarization of German politics during the numerous federal and state elections of 1932 whereby lesser, marginal parties lost support while the two ideological rivals, the Nazis and the Communists, gained strength.[12] Brüning finally acted against the Nazis' campaigning methods in the immediate aftermath of Hindenburg's re-election by banning the paramilitary organizations associated with the NSDAP, notably the Stormtroopers or SA. The SA played a central electioneering role by projecting an imposing martial image,

8 Ibid., Murphy–McCauley, 26 Aug. 1932. 9 NAI, DFA 34/125, McCauley–Walshe, 7 Apr. 1932. 10 Ibid., 11 Apr. 1932. 11 Ibid., 7 Apr. 1932. 12 Ibid., 25 Apr. 1932.

intimidating political opponents, and amplifying the German political crisis through provoking street battles with Communist opponents. McCauley approved of Brüning's suppression of the SA:

> the Government has at last decided to grasp the nettle firmly, but it may well be they are no longer strong enough to carry out their intention effectively ... if it fails the position of the Government will be seriously weakened and the strength of the Nazis enormously enhanced.[13]

Subsequent events justified his concern about the tardiness of the chancellor's reaction to the Nazi challenge. Brüning's decree was a political tactic to undermine Nazi strength in the upcoming election in the key German state of Prussia. But the belated ban failed to stem the upsurge in popular support and the NSDAP won a 'sensational' victory in the Prussian state elections of 24 April 1932. In a meteoric rise it became the largest party in the Prussian Landstag, increasing its holding from nine seats in the previous assembly to 162 seats.

McCauley properly interpreted the Prussian election result as an indicator of the decline in small parties. The German electorate increasingly sought a stable and decisive single party government rather than a succession of unstable multiparty coalitions blamed for stoking the continued political crises of Weimar. It was clear to McCauley that since neither the seriously depleted Weimar Coalition nor the Nazis had the necessary majority to control the Prussian Landstag, the formation of a future coalition was dependent on who the Nationalist party (DNVP) decided to support.[14] However, DNVP leader Alfred Hugenburg proved to be unwilling to form a coalition with either side, leaving the weakened Weimar Coalition to form a minority government in Prussia.

Prussia then became a testing ground for Hitler's tactic of creating maximum political turmoil by refusing to join government, preventing the formation of majority governments, or by obstructing the efficient working of minority governments in the Landstags and in the Reichstag. By refusing to participate in the coalition politics of Weimar at either regional or federal level, he made the country ungovernable, strengthening the appeal of his call for the election of a strong, majority Nazi government.

By late May 1932 McCauley reported that the German political situation was at a 'critical' juncture. The electoral rise of the Nazis, as indicated by the Prussian elections, had sapped Brüning's remaining support within the Reichstag to such a degree that it was 'rapidly becoming impossible for him to continue as head of the government'. He was unable to find willing and able candidates to fill the vacant portfolios of foreign affairs, defence, interior affairs and economic

---

13 Ibid., 14 Apr. 1932.   **14** Ibid., 25 Apr. 1932.

affairs so the Brüning cabinet appeared to be 'on the verge of dissolution'. Again McCauley accurately recorded the prevalent belief in Berlin that Brüning would only remain in office until the end of the Lausanne conference, which was meeting to discuss a moratorium on German reparations payments.[15] In a bitter irony, Brüning lost the confidence of President Hindenburg, the government-maker whom he had been responsible for re-electing. Brüning resigned a few days before the beginning of the Lausanne conference which achieved the final cancellation of all German reparations payments. The Irish chargé was aware that the archschemer behind Brüning's downfall was General Kurt von Schleicher and said:

> He could, at any time, have become a member of Brüning's Cabinet but refused to do so, partly because he did not see any hope of the Cabinet having a long life. He would not strike one personally as being such a redoubtable personality. He always seems to be too cheery, happy and optimistic to be a dangerous figure.[16]

Schleicher became the minister of defence in the new cabinet of a 'transition government' prior to the general election of 31 July 1932.

DÉNOUEMENT OF PRESIDENTIAL GOVERNMENT

New Chancellor Franz von Papen was an aristocratic troublemaker and nominally a member of the Centre party. McCauley's report of Papen's appointment by Hindenburg captures the universal surprise that the event evoked. Papen had never even been considered as a contender for the chancellorship because he had no experience of government and his authoritarian views had made him an outcast from the Centre party.[17] Papen oversaw a conservative nationalist caretaker government that rescinded the ban on Hitler's Stormtroopers (SA) wearing uniforms. The unleashed triumphalist Nazi violence rose to a crescendo in the immediate run-up to the general election. Papen's rescinding order provoked a serious federal–state conflict with the federal decision to lift the ban on uniforms being resisted by the states of Bavaria, Württemberg and Baden.[18] McCauley faithfully drew attention to these developments but failed to discern that Papen was simply the front for an authoritarian regime choreographed by Schleicher.

McCauley was absent from Berlin on annual holiday during July when the next momentous event in German politics occurred, the dissolution of the Prussian government and the declaration of martial law in Brandenburg on the grounds of a suspected Communist uprising. In Prussia the conservative ethos

---

15 Ibid., 27 May 1932.   **16** Ibid., 1 June 1932.   **17** Ibid.   **18** Ibid., 29 June 1932.

of Papen's presidentially-privileged federal cabinet was opposed by the democratic, republican and collectivist policies of the main constituent of the
Prussian coalition, the socialist SPD.[19] Papen, therefore, dissolved the Prussian
government and appointed himself as federal commissioner to govern Prussia
indefinitely. More than a month earlier McCauley had speculated that: 'The
Prussian problem will probably be solved by the appointment of a
Reichskommissar; and *the same problem, should it arise for Germany as a whole,
would probably be solved by dictatorship* [author's italics].'[20]

McCauley also foresaw that the Nazis, although capable of making substantial electoral gains in the federal elections of late July 1932, would

> not command an absolute majority. The situation would then be that a
> party organised for violence and committed to an extreme programme
> [i.e., the NSDAP] will be in the position of having either to compromise,
> in which case it would lose many of its followers, or else disregard the
> Constitution and install a dictatorship by force.[21]

He knew that the future of Weimar democracy was delicately balanced. The
general election of 31 July 1932 'settled nothing',[22] although the NSDAP
became overwhelmingly the largest party, increasing its number of seats from
107 to 230.[23] But the NSDAP still did not have an absolute majority to form a
government. Hitler, however, judged that the electoral climate was still in his
favour and refused Hindenburg's proposal that the NSDAP form a coalition
cabinet with Papen as chancellor. Hindenburg, unwilling to concede Hitler's
demand to be made chancellor and take full control of the cabinet, pleaded with
him 'to conduct his opposition in an honourable and responsible manner'.[24]

McCauley again captured the turmoil of this period well. His reports showed
how power reverted to the Hindenburg-supported Papen 'cabinet of barons',
which lacked democratic legitimacy. None of Papen's cabinet were members of
the Reichstag so '[t]hey are a presidential Cabinet and derive their authority
solely from the President'. That Reichstag proved to be the 'shortest-lived in
German history', but McCauley judged it to have, notably, achieved the reform
of the German civil service to increase efficiency and the 'taking up with France
in a definite manner' German demands for international equality. Curiously,
McCauley regarded the suspension of Prussian democracy and the imposition of
direct federal rule as '[a]nother great achievement'.[25] In reality, the *coup d'état* of
20 July 1932 was 'the beginning of a switch from the liberal and democratic state

---

19 E. Kolk (translated by P.S. Falla), *The Weimar Republic* (London, 1988), pp 185–6.
20 NAI, DFA 34/125, McCauley–Walshe, 9 June 1932. 21 Ibid., McCauley–Walshe,
29 June 1932. 22 Ibid., McCauley–Walshe, 4 Aug. 1932. 23 Kolk, *Weimar*, pp 194–5.
24 NAI, DFA 34/125, secretary of state for dominion affairs–de Valera, 16 Aug. 1932.
25 Ibid., McCauley–Walshe, 16 Sept. 1932.

of the Weimar Republic to the totalitarian dictatorship of the Third Reich' in which the republican constitution was undermined and the political police in Prussia were re-organized as an instrument of an authoritarian regime.[26] McCauley's view in September 1932 was that the development was beneficial because '[i]t has always been a source of weakness in the German administration that two governments had their seat in Berlin, namely, the Government of the Reich and the Government of Prussia'.

The Nazi representatives in the Reichstag engineered a vote of no confidence in which the government received only 42 votes. A second federal election was called for 6 November 1932 but it, too, failed to resolve the political impasse in line with McCauley's gloomy pre-election prediction 'that parliamentary government in the ordinary sense of the term will continue to be impossible'. The crisis was exacerbated by the rumour that the president was unwell.[27] McCauley noted that the 'most striking feature in the elections' was the decline in the Nazi share of the vote, reflected in a fall in the number of seats it held from 230 to 195. Meanwhile there was a corresponding 'significant ... increase in the number of seats secured by the Communists from 89 to 100'. He argued this inverse electoral relationship between the two extremist parties' political fortunes substantiated the widespread opinion that the NSDAP's previous startling electoral successes arose from its attraction of young working-class men who would normally have voted Communist. However, as McCauley pointed out this electoral oscillation failed to break the political stalemate in Germany and Papen still could not establish a government.[28]

McCauley pinpointed the beginning of the NSDAP's relative decline to a single event in August 1932: the trial of five Stormtroopers charged with murdering a young Communist in Potempa 'in circumstances of revolting cruelty'.[29] On 22 August, the five SA men were sentenced to death for the crime. Hitler then undermined his claim that the NSDAP sought power through legal methods when he publicly announced his solidarity with the murderers by publishing a telegram of support. McCauley translated the telegram. It read, 'Comrades, I feel myself linked to you by infinite infidelity by reason of this atrocious and bloodthirsty sentence. From this moment your liberty is a question of honour for us, and the struggle against a government under which this is possible is our duty.' This 'open identification by Hitler of himself with the condemned men ... shocked public opinion', in McCauley's estimation.[30]

Papen's attempt to form a new cabinet after the November Reichstag election was doomed by the failure of any other single party to emerge as a potential party of government. His cabinet resigned as soon as it was formed on 17 November, prompting a new round of negotiations to form a cabinet with a

26 Graf cited in Kolk, *Weimar*, p. 186. **27** NAI, DFA 34/125, McCauley–Walshe, 21 Oct. 1932. **28** Ibid., 7 Nov. 1932. **29** Ibid., 7 Dec. 1932 & 24 Aug. 1932; Burke, *Sackett*, p. 253. **30** Ibid., 24 Aug. 1932; J.C. Fest, *Hitler* (London, 1974), p. 342.

semblance of popular support. McCauley's telling comment at this stage was that, 'It is clear that Hindenburg is once more bearing a very heavy responsibility and that much depends on his firmness and tact in handling the present situation'.[31] In retrospect, this ailing octogenarian had too much responsibility thrust on him at a time when his rapid physical and mental decline made him malleable to his conspiratorial entourage. Hindenburg turned reluctantly to Hitler as the leader of the largest party in the Reichstag to form a majority coalition government. But Hitler remained unwilling to enter a coalition government in which he was not chancellor and Hindenburg was forced to return to the former style of presidential cabinets since no other political party could form the core of a working majority in the Reichstag.[32] By now McCauley, like Binchy before him, had diagnosed the 'root cause' of Weimar's political instability as the 'multiplication of political parties',[33] a view that tended to ignore the aggregation of factors contributing to the general crisis of late Weimar.

A defining moment had arrived. Through intrigue General Kurt von Schleicher outflanked Papen, gained the ear of Hindenburg and was appointed chancellor on 2 December 1932. McCauley had mixed views. He drew an analogy between Schleicher and Cromwell, in that both proffered military and authoritarian solutions to political instability. McCauley recorded Schleicher's belief that 'the ills in the German body politic can be cured by the timely application of a lieutenant and platoon of soldiers'. But Schleicher was, from McCauley's perspective, also a paragon of law and order who had the potential to stabilise Weimar but had come to power too soon. Schleicher, however, was as unsuccessful as Papen had been in his attempts to court a cross-party mass following inclusive of the trade unions and the radical Strasser[34] left wing of the Nazi party. Schleicher had hoped to split Strasser's wing from the NSDAP and had repealed anti-labour legislation to entice Strasser, but this convinced conservative and economic elites that an NSDAP government was preferable. The old anti-democratic elites ended up bargaining with the Austrian corporal who represented the largest party in the Reichstag. Simultaneously, Hitler compromised on forming a coalition government because the NSDAP's election performance was ebbing.[35] Its electoral decline in the general election of 6 November was confirmed in local government elections in Thuringia on 4 December 1932, despite Hitler's vociferous personal campaign.[36] Nazism was sliding into 'the rubbish pile of history' but external circumstances saved Hitler from possible oblivion.[37]

---

31 Ibid., 19 Nov. 1932.   32 Ibid., 26 Nov. 1932.   33 Ibid., 22 Nov. 1932.   34 Gregor Strasser, a leader in the Nazi party before 1933, adhered to radical socialist ideas but resigned his positions in December 1932 after Hitler accused him of treachery.   35 Peukert, *Weimar Republic*, pp 264–5.   36 NAI, DFA 34/125, McCauley–Walshe, 7 Dec. 1932.   37 D. Orlow, *The history of the Nazi party*, vol. 1, *1919–1933* (Newton Abbot, 1971).

HITLER IN POWER

Schleicher's cabinet collapsed in January 1933 because it had lost the support of the old elites and lacked a popular base. A Nazi government option was pursued energetically. The alienated Papen sought his revenge against Schleicher. The conservatives led by Papen and Hindenburg's nephew, Oskar, convinced the impressionable Hindenburg that the recent decline in the NSDAP vote would convert Hitler into a tempered political exponent of traditional authoritarian, monarchical, and business interests. Hindenburg appointed Hitler chancellor of a coalition cabinet on 30 January 1933 by presidential decree under Article 48 of the Weimar constitution. The Nazis filled only three of the 12 ministerial port-folios so that Papen, the new vice-chancellor, boasted that in just two months, 'we will have pushed Hitler so far into a corner that he'll squeak'.[38] Most con-temporary bourgeois commentators underestimated Hitler's guile, opportunism and political intelligence. Their complacency was soon confounded.

When appointed as chancellor, Hitler had extracted a promise to hold another federal election on 5 March, on the pretence that the electorate needed to sanction the national coalition. In reality he was hoping to secure an increase in Nazi support to allow him to govern alone. Hitler presented himself publicly as a democratic and reasonable nationalist while simultaneously manipulating the coercive forces of the state apparatus to prevent the opposition parties of the centre and the left from campaigning in the run-up to that March election. Although there were only two other Nazis in the cabinet (Frick, as minister of the interior, and Göring, as minister without portfolio and Prussian minister for the interior) they used the police forces to repress the opposition campaign.[39] Hitler used presidential power under Article 48 to introduce a series of emer-gency decrees dissolving the Prussian Landstag, banning political meetings and opposition newspapers. On 27 February 1933, McCauley astutely remarked that '[i]t has been said of Hitler and Papen that one of them is the cuckoo in the nest'. He predicted that if the Nazi–Papen coalition failed to gain a majority in the forthcoming elections 'they will continue to hold office, if necessary by force'.[40]

McCauley took the opportunity in February to attend one of Hitler's public speeches but, like most foreign commentators, he was disappointed by the shrill anti-Marxist 'rave' to which he was exposed. The speech was illogical and lacked any content. Nonetheless, McCauley noted that Hitler's theatrical ora-tory was obviously 'carefully prepared' to instill 'the wildest enthusiasm' in a German audience. Hitler was quite 'a different person behind the scenes' according to McCauley. His public persona was at odds with the unscrupulous,

---

38 Bracher, *German dictatorship*, chapter 4. Binchy, now returned to academic life, held a similar opinion. Binchy, 'Adolf Hitler', p. 46; Keogh, *Ireland & Europe*, p. 33. **39** Carr, *History of Germany*, p. 359. **40** NAI, DFA 34/125, McCauley–Walshe, 27 Feb. 1933.

secretive and effective organiser who had built up the Nazi movement. McCauley presented Hitler as a 'mystical and mysterious figure: no one knows what his principles and true policy really are, and one can only speculate as to his statesmanship'. He accurately foretold that, 'It is probable that the Hitler movement will not show its hands until after the results of the forthcoming elections are known. Up to the present its actions have mainly been of a repressive nature, for the purpose of silencing the opposition'.[41]

On the evening of 28 February, an act of arson destroyed the Reichstag and conveniently furnished Hitler with the justification he needed to fight the 5 March 1933 federal election with 'no pretence whatever at impartiality', according to McCauley.[42] McCauley's assessment of Hitler the individual and Hitler the politician accords with mainstream historical analyses.[43] Writing on the day after the Reichstag Fire, McCauley highlighted the destruction of the Reichstag as 'a serious inconvenience' for democrats. It would favour authoritarian government. Indeed, chancellor Hitler used the emotive accusation that the Reichstag had been burned by a Dutch Communist as a first step in a general communist revolution, to proscribe KPD and SPD rights to hold public meetings or to conduct an election campaign. Hitler persuaded Hindenburg to proclaim an emergency 'Decree for the Protection of People and the State' which effectively repealed most civil and political liberties. The decree, supposedly temporary, remained in force until 1945 permitting the federal government to arrest people, suspend state legislatures, censor private correspondence and search private property at will.[44] In retrospect, it was the so-called Reichstag Fire Decree which permitted the entrenchment of the Nazis in government. This decree was indeed the fundamental law of the Third Reich. McCauley noted that the government ran its election campaign on the assumption that 'they were the representatives of the whole German people' and treated the opposition 'as if it were non-German or anti-German'. 'A state bordering on a state of terror now prevails among the Communists and the Socialists' was how McCauley graphically recorded the situation.

Even under the artificially advantageous conditions in which the NSDAP and German nationalists monopolised air time on the wireless and prevented an effective opposition electoral campaign, McCauley and other observers noted that the NSDAP failed to achieve an overall majority in the general election on 5 March.[45] It gained only 43.9 per cent of the vote (288 seats). But, with the support of the traditionalist German National People's Party (DNVP), the Nazis could command a majority in the new Reichstag. As McCauley recognised, the result was disappointing for the Nazis who claimed to speak for the 'overwhelming majority of the German people'.[46] Once the new Reichstag

41 Ibid., 28 Feb. 1933.   42 Ibid., 6 Mar. 1933.   43 For example, Carr, *History of Germany*, pp 353–61.   44 Williamson, *The Third Reich*, p. 9.   45 NAI, DFA 34/125, McCauley–Walshe, 6 Mar. 1933, p. 2.   46 Ibid., 6 Mar. 1933.

convened, it committed what McCauley described as 'political suicide'.[47] After excluding the Communist deputies by force, Hitler coerced the rump Reichstag into passing the Enabling Bill on 23 March 1933. The bill, formally entitled the 'Law for removing the distress of the People and the Reich', was designed to transfer the power of the legislature to the executive. The chancellor and his Nazi government now drafted and made law, reducing the Reichstag and the Republic to a democratic fiction. Even the Centre Party could not resist the intimidation in which the Reichstag was surrounded by Brownshirts chanting, 'We want the bill-or fire and murder!' The chancellor delivered a disingenuous justificatory speech, stating that he needed the temporary authority to tackle recession, unemployment and to ensure peace with foreign powers, but that he would use the authority with restraint and only for vital measures. Simultaneously, he threatened the Reichstag with physical force if he did not get his bill passed: 'It is for you, gentlemen of the Reichstag, to decide between war and peace'. The Enabling Bill was passed by the two-thirds majority under Article 76 necessary to make it law.[48] McCauley noted the symbolic demise of Weimar when the Republic's black-red-gold flag[49] disappeared and the old imperial flag of Wilhelmine Germany was flown alongside the Nazi swastika.[50]

'GLEICHSCHALTUNG'

Hitler was now well advanced in establishing Germany as a one-party state. As chancellor he ruled by decree – the Reichstag was suspended and the constitution ignored although not formally withdrawn. Hitler maintained the myth of a 'legal revolution'. It was after all the *modus operandi* of the Weimar constitution that had allowed Hitler to take over. The authoritarian permissiveness of Article 48 permitted Hitler to gain power while Article 76 allowed fundamental constitutional rights to be abrogated by a two-thirds majority in the Reichstag. Hitler could claim to have technically obeyed the letter of constitutional law, except of course that the substantive methods he used to attain power in the first place were undemocratic and included physical intimidation of opponents. Some contemporary commentators, however, were beginning to accept the emergence of fascist dictatorships across Europe as a solution to the apparent ungovernability of many states during the interwar years. Mussolini's fascist Italy was a case in point. With this widespread contemporary ambivalence towards the emergence of fascistic dictatorships in central, eastern and southern Europe, how did McCauley interpret the troubled transition of Germany from democracy to dictatorship?

---

47 Ibid., 27 Mar. 1933. **48** J. Toland, *Adolf Hitler* (New York, 1976), pp 306–7. **49** NAI, DFA 34/125, McCauley–Walshe, 6 Mar. 1933. **50** Ibid., 15 Mar. 1933.

McCauley's diplomatic reporting presents an interpretative dilemma. His reports on the initial months of Hitler's rule, like those of many other observers of the early years of the Nazi regime, betray some degree of ambivalent admiration for the vitality of new regime compared with the stagnation of the previous one.[51] For example, the *Irish Times* greeted Hitler as 'Europe's standard-bearer against Muscovite terrorism'.[52] After more than a decade of political impotence, the new regime transformed the government overnight. After the instability of the Weimar Republic, McCauley shared the popular presumption that Germany needed strong government and reform. He constantly referred to the obvious 'difficulties' that Germany's complex party system had created for the normal functioning of democracy in Weimar. Hitler ended this situation in McCauley's opinion.[53] McCauley was 'almost' amused, in a sarcastic way, by what he saw as the hypocrisy of other foreigners resident in Germany, particularly foreign newspaper correspondents and diplomatic staff. They had reacted with hostility to the new regime, contradicting their past utterances that 'the Germans ... really required a highly centralized government and a strong hand to rule them'.[54]

Gleichschaltung (literally co-ordination or unification) was the policy of creating a centralised one-party state which required passing a large amount of Nazi legislation during 1933. The first expression of *Gleichschaltung* was the March 1933 Enabling Act, and the process continued with the termination of the rights of the states, the nazification of the education and legal systems, the dissolution of democratic opposition parties, and the eradication of Communism from public life. Arguably, McCauley's otherwise faithful factual record of *Gleichschaltung* is infused with the ambiguity of a confused observer close to enigmatic historical events, without the benefit (or hindrance?) of retrospection. In May 1933, McCauley claimed that '[e]vents have moved so rapidly' that it was difficult to even summarize them.[55] But from the outset he hinted at the symbolic menace of Hitler's choice of Potsdam as the meeting place for the new Reichstag in March. The militaristic and authoritarian overtones of this Prussian royal site, the final resting place of Frederick the Great, were unavoidable. He said the non-Prussian states regarded 'the Garrison church in Potsdam as the shrine to Prussianism, which indeed it is'.[56]

McCauley revealed, too, that most of the diplomatic corps feared that once Hitler had consolidated his position domestically he would then turn 'his own amazing energy and the enthusiasm of his following to foreign affairs'.[57] In early

---

51 See for example: R. Griffiths, *Fellow travellers of the right: British enthusiasts for Nazi Germany* (London, 1980), chapter 1. **52** C. Cruise O'Brien, 'Passion and cunning: an essay on the politics of W. B. Yeats', in C. Cruise O'Brien, *Passion and cunning: essays on nationalism, terrorism & revolution* (London, 1988), p. 42. **53** NAI, DFA 34/125, McCauley–Walshe, 6 July 1933. **54** Ibid., 15 Mar. 1933. **55** Ibid., 11 May 1933. **56** Ibid., 8 Mar. 1933. **57** Ibid., 15 Mar. 1933.

May 1933, he reviewed anxious international reaction to Hitler's rise to power, noting that the 'national resurgence' of Germany had 'reinfected' the Sudeten Germans of Czechoslovakia. Demands that the 'whole German race' should be brought 'under one roof' provoked a severe deterioration in Austro-German relations, not least because Austria had its own large Nazi party. Denmark was similarly nervous that the Reich would seek to reclaim the contested region of north Schleswig that it had gained from Germany following a plebiscite after the 1914–1918 war. There was, however, little German government activity to report in foreign affairs generally because the new regime was preoccupied with domestic consolidation. But McCauley was aware of the paradox created by Nazism's anti-Communist ideological basis (which involved the domestic suppression of Communism) and Hitler extending conciliatory feelers to the Soviet Union in foreign policy. His only explanation for this contradiction between Nazi theory and practice was that 'German industry cannot do without Russian orders'.[58]

The Reich's subjugation of the last remaining anti-Nazi stronghold in predominantly Catholic Bavaria was the death knell of Catholic southern Germany's federal resistance to Hitler's ideal of 'Ein Volk, ein Führer'[59] according to McCauley. He was aghast at the installation of General Ritter von Epp, one of the earliest National Socialists, as general state commissar for Bavaria. The move violated directly Hindenburg's assurances that the Reich government would not interfere in Bavaria.[60] The rapidly weakening Hindenburg had been 'reduced to a rubber stamp' for whom 'it would have been far better for his great reputation if he had not allowed himself to be nominated for the presidency at the last election'. There was an implicit hint of regret in McCauley's report of July 1933 about the dissolution of the Centre party, the last democratic party in the Reich. The Zentrum had 'clung stubbornly to life', he said, and 'it began to seem likely that, with the backing of the Bishops, it would succeed in surviving'.[61]

Conversely, McCauley was captivated by Germany's newfound dynamism. He recorded that, '[n]ew history is being made daily'[62] and commented that '[i]t would be difficult to find a parallel in history for such a burst of administrative energy'.[63] McCauley was overawed by the new government's initial vigour, by its 'ability to impose its will', and by its attention to administrative detail.[64] McCauley was not alone in being mesmerized by the Nazi rejuvenation of Germany. Walshe, the secretary of the department of external affairs who received heart treatment at a health spa in Cologne for several weeks in July and August 1933, was similarly impressed. From Germany he wrote to de Valera enthused about the 'great experiment' being undertaken adding 'the essentials of which we may well have to initiate in Ireland'. He was seduced, too, by Nazi

58 Ibid., 11 May 1933. **59** Bracher, *German dictatorship*, pp 259–63. **60** NAI, DFA 34/125, McCauley–Walshe, 15 Mar. 1933. **61** Ibid., 6 July 1933. **62** Ibid., 15 Mar. 1933. **63** Ibid., 11 May 1933. **64** Ibid.

arguments about the ineffectiveness of democratic government and advised de Valera: 'It seems to me inevitable that if you are to get leisure to think for yourself and your Ministers, as well as time to work you will have to give Parlt. [parliament] a holiday for an indefinite period'. He even went so far as to advise the use of force to achieve national unification as 'there is no reason why you should not succeed by other and better methods than those employed elsewhere'. He also thought that the Irish education system was 'deplorable' by comparison to the German one. Radical reform of education was necessary to implement social change in Ireland. He wrote, 'How different it is here where there is at least one intelligent, well educated and cultured person in the smallest community ready to form a link in a great national movement.'[65] However, Walshe's private intimations need to be read cautiously. He was disillusioned by the bitter, partisan parliamentary politics in the Saorstát as a result of the Irish Civil War.[66]

McCauley was similarly susceptible to the typical contemporary rationalization that Hitler was politically temperate and sought to control the wild men in the Nazi movement. On 15 March 1933, McCauley reported to Dublin that Göring was the reputed 'morphine addict' commonly alleged to be 'Hitler's evil genius'. McCauley characterized him as the 'most violent man in the new Government' who made speeches that were 'certainly very violent and unrestrained'.[67] In contrast, McCauley presented Hitler's keynote speech on German foreign policy to the rump Reichstag of 17 May 1933 as showing 'a new moderation and prudence'. Hitler presented the treaty of Versailles as the cause of all the post-war disasters and made a solemn 'declaration of friendship' to all other peoples. However, McCauley was not persuaded by Hitler's bid to convince foreign observers (and probably the German army or Reichswehr) that the Stahlhelm and the SA were not a reserve of the Reichswehr and did not increase Germany's military strength.

Hitler claimed that Germany was not an 'aggressive' power, was defenceless and disarmed relative to its neighbours, and was the country most vulnerable to invasion. Hitler proposed the destruction of all Germany's offensive weapons if other countries did the same. McCauley failed to appreciate the threat implicit in Hitler's assertion that Germany would leave the League of Nations if Germany continued 'to occupy a position of inferiority and degradation'.[68] Five months later on 14 October 1933, Hitler announced Germany was leaving the League, ostensibly because little progress had been made on disarmament and the international rehabilitation of Germany.

---

65 Franciscan Archives, Killiney, de Valera Papers, 1529, Walshe–de Valera, 28 July 1933. Cited in A. Nolan, 'Joseph Walshe and the management of Irish foreign policy, 1922–1946: a study in diplomatic and administrative history' (PhD thesis, UCC, 1997), pp 61–4. 66 Ibid., pp 65–6. 67 NAI, DFA 34/125, McCauley–Walshe, 15 Mar. 1933. 68 Ibid., McCauley–Walshe, 19 May 1933.

THE JEWISH QUESTION

The turmoil in Germany during 1932 and 1933 held major implications for the Saorstát in terms of cultural relations, refugee policies, foreign relations and commerce. From the Irish perspective, the presence of an Irish representative in Berlin since 1929 had afforded considerable advantages. As the only dominion government represented in Berlin, the autonomy and independence of Ireland in foreign affairs had been tangibly underlined. A permanent representative in Berlin facilitated the Saorstát's attempts to build closer economic, cultural and political ties with Germany. And by late 1932 despite the political instability in Weimar, there were signs of increased intimacy between Ireland and Germany.[69]

However, Hitler's accession to power in January 1933 heralded the introduction into Irish-German relations of substantive issues. The repressive methods Hitler used to consolidate his power in the spring and summer of 1933 could not be totally hidden from foreign commentators, although these 'bullying tactics'[70] and excesses tended to be concealed in the sanitised language of diplomatic reports normally received in the foreign offices around the world. International journalists were not so coy in their critiques of how the Nazis achieved their *Gleichschaltung*. William L. Shirer commented 'parliamentary democracy was finally interred'[71] and most powerful institutions were coerced one by one out of existence.[72] This outcome was often achieved by the most brutal methods. Hitler had unleashed the Brownshirts or SA to repress political opponents, in particular Social Democrats and Communists, resulting in widespread violence, murder, torture and extra-legal internment in makeshift backstreet concentration camps. These first so-called wild camps were simply called beating stations and there were approximately 50 of them in Berlin alone in 1933–4.[73] Berlin was caught up in an 'epidemic of fear'. It was a city full of whispers telling of 'illegal midnight arrests, of prisoners tortured in SA barracks, made to spit on Lenin's picture, swallow castor oil, eat old socks'.[74]

Reports printed in the Irish press demonstrated how the first months of Hitler's rule had negative implications for human rights, religious freedoms, and political rights as well as for international relations. There was considerable uneasiness about the Nazis' treatment of religion and of the Catholic Church in particular. The banning of the German Catholic press and violent clashes between the Nazis and the Centre party were reported in the run up to the

---

69 One such was the Irish military horse jumping team's attendance for the first time at the international tournament in Berlin in February 1933. NAI, DFA, Berlin letterbooks, Fahy–McCauley, 5 Nov. 1932. 70 I. Kershaw, *Hitler 1889–1936: hubris* (London, 1998), p. 468. 71 W.L. Shirer, *The rise and fall of the Third Reich: a history of Nazi Germany* (London, 1998), p. 199. 72 Ibid., pp 200–2. 73 A. Ritchie, *Faust's metropolis: a history of Berlin* (London, 1999), p. 412. 74 C. Usherwood cited in P. Brendon, *The dark valley: a panorama of the 1930s* (London, 2000), p. 243.

elections of 5 March 1933.[75] The 'new iron regime' in Germany after the Reichstag Fire made Germany a 'virtual dictatorship' with an almost arbitrary use of capital punishment, according to the *Irish Press*.[76] But there was relatively little pointed criticism of the new Nazi regime in the Irish papers.

The issue that placed immediate pressure on the Irish government and public opinion for a response was the Jewish question. On 15 March 1933, McCauley highlighted that anti-Semitism was the 'principal plank in the Nazi platform'.[77] Nazi radicals attacked individual Jews and their property without fear of retribution.[78] Atrocities were numerous and widespread. McCauley found it difficult to establish the extent of such actions and thought they had been 'very much exaggerated'. Nor did he accept that 'such attacks were the result of personal enmity between individual Nazis and individual Jews ... though it probably is true that the attacks were the result of individual action and were not official'.[79]

The ferocity and extent of anti-Semitic violence provoked a reaction among Jewish communities throughout the world who instigated a boycott of German goods. The protest spread to Jewish traders in Dublin but the notices asking customers to 'Boycott German goods,' ceased to be displayed at the request of the chief rabbi, Dr Isaac Herzog, after he had been reassured by Dehn-Schmidt.[80] According to the official German version the violent attacks on Jews were individual actions by irresponsible elements and would be quashed. The damaging impact of the anti-Semitic outrages on significant elements of German and non-German opinion and on the German economy prompted Hitler to order that individual direct action taken against Jews by 'irresponsible members of the movement' should be halted.[81] Hitler, however, took the opportunity to allow his party radicals to vent their frustrations by calling a one-day national counter-boycott against the Jews in Germany for 1 April 1933. But his tactic backfired when the action further fuelled international press condemnation of the regime, met with the disapproval of many Germans (to Hitler's great disappointment) and undermined the faith of foreign bankers.[82]

Thereafter, many Irish newspapers printed Nazi justifications of their actions and Nazi critiques of international complaints. One example was the synopsis of a speech by Seldte, the minister of labour, dealing with the alleged anti-German propaganda that appeared in the *Cork Examiner* on 12 April 1933,

---

75 IP, 20 Feb. 1933; IP, 21 Feb. 1933.   76 IP, 1 Mar. 1933.   77 NAI, DFA 34/125, McCauley–Walshe, 15 Mar. 1933.   78 The climate of extreme fear and violence is well captured in contemporary accounts by Bella Fromm and Victor Klemperer. B. Fromm, *Blood and banquets* (Glasgow, 1943); Victor Klemperer, *The Klemperer diaries, 1933–1945* (London, 2000).   79 NAI, DFA 34/125, McCauley–Walshe, 11 May 1933.   80 PA, AA III, R 77500, 1 Apr. 1933; II, 1 Apr. 1933.   81 NAI, DFA 34/125, McCauley–Walshe, 15 Mar. 1933. 82 Kershaw, *Hubris*, pp 472–4.

in which he claimed that the current wave of reporting was comparable to 'that of the anti-German atrocity propaganda during the world war'. He argued that no 'previous revolution in the world's history has been brought about to the accompaniment of so little bloodshed', which was the product of the 'exemplary discipline' of the Nazi movement.[83] Denials of the critical press reports by Herman Göring, Hitler's appointed deputy, appeared in the *Cork Examiner* on 26 April 1933. He said Germany was undergoing a period of national revival or rehabilitation in line with the 'strictest possible discipline' arguing that the murder rate had not increased and that any terrorism that had occurred was the product of communist agent provocateurs. He argued that thousands of Communists and Social Democrats had been arrested for treasonable attacks on the authority of the new government and for waging an international systematic campaign of hostile propaganda. He added that Jewish Germans had no need for fear 'so long as they do not transgress the law'.

These denials of wrongdoing and the accompanying assertions of good intentions were hardly convincing. But this was an early stage in the regime and hopes were widespread, even in the discriminated-against German Jewish community, that the situation would improve as the new regime faced the realities of government and the constraints of international society. Nonetheless, as McCauley highlighted, Hitler's government still had a very serious difficulty. Anti-Semitism was the central cohesive force of the Nazi movement and Hitler had built expectations among his rank-and-file supporters that a solution to the Jewish question was imminent. They expected the government to 'seize Jewish property, expropriate their businesses and either banish Jews themselves from the country or deprive them of the ordinary rights of citizenship' thus presenting the regime with 'a nice legal problem'.[84]

The Nazi regime passed laws to Aryanize German society at all levels. Shortly after the April boycott, the 'Law for the Restoration of the Professional Civil Service' compulsorily retired Jews from the civil service, even although they were grossly under-represented. Further legislation followed quickly to Aryanize the professions, press, theatre, arts, universities and, to a lesser extent, business. Reporting on 11 May, McCauley considered the government 'faithful' to its anti-Semitic manifesto: 'The official actions of the Government are sufficiently severe'. The boycott of 1 April had also resurrected the yellow label that Jews had been required to wear in the middle ages. In effect, according to McCauley, the persecution was both counterproductive for Germany and a tragedy:

> The general effect of the Government's measures against the Jews has been to deprive Germany of the services of many men distinguished in

83 *Cork Examiner*, 12 Apr. 1933. **84** Ibid.

the sciences, in medicine and otherwise; and to reduce many ordinary inconspicuous people to poverty and despair. The Press has reported a remarkable number of suicides among such people.[85]

Nonetheless, betraying the widespread ambivalence towards Judaism prevalent in all Christian societies, he showed a lack of compassion, a misunderstanding of Jewish history and disregarded the fragmented nature of the Jewish people. He stated:

> To some extent the Jews brought this trouble on themselves. They made a display of wealth and prosperity when the average German was struggling for an existence. They filled the restaurants, theatres and seaside resorts more or less to the exclusion of the ordinary German citizens. The consequence is that scarcely a voice has been raised in their defence.[86]

This antipathy towards Jews reflected anti-Semitism throughout Irish society in the inter-war period that probably reflected the unthinking confessionalism of many Irish citizens. Similar feelings were present in most societies and among the diplomatic corps.[87] It was only after the Shoah (Jewish holocaust) that such attitudes would become widely viewed as politically inappropriate.

The crisis of the German Jews baffled Jews worldwide. Germany since the nineteenth century had been the least hostile to Jews of the major continental powers. Jews had contributed enormously to the construction of the German nation and identity in terms of culture, industry and learning. Germans and Jews had become entwined socially, culturally and economically. German Jews had fought loyally, in large numbers, with the German empire during World War I.[88] But the unfolding developments in Nazi Germany destroyed their complacency about being integrated and accepted in German society. The chief rabbi of Ireland, who had called off the boycott of German goods undertaken by some Dublin Jewish traders, paid a widely publicized visit on the afternoon of 4 May 1933 to de Valera, accompanied by the only Jewish member of the Dáil, Fianna Fáil deputy Robert Briscoe. Reportedly de Valera was 'deeply aggrieved' about the position of the German Jews and 'expressed his sympathy with the Jewish community in Ireland in their anxiety for their German brethren. He earnestly hoped that all cause for concern would soon be removed.'[89] The Irish government was apparently sympathetic but unwilling to

---

85 NAI, DFA 34/125, McCauley–Walshe, 11 May 1933.   86 Ibid.   87 When Sir Horace Rumbold, the British ambassador to Berlin (1928–33), first arrived he was 'appalled by the number of Jews in this place. One cannot get away from them. I am thinking of having a ham-bone amulet made "to keep off the evil nose", but I am afraid that even that would not be a deterrent'. M. Gilbert, *Sir Horace Rumbold: portrait of a diplomat, 1869–1941* (London, 1973), p. 319.   88 P. Johnson, *A history of the Jews* (London, 1995), p. 470.   89 IP, 5 May

interfere in the affairs of another sovereign state, even to alleviate the suffering of German Jews.

Another opportunity for the Irish government to clarify its position on the Jewish question arose when Dr Natzum Sokolow, president of the World Zionist Organization, arrived in Dublin later that month seeking Irish support for the establishment of a Jewish state in Palestine. Sokolow argued that 'Ireland was perhaps next to Israel in martyrdom and heroism' and hoped that the Irish people who were 'very friendly to Germany, would call the attention of the German government to the consequences' of its persecution policy.[90] De Valera received Dr Sokolow on 18 May and was 'asked to use his influence with the League of Nations to secure a larger quota for Jews entering Palestine, especially in view of the situation in Germany'. The *Irish Press* reported that de Valera was 'deeply interested in the whole question' and 'promised to do his best'.[91]

The suspension of Professor Julius Pokorny from Kuno Meyer's chair of Celtic in Berlin University drew the attention of the Irish government to the practical consequences of Nazi policy towards Jews. Regardless of de Valera's sympathies with the plight of the Jews, it appears that he considered it unwise in both the state's interests and in Jewish interests to intervene directly and formally. Pokorny, it will be recalled, had volunteered his services to the unofficial Irish mission in Germany during the Anglo-Irish War. His services to Irish nationalism, his extensive contacts with the Irish academic world, and his contribution to Celtic Studies offered no protection from the racial laws of the new German regime. He became the subject of investigations following his defence of a Jewish colleague, Ernst Lewy.[92] The subsequent discovery that his maternal grandfather was 'non-Aryan' led to his suspension from the prestigious academic post which he had occupied since Kuno Meyer's departure in 1920.[93] Pokorny contacted McCauley in Berlin who 'promised me to ask the Irish government for permission to intervene on my behalf, pointing out, that my person was an important link between Germany and Ireland'. He also contacted Richard Irvine Best, director of the National Library of Ireland, who occupied a central role in the transnational Celtic Studies network. Pokorny used Best's name and those of several other prominent members of the Irish and Celtic Studies academic community, including Eoin MacNeill and Osborn Bergin, to demonstrate his vital role in Irish-German relations and Celtic scholarship to the Nazi regime.[94]

Pokorny remained determined to stay in Germany and to secure his reinstatement although others had 'lost their nerves and left the country'. He recognized that the chaotic and contradictory nature of the new 'race' laws placed him in a 'funny position'. As a 'non-Aryan' he was 'forbidden from marrying a

1933. **90** IP, 19 May 1933. **91** IP, 19 May 1933. **92** Keogh, *Jews*, p. 103. **93** NLI, Richard Irvine Best papers, MS 11,996(2), Pokorny–Best, 5 May 1933. **94** NLI, Best papers, MS 11,003 (8), Pokorny–Best, 4 May 1933.

pure Aryan'. As a public servant (although suspended), however, he could not marry a 'non-Aryan' either, because 'according to a recent law *everybody* who marries a non-Aryan loses his job without any pension'.[95]

Irrespective of Pokorny's contribution and his plight, neither the Irish government nor Irish academia deemed it advisable to interfere formally in the domestic affairs of Germany.[96] McCauley was instructed by Seán Murphy, assistant secretary at the external affairs department, that:

> the Minister does not feel disposed to intervene in this matter. He feels that any interference on the part of the Saorstát Government in connection with a purely internal question of this kind might well be resented by the German Government and, far from assisting Professor Pokorny, might rather serve to injure any prospects he may have of re-instatement in his position.
>
> The German Minister, to whom I took an opportunity of mentioning the matter, is definitely of the opinion that no representation on our part could be of any avail.[97]

In late August, de Valera indicated to the legation 'that should an opportunity present itself you might refer unofficially to the long association of Professor Pokorny with Celtic scholarship and the debt of gratitude which so many students find themselves in. The Minister merely desires to have it made clear to all concerned, as occasion arises, that the Government here would do everything they could usefully do in Professor Pokorny's interest'.[98] Unofficial, informal intervention was deemed the safest course of action.

During the hiatus of Professor Pokorny's suspension, awaiting the outcome of the police investigations into his 'racial' background, Professor Ludwig Mühlhausen made a determined effort to acquire the post.[99] Mühlhausen, who had founded Hamburg University's department of Celtic Studies in 1928,

---

95 Ibid. 96 Pokorny as an individual is enigmatic according to recent detailed research by Lerchenmüller who argues that Pokorny himself may have been prone to anti-Semitic utterances in the early 1920s until he discovered he may have had Jewish ancestry (J. Lerchenmüller, *'Keltischer Sprengstoff': eine wissenschaftgeschichtliche Studie über die deutsche Keltologie von 1900 bis 1945* (Tübingen, 1997), pp 245–6). While Lerchenmüller is quick to denounce Pokorny for his vices, it nonetheless illustrates the prevalence of anti-Semitism in central Europe, particularly in Vienna, in the early twentieth century. Lerchenmüller's research does indicate however, how otherwise mediocre German academics such as Mühlhausen opportunistically used Nazism and anti-Semitism to progress careerwise in the field of Celtic Studies in Nazi Germany. In this regard see also D. Ó Cróinín's insightful review article of publications pertaining to the history of Celtic Studies in Germany in *Peritia*, 12 (1998), pp 424–30. 97 NAI, DFA, Berlin letterbooks, Murphy–McCauley, 16 May 1933. 98 Ibid., Hearne–Bewley, 26 Aug. 1933. 99 NLI, Best papers, MS 11,003 (8), Pokorny–Best, n.d. (late 1933?).

joined the Nazi party in 1932 and became a member of the SA or Storm-troopers. He used his Nazi credentials for career advancement purposes after Hitler came to power.[1] The new regime's Aryanization of universities offered party members unprecedented opportunities after the summary dismissal of hundreds of non-Aryan academics during its initial years. In Ireland, the department of external affairs maintained its unofficial and nuanced approach to Pokorny's suspension and instructed the Berlin legation:

> should you be approached in regard to the appointment of Professor Mühlhausen to the Professorship of Celtic Languages in Berlin University, the Minister sees no objection to your stating that the Government should be glad to see such an eminent scholar appointed to the post. You should, of course, avoid giving the impression that the supercession of Professor Pokorny in this appointment is welcomed by the Irish Government.[2]

In Pokorny's view this limited intercession by the Irish government and by scholarly colleagues was responsible for his restoration to the chair of Celtic in Berlin University in late 1933 after seven months suspension.[3]

In general on immigration and asylum policy, the Irish government adopted a regressive line that can be traced back to the unofficial Irish mission to Berlin in 1922. In April 1922, Nancy Power reported, '[i]f it becomes generally known that Ireland is available, it means that in a short time our country will be flooded, not only by Germans, but also by Jews, who will be glad to acquire a new field of operations.'[4] This tainted Judaeophobic perspective informed Irish policy on immigration from the very beginning.[5] It was confirmed in April 1933 when McCauley reported that as a result of the treatment meted out to Jews by Nazis he had received many inquiries and applications for visas. German and Irish citizens needed no visas at this stage to reside in each other's country. Many of the enquiries and applications involved non-German Jews resident in Germany, for example Poles, so he discouraged them from going to Ireland 'as they are really only refugees'.[6] In a matter of days, J.V. Fahy, a department of external affairs official, replied to affirm that the minister approved of McCauley's action and directed 'As far as possible such persons [Jewish refugees] should be discouraged from coming here.'[7] In the succeeding months several Jewish applicants

1 O'Donoghue, *Hitler's Irish voices*, pp xvii, 3.　2 NAI, DFA, Berlin letterbooks, Walshe–Bewley, 1 Dec. 1933.　3 NLI, Best papers, MS 11,003 (8), Pokorny–Best, 27 Dec. 1933 & 21 Obst 1935.　4 NAI, DFA, ES, Box 34, File 239, Power to Duffy, 10 Apr. 1922.　5 NAI, DFA, ES, Box 17, File 114, Walshe–Collins, 1 May 1922. The priorities set by Walshe/Duffy at this early stage for Irish immigration policy remained largely unchanged for the forty years.　6 NAI, DFA 102/9, McCauley–Walshe, 7 Apr. 1933.　7 Ibid., Fahy–McCauley, 19 Apr. 1933.

were refused visas to work or live in Ireland on various grounds. Applicants had to prove they had been domiciled in the 26 counties on 6 December 1922 when the Saorstát officially came into existence.[8] Visas for residency were also refused on the grounds that applicants could not show how they proposed to maintain themselves in the Saorstát. As Fahy informed McCauley: 'It is not unlikely that numerous applications ... may be received from Jews in Germany who are likely to lose their employment and it is considered undesirable to grant permission to these aliens to enter this country.'[9] The official policy was clear: the Free State was not willing to provide sanctuary for Jews fleeing Nazi persecution. In truth, like many other states, the situation of Jews under Nazi rule was not considered a policy priority but a threat to national interests.

TRADE

In 1932 Irish-German trade relations were in an embryonic state. Although the Treaty of Commerce and Navigation of 12 May 1930 was designed to encourage the growth of Irish trade with Germany,[10] it was only after the change of Irish government in March 1932 that this was acted on consistently. A special agreement for the avoidance of double taxation for Irish and German shipping company profits from trading between the two countries was finally signed in 1932, having been negotiated and deliberated over during the Cumann na nGaedheal period of government.[11] The agreement meant a net loss of approximately £1,000 in revenue to the Irish exchequer,[12] but the department of industry and commerce believed it was worthwhile in order to encourage direct trade and shipping between Germany and Ireland.[13] The department of finance had not been convinced and it took the transition from a Cumann na nGaedheal to a Fianna Fáil government to overcome its objections.

It was the outbreak of the Anglo-Irish Economic War in July 1932 that endowed Irish-German economic relations with significance. While one of the oft-noted general effects of that trade conflict was to reinforce Fianna Fáil's policy of self-sufficiency, it also stimulated Ireland's search for alternative markets. The Economic War was the result of British retaliation for de Valera's decision to withhold payment of land annuities and possibly his dismantling of the Saorstát's ties with Britain and the Commonwealth, which began with the abolition of the oath of allegiance in 1932. De Valera saw his policy merely 'as a means of eroding British restrictions on Irish sovereignty'.[14] He had already drawn a parallel between the payment of land annuities and Germany's forced

---

8 NAI, Berlin letterbooks, Fahy–McCauley, 23 May 1933.   9 Ibid., Fahy–McCauley, 16 May 1933.   10 NAI, DFA 314/49, untitled & unsigned memo, n.d.   11 NAI, DFA 314/49. 12 Ibid., Leydon–Ferguson, 11 May 1931.   13 Ibid., Ferguson–Leydon, 21 May 1931. 14 O'Malley, 'The origins of Irish neutrality' (Ann Arbor, Michigan, 1980), p. 196.

reparations in the Fianna Fáil manifesto for the February 1932 election campaign. He said the annuities 'impose on the Irish people a burden relatively heavier than the burden imposed on the German people by the war reparation payment'.[15] Britain retaliated for de Valera's refusal to pay with the introduction of a 20 per cent tariff on imported Irish agricultural commodities.[16] The Saorstát counter-retaliated by imposing duties on British cement, coal, electrical machinery, and also iron and steel manufactures. As a producer of mainly agricultural goods, dependent on exports for generating national wealth, the restrictions on Ireland's major export market combined with falling prices and the Great Depression signalled economic disaster.

Alternative markets to Britain had to be created. Continental markets, in particular urban-industrial societies dependent on sizeable agricultural imports such as Belgium and Germany, were targeted. As a market leader in several manufacturing fields Germany was seen as a strong potential trading partner for Ireland. Furthermore, Germany was a substantial net importer of basic dairy and beef products. Irish officials saw the prospects for a beneficial reciprocal trading arrangement between Germany and Ireland as being strengthened by the trade promotion activities of both the AA and private firms in Ireland during 1932 and 1933. In January 1933 an AA official travelled to Ireland in an attempt to interest private firms and the government in importing German goods. Having met Dr James Ryan, minister for agriculture, and Seán Lemass, minister for industry and commerce, the official submitted an optimistic report to his superiors outlining the possibilities for increasing German exports to the Free State. Then J.W. Fäsenfeld and his son, Georg, who owned a large slaughterhouse in Bremen, showed interest in importing Irish cattle. Fäsenfeld's friendship with Robert Briscoe TD gave him access to de Valera[17] and he won the right to manage meeting the quota of 6,000 cattle to be sent to Germany in 1933.[18] Siemens, the company that had played the central role in developing the Shannon hydroelectric scheme, was at the same time lobbying the Irish government for a significant stake in constructing a second proposed hydroelectric project on the Liffey.[19] There appeared to be sufficient German interest in expanding Irish-German commercial relations to satisfy emerging Irish trade requirements.

Immediately following the outbreak of the Economic War in July 1932, de Valera instructed McCauley speedily to explore the possibilities of opening new markets for agricultural and manufactured produce in Germany.[20] As if to underline the importance of Germany as a new market, especially for live cattle,

15 Cited in D. McMahon, *Republicans & imperialists: Anglo-Irish relations in the 1930s* (London, 1984), p. 4. **16** Ibid., pp 68–9. **17** Dickel, *Aussenpolitik*, p. 30 f. 93. **18** NAI, DFA, 17/160. The 'most favoured nation' clause in the commerce and navigation treaty entitled the Free State to export to Germany 6,000 head of cattle a year. **19** Dickel, *Aussenpolitik*, p. 30. **20** NAI, DFA, Berlin letterbooks, Murphy–McCauley, 26 July 1932.

the treaty of commerce and navigation between the two states which had been signed two years earlier was registered with the League of Nations by the Free State later that month on 28 July 1932.[21] The Irish Free State simultaneously pressured Germany to accept an increased amount of Irish agricultural goods 'to adjust the adverse trade balance'.

While the Irish zeal to acquire enlarged export markets in Germany considerably added to McCauley's workload,[22] the initiative was launched in the most unfavourable German economic circumstances. The German economic situation was even more precarious than that of the Saorstát. Even before Hitler's accession to power, Germany was moving in the direction of protectionism. McCauley feared the Germans would impose tariffs on agricultural imports, especially cattle, which Ireland wanted to export.[23] But it was herring, not cattle, that became the first tariff target. In late 1932 German tariffs on salted herring imports were increased causing 'considerable dislocation' to the Irish fishing industry.[24] By late 1932, butter was the only product that the Free State could sell profitably on the German market.[25]

In Germany the unemployment rate was more than 30 per cent and, with the collapse in international demand for industrial products, Germany lacked the currency to purchase foreign products. In 1929 the Irish Free State imported £1.549 million worth of goods from Germany. By 1932 this had fallen to £1.303 million (a 15.9 per cent decrease). Over the same period the value of Irish exports to Germany fell from £661,000 to £70,000 or by 89.4 per cent,[26] benefiting Germany's balance of trade with Ireland. Ireland required high quality mechanical and electrical expertise and products more than Germany needed Irish agricultural produce. In 1933 unfavourable prices and tighter regulations to protect German agriculture and encourage autarky, virtually excluded Irish goods from the German market that year.[27]

Irish producers and suppliers, therefore, were at a considerable competitive disadvantage but the gravity of the Irish economic situation impelled the Irish government to continue to seek ways to penetrate the German market despite these inhospitable trading conditions. In particular, the government was determined to reverse the trade deficit Ireland had with Germany. Efforts made by McCauley and from Dublin failed. In 1933 only £170,000-worth of Irish goods was exported to Germany, while £1,750,000-worth of German goods was imported.[28] In July of that year, the attitude of the department of industry and commerce had noticeably hardened in response to the lack of progress made in overcoming German quantity restrictions and tariffs. As the official J.V. Fahy

21 Ibid., Cremins–McCauley, 12 Aug. 1932. 22 Ibid., Walshe–McCauley, 15 Nov. 1932. 23 NAI, DFA 19/10A, McCauley–Walshe, 6 Sept. 1932. 24 NAI, DFA, Berlin letter-books, Fahy–McCauley, 18 Oct. 1932. 25 Ibid., 22 Nov. 1932. 26 NAI, DFA 314/10/6/3, brief note on Saorstat–German trade negotiations, 10 Oct. 1934. 27 Dickel, *Aussenpolitik*, p. 30. 28 NAI, DFA 314/10/6/3, 'German-Saorstát trade agreement', n.d.

commented: 'If any trade is to be got in Germany it will not be got by more representations but by much more drastic action towards German imports here.'[29]

In Germany, the foreign policy aim of not alienating Britain meant Berlin
should not take advantage of London's difficulties with Dublin in trade matters.
German officials also believed that the Anglo-Irish trade dispute would be
short-lived. Baron Hans von Plessen, the AA official with responsibility for
liaising with the Irish legation and for 'all matters relating to the Saorstát and
Great Britain', told McCauley the 'strained economic relations at present existing between Great Britain and ourselves ... would not last very long because it
was in the interests of both parties to reach an agreement'. McCauley believed
this view had negative implications for closer trade relations: 'The Germans
would probably feel that we were asking them to help us out of a temporary difficulty and were offering them as an inducement trade advantages which would
also be temporary.'[30] The failure of their efforts led the departments of trade
and commerce, external affairs and agriculture to formulate a tougher strategy,
threatening to exclude German exports from the Saorstát as a lever to gain
increased access to German markets. Responsibility for implementing this
policy in Berlin would be largely left to McCauley's successor, Charles Bewley,
after August 1933.

CONCLUSION

McCauley's extended tenure in his supposedly temporary post finally came to
an end in July 1933. In his final report he noted that 'Hitler's idea of "One Party,
One State" has now been achieved',[31] although Hitler was not to proclaim the
'unity of party and state' until December.[32] On balance, any appraisal of
McCauley's performance during 1932 and 1933 should be positive. He stepped
into the position at short notice and in a period of turmoil in Irish, German and
international affairs. While Irish-German relations were mainly limited to trade
matters, it nevertheless benefited the Free State to have a diplomatic representative resident in Berlin, observing firsthand the momentous political transition
in Germany.

Few historians today would quibble with his view in February 1933 that
'[s]ince the resignation of Dr Brüning and his Cabinet in May last there has
been no pretence whatever at parliamentary government; and even before that
date the government had been carried on by decree'.[33] McCauley's recounting
of political events during the transition period was exemplary, whether one

29 NAI, DFA, Berlin letterbooks, Fahy–McCauley, 17 July 1933.   30 NAI, DFA 19/10A,
McCauley–Walshe, 6 Sept. 1932.   31 NAI, DFA 34/125, McCauley–Walshe, 6 July 1933.
32 Bracher, *German dictatorship*, p. 266.   33 NAI, DFA 34/125, McCauley–Walshe, 28 Feb.
1933.

considers his analyses of the many regional and federal elections, the popular mood, the economic situation or the main politicians. His detailing of the events and developments after Hitler's appointment as chancellor (January 1933) could leave no reader of his reports in Dublin complacent about the implications of *Gleichschaltung* for democracy and basic human rights in Germany.

He played a key role in the burdensome and protracted negotiations leading to the first Irish-German bilateral trade agreement in 1932, fulfilling his dual trade and political reporting role admirably. It was largely in recognition of his heavy workload and responsibilities that, in April 1933 the secretary of the department of external affairs and the minister of external affairs finally recommended that McCauley receive 'additional remuneration' over and above his normal salary as secretary.[34] This recommendation was a highly significant reflection of the department's satisfaction with McCauley's performance as the ministry was under severe pressure to make sizeable budget cuts. The department of finance's decision to reduce spending on international and other external bodies and conferences by 20 per cent in 1933–34 and by 50 per cent in 1934–35 underlined the dire need of the Irish government for economies. It had even suggested that the Irish office to the League of Nations in Geneva should be closed,[35] in contradiction to de Valera's explicit policy of Ireland's high profile policy of internationalism.[36]

But McCauley did prove to be an unsound analyst to the extent that Nazi government successes and dynamism beguiled him after January 1933. While attentive to the negative aspects of Nazism, notably its use of domestic oppression and authoritarianism, he admired its firmness. There was some evidence, too, that he and his superiors lacked empathy for the predicament of Jews in Germany. The Irish government and the legation in Berlin tightened immigration and visa criteria against Jews fleeing Nazi persecution. Nor was there a formal intervention against the dismissal of Professor Pokorny from the University of Berlin. The Irish official position was that conventional diplomacy required all states to deal with the new regime, no matter how distasteful it was, in pursuit of their own national interests.

On 10 July 1933, the *Cork Examiner* presented the 'Case for Hitler' by an anonymous German correspondent. It argued that political rule differed from country to country and what was suitable for Germany need not be suitable elsewhere.[37] The report appealed to anti-Communist sentiment in many western democracies and in Catholic-dominated societies where Communism was equated with atheism and the suppression of Christianity. It held that the Nazi regime was the bulwark of western Europe against the infiltration of Communism from the east. The report also claimed that it was only a minority

34 NAI, DFA 17/18, Walshe–secretary, department of finance, 24 Apr. 1933. 35 D. Gageby, *The last secretary-general: Seán Lester and the League of Nations* (Dublin, 1999), pp 45–7. 36 Keogh, *Ireland & Europe*, pp 39, 41. 37 *Cork Examiner*, 10 July 1933.

in the German Jewish population who were seen as a malign influence and claimed that not one Jew had died violently during the Nazi revolution. By August 1933 it was up to McCauley's successor, Charles Bewley, to deal with the challenges presented by the Berlin posting.

4

Consolidating the Hitler state,
September 1933–July 1934

'Germany I really only know in its old state of about five years ago, but already, after three weeks here, I can say that one can perceive a new hope in the people which was not perceptible' (Bewley).[1]

'[T]he word [Aryan] survives in modified form in the name 'Erin', the Celtic name for Ireland, the green isle, which has preserved for us so much of the best in Aryan tradition' (*Lokalanzeiger*).[2]

In July 1933, Bewley, the former Sinn Féin trade envoy to Berlin (1921–3), finally gained the Berlin posting he had always sought. Bewley was apparently well qualified, being fluent in French, German, Italian, and Latin,[3] and able to learn languages easily.[4] The Germany he arrived in was a racialist police state that attempted to veil oppression behind legal legitimacy.

Bewley's stay in Berlin for most of the peacetime period of the Hitler state is a valuable record of how it evolved, matured and contributed to the outbreak of World War II, bearing in mind that Bewley developed his own unique analysis of this crucial crossroads in twentieth-century history. But Bewley's key role was initially purely commercial – to facilitate Irish exports to Germany thereby reducing dependence on Britain during the Economic War. However, Bewley the individual and diplomat is the subject of debate on whether he had pro-Nazi inclinations from the outset or when precisely his critical faculties towards the Third Reich failed him.[5] To assess his suitability as a diplomat in Berlin after 1933 his background requires examination.

After Bewley's resignation as an 'unaccredited representative of a half-independent state' in Berlin in the spring of 1923, he returned to the practice of

1 Translated from *Deutsche Allgemeine Zeitung*, 20 Aug. 1933. 2 Cited in NAI, DFA CRS 19/50, McCauley–Walshe, 20 May 1933. 3 Keogh, *Ireland & Europe*, p. 28. 4 II, 8 Nov. 1943. 5 His role in the collapse of the troubled Irish mission to Germany in 1922 and 1923 seems to have been disregarded. Evidence that might explain the rationale for Bewley's appointment to Berlin in 1933 is limited. Existing interpretations are also contradictory. Roth has asserted that there has been no speculation as to why Bewley was appointed. Although he has added some new detail, his assertion is inconclusive. Bewley's appointment and background have attracted considerable comment. But since there are no details regarding his appointment available in the NAI, comment on his appointment is dependent on German and British sources, or speculation. See Roth, *Mr Bewley*, p. 21; Duggan, *Neutral Ireland*, pp 27–8; Keogh, *Ireland & the Vatican*, pp 106, 153n; M. Kennedy, 'Our men in Berlin: some thoughts on Irish diplomats in Germany, 1929–39', ISIA, 10 (1999), pp 61–70.

law in Ireland. When he re-entered the diplomatic world in 1929 to go to the Vatican, his anti-Britishness was expressed in his view that a close Anglo-Irish relationship was inimical to the representation of Irish independence. He believed that the emergence of separate diplomatic services and foreign policies in the British dominions undermined British superiority in world affairs. But the relationship between the dominions and Britain confused outsiders because of its evolving and intricate nature and was 'embarrassing' for the Irish and the British.[6] In Rome he bristled at the British embassy's tendency 'to treat me as a subsidiary member of the British representative in Rome'. Bewley exacerbated the unease between the Irish and British representatives to the Vatican by scoring points over the British embassy in Rome to assert Ireland's independent status.[7] Bewley's inveterate hostility to the British embassy is unmistakable in his reports to Dublin.[8]

Further evidence of Bewley's declining utility[9] included external affairs secretary Walshe's criticism of his lapses in submitting reports on at least two occasions,[10] a problem that re-emerged during Bewley's posting in Berlin. On the first occasion (23 December 1930), Walshe said that without regular and extensive reporting effective foreign policy decisionmaking was prevented.[11] On the second occasion (24 February 1931), Walshe was forced to ask Bewley directly: 'Does the position suit you or do you feel that another post would give you better scope? The Minister is beginning to fear that the absence of reports from you may be an indication of your dislike for the work'.[12] Bewley's response was that he did not want to remain in Rome 'indefinitely', and he hoped he could transfer to 'some more northern climate' in the future.[13]

Bewley was a 'diminishing asset in Rome' but his superiors could not sack him nor recall him to Dublin as that would have precipitated his promotion. Dublin's solution, according to Keogh, was a transfer to Berlin.[14] J.P. Duggan suggests Bewley charmed and outwitted the new president of the executive council, Eamon de Valera, on the occasion of the latter's visit to the Holy See in July 1933, to secure his transfer to Berlin.[15] More recently Andreas Roth presents Bewley as the only credible candidate for the Berlin post.

There is no single explanation for Bewley's transfer to Berlin. Walshe was dissatisfied with Bewley's performance and the Vatican rated far higher in Walshe's estimation than Berlin. Bewley had always hankered after a Berlin posting. Nazi Germany was an unknown quantity in 1933 so the centrality of Berlin to international affairs was still not obvious. Could it, therefore, be that Bewley's transfer in 1933 was simply a rational personnel decision? Suitable

6 Bewley, *Memoirs*, pp 104–5. 7 Roth, *Mr Bewley*, pp 18–21. 8 NAI, DFA B12/32, Bewley–Walshe, 16 Apr. 1931. 9 Ibid. 10 Cf. Roth, *Mr Bewley*, p. 18. 11 NAI, DFA, B7/32, Walshe–Bewley, 23 Dec. 1930. 12 NAI, DFA, B7/32, Walshe–Bewley, 24 Feb. 1931. 13 NAI, DFA, B12/32, Bewley–Walshe, 2 Mar. 1931. 14 Keogh, *Ireland & the Vatican*, p. 106. 15 Duggan, *Neutral Ireland*, p. 27–8.

linguistically qualified diplomats were in short supply, so the service had to uti-
lize the personnel at its disposal to best effect.[16]

ACCLIMATIZING TO BERLIN

In July 1933, Bewley drove from Rome to Berlin.[17] Like his predecessor, Bewley
encountered difficulty in presenting his credentials to President Hindenburg
who was on vacation at his estate in Neudeck, East Prussia.[18] Instead, Bewley
spent the month of August studying Irish-German trade matters, while the AA
extended *de facto* recognition to Bewley as Irish minister plenipotentiary and
envoy extraordinary.[19]

Before his formal accreditation, Bewley granted an interview to the *Deutsche
Allgemeine Zeitung* in August 1933 revealing that he was impressed by the Nazi
reinvigoration of Germany.[20] He continued this charm offensive at his accreditation ceremony with President Hindenburg on 31 August.[21] Bewley, although
communicating the usual diplomatic courtesies,[22] inadvisedly applauded the
Nazi takeover of the German state by translating one passage of the text which
the department of external affairs had given him 'rather freely' to make reference to the 'national rebirth of Germany'.[23]

In reporting back to Dublin, Bewley justified his liberal translation of the
prepared script he had received by reference to his predecessor Binchy's recent
Studies article, critical of Hitler and National Socialism (see chapter 2). Bewley
said: 'I thought it better to make it clear at once that the position therein taken
up was not that of the Irish Government.'[24] The article had received a very hostile reception in Berlin and Bewley felt it was 'particularly deplorable when it is
remembered that it was written by an Ex-Minister here, and was ... not calculated to make the task ... afterwards of myself any easier'. According to Bewley's
sources in Berlin, Binchy had made clear his dislike of German people and institutions during his Berlin posting. Binchy preferred the British.[25]

Immediately after the accreditation ceremony, Bewley went to Nuremberg to
attend his first Nazi Party congress. During the Third Reich this annual congress served to rally the party around the Führer, reinforcing participants' belief
in Hitler and the Nazi movement. Bewley went of his own volition each year
subsequently while he was Irish minister to Berlin.[26] In his memoirs Bewley

---

16 De Valera must have known about Bewley's contribution to the implosion of the unofficial Irish mission to Berlin in 1922 and 1923, since Briscoe was an influential backbencher
in the Fianna Fáil government.   17 NAI, DFA 217/28, Bewley–Walshe, 30 June 1933.
18 Ibid., 25 July 1933.   19 Ibid., 31 July 1933.   20 *Deutsche Allgemeine Zeitung*, 20 Aug.
1933.   21 NAI, DFA 217/28, Bewley–Walshe, 4 Sept. 1933.   22 Ibid., Bewley–
Hindenburg, n.d. & ibid., Hearne–Bewley, 18 Aug. 1933.   23 Ibid., Bewley–Walshe, 4 Sept.
1933.   24 Ibid.   25 NAI, DFA 5/88B, Bewley–Walshe, 9 Sept. 1933.   26 He reported on

correctly noted the annual congress was 'strictly speaking … not a state function', but that of the NSDAP, the only official political party in the German
state.[27] On this basis, diplomatic representatives from the main democratic
states – the US, Britain, and France as well as the sworn ideological rival of
Nazism, the USSR – did not attend the Nuremberg rallies during the 1930s.
Later, in 1936, Bewley took exception to this interpretation recording that, 'In
the case of England and America, I am informed that the reason assigned is that
the Congress is the affair of a party and not of the State, a point of view which
is technically incorrect and in any event pedantic.'[28] Bewley retrospectively
claimed National Socialism was 'an unknown quantity' initially and 'the *Parteitag*
[party rally] had not yet assumed the militaristic character of subsequent
years'.[29]

The 1933 congress gave him the opportunity to examine firsthand the nature
of the Nazi movement and the 'unanimous enthusiasm for one man'. On 4
September 1933, he wrote: 'it is a personal devotion hard to realize by those who
have not come into personal contact with it'. The Führer cult was spreading.
Having attended two of the chancellor's speeches, Bewley adjudged Hitler as
'incomparably the finest orator that I have heard'. After the Führer visited the
diplomatic train laid on for diplomats attending Nuremberg, Bewley followed
his advice to mingle with the German people and see if they were as 'outraged'
as the foreign press reported.[30] This evidently had an affect on him.

'PAPER WALL'

The negative Nazi reactions to Binchy's *Studies* article at the very commencement of Bewley's tenure in Berlin apparently made him hypersensitive about
any critical Irish press comment on the Nazis. Bewley disapproved of what he
viewed as the Irish newspapers' inaccurate and deceptive portrayal of the
Nuremberg rally. Taking exception to a report that the only embassy represented was that of Italy, he reported to Dublin that Turkey's chargé d'affaires
was also present. He also claimed the Reuter's report used in the Irish papers
deliberately belittled the rally. He listed all the countries that were represented
to counter what he perceived was an attempt to play down the *Parteitag*'s importance.[31] In his memoirs, however, Bewley was cynical about the *Parteitag* and
wrote: 'If banners and searchlights could have made proselytes to National

it annually in NAI, DFA, CRS 19/50 and 19/50A. Unlike William Warnock, the chargé
d'affaires who succeeded him in 1939, he did not request departmental permission to attend
(NAI, DFA 235/65, Warnock–Walshe, 19 Aug. 1939; NAI, DFA 217/28, Bewley–Walshe, 17
Aug. 1933). **27** Bewley, *Memoirs*, p. 119. **28** NAI, DFA, CRS 19/50A, Bewley–Walshe,
16 Sept. 1936. **29** Bewley, *Memoirs*, p. 122. **30** NAI, DFA 217/28, Bewley–Walshe, 4
Sept. 1933. **31** Ibid.

Socialism, not one of us would have remained outside the fold',[32] and 'the
German mentality is not adapted to make converts outside its own race; some of
the methods adopted had the opposite effect to that intended'.[33] He referred to
the 'pretentious theatricality' of Hitler's oratorial dramatics at Nuremberg in
1933, declaring their total lack of impact on foreigners such as himself and
describes Hitler as 'a commonplace figure mouthing sentiments with the self-
sufficiency of the half-educated'.[34]

Later in September 1933 Bewley submitted another report highly critical of
Irish newspaper coverage of German affairs. He recalled Arthur Griffith's
famous reference to the so-called 'paper wall' Britain had constructed to prevent
outsiders understanding Anglo-Irish difficulties and to maintain dominance by
controlling what appeared in newspapers. Bewley feared British news agencies
unduly influenced Irish perceptions and he condemned Irish dependence on
British sources such as *The Times* and the Reuters news agency as damaging to
Irish–German relations.[35]

Despite assertions by the Irish press and government that Irish newspapers
were impartial, Bewley claimed the newspapers substantiated Nazi allegations
that Ireland was hostile and reinforced Germany's perception of the Saorstát as
that of an English province.[36] Bewley's allegations that the Saorstát's access to
foreign news stories was limited to British-based sources were not without substance. But was the alternative to switch allegiance to the propagandistic and
censored reports transmitted by the German authorities? As soon as Hitler had
come to power, the Nazis took control of all media. By March 1933 Goebbels
had established control over radio broadcasts.[37] Then Communist and Socialist
press outlets were crushed. Next came the Aryanization of the many publishing
houses owned by Jews which meant the businesses were forcibly acquired at an
artificially low price or had their directors replaced so that ownership and control passed to Nazis. The staffs of all newspapers were vetted.[38] In October
1933, Goebbels promulgated the Editors' Law which 'set the cornerstone of
state and party control of the press'.[39] The content of all publications had to
abide by Nazi policy or editors, journalists and proprietors would suffer punishment. Only the Catholic confessional press remained under the protection of
the July 1933 concordat signed by Hitler and the pope although this, too, was
progressively eroded in succeeding years.

The state now held a monopoly of the news in Germany. The Third Reich
constructed its 'paper wall' in line with Hitler's views in *Mein Kampf* that the
mass of the population was credulous and their minds were susceptible to poi-
soning by the 'Jewified' liberal-bourgeois or 'respectable press'.[40] The loss of

32 Bewley, *Memoirs*, p. 120. 33 Ibid. 34 Ibid., p. 123. 35 NAI, DFA 5/88B, Bewley–
Walshe, 9 Sept. 1933. 36 Ibid. 37 M. Burleigh, *The Third Reich: a new history* (London,
2000), pp 206–7. 38 Ibid., pp 207–8. 39 O.J. Hale, *The captive press in the Third Reich*
(New York, 1973), p.83. 40 A. Hitler, *Mein Kampf* (London, 2001), pp 219–22.

this fundamental freedom was a loss that Bewley failed to take fully into account during his posting in Berlin.

NAZI PERCEPTIONS

As Bewley discovered on arriving in Berlin, the German newspapers' interpretation of developments within the Saorstát and of Irish foreign policy tended to be based on the simplistic Nazi worldview or *Weltanschauung*, taking little account of the complexities and nuances of Irish political developments. The central tenets of Nazi ideology – namely a disdain for parliamentary democracy, the hierarchy of races, anti-Communism, and fraternity with their Aryan Anglo-Saxon brothers – were applied indiscriminately to the Saorstát. During 1933 and 1934 the actions of the anti-Fianna Fáil opposition unhelpfully corroborated some of the Nazis' perceptions of the Saorstát. The foundation of the Blueshirts and their opportunistic adoption of many of the externalities of continental fascism, including the blue shirt and the 'Hitler salute' as well as some of its anti-parliamentarian language further confused matters.

It is not unsurprising that Ireland played a very marginal role in Nazi thought. Indeed, Hitler's attitude to the 'Irish question' can only be deduced from his attitude towards 'England' that he recorded as early as 1925 in *Mein Kampf*. On one hand, he admired the English as a superior race and nation that had determinedly built and defended the British empire using whatever means necessary, ranging from trade and sea power to diplomacy and the use of force.[41] On the other hand, Hitler feared parliamentary democracy had permitted Jewish influence to adulterate Britain's traditional statesmanship, shifting interests away from its maritime empire to the defeat of Germany in the Great War. Thus, the Jews had temporarily conspired in the British defeat of her German brothers.[42] Anglo-German antagonism was, Hitler believed, an aberration and traditional British statesmanship would overcome Jewish infiltration and lead to the imminent reconciliation of the British and German sister nations. Germany should have unequivocally renounced seapower and colonies to ensure English acquiescence in the German expansion eastwards into Russia.[43] Hitler's prescription for future German success was to avoid a repeat of a two front war by guaranteeing British interests and by making Germany *bündnisfähig* (a worthy ally).[44]

The pre-eminence of Britain in Hitler's combination of nationalist–racialist (*völkisch*) and military–strategic notions was profoundly limiting for Irish-German relations after 1933. It meant the Saorstát could never be allowed to interfere with Hitler's objective of furthering Anglo-German relations unless

41 Ibid., p. 132. 42 Ibid., pp 567–9. 43 Ibid., pp 128–9. 44 D.C. Watt, 'Introduction', in ibid., p. xxxii.

there was no prospect of reconciliation with Britain. Only the Nazi ideologue Alfred Rosenberg, a German from Riga, had devoted any time to the subject of Ireland before 1933. An aggressive anti-Christian, Rosenberg was considered a leading Nazi theorist during the 1920s and the first half of the 1930s. He was the editor of the chief Nazi press organ, the *Völkischer Beobachter*, and contributed a number of articles in the early 1920s on the Irish question. During the 1921 ceasefire that led to the Anglo-Irish Treaty, he wrote that although sympathetic to the Irish freedom struggle he discerned the hand of international Jewry, Bolshevism and the Catholic Church behind Sinn Féin. De Valera was nothing but a half-Jew and the Irish freedom struggle was a means by which Jewish internationalists sought to undermine the British empire.[45] The Treatyites and their successors, Cumann na nGaedheal, were viewed sympathetically because they had come to terms with Britain and remained within the British empire. The anti-Treatyites (and later Fianna Fáil) were contaminated by their perceived role in a Jewish world plot to destroy the British empire.[46]

Nazi and general German opinion otherwise remained perplexed by the Irish question and at first attempted to apply continental fascist or German Nazi presumptions to the Irish situation. During 1933 some thought went into what position Irish people occupied in the Nazi racialist *Weltanschauung*. In May 1933 the *Lokalanzeiger* published an article which claimed the word 'Aryan' was preserved in the Indian and Iranian languages. It continued:

> It is the expression of a proud consciousness of race and means 'members of the clan', 'the persons worthy of honour', the 'honourable ones', the 'lords'. Formerly all Aryan peoples called themselves thus: for example, the word survives in modified form in the name 'Erin', the Celtic name for Ireland, the green isle, which has preserved for us so much of the best in Aryan tradition.[47]

But in December 1933 Bewley noted that Rosenberg regarded the Irish as corresponding to the Letts of Lithuania,[48] a lower order race destined to be ruled by Germans. Bewley implied that, according to Rosenberg, the Irish were inferior to 'Aryan' Anglo-Saxons and were destined to be subordinate to the English. Bewley's suspicions were verified when he attended a lecture delivered by interior minister, Dr Wilhelm Frick, to the diplomatic corps and foreign press. Frick, the 'most fervent advocate of racial theory' in the NSDAP, classified the Celts, Latins and Slavs as 'Indogermanen'. They were associated with

---

45 *Völkischer Beobachter*, 14 Sept. 1921.   46 Dickel, *Aussenpolitik*, p. 28. Certainly, confusion reigned within the Nazi movement during the 1920s concerning how it should view Irish independence and Irish republicanism. Sometimes Nazis supported the rights of 'little peoples' to self-determination.   47 NAI, DFA CRS 19/50, McCauley–Walshe, 20 May 1933. 48 Ibid., Bewley–Walshe, 11 Dec. 1933.

the 'Germanen' (Germans, English, Dutch and Scandinavians) but did not possess 'the peculiar qualities of the Germanic race properly speaking in the same degree'.[49] The Irish place in the Nazi racial pyramid was inferior to the Aryans but not subhuman like Jews. The few Nazis who bothered to consider the Saorstát between 1932 and 1934 estimated that it was undergoing a fascist upheaval similar to the recent 'Nazi revolution' in Germany, although there was a degree of uncertainty about whether O'Duffy or de Valera was the Irish 'Führer'.

The internal political situation in the Saorstát during the first months and years of Fianna Fáil government was heated and unpleasant as civil war politics came to the fore. Attempts by the preceding Cumann na nGaedheal government to besmirch de Valera, Fianna Fáil and the IRA as Bolshevik internationalists during the Red Scare in 1931 and 1932 retained their credibility among the opposition to de Valera's government.[50] To some Nazi and German eyes it was tempting to cast Eoin O'Duffy's Blueshirts as the Irish equivalent of the NSDAP. Originally founded and seen as legitimate protection for Cumann na nGaedheal against IRA thugs who supported Fianna Fáil, it grew into an organization that challenged the Fianna Fáil government. Many victims of de Valera's Economic War with Britain became supporters and the organization came to use street violence superficially comparable to that employed by the Brownshirts (or SA) in Germany. The Blueshirts even began to address O'Duffy in Hitlerite fashion, as 'Hoch O'Duffy'.[51] The green Duce's[52] Blueshirts merged with Cumann na nGaedheal and the Centre Party to found the United Ireland (Fine Gael) party in September 1933 which questioned the legitimacy of the de Valera government on the grounds that it was communist orientated but, more specifically, that it had illicitly relied on the extrajudicial violence of the IRA to attain and retain power. External commentators might be forgiven for considering that the Irish conservatives would ease O'Duffy into dictatorship in the same way a hapless Papen and Schleicher had done for Hitler in 1932 and early 1933.[53] The outburst of a future Fine Gael taoiseach, John A. Costello, in Dáil Éireann on 5 February 1934 that 'the Blueshirts will be victorious in the Irish Free State' like 'the Blackshirts were victorious in Italy' and the Brownshirts were in Germany added to such German speculation.[54]

But the Blueshirts were not fascist and/or Nazi. At most they were comparable to clerico-fascist movements[55] in less developed regions of eastern and

49 Ibid., 19 Feb. 1934. 50 See D. Keogh, 'De Valera, the Catholic Church and the "red scare"', pp 134–59. 51 M. Cronin, *The Blueshirts & Irish politics* (Dublin, 1997), p. 48. 52 Keogh, *Twentieth-century Ireland*, p. 81. 53 Cronin, *Blueshirts*, p. 67. British commentators considered de Valera as a 'transient apparition' who would soon lose power, in the hope that Anglo-Irish relations would revert to the relatively halcyon days of Cumann na nGaedheal government. See: D. McMahon, ' "A transient apparition": British policy towards the de Valera government, 1932–5', IHS, 22: 88 (1981), pp 331–61. 54 Lee, *Ireland*, p. 183. 55 Keogh, *Twentieth-century Ireland*, p. 81.

southern Europe, such as Salazar's Portugal. Although the Blueshirts may have
draped themselves in fashionable fascist paraphernalia, their inspiration and
sustenance came from civil war enmities. De Valera's dismissal of General Eoin
O'Duffy as Garda commissioner in 1933 accorded the latter the status of martyrdom in Cumann na nGaedheal, the presumption being that he had been
expunged because of his pro-Treaty stance and anti-republican policies.[56] The
street clashes with the IRA owed as much to the long tradition of Irish faction
fighting than to the example of the organized political violence of fascist movements. Nor did the Blueshirts have a politically astute leader. Although many in
the Blueshirts and even in the Irish government and civil service held a certain
regard for Mussolini's Italy,[57] as did many in Britain and France, their primary
declared grievance with the government was not that it was democratic but that
it was not sufficiently democratic. Moreover, if the Blueshirt movement and the
United Ireland party were influenced by any ideology it was not primarily
derived from Mussolini's fascist conceptions (and definitely not from Hitler's
'mumbo-jumbo' *völkisch* ideas).[58] Its corporatist prescription for Irish society
was based on Pope Leo XIII's encyclical, *Rerum Novarum*, and Pope Pius XI's
encyclical, *Quadragesimo Anno.*[59]

Therein lies the central difference between the Blueshirts and the
Brownshirts: the Blueshirts and their democratic colleagues in the United Irish
party were a product of an intensely Catholic society. From this stems their
generic anti-communism. It is unlikely the vast majority of Blueshirt members
understood fascism or Nazism. O'Duffy and perhaps one or two of his lieu-
tenants were more sinister, however. But most in the United Ireland Party
distanced themselves from the 'mad mullah' before it was too late,[60] eventually
realizing he was more of an embarrassment to them than the IRA was to Fianna
Fáil. O'Duffy had begun to incite revolution advocating the overthrow of parliamentary democracy. Thus by early 1934 his parliamentary friends were
moving to terminate the relationship.

De Valera's criminalization of the Blueshirts, through repeated banning
orders and the use of ex-IRA men in the Auxiliary Police Force to defeat them
on the streets, was also beginning to take effect. By September 1934 O'Duffy
was quoted in one newspaper as saying, 'Hitler had done more for Germany
than any other leader in the world had done for his country'.[61] The further he
was distanced from mainline political discourse in the Saorstát the more he
sought to establish connections between the Blueshirts, fascism and Nazism. He
was effectively in the political wilderness with a small residual Blueshirt (later

56 F. McGarry, *Irish politics & the Spanish Civil War* (Cork, 1999), pp 18–9. 57 Keogh,
Ireland & Europe, pp 42–6. 58 Watt, 'Introduction' in Hitler, *Mein Kampf*, p. xxxiv.
59 Cronin, *Blueshirts*, pp 81–3, 86–7. 60 J.M. Regan, *The Irish counter-revolution, 1921–
1936* (Dublin, 1999), p. 343. 61 NAI, MS 1065/2/4, Frank McDermot papers,
Dillon–McDermot, 25 Sept. 1934.

Greenshirt) membership. During its mass movement and most successful stage, Blueshirts were probably not fascists in the continental sense,[62] but were 'potential para-fascists', that is, 'a movement which skirted around the ideologies of generic fascism' having a core membership that supported the democratic institutions of the Saorstát.[63] O'Duffy, however, transformed into a fully-fledged fascist after his marginalization in Irish politics.[64]

A superficial comparison of the post-war histories of Ireland and Germany could be used to argue that immediately after the Great War Germany and Ireland experienced revolutions, the establishment of parliamentary democracies (Weimar Republic and the Irish Free State), and had reluctantly signed domestically divisive end-of-war treaties (the Versailles treaty and the Anglo-Irish Treaty).[65] In the 1920s both faced the challenges of new statehood in an adverse international climate where their status was ambiguous and uncertain as a result of the humiliating treaties they had signed. The Wall Street Crash ultimately crippled their economies and fuelled the rise of anti-Treaty political parties (the Nazis and Fianna Fáil) which adopted democratic methods after the earlier failure of force to gain power. Both the NSDAP's and Fianna Fáil's election manifestos suggested an agenda for foreign policy revisionism and autarchy. The NSDAP's determination to end reparations was paralleled by Fianna Fáil's resolve to end land annuities paid to Britain.[66] These parties ultimately gained power in the early 1930s. Arguably both adopted authoritarian political styles although Saorstát/Éire did so within the democratic fold and the Third Reich in an openly dictatorial mode. De Valera could then be seen as simply masterminding the overthrow of a 'Gaelic Weimar'.[67]

What German commentators failed to realize was that the Irish situation was unique and analogies between mainland Europe and Ireland were forced, if not erroneous.[68] In contrast to Germany, Ireland was technically victorious in the Great War by virtue of being part of Britain. A further difference was that Italy and Germany had been nation-states in 1914, while Ireland was not. Although the Saorstát had irredentist inclinations after partition, unlike Germany it evolved a stable parliamentary democracy during the 1920s which was maintained on Fianna Fáil's accession to power in 1932. Hitler, however, had undermined the rule of law, eroded civil liberties and inaugurated a one-party state.

So in late 1933, Bewley was about to discover that it would be easier to educate the Nazis and Germans about the internal dynamics of Irish politics than to change their geopolitical commitment to giving special consideration to

---

62 See Lee, *Ireland*, pp 181–4; Manning, *Blueshirts*, pp 232–44. 63 Cronin, *Blueshirts*, p. 13. 64 Ibid., pp 51–2. 65 Dickel, *Aussenpolitik*, p. 33 n. 111. 66 De Valera and the department of finance used this comparison (McMahon, *Republicans*, pp 57–8). 67 Lee, *Ireland*, p. 184. Bewley drew such a parallel (Bewley, *Memoirs*, p. 107). 68 See Cronin, *Blueshirts*, p. 44.

Britain. On arrival in Berlin, Dublin instructed him to protest formally to the AA about the portrayal of de Valera as a half-caste Jew in the 16 July issue of the *Deutsche Wochenschau*.[69] Deprecatory remarks were also made about Irish republicanism, linking it to a Jewish world conspiracy, taking advantage of the fact that Robert Briscoe, a Fianna Fáil TD, was Jewish. Bewley demanded retractions from the *Deutsche Wochenschau*, and other German papers which published such incorrect and distorted statements.[70] His complaints failed to prevent the *Hammer*, another Nazi publication, from accusing de Valera in early August of being a member of a universal Jewish conspiracy.[71]

On 6 September 1933, as a result of pressure on the AA, the *Völkischer Beobachter* and the *Hamburger Tageblatt* published articles condemning crude parallels between Irish and German political developments, in particular the portrayal of the Blueshirts as Nazis.[72] Bewley told Rosenberg in early December that he 'was glad to see that Irish affairs were now being treated in the German press with more understanding than some time ago'. By early 1934 Irish lobbying of German authorities, de Valera's crackdown and the ebbing of the Blueshirt's fortunes ensured that the number of newspaper articles drawing specious parallels between the Nazis and Blueshirts fell dramatically.[73] AA officials wanted to avoid the appearance of German interference in the Saorstát. Nor did they want to intervene in the developing Anglo-Irish conflict for fear of annoying the British. But they did hope to benefit economically from the Anglo-Irish Economic War.[74]

TRADE TRIANGLES

One of Bewley's primary functions was trade promotion and the establishment of a balance-of-trade reciprocity between the Saorstát and Germany.[75] The Irish government's forced industrialization policies and the fallout of the Anglo-Irish Economic War had already created opportunities for German exporters, and the expectation was aroused in Irish official circles that these gains for German industry could be used to prise open German agricultural markets. Germany was the best market other than Britain affording possibilities for the export of Irish agricultural products.[76] The Irish government had been anxious since the

69 NAI, DFA, Berlin letterbooks, Hearne–McCauley, 29 July 1933. **70** Ibid. **71** Dickel, *Aussenpolitik*, p. 34. **72** Ibid., p. 34 n. 113. **73** NAI, DFA, CRS 19/50, Bewley–Walshe, 11 Dec. 1933; NAI, DFA 5/88B, Bewley–Walshe, 9 Mar. 1934, 19 Mar. 1934, 9 July 1934. **74** Dickel, *Aussenpolitik*, p. 34. **75** NAI, DFA 217/28; *Deutsche Allgemeine Zeitung*, 20 Aug. 1933; NAI, DFA 217/28, Bewley–Walshe, 4 Sept. 1933. Dickel argues that the AA regarded Bewley with mistrust because he aroused inflated expectations in Dublin about the capacity of the German market to import Irish agricultural products. Dickel, *Aussenpolitik*, p. 35. **76** NAI, DFA, Berlin letterbooks, Walshe–Bewley, 18 Jan. 1934.

outbreak of the Economic War to achieve greater trade between Ireland and Germany. Bewley, like McCauley, found this to be an extremely difficult brief. Indeed, the Irish balance of trade with Germany was deteriorating. The trade deficit with Germany had increased unrelentingly from £614,137 in 1930 to £1,566,099 in 1933.[77] In July 1933 de Valera had set out his position on developing new markets to the Dáil:

> our representatives abroad ... have been very busy in trying to extend our markets to redress what is at present the adverse balance against us in most of these countries ... if countries outside want to get goods in here to the extent of £1,500,000 they will have to take from this country in return a very considerable portion of that amount in goods. If they do not it will be necessary to take steps to prevent their goods coming in as freely as at the present moment.[78]

Questions by the opposition in the Dáil led de Valera to confess his dissatisfaction with the adverse balance of trade with Germany.[79] His objective was to increase cattle exports to Germany significantly beyond the 6,000 head guaranteed under Ireland's 'most-favoured-nation' status in the Irish-German trade agreement. The glut of cattle in the country as a result of the Anglo-Irish Economic War made this an imperative. But Irish expectations of increased agricultural exports were to be disappointed throughout the remainder of 1933. Meanwhile, German exports entered the Saorstát unimpeded as the Irish-imposed retaliatory tariffs on British commodities delivered a competitive advantage to German exporters.[80]

The leakage of currency resulting from the unbalanced Irish-German trade relationship required immediate rectification. The Saorstát's tactic was to threaten to end free entry for German products as a means to bargain for increased Irish access to the German market. Bewley was instructed to approach German manufacturers who exported to the Saorstát to explain the dangers their trade faced because of the German government's failure to reciprocate in permitting Irish exports into the German market. The objective was 'to induce those persons interested in export trade from Germany to bring pressure to bear on the German Government'.[81]

In October 1933 the Saorstát eventually commenced negotiations with a German delegation in Dublin on the size of German import quotas for Irish butter and eggs for the following year.[82] Simultaneously, the Saorstát ordered

---

77 NAI, DFA, 314/10/6/3, Statement made by Irish delegation at opening meeting of Saorstát–German trade negotiations, 16 Oct. 1934. 78 *Dáil Debates*, vol. 48, col. 2150, 11 July 1933. 79 Ibid., cols. 2149-53, 11 July 1933. 80 NAI, DFA, 314/10/6/3, 'German Saorstát trade agreement', n.d.(*c.*mid–1934). 81 NAI, DFA Berlin letterbooks, Fahy–Bewley, 20 Aug. 1933. 82 Ibid., 17 Oct. 1933.

£600,000-worth of sugar factory machinery from Germany.[83] But the AA failed to agree terms to narrow the unfavourable trade gap, so the Irish government terminated the Dublin negotiations.[84] In December an Irish delegation went to Berlin to resume the negotiations, hoping to use the sugar factory contract to gain a quid pro quo in the form of the export of Irish butter and eggs to Germany in 1934.[85] Reports in the *Irish Press* raised public expectations of success.[86]

The Irish government was seeking increased quotas and lower tariffs for existing Irish imports entering Germany, not for future or new trade. Walshe was aware the AA 'think ... it is Government policy ... to pay any price for trade she enjoys' as a result of the Anglo-Irish Economic War. Bewley was instructed to adopt an uncompromising position since the department of industry and commerce could impede German imports by using liberally its power to license British goods free of emergency tariffs if deemed necessary. Bewley was sanctioned to 'use every threat to strengthen the Saorstát's bargaining position'. Unfortunately, as Walshe admitted, German officials knew there was 'little likelihood of procuring a market for Saorstát agricultural products in any other country' other than Germany.[87] The Irish refused a derisory German offer on increased butter and egg quotas made in December 1933 which excluded any offer to increase the cattle quota[88] and the Berlin negotiations were terminated. The Irish government resolved never again to award a large contract to Germany without first securing a reciprocal compensation agreement. The Irish failure to procure such an agreement in December 1933 meant the 1934 trade deficit with Germany amounted to £2.15 million, the largest ever adverse balance of trade between the two.[89]

By the first half of 1934, therefore, the economic nationalist course advocated by de Valera was 'under increasing pressure' from Lemass and MacEntee. Both were calling for a reconsideration of economic policy towards Britain because of the enormous damage it was causing the Irish economy.[90] The government's efforts to redirect trade to Germany had failed but the widely publicized initiatives to develop new export markets had created unfulfilled domestic expectations,[91] strengthening criticism of de Valera's government.[92]

On 22 January 1934 de Valera met a high-powered German delegation led by

83 NAI, DFA 314/10/6/3, Bewley–Walshe, 7 Nov. 1934.   84 Dickel, *Aussenpolitik*, p. 36. 85 NAI, DFA 314/10/6/3, Bewley–Walshe, 7 Nov. 1934; IP, 12 Dec. 1933.   86 IP, 12 Dec. 1933; IP, 15 Dec. 1933; IP, 19 Dec. 1933; IP, 28 Dec. 1933. Throughout 1933 hopes of an increased cattle trade with Germany were inspired by the high profile activities of the Bremen firm of Wilhelm Fäsenfeld, and his son Georg, in the Irish cattle markets, which was responsible for filling the existing 6,000 annual quota (IP, 22 Dec. 1933).   87 NAI, DFA, Berlin Letterbooks, Walshe–Bewley, 12 Dec. 1933.   88 Ibid.; NAI, DFA, 314/10/6/3, Brief note on Saorstát–German negotiations, 10 Oct. 1933.   89 NAI, DFA 314/10/6/3, German Saorstát trade agreement, n.d. (*c*.mid-1934).   90 McMahon, *Republicans*, pp 138–9.   91 IP, 30 August 1933.   92 For example, *Dáil Debates*, vol. 50, col. 1350–1, 14 Feb. 1934.

the German minister Dehn-Schmidt. The president made 'a general remark that the desire of his government was that Irish Free State imports be divided ultimately as follows: one-third from Germany, one-third from Great Britain and one-third from US and that on the basis of reciprocity Irish Free State exports should be divided in like proportion between these three countries'.[93] Dehn-Schmidt evidently took this to be a formal proposal and communicated with the AA. Hemmen, the chief trade negotiator, contacted Bewley in Berlin to indicate the German government was considering de Valera's proposal. A surprised Bewley, made aware of the proposal for the first time, requested clarification from the department of external affairs. Until then Dublin 'had no knowledge that Herr von Dehn-Schmidt had interpreted the president's words as being in the nature of a proposal nor had the president intended them as being other than general remarks'. Dehn-Schmidt's 'rather specific interpretation' of de Valera's 'very general remarks' placed Bewley in an awkward position. Nonetheless, de Valera and Walshe decided to take advantage of this unexpected development and instructed Bewley not to disabuse the AA of its illusions. It should be permitted to consider the so-called proposal and the German response to it 'would afford a very good indication of how far Germany is prepared to go in an ultimate agreement'. By this stage Bewley had formed the impression that unless Ireland was able to offer 'some definite and considerable material advantage' such as an export market worth £10 million, Germany would not risk offending Britain.[94] In any case the AA failed to respond positively to de Valera's informal suggestions.

In late March 1934, the Irish government again broke off talks because it could not secure a larger cattle quota. Bewley was instructed to communicate the Irish government's extreme dissatisfaction about the import of Danish cattle which it regarded as a breach of the 1930 'most favoured nation' agreement between Ireland and Germany. The Saorstát threatened to rescind the most-favoured-nation status it had extended to Germany and to curtail German imports.[95] The fact that many Irish businesses were experiencing delays in payment because Germany lacked sufficient stocks of sterling further angered the Irish side.[96] A complete breakdown in Irish-German trade relations was imminent.

The Nazi policy of protecting domestic agriculture to ensure German self-sufficiency led many of Germany's other trading partners to retaliate by cutting imports of German manufactured goods. Consequently Germany lacked the will and the foreign currency to pay for additional agricultural imports.[97] Meanwhile the German government's extensive and expensive job creation and

93 NAI, DFA Berlin letterbooks, Walshe–Bewley, 10 Feb. 1934.　94 NAI, DFA CRS 19/50, Bewley–Walshe, 26 Feb. 1934.　95 NAI, DFA Berlin letterbooks, Fahy–Bewley, 24 Mar. 1934.　96 Ibid., 1 Jan. 1934.　97 NAI, DFA CRS 19/50, Bewley–Walshe, 11 May 1934.

public works programmes, such as autobahn construction and covert rearmament, added to the need to import raw materials while demand for German
exports remained low. This exacerbated the shortage of foreign currency with
which to purchase foreign commodities.[98]

As a consequence of the acute currency shortages the minister of economics,
Dr Hjalmar Schacht,[99] inaugurated the New Plan of 1934 which led to an
increased and deeper bilateralization of trade as begun by Papen and
Schleicher.[1] The New Plan from September 1934[2] cut imports of raw materials
and live animals (for example, cattle).[3] Next was a moratorium on Germany's
payment of foreign debts to halt the foreign currency haemorrhage.[4] Then,
using the concept of *Grossraumwirtschaft*, or the theory of the relative advantage
of large economic blocs (a form of common market trading system), Germany
moved to create a German-dominated trading bloc, particularly in eastern and
central Europe.[5] Imports to Germany were to come from countries in the
Balkans (and Latin America), which had a large surplus of primary produce that
could not be sold on the world market. In return those weaker economies had to
accept German goods, in effect setting up a barter system.[6] Germany also tightened foreign exchange controls significantly and required the state to sanction
all imports. Schacht began to introduce clearinghouse arrangements that meant
the government had total control over foreign trade.[7]

Bewley's report of Schacht's landmark New Plan speech to the AA and
diplomatic corps on 21 June 1934 spelled out the bilateral, protectionist, refla-
tionary and clearinghouse direction in which German trade and economic
policy was moving. The Irish side was concerned, too, about the implications of
Anglo-German economic disputes for Irish-German trade. Bewley inferred
from Schacht's statement:

> if England which has an unfavourable trade balance with Germany were
> to institute a clearing-house, Germany would cease to trade not only with
> England but with the whole British Empire: the plea that the Dominions

---

98 NAI, DFA Berlin letterbooks, Fahy–Bewley, 1 Jan. 1934; ibid., Fahy–Bewley, 23 Mar.
1933; ibid., Walshe–Bewley, 8 Aug. 1934. 99 Reichsbank president 1933–9 and economics
minister 1934–7. 1 NAI, DFA CRS 19/50, O'Donovan–Walshe, 29 Mar. 1934; ibid.,
Bewley–Walshe, 9 Apr. 1934; ibid., Bewley–Walshe, 15 June 1934; ibid., Bewley–Walshe, 22
June 1934. 2 W. Michalka, 'Conflicts within the German leadership on the objectives and
tactics of German foreign policy, 1933–9', in W. J. Mommsen & L. Kettenacker (eds), *The
fascist challenge and the policy of appeasement* (London, 1983), p. 53. 3 NAI, DFA CRS
19/50, Bewley–Walshe, 15 June 1934. 4 This was presaged in: NAI, DFA CRS 19/50,
Bewley–Walshe, 22 June 1934. 5 A.S. Milward, 'Fascism and the economy', in W.
Laqueur (ed.), *Fascism: a reader's guide* (London, 1979), p. 438. 6 W. Carr, *Arms, autarky
and aggression: a study in German foreign policy, 1933–1939* (London, 1981), p. 40. 7 R.
Munting & B.A. Holderness, *Crisis, recovery and war: an economic history of continental
Europe, 1918–1945* (London, 1991), pp 143–4.

were independent could not be accepted in view of the real nature of their relations to England. He compared England to one German province and the Empire to the whole of Germany, and refused entirely to consider Great Britain as apart from her dominions ...

Bewley concluded that if Irish sovereignty and membership of the League could not protect the state 'from economic reprisals against England even in time of peace, it would follow that in time of war Ireland would be subject to belligerent treatment as a part of the British Empire'.[8] Dublin was angered by Schacht's 'belittling' portrayal of Ireland. De Valera considered Schacht to be 'under a grave misapprehension' regarding the status of a dominion and instructed Bewley to protest to the AA.[9] Bewley informed the AA that Schacht's 'gross' 'misconception' of Irish status was 'a statement of Government policy'. The AA's Ministerialdirektor Dieckhoff was forced eventually to excuse Schacht as an economic rather than a political expert, adding that the economics minister's statement 'did not represent the view of the German Government'.[10]

Meanwhile the Irish government, despite its earlier protests and threatening posture, decided in May 1934 to accept the earlier German quota offer on eggs and butter for 1934.[11] Dehn-Schmidt was also told that Irish importers would be allowed to purchase up to half a million tons of coal from Germany rather than Poland and that, of the Saorstát's total annual imports of wheat worth about £2.5 million, at least £1 million-worth could be transferred to Germany provided it was 'prepared to purchase 50,000 extra cattle'. The minister of industry and commerce, Seán Lemass, informed Dehn-Schmidt the Saorstát could purchase up to £10 million-worth of German goods. Lemass was adamant in his conversations with Dehn-Schmidt that he wanted to dispose of £1 million worth of cattle. Dehn-Schmidt replied, 'he did not think it possible for Germany to take so much'.[12]

The AA rejected the belated Irish acceptance of the eggs and butter quotas it had offered in December 1933 and January 1934 indicating they had been filled from other sources following Dublin's objections.[13] De Valera's efforts to seek alternative markets had achieved little success. Only 6,000 head of cattle would be exported to Germany in 1934, accounting for the vast majority of Irish exports to Germany that year, and there was to be no deal on eggs or butter.

---

8 NAI, DFA CRS 19/50, Bewley–Walshe, 22 June 1934.   9 Ibid., Walshe–Bewley, 26 June 1934.   10 Ibid., Bewley–Walshe, 30 June 1934.   11 NAI, Berlin letterbooks, Fahy–Bewley, 24 May 1934.   12 Ibid.; NAI, Berlin letterbooks, Fahy–Bewley, 13 June 1934.   13 NAI, DFA 314/10/6/3, brief note on Saorstát–German trade negotiations, 10 Oct. 1934.

INTERDEPENDENT DOMESTIC AND FOREIGN POLICIES

Throughout these tortuous negotiations, the Nazi regime matured. The central goal of the Nazi state during its first two years of existence was to develop the economy and reduce unemployment, while avoiding international complications and thoroughly embedding Nazism in the society, institutions and identity of Germany. This was a precarious period for Hitler: old conservative bastions of Weimar and the aristocracy still maintained a grip on the presidency, the AA and the Reichswehr. He had yet to fulfil his manifesto pledges to reduce unemployment and strengthen the economy. Nor could the German chancellor embark on an aggressive foreign policy to break the shackles of Versailles because Germany was still vulnerable to outside intervention.

Bewley did not arrive in Berlin until after the end of the first phase of Nazi foreign policy, during which the Nazis had tried to convince other governments that the Nazi takeover would not alter German foreign policy. Towards the end of 1933, however, the second phase of Nazi foreign policy commenced. Hitler adopted the strategies of multilateral disengagement and bilateral diplomacy leading to the unilateral renunciation of pre-Nazi German commitments. Germany followed Japan's May 1933 precedent by seceding from the League of Nations on 14 October. Thereafter Hitler withdrew progressively from all international fora. Hitler even withdrew from the Disarmament Conference while feigning an interest in total disarmament and talking peace to allay international fears.

Behind this foreign policy façade Nazi Germany began to rearm. Although Weimar had undertaken limited covert rearmament, Germany remained militarily feeble in 1933 and 1934. Simultaneously, Hitler commenced his own programme to revise the Versailles treaty. His aim was to win Germany's sovereign right to an independent foreign policy and to an unrestricted military establishment. He also sought the incorporation of other German-speaking states (Austria) and German minorities (Danzig, Baltic States, Sudetenland) in the long term. But in the short term he looked forward to the remilitarization of the Rhineland and the return of the contested Saar region.

Bewley reported little on German foreign policy to Dublin during this period and therefore major oversights occurred. He did not mention Germany's withdrawal from the Lausanne Disarmament Conference and the League.[14] He also failed to report on the non-aggression pact between Germany and Poland signed in January 1934. In February 1934, Walshe had to instruct Bewley to send regular reports on German foreign policy additional to his regular reports on the domestic situation.

Such was the enormity of reinvigorating the German economy and so slow

14 NAI, DFA, CRS 19/50, Bewley–Walshe, 11 Dec. 1933.

the results that public apathy developed. Evidence from various sources indicated to Bewley that 'the Government does not feel itself secure' and was 'being stampeded more and more to the left' as Hitler seemed unwilling to prevent his minions such as Dr Goebbels and some leaders of the Hitlerjugend expressing state socialist sentiments 'more in harmony with the sentiments of Moscow' in an effort to retain popular support. Bewley feared the socialist and anti-clerical radicals in the party were now 'dictating the course of events'.[15] Anti-Catholicism and anti-Semitism were the Nazi leadership's tactical tools used to divert popular attention from unfulfilled economic expectations.

NAZI ANTI-CATHOLICISM

On Nazi treatment of both the Catholic Church and of Jews, Bewley kept Dublin relatively well informed. He did, however, display ambivalence and agreed with Nazi anti-Jewish policies on occasion. But this was not out of line with Vatican thought at the time or the Christianity induced anti-Semitism that permeated western societies in the pre-holocaust era. Bewley's interpretations were largely unexceptional, if somewhat disturbing to modern readers. His impressions of the religious-political conditions prevailing in Germany were formed during his Vatican posting. In a report to Dublin of 12 March 1932, he revealed the views that later permeated his Berlin reports.[16] Bewley argued the Catholic Centre party (Zentrum) had been hostile to National Socialism during Weimar and this had unduly influenced the views of the papal nuncio in Germany, Cardinal Pacelli and, in turn, the Vatican.[17] Only a third of the German population were Catholics although as a faith it was 'better organized' than fragmented Protestantism to deal with the predations of Nazism.[18] The sense of vulnerability induced by Bismarck's church–state conflict in the 1870s (the Kulturkampf) had imprinted itself in the consciousness of the Catholic hierarchy and on the Vatican. Their objective was to protect the rights of the Catholic Church in Germany while accommodating German nationalism.

Bewley thought National Socialism had many characteristics appealing to the Church, notably its strong stance against moral abuses and its opposition to the licence of the press and stage permissible under the liberal Weimar constitution. His characterization of Catholicism in Weimar Germany was substantially accurate. The Centre party was crucial to the 'balancing act' of coalition politics during Weimar and it allied with the Social Democrats when necessary. The Centre party was a confessional party, adhering strictly to its denominational

---

15 Ibid., Bewley–Walshe, 22 June 1934. **16** NAI, DFA, CRS 19/1, Bewley–Walshe, memo on the present policy of the Holy See, 12 Mar. 1932. **17** Ibid. **18** J. Cornwell, *Hitler's pope: the secret history of Pius XII* (London, 1999), p. 107.

beliefs, and neither it nor its Catholic followers condoned the much demonized licentiousness of Weimar. But Bewley forgot the pluralist atmosphere of Weimar permitted a Catholic renaissance in Germany when Catholic associations and intellectual life flourished under the protection of the state.[19]

Hitler, while declaring himself a Catholic, was ambivalent about the Catholic Church. In *Mein Kampf* he suggested National Socialism could benefit from studying Catholicism which he admired for its ability to maintain a 'doctrinal edifice' as a powerful cohesive force.[20] However, he was also hostile because he believed German Catholics needed to be Germans first and Catholics second, or preferably not Catholic or Christian at all. Hitler thought Christianity weakened the natural impulse of the *Volk* by infecting the popular mentality with ethical and moral issues thus endangering the survival of the German people.[21] He nonetheless feared engaging in a direct conflict with Catholicism due to its power.[22] For tactical purposes he criticized political Catholicism for interfering in national politics, while conceding that spiritual Catholicism was acceptable and was private to the individual. The Nazis accused the Centre party of collaborating with the socialist enemies of the German people, the Social Democrats, who in the Nazi view had surrendered the German nation to the Allies in 1918. The need to end such political Catholicism was a clear aim of Hitler's. However, he was less clear in public on the future of non-political or spiritual Catholicism. Privately, Hitler admitted that Christianity and Nazism were incompatible, so Christianity had to be removed.[23]

Between 1928 and 1933 the Catholic hierarchy opposed the Nazi notion of 'positive Christianity' as a meaningless term to camouflage 'fanatical' nationalism. However, the German episcopate was not united and failed to agree on a single condemnatory policy towards the Nazis, although the majority of individual bishops advised their congregations not to join the NSDAP and criticized it harshly.[24] That situation changed when Hitler acceded to power by, nominally, legal means.

Catholicism was generally hostile towards Nazism prior to 1933. When Bewley arrived in Berlin, Hitler and the Vatican had recently signed the concordat of 20 July 1933. Pius XI, the 'Pope of Concordats',[25] supported by the cardinal secretary of state Eugenio Pacelli (the former papal nuncio in Germany), had a longstanding pragmatic policy to reach an accommodation with any regime –

---

19 G. Lewy, *The Catholic Church and Nazi Germany* (New York, 2001), pp 1–8; J. Zender, 'Germany: The Catholic Church and the Nazi regime, 1933–1945', in R.J. Wolff & J.K. Hoensch (eds), *Catholics, the state, and the European radical right, 1919–1945* (Boulder, 1987), pp 92–3; Cornwell, *Hitler's pope*, pp 106–7; K. Lönne, 'Germany', in T. Buchanan & M. Conway (eds), *Political Catholicism in Europe, 1918–1965* (Oxford, 1996), pp 158–67. 20 Hitler, *Mein Kampf*, p. 417. 21 Ibid. p. 104. 22 Cornwell, *Hitler's pope*, p. 105. 23 Ibid., p. 106. 24 Lewy, *Catholic Church*, pp 9–15. 25 F.J. Coppa, 'The Vatican and the dictators between diplomacy and morality', in Wolff & Hoensch, *Catholics*, p. 208.

whether fascist, Socialist or liberal democratic – to secure the rights of the Catholic Church in all countries.[26] In March, the all-German Catholic bishops' conference had reversed its previously condemnatory attitude towards Nazism and confirmed that it was the duty of all Catholics to support the regime,[27] because 'The German bishops did not ... regard the Nazi party as a clear and present danger to their church in the way that they did the Communist party and its mentor, the Soviet Union.'[28] The pope distrusted the demeaning nature of democratic politics as an enterprise that diverted Catholics from their Catholic duties.[29] The papacy wanted to avoid arguments about the value of different political systems (except Communism which it opposed) and instead postulated certain clear and important preconditions for all regimes, 'namely, that not only the rights of the church, but the rights of God and the Christian conscience, must be safeguarded'.[30] Pius XI advocated securing the Catholic Church's interests through the development of Catholic associations to meet spiritual, social and economic needs, rather than through political Catholicism.

Both Pius XI and his subordinate Pacelli were willing to see the successful Centre party disbanded and to renounce any political role for the Catholic Church or its members if papal control of German Catholicism was guaranteed; religious Catholic associations were safeguarded; and Hitler accepted that Catholics should receive a full Catholic education. The two sides were unable to agree a definition of religious associations but signed the concordat, postponing negotiations on a definition until later.[31] The Vatican believed the position of the Catholic Church in Germany had been safeguarded, at least temporarily. Pacelli considered it was preferable to have an agreement with Hitler rather than to not have one. He also realized the concordat might be violated, but he 'doubted that even the Nazis would violate all of its articles at once'.[32]

Bewley's attitudes to Nazism and to the Catholic Church during his first years in Berlin resemble the position of the Vatican; not surprising given that he was a practising Catholic who had just spent three years at the Vatican. He evidently approved of the Holy See's position. After arriving in Berlin, Bewley continued to pay attention to the treatment of the Catholic Church, reflecting Irish interest in Catholicism generally and his own religious convictions. He initially denounced Alfred Rosenberg's *Myth of the twentieth century* (which had become the second bible of Nazism after Hitler's *Mein Kampf*) as 'historically of no value whatever' in its attempts to establish a theological doctrine of Nordic racial superiority and to establish a German state religion. Rosenberg had established the German Faith Movement which renounced the title of Christianity

---

26 Ibid., pp 202–6. 27 Lewy, *Catholic Church*, pp 36–41. 28 Zeender, 'Germany: the Catholic Church', p. 96. 29 Coppa, 'The Vatican and the dictators', pp 200, 202. See also Lönne, 'Germany', p. 165. 30 B.R. von Oppen, 'Nazis and Christians', *World Politics*, 21: 3 (1969), p. 405. 31 Zeender, 'Germany: The Catholic Church', pp 97–9. 32 Coppa, 'The Vatican and the dictators', p. 208.

and was opposed to 'dogmatic Christianity of any kind, and of course princi-
pally to the Catholic Church'.[33] Bewley correctly saw Rosenberg's movement
was one of many in Nazi Germany that attacked Christianity because 'its protection of the weak and its elevation of charity as a virtue' were 'calculated to
destroy heroic qualities'.[34] Unsurprisingly, the Holy See placed *Myth of the
twentieth century* on its Index of proscribed books.[35]

Despite his denunciation of Rosenberg's ideas, Bewley saw little in the
NSDAP programme harmful to the Catholic Church, except perhaps the
Sterilization Law applied to the physically and mentally infirm. He argued erroneously that Papen's position as vice-chancellor was a 'guarantee' that Catholic
interests would be protected. Bewley's view was that clergy previously active in
the Centre party who maintained their opposition to National Socialism were
political activists and were breaching the concordat's stipulation that clergy
should not participate in politics. He said, 'It would, I think be entirely incorrect
to suggest, as has been done, that there is any sort or kind of persecution of
Catholics'. The evidence for this he believed lay in the loyalty of the majority of
Catholic priests to 'the present regime'. Catholics were grateful to the Nazis for
the 'miracle' of 'the purification of the stage, literature and the general life of
the German cities', and the attempted 'suppression of Freemasonry' with the
abolition of Grand Orient lodges in Germany.[36] Bewley's views were in line with
the contemporary popular Catholic aversion to the triple evils of freemasonry,
communism and immorality.[37]

By late February 1934 both Bewley and the Catholic Church were forced to
revise their original sanguine attitude.[38] Cardinal Faulhaber, archbishop of
Munich, had already during Advent in 1933 and the New Year 1934 criticized
certain aspects of the Nazi regime from the pulpit stating, 'it was useless to be
rescued from Russian barbarism if the country was only to relapse into
Germanic savagery'. On 22 February Rosenberg addressed the diplomatic corps
in Berlin and condemned Faulhaber saying that a member of the NSDAP had
only the religion of 'national honour'. Then, Hitler Youth leader, Baldur von
Schirach, said in a speech that Catholic youth organizations would be dissolved
and incorporated into the Hitler Youth and Bewley reported that 'one cannot
help feeling that the misgivings of the Holy See [about the Nazis not adhering
to the concordat] are to a great extent justified'.[39]

By April Bewley was speculating about a possible conflict between Catholic

33 NAI, DFA, CRS 19/50, Bewley–Walshe, 23 Jan. 1934.   34 Ibid.   35 Ibid., 26 Feb.
1934.   36 Ibid., 23 Jan. 1934.   37 Lewy, *Catholic Church*, pp 98–9.   38 A concealed diplomatic conflict had already been raging between the Vatican and the Nazi government since
late 1933 as it became clear that the 'totalitarian claims of the state' on the individual and family life, as well as its actions relating to the Catholic press and the persecution of Jewish
converts, undermined the spirit and substance of the concordat.   39 NAI, DFA, CRS
19/50, Bewley–Walshe, 26 Feb. 1934.

youth organizations and the Hitler Youth. He foresaw serious difficulties ahead for the Catholic Church, because the incorporation of the Catholic Youth into the Hitler Youth could not be achieved in the same way as the Catholic youth had been absorbed into the fascist youth movement, or Ballilla, in Italy because 'Germany is non-Catholic, the Catholic children would find in the Hitlerjugend a non-Catholic, and often a bitterly anti-Catholic atmosphere'.[40] Then in April 1934 Bewley reported a case of the Hitler Youth absorbing a Catholic youth group in Stuttgart[41] and unsettling incidents in Danzig where the Nazi government accused the Danzig Centre party priests of political acts of provocation. Bewley concluded that cumulatively these events marked the inauguration of a general campaign against the Catholic Church, whereby 'any indiscretions on the part of the representatives of the Church are being seized on to justify it'.[42] The steady deterioration in church–state relations led Bewley to believe that 'something in the nature of a *Kulturkampf* against the Catholic Church' was possible.[43] Goebbels confirmed Bewley's worst suspicions with an anti-clerical speech on 11 May 1934. Bewley nonetheless remained convinced that the campaign did not seem to be approved by the 'intelligent elements' in the Nazi Party.[44]

Bewley, German Catholics and the Vatican, who had initially welcomed the July 1933 concordat, discovered that the regime's racially based nationalism and totalist claims on the individual and society were determined to undermine the Catholic Church in particular and Christianity in general. The concordat had served Hitler's purposes well because it had helped to legitimize his power. The Vatican, however, was reluctant to renounce the concordat for fear of unleashing a Nazi onslaught on Catholicism. It continued to believe Catholics were better protected than other groups within German society against extensive Nazi predations. Jews, the most exposed, vulnerable and demonized element in Germany, lacked any protection.

JEWS

Bewley was fully aware of the practical consequences of Nazi anti-Semitism. In February 1934 Bewley sent Dublin an extensive report on the Jewish question warning of the likely prohibition on Jews practising in many professions, the likelihood that Jewish emporiums would 'be compelled to go out of their business', and the possibility of a legal prohibition against marriages between Jews and 'Aryans'.[45] Next in May 1934 he predicted an intensification of anti-Semitic practices in Germany to counter the growth of economic pessimism in the public.[46] He reported attacks on Jewish shops, businesses, and synagogues; the painting of 'anti-Semitic inscriptions' on their premises; the banning of Jews

---

40 Ibid., 9 Apr. 1934.   **41** Ibid., 11 Apr. 1934.   **42** Ibid., 17 Apr. 1934.   **43** Ibid., 11 May 1934.   **44** Ibid., 14 May 1934.   **45** Ibid., 19 Feb. 1934.   **46** Ibid., 11 May 1934.

from certain public areas; the boycott of Jewish businesses;[47] and physical violence and intimidation of anyone who dared to associate with Jews.[48]

Bewley reported, however, the Nazis had taken a more moderate stance than their rabid anti-Semitism before 1933 would have indicated. The severity of Nazi anti-Semitism had been lessened by concerns about economic dislocation and the negative impact on foreign opinion.[49] Anti-Semitism, Bewley said, was not a Nazi imposition because German opinion was anti-Semitic by nature, and the Nazis' anti-Semitism increased their popular appeal especially among the working-class.[50] However, this was a gross generalization. The German public was not uniformly anti-Semitic and the lack of public enthusiasm for the 'boycott' of Jewish businesses on 1 April 1933 had seemed to prove that ill-treatment of Jews could not be carried out on a mass, public scale.

Bewley also drew attention to the Nazis' dual approach to the so-called Jewish question.[51] They combined thuggery, emotionalism and street violence long associated with the Nazi movement before 1933, with the legal and systematic framework of the traditional German state. He recognized the appeal of anti-Semitism in Germany, as in most Christian-dominated societies, which retained a view of Jews as 'Saturday people'[52] and murderers of Christ. He seemed to perceive, if dimly, that the pseudo-racialist justifications for anti-Semitism in Nazi Germany added a new element absent in the persecution of the Jews in the middle ages and early modern times.

Bewley did fulfill the role of information gatherer reasonably well on the issue of the Jews in this early phase of his posting in Berlin, as Michael Kennedy has argued,[53] but this was not value-free reporting. A closer examination of his early reports, important to interpreting his later career, reveal Bewley was an anti-Semite. Some of his actions as unofficial trade envoy in Berlin in the early 1920s indicate that his innate anti-Semitism had been activated at least momentarily then. It is not satisfactory to downplay this aspect of his character as inconsequential as long as he fulfilled his role as an information gatherer, because Bewley was the official representative of the Irish government to a regime whose core ideological tenet was anti-Semitism. Furthermore he was responsible for processing and offering significant advice to Dublin on whether or not to accept applications for visas from Jews fleeing persecution in Germany, whose numbers

47 NAI, DFA, CRS 19/50A, Bewley–Walshe, 19 July 1935. 48 Ibid. 49 Ibid. Domestic political considerations also played a role in limiting Nazi radical anti–Semitic action. The conservatives, such as Schacht (finance), Hindenburg (president), Neurath (foreign) and even Frick (interior) constrained the full effects of Nazi anti-Semitism in their desire to the maintain a stable economy, administration and government (Burrin, *Hitler and the Jews*, p. 42). 50 NAI, DFA, CRS 19/50, Bewley–Walshe, 11 May 1934. 51 P. Johnson, *A history of the Jews* (London, 1995), p. 483. 52 D. Vital, *A people apart: a political history of the Jews in Europe, 1789–1939* (Oxford, 2001), p. 748. 53 Kennedy, 'Our men in Berlin', p. 62.

would increase throughout the 1930s as Nazi anti-Semitic policies became more severe.

His reports on the Jewish question require close analysis. On 6 June 1934 Bewley summed up 'the belief of a very large number (I think personally a great majority) of the German people' as follows: since the Jews regarded themselves as the chosen people they treated non-Jews as sub-human and inferior. Many Germans believed that Jews' relations with non-Jews was 'in no way bound by the ordinary moral law'. In addition, Bewley, apparently representing the views of the German people, stated Jews were hostile to non-Jewish nationalism and religion taking advantage of the principle of equality in democratic societies. Thus any Jew should 'be removed from all positions enabling him to exercise his demoralizing influence'. It was on the basis of this theory that all the measures against the Jews were taken by the Nazi government, Bewley said. He added that accusations of ritual murder were used to support the general theory. 'This belief is held to my own knowledge by many well educated and intelligent people.' Some of the alleged ritual murder cases, he said:

> have been the subject of very copious literature, and ... full reports of the trials have been reprinted, from which in some cases the impartial reader gets the impression that the person in question was killed by Jews in a manner corresponding to the Jewish rite in slaughtering animals.

Is the inference here that Bewley was 'an impartial', 'educated' and 'intelligent' observer who had sympathies with the common, Nazi, anti-Semitic charge of ritual murder? He drew attention next to what he considered to be the half-hearted defences against the charges mounted by Jews. He wrote that:

> In the circumstances, on the assumption that ritual murders do not in fact take place, it seems regrettable that the Jewish authorities do not deal more circumstantially with the very detailed charges made. A general denial or denunciation of 'medieval superstition' is an unsatisfactory method of meeting accusations that give dates and names, nor does it explain why at all periods and in all countries this particular charge should have been fastened to the Jewish race alone.[54]

Bewley questioned modern official Catholic statements which denied the existence of ritual murder, by highlighting the canonization of alleged victims of ritual murder in the fifteenth century. He added that papal bulls had been published on particular cases of ritual murder in the later medieval period. Bewley's indictment of the Nazis' virulent anti-Semitic propaganda was not

---

54 NAI, DFA, CRS 19/50, Bewley–Walshe, 6 June 1934.

because it was anti-Semitic *per se*, but because its general nature and extremism had negative international repercussions for Germany and allowed Jewish propagandists to escape a reasoned debate. Bewley tellingly added:

> It can, however, be readily understood that the vulgarity and over-emphasis with which the case is presented in the *Stürmer*, while no doubt of assistance in making propaganda in Germany, must affect non-Germans unpleasantly and on the whole facilitate Jewish propagandists in their desire to avoid a detailed controversy on the subject.[55]

The tone of Bewley's reportage and his references to Jewish propagandists avoiding the subject suggests he considered there to be an element of truth in the ritual murder charges. The persistent myth of ritual murder, in fact a twelfth-century invention of the Christian world,[56] still had many adherents in European societies although the Catholic Church and Protestant churches had rejected it as a falsehood. Bewley, however, revealed a distinct lack of sympathy for the plight of German Jews or any understanding of their precarious position.

In fact, the German Jewish population was generally fragmented, dispersed and law abiding. They had no natural allies to support their cause domestically and Christian denominations were more concerned with defending their own interests than those of a Jewish minority to whom they were theologically hostile. As there was only one official political party, the NSDAP, Jews had no access to politics. Nor was there an effective Reich-wide Jewish organization because German Jews had struggled for centuries to win acceptance and the status of loyal Germans.[57] Bewley's apparent ignorance about the predicament of Jews in Germany had been displayed, too, when in May 1934 he told Dublin that the 'vast majority of Jews in Germany' were left 'untouched' and were 'living exactly as they did before, although excluded from some public positions'.[58] In fact, a large number of Jews who held positions in German universities or were doctors and lawyers were having their academic careers and source of earnings destroyed. This affected a sizeable proportion of the Jews of Germany and Bewley had firsthand knowledge of the pernicious Nazi legislation which Aryanized the universities, professions and arts. The majority of Jews managed to survive in the early years of the Nazi regime but they were under intense pressure from the party-state. Arbitrary street violence against Jews was constant[59] and Jews underwent a process of humiliating vilification, separation and exclusion from normal life.[60]

Many Jews had embraced cultural embourgeoisement and thought that their contribution to the cultured German nation would bring them respectability. They remained loyal to Germany having committed themselves to the German

---

55 Ibid.   56 Vital, *People apart*, p. 233.   57 Ibid., p. 829.   58 NAI, DFA CRS 19/50, Bewley–Walshe, 11 May 1934.   59 Vital, *People apart*, p. 816.   60 Ibid., p. 812.

nation after the German Enlightenment (*Aufklärung*) in the late eighteenth and early nineteenth centuries. They were attracted by the humanistic ethic of *Bildung*, or 'self-cultivation of one's intellectual and moral facilities through' education,[61] the ideas of cosmopolitanism and tolerance preached at that time. Unfortunately, the acculturation strategy failed as German identity became increasingly identified with blood and *Volk*, particularly after the Great War. The Nazis rejected modernity and the German Enlightenment as softening the German soul. Thus Hitler's capture of the German state in 1933 was a rejection of German Jews conception of Germany as well as their contribution to it.[62] While some Jews emigrated, there was no massive flight. Maybe Hitler would lose power? Perhaps Hindenburg and the old conservatives in government and the civil service would continue to moderate the Nazi party's anti-Semitism and force it into retreat? Bewley skims over these complexities.

Bewley's attitude towards Jews may have been of religious origin. Concern for baptized or converted Jews as opposed to practicing Jews was a central tenet in Christianity.[63] Both Protestant/Lutheran and Catholic traditions differentiated between 'Christian' Jews and 'Jewish' Jews and this distinction later suffused Ireland's parsimonious Jewish immigration policy in the late 1930s.[64]

COMPLETING THE DICTATORSHIP, JUNE–JULY 1934

This then was the state of Nazi internal rule in the first half of 1934. Hitler's internal freedom of action to deal with Christianity and the Jewish question was dramatically increased after the Night of the Long Knives on 30 June and Hindenburg's death soon afterwards. Many of the obstacles erected by the political partners of 30 January 1933 in an attempt to control Hitler were destroyed and his seizure of power was complete.[65] When Hindenburg died in August the way was cleared for Chancellor Hitler to assume the presidency and to truly become Germany's Führer.

The Night of the Long Knives was the turning point. It marked the temporary abandonment by the Nazi leadership of a legal façade. On Hitler's orders, one of his oldest friends and only serious rival, Ernst Röhm, the Brownshirt leader,[66] most of the other Brownshirt or SA leaders and various influential

61 P. Mendes-Flohr, *German Jews: a dual identity* (London, 1999), p. 26. 62 Ibid. 63 J. Shaver cited in D.L. Bergen, 'Catholics, Protestants, and Christian anti-Semitism in Nazi Germany', in *Contemporary European History*, 27: 3 (1994), p. 331. 64 Keogh, *Jews*, pp 115–52; Keogh, *Ireland & Europe*, pp 99–112; Katrina Goldstone, ' "Benevolent helpfulness"? Ireland & the international reaction to Jewish refugees, 1933–9', in Skelly & Kennedy, *Irish foreign policy*, pp 116–36. 65 Bracher, *German dictatorship*, p. 304; A. Tyrell, 'Towards dictatorship: Germany, 1930–1934', in C. Leitz (ed.), *The Third Reich: the essential readings* (Oxford, 1999), p. 47. 66 Ritchie, *Faust's metropolis*, p. 419.

figures who had impeded his ascension to power were murdered.[67] The purge
cleared Hitler's path to the presidency and to becoming commander-in-chief of
the Reichswehr (army) by eliminating potential rivals and those of his more
unsavoury past associates to gain the support of the Reichswehr's generals. The
power of the SA was broken and Hitler would now rely on the army. The rise
of Himmler, Heydrich and the SS was also ensured.[68]

In the months before the purge Bewley had reported a cooling of public
enthusiasm for the regime in a 'considerable wave of pessimism'[69] as the
German economy deteriorated and hard currency disappeared. Talk of a 'second revolution' had become common and the SA had simultaneously adopted a
more unruly, aggressive stance. These 'old fighters' resented having no formal
role in the government nor reaping the rewards which other senior members of
the party and Hitler's entourage had received. Röhm sought to establish the SA
as a *Volksheer* (people's army) to the dismay of the regular German army's commander-in-chief, General Werner von Blomberg. Blomberg and the Reichswehr
wanted the SA disbanded. Röhm's party rivals, Göring, Himmler and Hess,
conspired against him to benefit their own careers. Hitler had to make a choice
between the Reichswehr and the SA, and as the year progressed he sided with
the regular army since his ambitions for a strong German state required an
enlarged regular army, not a paramilitary, irregular force. To reduce the palpable
tensions Hitler ordered the SA on an enforced month's leave in June.[70]

Meanwhile conservatives such as vice-chancellor Papen and economics minister Schacht were increasingly disillusioned with the Hitler regime.[71] Papen, on
instructions from a very ill Hindenburg, decided to intervene and delivered an
unprecedented speech critical of the regime at the University of Marburg on 17
June. He accused the government of treating the people like 'morons' with their
outrageous propaganda in the German press and pointedly added that 'Great
men are not created by propaganda'.[72] Papen attacked the creation of the Hitler
personality cult and accused the Nazi revolution of 'selfishness, lack of character, insincerity, lack of chivalry and arrogance'. He also targeted Röhm's talk of
a 'permanent revolution'.[73] Goebbels banned coverage of the speech and Bewley
had to read about it in the international press.[74]

Papen's speech enraged Hitler who knew he would have to make a choice
between the SA and the conservatives, more particularly the Reichswehr. Then,
on 21 June, Blomberg as army commander-in-chief delivered an ultimatum to
Hitler that unless he dealt with the SA, Hindenburg would transfer control of

---

67 Fest, *Hitler*, p. 467.   68 H. Krausnick & M. Broszat, *Anatomy of the SS state* (London,
1982), p. 166.   69 NAI, DFA, CRS 19/50, Bewley–Walshe, 11 May 1934.   70 Kershaw,
Hubris, pp 499–512.   71 Ibid.; K.P. Fischer, *Nazi Germany* (London, 1995), p. 288. Bewley
had recognized some disturbing elements of the Nazi state in his confidential reports despite
his own ambivalence.   72 Shirer, *Rise and fall*, p. 218.   73 Kershaw, *Hubris*, p. 509.
74 NAI, DFA CRS 19/50, Bewley–Walshe, 22 June 1934.

the state to the Reichswehr. With some further encouragement and false information supplied by Göring and Himmler, that Röhm was planning an imminent coup d'état, Hitler was overcome by a paranoid rage and unleashed the blood purge (codenamed Hummingbird) to end the perceived threat to his regime and position. No such putsch had been planned. The SA leadership remained loyal to Hitler even as the SS and Gestapo summarily executed them on 30 June and 1 July. Hitler (or his followers on their own initiative) also took the opportunity to settle old scores with some of the conservatives in Papen's circle, whom Hitler called 'dwarves'.[75] The three men who had collaborated on preparing the Marburg speech: Herbert von Bose (Papen's press secretary), Edgar Jung (the main writer of Papen's Marburg speech), and Erich Klausener (the leader of Catholic Action) were all murdered. Papen, 'the little worm'[76] and nominal vice-chancellor, was placed under house arrest. Other individuals who knew too much about Hitler's earlier career and private life were also butchered.[77]

Like most other commentators Bewley had not foreseen the bloodshed. Bewley was disoriented in the days immediately following the purge, the result of living in a censored climate of fear. Many Germans in the street immediately after the purge adopted the sarcastic greeting 'Lebst du noch?' ('Are you still among the living?').[78] The German media created the impression that an incipient revolution had been suppressed. Verification of rumours and propaganda statements was impossible, leaving arch-propagandists Goebbels and Hitler free to supply rationalisations for their actions in the certain knowledge they could not be contradicted.

Although Bewley was a foreign diplomat with access to external critical opinion he still found it extremely difficult to write a coherent report on the events.[79] He considered the truth 'will possibly never be known for certain' and that there was 'no definite information available, even to the best-informed journalists'.[80] On 2 July, with the wisdom of hindsight, he recalled that '[i]t had been obvious for some days [before the purge] that things were not normal' as had other contemporary observers who felt an increase in tension in Berlin.[81]

After details of the purge became known, Bewley began to accept the party-state's official account of events repeating the Nazi mantra that an 'incipient revolution had been crushed'.[82] He denounced Röhm's 'character', 'proclivities' and lifestyle concurring with Nazi propaganda which contrasted Röhm's behaviour to the allegedly laudable 'puritanical and ascetic personality of Hitler'.[83] It suited Nazi propaganda to emphasize this aspect of Röhm's and his associates' private lives after they were murdered.[84] The homosexuality of some of the SA's

---

75 Kershaw, *Hubris*, pp 512–71. 76 Ibid. 77 Fischer, *Nazi Germany*, pp 291–2. 78 M. Dodd, *My years in Germany* (London, 1933), p. 133. 79 NAI, DFA CRS 19/50, Bewley–Walshe, 2 July 1934. 80 Ibid., 5 July 1934. 81 Ibid., Bewley–Walshe, 2 July 1934. 82 Ibid. 83 Ibid. 84 A. Bullock, *Hitler: a study in tyranny* (London, 1968), pp 291–2.

leadership and their ostentation were exposed to strengthen Hitler's position. That Edmund Heines, the SA Obergruppenführer for Silesia, was caught in bed with a young man was used to maximum effect in Goebbel's propaganda. The view that Hitler was a 'moral cleanser' eliminating a notorious group of 'pederasts' gained popular currency, as did the insight that he had crushed 'Bolshevism'.[85] As Bewley noted, 'I have not heard a world of regret for Röhm ... and it is more or less admitted that the fate of the various persons executed was inevitable'.[86]

Dublin took an understandable interest and de Valera, who did not normally read Bewley's diplomatic reports, was keen to read Bewley's initial report on the subject on 2 July and then his analysis of Hitler's 13 July 1934 speech to the Reichstag.[87] Bewley initially thought it 'remarkable' that the alleged putsch consisted of two groups who were 'not by any means natural allies'; that is, members of the former ruling classes led by General von Schleicher, and the SA leaders.[88] Yet he rejected foreign opinion that 'the Schleichers were murdered for political reasons' and naively accepted the Hitlerian line that they were involved in planning a putsch.[89] Hitler's self-exculpatory speech on 13 July impressed Bewley as 'a very fine piece of oratory and gave the impression of complete sincerity'.[90] All that sceptical diplomats and the foreign press could achieve was to point to some of the inconsistencies in the Nazi cover story. But Bewley was correct in concluding of Hitler's explanation was 'accepted by the vast majority of the country as a complete justification of the Government's action'.[91]

Röhm's wild talk of 'a second revolution' was a sufficient pretext for a preventive purge in Bewley's mind. Bewley repeated the propagandistic argument that Röhm left Karl Ernst, the SA leader in Berlin, to lead the rebellion in the capital while Röhm met other SA leaders in Bavaria.[92] In fact, Karl Ernst was in Bremen setting off on his honeymoon by boat to Madeira when he was arrested.[93] This was a man whom Hitler highlighted as one of the principal figures in the *coup d'état*. Bewley had again been misled by the propaganda.

The version of events presented to the Reichstag by Hitler on 13 July had Generals von Schleicher and von Bredow bringing 'a foreign power' (allegedly France) in to support the mythical *coup d'état*.[94] Bewley accepted this account of events,[95] although it was a piece of propaganda which later required the Germans to present a diplomatic note to the French apologizing for the groundless allegations against the French ambassador in Berlin.[96] Nevertheless, the lie

85 Klemperer, *The Klemperer diaries*, p. 72.   86 NAI, DFA CRS 19/50, Bewley–Walshe, 5 July 1934.   87 Ibid., 2 July 1934 & 16 July 1934 (annotations on both of these reports read 'Seen by secretary & president').   88 Ibid., 2 July 1934.   89 Ibid., 5 July 1934. 90 Kershaw, *Hubris*, p. 519.   91 Ibid. A similar observation is made in NAI, DFA CRS 19/50, Bewley–Walshe, 5 July 1934.   92 NAI, DFA, CRS, 19/50, Bewley–Walshe, 16 July 1934.   93 Bullock, *Hitler*, p. 295; Fest, *Hitler*, p. 464.   94 Bullock, *Hitler*, p. 294.   95 NAI, DFA, CRS 19/50, Bewley–Walshe, 16 July 1934.   96 Bullock, *Hitler*, p. 295.

had served its purpose domestically, as a pretext to decapitate both the conservative and SA irregular army opposition.

Bewley criticized the *Times* correspondent and the news agencies for ignoring Hitler's intention to arrest and bring to trial those responsible for outrages unconnected with the government's action.[97] In fact no one was brought to trial. Instead Himmler and the SS were rewarded for their role in the orgy of violence and all the SS were presented with 'honorary daggers' on 4 July in a ceremony in Berlin.[98] The Röhm Purge initiated the rise of the SS and on 20 July 1934, the SS was released from its subordination to the SA and permitted to train its own fighting forces independent of the Reichswehr.[99] Meanwhile, the purge left an estimated 150 to 200 people dead, most of whom were not connected to the SA or to Röhm. The SS and Hitler had taken the opportunity to exterminate all resistance to Nazification.[1]

Bewley expressed some doubts about why the government delayed so long in reprimanding Röhm and the leaders of the SA for their alleged proclivities. He sought a plausible explanation for the shooting of members of von Papen's vice-chancellery and speculated that those shootings might have been unauthorized.[2] But he tended to agree with Hitler's 'justification for the summary executions of the alleged putschists as the only way to prevent an outbreak of civil war'. As he said, 'That the Government believed in the necessity is, I think, clear; they may have been mistaken, but it is very hard for outsiders with a limited knowledge of the facts to dispute the necessity.'[3]

Bewley neglected a number of important considerations in arriving at this conclusion. He underestimated the significance of the deaths of people unconnected with the SA, and he made a very feeble attempt to explain why more people were murdered than admitted to in Hitler's speech.[4] In addition, if a *coup d'état* had been plotted and Hitler moved to prevent it, why had the alleged insurgents offered no resistance? Most disturbing of all was the retrospective legislation of 3 July which exonerated the purge as a justifiable act of 'self defence by the state'.[5] This was a legal sham whereby the new party-state judged itself and legalized its murderous actions. Bewley failed to notice all these oversights, which if acknowledged should have led to the conclusion that Hitler's cover-up was inconsistent and therefore suspect.

However, even Hitler's consummate oratory on 13 July could not suppress a couple of concerns Bewley had about Hitler's rationalization of the events. There were two particular questions that had 'not so far been satisfactorily answered'. First was 'why Röhm, whose proclivities were long known to government and public, was allowed to hold his post'. The second was why several

---

97 NAI, DFA, CRS 19/50, Bewley–Walshe, 16 July 1934. **98** Fest, *Hitler*, p. 470. **99** Broszat & Krausnick, *Anatomy*, p. 166; Fest, *Hitler*, p. 472. **1** Fest, *Hitler*, p. 470. **2** NAI, DFA, CRS 19/50, Bewley–Walshe, 16 July 1934. **3** Ibid. **4** Bullock, *Hitler*, pp 304–5. **5** Bracher, *German dictatorship*, p. 302.

individuals in the Papen circle had been disposed of.[6] So although he was not wholly gullible, Bewley generally accepted Hitler's explanations.

The international press, on the other hand, was horrified by the butchery[7] as were the Irish newspapers on the whole. However, like Bewley, the *Irish Times* initially misinterpreted the massacre believing Nazism was a 'passing phase'.[8] Hitler was portrayed as 'well meaning'[9] and courageous in subordinating 'his personal feelings' towards his friends 'to the national welfare and although the brutality of his methods has shocked the world, the sincerity of his purpose hardly can be questioned'.[10] Nevertheless, the *Irish Times* did criticize the brutal methods adopted by the Nazis ('Kid gloves do not seem to be included in the Nazi equipment')[11] adding, 'No people can be governed permanently by violence. Sooner or later revolt is inevitable.'[12] So while initially ambivalent, the newspaper became increasingly critical of the purge in a way that the Irish diplomat might have been expected to react but failed to do.[13]

The *Irish Press*, on the other hand, unreservedly condemned the whole event as a 'holocaust' from the beginning. It suspected the Third Reich's use of the terms 'shot while resisting arrest' and 'shot while attempting to escape', as 'the phrase[s] well known in Ireland as the pseudonym[s] for assassination'. Regarding the German authorities' use of the word 'suicides' in several cases, it concluded these were euphemisms for the result of a choice between execution and suicide. The *Press* stated 'these terrible events' were an act of 'paganism' whereby 'those who make a worship of the State turn back to the methods of Pagan Rome'. According to the *Press*, it was irrelevant whether some of the men killed were 'of evil character'. State sanctioned repression and the nature of the Nazi state itself were the real issues.[14]

Bewley's analytical weaknesses were again revealed in his reports on the death of Hindenburg. By the end of July Hindenburg was dying. Hitler's position with the Reichswehr and its generals had much improved since he had disposed Röhm and the SA as a competitor for the defence of Germany. Many conservatives believed Hitler was finally 'tamed' since he had purged his most unpleasant friends and allies. Even before Hindenburg had breathed his last, Hitler had drafted the 'Law on the Head of State of the German State' which was signed on 1 August immediately before Hindenburg's death. The law amalgamated the offices of president and chancellor in the person of Hitler, the Führer. The new head of state required all members of the Reichswehr to swear a personal oath of loyalty to him. Bewley again ignored the illegality of Hitler's actions. The new law violated the Enabling Act that had guaranteed the inviolability of the president's office in return for the powers it granted to Hitler as chancellor.[15] Bewley seemed not to notice this contravention.

---

6 NAI, DFA CRS, Bewley–Walshe, 16 July 1934.   7 Kershaw, *Hubris*, p. 517.   8 IT, 16 July 1934.   9 IT, 10 July 1934.   10 IT, 3 July 1934.   11 IT, 2 July 1934.   12 IT, 3 July 1934.   13 IT, 6 July 1934 & 10 July 1934.   14 IP, 6 July 1934.   15 Bracher, *German dicta-*

Bewley believed the plebiscite Hitler called to endorse the new law would 'lead to a tremendous majority for Hitler' because 'there is no alternative'.[16] On 19 August nearly 90 per cent of the German electorate sanctioned Hitler's arrogation of Hindenburg's office. F.T. Cremins, the Irish permanent delegate to the League of Nations, reported to Dublin that opinion in the League's headquarters in Geneva was apprehensive because 'Hindenburg and the Reichswehr remained the only really stable factors in Germany – a stable background to a very unstable front'. Now that Hitler had combined the offices of the presidency and chancellor, and had assumed control of the Reichswher some feared the regime would become more unstable than before.[17]

CONCLUSION

Although Bewley's reporting during these months in Berlin betrayed very limited sympathy for the plight of Jews and a certain consideration for National Socialism, he was not alone in this respect either in Irish diplomatic or government circles or internationally. He tended to place the onus for Nazi behaviour on Jews themselves and, perhaps like large sections of the German population, he began to succumb to Nazi indoctrination.[18] Bewley, too, was strongly anti-communist and as Kershaw, the eminent English historian of the Hitler regime, has commented the German population believed that while Nazism had its dark side 'Bolshevism would have been worse'. There was also a prevalent feeling that those who suffered most under Nazi rule, including Socialists, Communists and Jews, deserved it. Hitler remained popular and the life of ordinary Germans was improving if they were not members of a disliked minority.[19] Bewley was susceptible to this because of his anti-Semitic, his anti-Communist and anti-English point of view, and his sympathy for the German stand against the iniquities of the treaty of Versailles. However, until late 1935, he gave his superiors only limited reason to be dissatisfied with his reporting from the Third Reich.[20]

---

torship, p. 305; Fest, *Hitler*, p. 474. The Dáil duly passed a motion of condolence to the German people on the death of Hindenburg (*Dáil Debates*, vol. 53, cols. 2037–8, 2 Aug. 1934).   **16** NAI, DFA CRS 19/50, Bewley–Walshe, 3 Aug. 1934.   **17** NAI, DFA CRS 19/40, Cremins–Walshe, 3 Aug. 1934.   **18** Kershaw, *Hubris*, p. 508. See also R. Gellately, *Backing Hitler: consent and coercion in Nazi Germany* (Oxford, 2001), pp 31–3.   **19** Kershaw, *Hubris*, p. 508.   **20** On occasion Bewley had to be prompted to submit reports (NAI, DFA Berlin letterbooks, Walshe–Bewley, 16 Nov. 1933). Bewley incurred a reprimand from Walshe for failing to supply requested information on at least one other occasion (NAI, DFA Berlin Letterbooks, Walshe–Bewley, 12 Mar. 1934). On the other hand Walshe informed Bewley on two occasions that de Valera found his reports on the position of the churches in Germany and on internal conditions in Germany as 'very interesting' (NAI, DFA, CRS 19/50, Walshe–Bewley, 1 Feb. 1934, NAI, DFA, CRS 19/50, Walshe–Bewley, 16 May 1934).

5

Transition, August 1934–August 1935

'Ireland which so often had risen from defeat ... looks with genuine sympathy on this action of the German people which became possible only through unity of purpose. That Germany which in 1918 had to take on itself the Versailles Treaty had now thrown this dictated peace into a limbo of forgotten things where it belonged' (Seán MacEntee).[1]

'I would personally imagine that the aim of the Government is to secure the youth of the country is trained in anti-Christian doctrines in the Hitler Youth – when, like the Soviet Government, it can afford to ignore the older population' (Charles Bewley).[2]

By August 1934 Hitler and his followers were ensconced as masters of Germany. Hitler had established his dictatorial control of the state and the party, and the German economy was recovering. He began to concentrate on foreign policy matters. At the Nuremberg rally in September 1934 he declared the founding of the 'Thousand-Year Reich'.[3] The next two years were to be a testing period for Hitler's foreign policy as he struggled to strengthen his relatively weak foreign and military positions. While undertaking covert rearmament, he used the rhetoric of peace and international justice to test international resolve against German nationalist demands to revise the treaty of Versailles.

Hitler's failed intervention in Austria in July 1934 alienated the Italian dictator, Mussolini. But in a matter of months he won a majority in the plebiscite on the return of the Saar to German control. However the prospect of a resurgent Germany, led by such a provocative leader as Hitler and espousing irredentist claims, led his western European neighbours, particularly France and Italy, to combine with eastern European countries in mutual defence pacts, leaving Nazi Germany internationally isolated. Germany remained vulnerable militarily and Hitler sought to puncture this envelopment. He began to achieve that aim in 1935 with the signing of the Anglo-German naval agreement.

How did the Irish government and its representative in Berlin interpret these significant changes in Germany's foreign policy posture and the repercussions for international relations generally? Faced with increasing evidence of the nature of Nazi rule, what reactions were there from Irish quarters? Most impor-

---

1 Translation from *Kölnische Zeitung*, 26 Mar. 1935. 2 NAI, DFA, CRS 19/50A, Bewley–Walshe, 27 Nov. 1935. 3 Brendon, *Dark valley*, p. 259.

tant in any analysis of the day-to-day conduct of Irish-German relations at this stage (and routinely ignored in most of the existing literature) was the trade relationship. The period of 1934 saw the threat of a total breakdown in Irish-German trade as the Saorstát tried to deal with the bullying tactics that characterized German trade policy and sought to staunch the outflow of foreign currency from Irish coffers. Yet by early 1935 Irish-German trade was on its most hopeful and solid footing since the beginning of Irish-German diplomatic relations. An account of the fraught Irish-German trade negotiations provides insights into the implications of the Anglo-Irish Economic War for the Saorstát, the new economic dictatorship that was developing in Nazi Germany under Hjalmar Schacht and also the central role of Britain in Irish-German relations.

The over-arching British dimension was instrumental in frustrating the Saorstát's efforts to ensure Germany treated it as it would any other small, independent state. Contrary to the prevailing assessments of Bewley, and despite his undeniable weaknesses he provided a tolerably accurate analysis of the international climate at this time. On the whole he supplied his political masters and his department with relatively adequate assessments of the changes underway in Germany, given his undeniable prejudices.

AUSTRIAN PUTSCH

Bewley's international reporting throughout 1934 was substantially correct about both the evolution of Hitler's foreign policy and the Nazi use of supporting propaganda. German newspapers played on popular encirclement fears by referring to the world media's 'concentric fight against Nationalist Socialist Germany'.[4] Bewley noted criticism of Austria in the German press in June 1934,[5] in line with the general German resentment of the creation of a separate Austrian state through the treaty of Versailles. Anschluss or unification with Austria was a central tenet of all irredentist German nationalist opinion, even during the Weimar Republic.

The German dictator was convinced that the authoritarian regime of Austrian chancellor, Engelbert Dolfuss, was intrinsically weak and he maintained secret contact with the Austrian Nazis throughout 1933 and early 1934. On 25 July 1934 the Austrian NSDAP launched a coup, murdering Dolfuss. But the Austrian security forces remained loyal contrary to advice Hitler had received. The failed putsch caused Hitler's regime considerable international embarrassment and alienated Mussolini. The Italian dictator was determined to prevent the creation of a united powerful German neighbour on his northern borders and Italo-German relations deteriorated to the delight of France and

4 NAI, DFA CRS 19/50, Bewley–Walshe, 5 July 1934.   5 Ibid., 12 June 1934.

Britain. Hitler's incompetent meddling in Austria had isolated Germany further. Bewley's reports recognized this. He believed the Austrian fiasco had rendered 'a much more severe blow to the regime' than the brutality involved in the suppression of the Röhm putsch.[6]

Bewley reported on the Nazi propagandists' attempts to camouflage Hitler's foreign policy disaster from the German public. He revealed that the German press had been 'instructed not to mention the word National Socialist in connection with the mutineers' in the vain hope that the German public would 'be unable to guess the identity of the party in question'. The press used 'childish and disingenuous' special pleading intended for internal consumption to satisfy the 'docile German public'. Theo Habicht, a member of the German Reichstag, had acted as a spokesman for Nazi policy on Austria and as an agitator against Dolfuss. As Bewley wrote: 'Apparently Habicht made a statement in his broadcasting which in some way convicted National Socialism with the crime: why he should have done so, if in fact there was no connection, is not explained.'[7]

Bewley realized that Nazi Germany's protests of innocence would 'not convince anyone outside of Germany'.[8] The invented alibis designed to prove German Nazi non-involvement in the putsch were inconsistent. Bewley correctly concluded that the government's immediate dismissal of the German ambassador to Austria, Dr Rieth, was because he had compromised Germany.[9] Rieth had mediated between the rebels and the Austrian government, and he had 'guaranteed them [the rebels] a free passage to Germany'. Bewley refuted Rieth's long and unconvincing statement to the effect that he had acted as an individual and not as the German ambassador. The Irish minister cuttingly opined that the Nazi alibis were 'so childish as not to convince anyone' and 'would appear rather a proof of complicity than of innocence'.[10] His summation is demonstrative of a generally accurate appreciation of German Nazi entanglement in the Austrian putsch:

> the German Government, after having encouraged in every way, in the press and by radio, the most violent political and personal attacks on Dolfuss as a torturer of National Socialists and a traitor to the German race, and after having at last connived at the smuggling of arms into Austria, is alarmed at the inevitable effects of its policy and is trying without success to establish an alibi.[11]

A 'very great depression' settled on German public opinion, aggravated by poor economic results. In early August, Bewley told Dublin that Italian press

---

6 Ibid., 28 July 1934.   7 Ibid., 28 July 1934. Habicht was instrumental in attempting to destabilize the Dolfuss regime. See G.L. Weinberg, *The foreign policy of Hitler's Germany* (Chicago, 1970), p. 93.   8 Ibid.   9 Ibid. See Weinberg, *Foreign policy*, pp 101, 102, 104–5.   10 NAI, DFA, CRS 19/50, Bewley–Walshe, 28 July 1934.   11 Ibid.

attacks had a very negative impact on German public opinion because Italy had been the only Great Power that had 'consistently supported German claims', but now a 'foolish policy in Austria' had resulted in the loss of this valuable friendship. Bewley was surprised by the foolhardiness of the German press when it praised the 'heroic' conduct of Dolfuss' assassins as they were executed with the cry of 'Heil Hitler' on their lips. This was a volte-face from its initial editorial policy of denying any Nazi connection with the putsch. Bewley was incredulous: 'It is no wonder that the average German has come to distrust the Press and to wonder how far the attacks of foreign newspapers are justified.'[12]

Bewley was correct – the implications of the Austrian putsch were more far reaching than the execution of the SA leaders on 30 June 1934. Hitler had failed in his policy attempt to treat Austria as simply another domestic matter of *Gleichschaltung* (political co-ordination)[13] like Danzig.[14] Hitler the supreme opportunist did, however, salvage something positive from the disaster. It proved to be an excellent opportunity to dispose of his bothersome vice-chancellor, Papen, and use him to further his objectives. Papen, appointed as German ambassador to Vienna, was a Catholic and able to assuage Austrian fears about Nazi anti-clericalism. He was also to prove instrumental in the eventual achievement of the Anschluss in 1938.[15]

Following his international embarrassment in Austria, Hitler grew more cautious. Although he had experienced a summer of domestic and international crises, his domestic power base was unassailable. The Hitler cult grew within Germany. With the inauguration of practical Nazi socialism and economic growth, ordinary Germans (with the exception of those defined as racial enemies, outsiders or dissidents) entered a halcyon and complacent period lasting from 1935 to 1938. Hitler's initial failure in Austria proved to be only a temporary foreign policy setback, soon forgotten.

THE SAAR PLEBISCITE

The return of the Saar to German control in a landmark plebiscite on 13 January 1935 inaugurated a period of growing international success for Hitler. The Saar, in accordance with the treaty of Versailles, had been placed under League of Nations control for fifteen years giving France access to its resources. A plebiscite was scheduled when this mandate expired to allow the German speaking population to decide whether to rejoin Germany, merge with France or remain under League mandate. Bewley's analysis of events leading up to Saar plebiscite was broadly correct. The Nazi regime (anxious for a success to enthuse the population following the Dolfuss debacle) reduced its anti-clerical

12 Ibid., 3 Aug. 1934. 13 Weinberg, *Foreign policy*, p. 106. 14 Ibid., p. 92. 15 Ibid., pp 106–7.

and anti-Catholic outpourings to take account of the predominantly Catholic population of the Saarland. The revulsion induced by the 'Blood Purge' of 30 June 1934 also had to be overcome. A Nazi press campaign in the Saar high-lighted the advantages of National Socialism, as opposed to Communism, for Catholicism, printing atrocity stories about the Soviet Union and pointing to the relative stability and prosperity of Germany.[16]

Bewley recognized the Nazi tactic: 'Obviously it would be folly to attack the Catholic Church directly while awaiting the result of a plebiscite where 90 per cent of the voters are Catholic'. If a substantial section of Saar Catholics voted against reunification, Bewley suggested this would provide 'an excellent pretext for a general attack on the Church' in Germany. But this was not a likely out-come. As early as November, Bewley was predicting that 'Germany will have a majority, possibly a very large one'.[17] The Vatican, he correctly predicted, would not 'do anything ... to injure German prospects in the Saar' as its 'repercussions' would damage the interests of the Church in Germany.[18] Indeed, the German Catholic hierarchy and the Vatican not wishing to attract the further ire of the regime, later adopted an encouraging attitude towards the plebiscite. As Bewley recorded, the Vatican adopted a position of neutrality on the question. Although the Holy See was not 'any nearer to a reconciliation with the German govern-ment', it wanted to avoid creating the impression that it was 'hostile to legitimate German aspirations'.[19] For similar reasons the German hierarchy took a supportive line towards German nationalist aspirations to reacquire the Saar. The Catholic Church hoped this demonstration of loyalty might militate against Nazi persecution. Bewley confidently concluded three days before the vote that 'a majority in favour of returning to the Reich would seem to be assured'.[20]

Ultimately, 91 per cent of the Saar population voted for reincorporation into Germany, a distinct shock to most commentators and to the French in particu-lar. But the plebiscite had been scheduled to occur regardless of who held power in Germany, and the German ethnicity of the Saar population made it probable that they would vote for a return to the state from which they had been invol-untarily separated. The return of the Saar awoke German national pride for perhaps the first time since the Great War while Hitler's regime gained greater freedom of action both internally and externally.

---

16 Lewy, *Catholic Church*, p. 194.   17 NAI, DFA CRS 19/50, Bewley–Walshe, 8 Nov. 1934.
18 Ibid., 6 Dec. 1934.   19 Ibid., 10 Jan. 1934.   20 Ibid. See Lewy, *Catholic Church*, pp 182–201; G. Lewy, 'The German Roman Catholic hierarchy and the Saar plebiscite of 1935', *Political science quarterly*, 79: 2 (1964), pp 184–208.

REARMAMENT AND UNILATERALISM

After January 1935, Nazi foreign policy concentrated on exploiting all available opportunities to overcome its self-incurred isolation and encirclement arising from the failed Austrian putsch. Bewley realized that the Nazi regime was still in a weak transitional phase and while German rearmament was underway, it had not reached a stage whereby 'it could compare with the state of preparedness' of its possible opponents.[21] Bewley had already drawn the Irish government's attention to rearmament when he analysed the German budget of 1934. Spending on the army had increased, but it was the Luftwaffe that experienced a 'remarkable increase'.[22] By February 1935 Bewley was drawing Dublin's attention to the rise of General Blomberg and the Reichswehr from the ashes of the SA.[23]

Germany's undeclared rearmament increased international tension and was a breach of the treaty of Versailles. Bewley disagreed with those in the international press who speculated that the German government was planning war. German rearmament had not progressed far enough for the government to contemplate war, Bewley thought. If the Nazi elite was considering embarking on war at this stage it was 'sheer madness':

> My personal belief is that Germany is quite aware that for years, perhaps generations, to come she will be incapable of waging a war with any chance of success, and will therefore do everything to consolidate her position economically and politically while keeping the peace.[24]

Germany at this stage had only one ally, Poland, which Bewley identified as 'a very doubtful one'.[25] Francis Cremins, the Irish permanent delegate to the League, held similar opinions.[26]

Hitler refused to become involved in a multilateral straitjacket such as an eastern Locarno pact that would guarantee the Versailles borders of Germany's eastern neighbours.[27] He pursued a policy of bilateralism seeking to play off his opponents against one another. This was a high-risk strategy because the Versailles international order remained intact during 1934 and the first months of 1935. It was doubly so since German rearmament was poorly concealed and provocative. To all intents and purposes Germany was isolated internationally

---

21 NAI, DFA CRS 19/50, Bewley–Walshe, 8 Nov. 1934. **22** Ibid., 9 Apr. 1934. Göring extended his influence in military aviation during 1934, but Bewley failed to report that in May 1934 the air office of the defence ministry was brought under his control. See Overy, *Göring: the 'iron man'* (London, 1984), pp 32–3. **23** NAI, DFA CRS 19/50, Bewley–Walshe, 1 Feb. 1935. **24** Ibid., 6 Dec. 1934. **25** Ibid., 8 Nov. 1934. **26** Kennedy, *Ireland*, p. 196. **27** The original Locarno treaty of 1925 had safeguarded the borders of her western neighbours.

and kept in check by a concentric wall of alliances orchestrated by a fearful France. Hitler's enticement of General Pilsudski into the Polish-German anti-aggression pact of January 1934 had served to temporarily rupture France's attempts to build a defensive alliance of the new eastern European nations (the 'Little Entente') against Germany. But his tactic backfired because of the Soviet Union's sensitivity regarding German access to a direct route to Moscow, leading to a Franco-Soviet rapprochement, a mutual defence pact in February 1934 and, ultimately, to Soviet membership of the League of Nations in September. Hitler's alienation of Mussolini, his Italian ideological twin, through the failed Austrian putsch in July propelled Italy closer to France, to Paris' delight and to the Nazi regime's annoyance.[28]

Hitler cultivated a pacifist posture engaging in disarmament discussions with the British, in particular. He stalled British and French requests that Germany should return to the League of Nations before Germany's right to rearm could be recognized. The Führer claimed that disarmament could only occur when 'equality' of armaments had been achieved and, since Germany was already disarmed, the onus was on other powers to do the same.[29] Nonetheless, the British government was attracted to the idea of a naval treaty with Germany. In British minds, imperial overstretch and containment of Japanese expansionism in Asia were major drains on her naval assets. If some accommodation was possible whereby Germany agreed to restrict its *de facto* naval building to a proportion of British naval strength then Britain's global maritime reach could be secured. Encouraging signals emerged from Berlin in November 1934 that an Anglo-German naval agreement was possible. France, meanwhile, remained suspicious of German intentions. With Germany's two main opponents at odds on this issue, Hitler's government continued safely, and not so secretly, to rearm. Bewley's reports, silent on the covert discussions relating to naval matters, repeatedly drew attention throughout 1934 and 1935 to courtship of Britain being 'the guiding principle in German international policy'.[30]

Despite the maritime and global strategic concerns impelling the British government, it appeared that the prospects for an understanding with Germany were shattered by the immediate threat of German rearmament. Following Hitler's delaying tactics on disarmament talks, the British government announced increased military expenditure and limited rearmament measures in March as a precaution against Germany's unilateral rearmament. Germany's decision to make public its rearmament was taken to announce Nazi Germany's arrival as a Great Power deserving of equal treatment. Göring declared the existence of the Luftwaffe on 10 March, in open contravention of Versailles and, for effect, exaggerated the size of the German air fleet. Then on 16 March Hitler announced the reintroduction of German conscription to the consternation of

28 NAI, DFA CRS 19/50, Bewley–Walshe, 10 Jan. 1935. 29 Ibid., 1 Feb. 1935. 30 Ibid., 10 Jan. 1935.

France, Britain, Italy and most of the continental European states, but to the gratitude of General Blomberg, the Reichswehr and the German population generally. What appeared to be an open defiance of the provisions of Versailles appeared to most Germans as reclamation of legitimate rights. As Papen informed the British ambassador, 'Germany's recent bombshells' were 'merely quite natural steps away from the hated and impossible Treaty of Versailles'.[31] Göring's delivery of an 'aggressive speech' at Freiburg on 10 May, in which he condemned the alleged 'trickery of Geneva' and declared that Germany no longer recognized any 'frontier States', heightened international tensions.[32]

Bewley was well aware of the increasingly aggressive posture of the Nazi elite. At a reception in the propaganda ministry on 20 March he had overheard a conversation between Goebbels and a number of German journalists. Goebbels apparently forgot that outsiders were present and told the journalists:

> It was obvious to everyone that for the past 15 years no policy had had any success in Europe or elsewhere except that of the 'fait accompli', and the proclamation of their air force and the introduction of conscription were the result of the Government's realisation of this fact.

Germany's objective was to achieve international equality between sovereign states (*Gleichberechtigung*). Goebbels also intimated that 'We only deal with big powers', and that Nazi Germany sought agreement with her equals, 'her western neighbours but not with her eastern and southeastern ones with the exception of Russia'.[33]

APPEASEMENT

Contrary to its defiant rhetoric, the Nazi regime was in the midst of its most testing period. Rearmament and the development of the armed forces were not as far advanced as the regime pretended and the Anglo-French containment of Germany remained unbroken. The regime was uncertain about how the democracies would react to its brazenness. The initial omens were that Hitler's deceptive propaganda coup of announcing rearmament had reinforced the alliance of forces against Germany. On 11 April 1934 Britain, France and Italy formed the Stresa Front to enforce the 1925 Locarno pacts, which ensured the western borders of Germany and the maintenance of Austria as a separate entity. The League condemned German rearmament and a Franco-Soviet mutual assistance agreement was signed on 2 May. A Czech-Soviet treaty followed this

---

31 DBFP, 2nd series, vol. 8, 1934–6, Doc. No. 202.   32 Ibid., Doc. 212.   33 NAI, DFA CRS 19/50, Bewley–Walshe, 21 Mar. 1935.

on 16 May. Bewley commented that German opinion was depressed by the League's condemnatory resolution and resented 'the fact that England and Poland voted for it, showing that Germany is for practical purposes without a friend in the world'.[34] The League's action, the Stresa Front, the unanimity of European denunciations and the incorporation of the Soviet Union into European alliance politics against Germany cumulatively shocked German opinion, according to Bewley.

Despite surprise at Britain's action, the Nazis remained committed to the 'erroneous' race theory that Britain was fundamentally pro-German. Bewley commented caustically: 'German psychology appears to be the slave of its own theories.' The 'inflexibilty' induced by Nazi racial theories and the German belief in the rightness of its actions, apparent in dealings with the Great Powers, also affected dealings with small neutral countries. Bewley pointed to the irrefutable evidence that Nazis had 'kidnapped the Jewish journalist Berthold Jakob on Swiss soil'.[35] He noted kidnappings of other German émigrés in Czechoslovakia and Holland.[36] Bewley pinpointed the assumptions underlying Hitler's new forceful approach to foreign policy:

> Presumably the theory at the back of all this insistence on her claims is that no other powers will declare war on Germany, and that therefore Germany can more or less do what she wishes and, having consolidated her military position, can look around for allies in the future. There are two possible coalitions against her – in the first place the Franco-Russian alliance. But here Germany counts on the distaste in other countries, notably Poland, Italy and England, and in France itself for alliances with the Soviets. The second possibility is that of a pact between France, Italy, Poland and the Little Entente. But here again Germany counts on possible dissensions, the hostility of Czechoslovakia to alter German policy, which is based on the consideration that, if Germany herself does not declare war, no one else will, and that she therefore need not trouble herself over the susceptibilities of other states.[37]

Bewley also presciently noted that the regime 'hoped that Italy will be prevented by a war in Abyssinia from taking an active part in Austrian affairs'.[38] Bewley's characterization of Nazi thought on external relations at this juncture was astute. In spite of its bravado, the swastika regime was insecure internationally as private comments from Goebbels and Hitler reveal during this period. External military intervention in Germany was possible, but Hitler privately stated, 'I think we'll come through'.[39]

---

34 Ibid., 25 Apr. 1935.   35 Ibid., 2 May 1935.   36 Ibid., 16 May 1935.   37 Ibid., 2 May 1935.   38 Ibid., 16 May 1935.   39 Kershaw, *Hubris*, pp 553–5.

However, British strategic interests, popular pacifism, fear of the impact of a spiralling arms race on a fragile economy and desire to maintain a stable status quo, led the British government to respond positively to Hitler's repeated offers of a naval understanding. The brutality and depravity of Nazism were distasteful, but Hitler was not as repulsive in British eyes as Stalin. The British foreign office in particular became an advocate of the so-called new diplomacy of accommodation and reconciliation with Germany. British statesmen and, indeed, British public opinion had long been uncomfortable with the punitive Versailles treaty.[40]

The British recognized, too, the deterrence policy of the Stresa Front was innately weak. As Prime Minister Ramsay MacDonald admitted, 'the so-called "Stresa Front" was nothing more than a verbal reproof to Germany for past behaviour combined with an empty threat for the future'.[41] Nor was Hitler unduly concerned about Stresa.[42] Each of the three Stresa signatories, notwithstanding their shared antipathy to Hitler, pursued different objectives. The French attempts to contain Germany in the east were disapproved of by the British, who feared entanglements in eastern Europe could lead to a widespread European conflagration. Moreover both France and Britain remained suspicious of the Soviet Union, although the former was more willing to incorporate it into a Nazi containment system. Mussolini, for his part, was preparing for unilateral action: the invasion of Abyssinia.[43] The Stresa Front was simply declaratory, as Hitler recognized.[44]

Formal appeasement of Hitler commenced when Ramsay MacDonald declared in the house of commons that a statesman had to decide whether 'he is now to abandon his attempts to build up, on general confidence, a peace system in Europe or seek refuge in those combinations of sheer force which have never saved him from war and never will'. He added that appeasement despite its 'palpable dangers' had 'chances' of reaching a 'negotiated agreement' without upsetting the peace of Europe.[45] In this hopeful scenario, Britain would not need to rearm intensively, would protect its lacklustre economy and would play the role of European peacemaker. A satisfied Hitler would be reincorporated as an equal in the international order and his regime would moderate. If this appeasement ploy ultimately failed, Britain would still have purchased valuable time to strengthen itself for a conflict.[46]

Japanese repudiation of the Washington naval agreement in December 1934 ended naval limitation in the Far East and a new race for naval superiority threatened there. Britain's policy objective was to ensure predictability in the

40 P. W. Doerr, *British foreign policy, 1919–1939* (Manchester, 1998), pp 158–9. 41 R.A.C. Parker, *Chamberlain & appeasement: British policy & the coming of the Second World War* (London, 1993), p. 29. 42 Kershaw, *Hubris*, p. 555. 43 F. McDonough, *Neville Chamberlain, appeasement & the British road to war* (Manchester, 1998), p. 24. 44 Kershaw, *Hubris*, p. 555. 45 Parker, *Chamberlain*, p. 29. 46 Doerr, *British foreign policy*, p. 159.

European naval situation so as to be free to concentrate on the Japanese.
Furthermore, if an accord could be arrived at with Hitler on naval matters, then
a similar accommodation might be possible on air power. Göring's exaggerated
German air power claims exercised British public opinion. As the permanent
under-secretary of the foreign office, Sir Robert Vansittart, argued in April
1935: 'Air policy, in its broadest aspects, cannot now be divorced from foreign
policy.'[47]

The Anglo-German naval agreement of 18 June[48] limited German naval tonnage to 35 per cent of the total tonnage of the British Commonwealth, based on
British confidence that the German navy would take a considerable time to
attain that level.[49] Germany was jubilant, according to Bewley, because 'it would
appear that the chief German object has been realized, that is, the detachment
of Great Britain from the united front formed at Stresa'.[50] Germany's pursuit
of the agreement was 'a calculated bid to win Britain over and free Germany for
war against France and Russia in that order'.[51] The whole episode made Britain
complicit in Hitler's repudiation of the Versailles treaty and encouraged the
British belief that German grievances could be alleviated peacefully.

STORM CLOUDS

Bewley understood the transition in German foreign policy as Hitler adopted a
more assertive style, his confidence growing after the naval deal with Britain.
Soon Mussolini's designs on the east African independent state of Abyssinia
offered Hitler new foreign policy opportunities. Mussolini had resolved months
earlier to embark on an imperial quest and preparations were underway at both
a diplomatic and military level. Mussolini relied on French acquiescence in his
African conquest. Britain, however, remained circumspect and unhelpful. The
Anglo-German naval agreement outraged Mussolini. Britain's new Baldwin
government attempted to square the Stresa circle in August by offering
Mussolini territory in Ogaden, a desert, and compensating Ethiopian emperor
Haile Selassie with a corridor of land in British Somaliland to the port of Zeila.[52]
But this was insufficient to satisfy Mussolini who was determined to obliterate
the shame of 1896 when poorly equipped Abyssinian natives had defeated
would-be Italian imperialists at Adowa. Mussolini's designs on Abyssinia and
the discord it created within the already fatally wounded Stresa Front was a further opportunity for Hitler to undermine the crumbling Versailles order.

Bewley's reports for the summer months of 1935 are revealing. He saw the
Germans were confident about their improved relations with England.[53] He

47 DBFP, 2nd series, vol. 8, 1934–6, Doc. No. 127.   48 Doerr, *British foreign policy*, pp 170–
4.   49 Carr, *Arms*, p. 47.   50 NAI, DFA CRS 19/50A, Bewley–Walshe, 18 June 1935.
51 Carr, *Arms*, p. 48.   52 Brendon, *Dark valley*, p. 270.   53 NAI, DFA CRS 19/50A,

also discerned a more courteous tone in the German press towards Italy. The differences between Britain and Italy received 'painfully close attention, as it is realized that through the attitude of Britain the attainment of German aims on the continent of Europe may become possible far sooner than was ever thought possible'.[54] The possibility of an Italo-Abyssinian conflict was contemplated with satisfaction in Germany, Bewley revealed, because it would divert Italian attention from Austria and an Italian colonial success would bolster German claims for the return of its confiscated colonies.[55]

Bewley reported that Nazi racial theory underpinned the regime's international policy, particularly its aim to unify all German-speaking populations under the Third Reich. As in the case of Austria,[56] therefore, Germany would take advantage of any future opportunities to integrate the Germans of Bohemia and Memel. The maintenance of Polish-German entente remained indispensable since the Poles also had 'designs on the territory of both Lithuania and Czechoslovakia'.[57] In particular in early 1935, Bewley drew attention to violent Nazi propaganda against the Baltic states, 'which German opinion persists in regarding as incapable of independent survival'. The trial of 160 German-speaking irredentists by Lithuanian authorities was taking place in Memel and Bewley believed that the German nationalists there had 'received material help from the Reich'. Pan-Germanism was now rampant in Nazi Germany.[58]

Hitler's *Mein Kampf* was another indicator of the possible future trajectory of German foreign policy. Bewley emphasized the centrality of *Lebensraum* or 'living room', which expressed Hitler's concern that Germany's population had insignificant resources to meet its needs. The German dictator provided three potential solutions. The first was internal colonization through reclamation of wasteland which Bewley considered would offer only very limited population expansion. The second was the return of the colonies Germany had lost after the Great War, which Bewley concluded was impossible 'in view of the growing friendship with England, at whose expense the restitution would have to be' and because of British resistance. The acquisition of *Lebensraum* in eastern Europe as advocated in *Mein Kampf* was the 'only other possibility', according to Bewley, and this 'would lead to a war in Eastern Europe'.[59]

TOTALITARIANISM

Bewley was fully cognisant of the totalitarian nature of the Nazi state, and the mechanisms by which it maintained and increased its control over the German population. Hitler was the supreme leader and arbiter with the ultimate power of decisionmaking in line with the Nazi *Führerprinzip*.[60] Bewley understood

Bewley–Walshe, 19 July 1935. **54** Ibid., 24 Sept. 1935. **55** Ibid., 19 July 1935. **56** Ibid., 10 Jan. 1935. **57** Ibid., 1 Feb. 1935. **58** Ibid., 1 Feb. 1935. **59** Ibid., 5 July 1935.

Hitler was 'a mere opportunist' who allowed opposing factions beneath him adopt different policies until such time as he was finally forced to make a decision, or when one of the opposing factions emerged supreme of its own accord.[61] Only this hypothesis, Bewley believed could 'reconcile ... various apparently contradictory facts' within the regime.[62]

Bewley also understood National Socialism's ideological fundamentals. On 22 June 1936, he said: 'the real driving force of National Socialism is its hatred and distrust of Communism'.[63] To this he added nationalism and anti-Semitism, an integral ingredient of German nationalism especially among the working-class. The SA and the working-class, Bewley believed were, however, 'for all practical purposes communist' in their economic intentions. Therefore, Nazism implemented socialistic measures such as price fixing, the protection of tenants from eviction, and the introduction of Winterhilfe to 'placate' them.[64]

Bewley constantly reminded Dublin in his despatches that state censorship hindered his reporting. With almost total political control of newspaper content and radio broadcasting, the Nazis were in a position to influence the thoughts and actions of the population and prepare Germans for possible future foreign policy initiatives.[65] More startling was his acknowledgement that the Nazis used anti-Semitism in a cold, manipulative fashion to stimulate support for the regime when it experienced difficulties. He noted that 'things must be going badly from the economic point of view if the Government thinks it necessary to create enthusiasm by campaigning against the Jews'.[66] Bewley recognized, too, that party fanatics could rely on justifying their excesses against organized Christianity and minorities as the fulfillment of Hitler's racial and cultural guidelines. He paid particular attention to the cynical Nazi policies towards the Catholic Church during 1935.[67] After the successful Saar plebiscite, despite the patriotism of Catholics in Germany and in the Saar in overturning at least part of the 'dictated peace' of Versailles, the church–state conflict was rejoined with renewed intensity as Bewley had already predicted in late 1934 during the Saar campaign.[68] He had identified Rosenberg, Goebbels and Himmler as anti-clerical and anti-Christian. Then, in June 1935, Bewley noted, 'the campaign against the Churches continues to become intense and, if possible, more offensive to any kind of Christian sentiment'.[69] He considered that 'while the German Government does not wish to prohibit any form of Christianity, it is

60 Ibid., 10 Jan. 1935.   61 Ibid., 1 Feb. 1935.   62 Ibid.   63 Ibid., 22 June 1936.   64 NAI, DFA, CRS 19/50, Bewley to Walshe, 6 Dec. 1934; ibid., 11 May 1934.   65 NAI, DFA, CRS 19/50A, Bewley–Walshe, 10 Jan. 1935.   66 Ibid., Bewley–Walshe, 19 July 1935. See also NAI, DFA, CRS 19/50, Bewley–Walshe, 14 May 1934.   67 See NAI, DFA, CRS 19/50A, Bewley–Walshe, 25 Apr. 1935, 2 May 1935, 11 June 1935, 19 July 1935, and 26 July 1935.   68 Lewy, *Catholic Church*, presents a similar analysis.   69 NAI, DFA CRS 19/50A, Bewley–Walshe, 11 June 1935.

determined to exercise any means in its power to render it odious or ridiculous in the eyes of the German people'.[70]

Bewley recorded several disturbing developments: Himmler's order to SS members to resign from the Christian Churches;[71] the deliberate scheduling of Hitler Youth parades at times to interfere with its members attendance to religious duties;[72] the prosecution of Catholic clergy for minor currency law transgressions;[73] civil servants' tendency to remove their children from confessional organisations in order to safeguard their jobs; and the prohibition on Catholic associations' members wearing uniforms.[74] By May 1935 Bewley was reporting that 'confessional papers can no longer exist'.[75] Demonstrations with effigies of priests and nuns suspended from gallows intimidated clerics, in conjunction with a defamatory press campaign.[76] These measures were, he said, part of an orchestrated party-state crusade to discredit all churches but especially the Catholic Church. He also remarked that the German government was cynically involved in using the Hitler Youth to indoctrinate the younger generations and was using every means at its disposal to close down Catholic youth associations.

By mid-1935 Bewley anticipated that the Catholic Church would experience 'a very grave situation' in the course of the autumn.[77] Goebbels in a speech on 29 June compared clergy to 'quarrelsome marketwomen' and continued: 'We are not desirous of going into their pulpits, but we want them not to come on our platforms. We do not wish them to propagate Christianity.'[78]

Bewley, therefore, could not deny the true nature of the Hitlerite regime in relationship to its systematic abuse of individual liberty, human rights and freedom of belief.

THE IRISH INTERNATIONAL ROLE

While Nazi Germany was becoming increasingly active in international affairs, the Saorstát was busily establishing a reputation as an independent and model international citizen, particularly at the League of Nations. De Valera constructed a positive image of Ireland through his contributions to the League. His equivocal speeches supporting the Soviet Union's membership of the League were a masterly compromise between two seemingly irreconcilable opinions. On the one hand, he recognized Soviet membership as essential to the League's credibility as an international body and in maintaining peace and equality between nations,[79] satisfying League supporters and international

---

70 Ibid., 11 June 1935.   71 Ibid., 10 Jan. 1935.   72 Ibid., 1 Feb. 1935.   73 Ibid., 19 Nov. 1935 & 27 Nov. 1935.   74 Ibid., 26 July 1935.   75 Ibid., 2 June 1935.   76 Ibid., 24 Sept. 1935.   77 Ibid., 5 July 1935.   78 Ibid.   79 E. de Valera, *Peace & war: speeches by Mr de Valera on international affairs, 1932–1938* (Dublin, 1944), pp 21–6.

idealists. On the other hand, he placated the Vatican by establishing a direct link between international relations and religion: the League of Nations depended on trust between states, and if the Soviet Union failed to extend religious freedom it would not gain the confidence of Christians and Christian nations.[80]

Another sign of growing international acceptance of the Saorstát came when an Irish high court judge, James Creed Meredith, was appointed by the League as vice-president of the Saar supreme plebiscite tribunal which officiated over any disputes.[81] The League of Nations had also seriously considered the Saorstát as a fallback member of the international force responsible for upholding law and order during the Saar plebiscite if Sweden or the Netherlands were unable to take on that duty. The Saorstát was increasingly viewed as an impartial and constructive contributor to international matters. A high level of Anglo-Irish cooperation and consultation on many international issues overcame any immediate bilateral difficulties and led to a realization that the two countries often had a similar approach to many international problems.[82] Moreover, the secondment of Ireland's permanent representative to the League of Nations, Seán Lester, as high commissioner to Danzig in early 1934 affirmed this maturing perception of the Saorstát as an impartial mediator in international affairs.[83]

But by virtue of geography and history Ireland had little direct interest in or influence over the major international questions involving Germany except for the general strategic consideration of Ireland's relationship with Britain. As de Valera informed the League Assembly on 21 September 1934, the Irish were a people 'more or less looking at Europe from outside'.[84] As long as Hitler sought British acquiescence to revision of the treaty of Versailles during the mid-1930s, the Saorstát remained relegated to a minor position in the Nazi foreign policy pantheon. The Nazis did not encourage de Valera's progressive sundering of the Anglo-Irish Treaty because it endangered the chances of Anglo-German rapprochement. In any case de Valera's revisionist government was viewed from Berlin, to some extent under the influence of hopeful British forecasts, as 'a transient apparition' until at least 1934.[85] The speculation in Germany was that de Valera would have to moderate his demands and sue for peace with London[86] and, on the whole, German sources remained muted on the Irish question throughout 1934 and 1935.

80 Ibid., pp 32–4; Kennedy, *Ireland*, p.201; NAI, DFA 5/88B, O'Donovan–Walshe, 1 Oct. 1934.   81 IP, 12 Mar. 35; Michael Kennedy, 'Prologue to peacekeeping: Ireland and the Saar, 1934–5', in IHS, 30: 19 (1997), pp 421–2.   82 Ibid., passim.   83 Kennedy, *Ireland*, pp 189–90, 192; Gageby, *Last secretary general*, pp 46–7.   84 De Valera, *Peace*, pp 27–8.   85 D. McMahon, 'A transient apparition', pp 331–61.   86 NAI, DFA 5/88B, Bewley–Walshe, 23 Apr. 1934; ibid., Bewley–Walshe, 13 July 1934; ibid., O'Donovan–Walshe, 29 May 1934; *Berliner Tageblatt*, 11 July 1934.

A SECRET UNDERSTANDING?

The advisability of both sides preserving a low-key approach to German-Irish relations was underlined by the erroneous allegations levelled by a Northern Ireland law professor, J.H. Morgan. Morgan pursued a campaign against the Saorstát in the British media after speaking to the Irish Loyalists' Imperial Federation in London on 14 November 1934. In the midst of attacking de Valera's dismantling of the Anglo-Irish Treaty and highlighting that de Valera would shortly be in a position to declare an independent Irish republic, Morgan pointedly alleged that 'strange and mysterious' cargoes were being unloaded from Irish steamers at Irish ports.[87] In a subsequent statement to the *Sunday Chronicle*, Morgan suggested that the recalcitrance of the Saorstát needed to be dealt with urgently or both Germany and the Saorstát acting in concert could seriously disrupt the British empire. Playing on the British public's fear of the Luftwaffe, Morgan asserted: 'We may find the territory of the Irish Free State placed at the disposal of Germany as an aviation base against this country'.[88] De Valera denied these speculations instantaneously, but this failed to prevent their spread.[89]

Morgan's melodramatic conjectures about the prospect of a German air base in Ireland had a limited connection to reality. Since the late 1934 termination of the Irish-German air agreement (which had permitted German use of Irish air space for experimental transatlantic flights) Berlin had sought to extend the agreement for a new term. The department of external affairs was reluctant to agree an extension at a time when Britain's and Germany's neighbours were sensitive about the German 'air menace'.[90]

Suspicions about the existence of a secret Irish-German understanding received further anecdotal sustenance with the announcement that Ernst Toller, a socialist, writer, dramatist and an exile from Hitler's Germany, was scheduled to speak at an anti-Nazi meeting of the Irish Labour League against Fascism in Dublin on the evening of the Saar plebiscite, 13 January 1935.[91] Toller was scheduled to lead the anti-fascist Irish organization in an appeal on behalf of mistreated prisoners held without trial or charge in German concentration camps. He provided Hitlerism with a stereotypical *bête noire* figure: a Jewish socialist revolutionary who had played a prominent role in the shortlived Munich soviet republic of April 1919. Following representations from the German minister in Dublin, Toller was evidently persuaded by the Irish authorities not to speak in Dublin.[92] The Press Association in London speculated that

---

87 IT, 15 Nov. 34. 88 NAI, DFA 5/88B, Dulanty–Walshe, 26 Nov. 1934. 89 Dickel, *Aussenpolitik*, p. 51; IT, 15 Nov. 1934. 90 Dickel, *Aussenpolitik*, pp 51–2. 91 The refers to the anti-fascist Irish Labour Defence League a socialist republican organisation in which Peadar O'Donnell played a role. See D. Ó Drisceoil, *Peadar O'Donnell* (Cork, 2001), pp 82, 84, 87. 92 IT, 14 Jan. 35 & 15 Jan. 35; IP, 14 Jan. 35 & IT 15 Jan. 35; Dickel, *Aussenpolitik*, p.

the Irish Labour League against Fascism's meeting, and Toller's scheduled address, were 'viewed with disfavour in official quarters on the ground that it might prejudice' trade negotiations in progress between the Saorstát and Germany.[93] German newspapers including *Der Angriff*, Goebbels' Berlin based Nazi newspaper, complimented the actions of de Valera's government.[94]

The apparent compliance of the Irish authorities with Nazi wishes served to substantiate suspicions in some quarters of a secret arrangement. Taken together with de Valera's independence rhetoric, his progressive dismantling of the Anglo-Irish Treaty and the Anglo-Irish Economic War, the suspicion served to heighten expectations that the declaration of an Irish republic was imminent. The Statute of Westminster had given the Dáil authority to act as it wished without reference to the commonwealth. Conspiracy theorists among detractors of the Fianna Fáil government such as Northern Ireland unionists could claim to have some superficial evidence to suppose, mistakenly as it transpired, that an agreement existed between de Valera and Hitler. The German government became concerned that media speculation arising out of Morgan's conspiracy theories and the Toller incident might create a misleading impression of Irish-German intimacy in British circles. Goebbels directed the German press not to mention too much about German-Irish relations. He wanted it known that the bilateral relationship was certainly excellent, but that it should not be exaggerated because of the possible political repercussions for German relations with Britain.[95]

Europe was now caught in a spiral of mistrust which had repercussions for the Saorstát. British plans for increased armaments in the face of German covert rearmament; France's renewal of its 1921 mutual security agreement with Belgium; and a formal announcement of the existence of the German Luftwaffe on 10 March 1935 in direct contravention of the provisions of the treaty of Versailles, all heightened international tensions. France declared that the period of compulsory military service would increase from one to two years and Hitler used the French action as a pretext to announce conscription in Nazi Germany.[96]

The whirlwind of events in early March was reported on 18 March in the *Irish Press*. An article summarized the new German military law and the accompanying proclamation that justified German conscription on the basis of Russian rearmament, the French introduction of two-year conscription and German objections to the treaty of Versailles.[97] An accompanying editorial was sympathetic to the German actions. Germany's decision to raise an army of 36

---

51. The Irish high commissioner in London, Dulanty, allegedly approached Toller and 'advised' him not to go to Ireland (IT 14 Jan. 35).   **93** IT, 14 Jan. 1935.   **94** NAI, DFA 5/88B, Bewley–Walshe, 18 Jan. 1935.   **95** II, 25 Feb. 1935; NAI, DFA, Berlin letterbooks, Walshe–Bewley, 26 Feb. 1935; Dickel, *Aussenpolitik*, p. 51.   **96** Bullock, *Hitler*, pp 331–3; Kershaw, *Hubris*, pp 549–50.   **97** IP, 18 Mar. 1935.

divisions was portrayed as an unsurprising consequence of rearmament by other powers. It argued Germany was virtually defenceless as a result of the treaty of Versailles as other powers refused to disarm. Germany, like Britain, was simply acting in good faith and fulfilling its national duty of taking 'the necessary precautions for its own defences'. The *Irish Press* accepted, almost without reservation, Hitler's pacific and disarmament rhetoric since 1933.[98] That same evening the minister for finance, Seán MacEntee, addressed the annual meeting of a manufacturer's association. Alluding to developments in Germany, he said:

> that they in Ireland, who had been so often broken in defeat, could not remain unmoved at the spectacle of what a great nation had achieved by unity of purpose. The vanquished of 1918 was today the peer of the conqueror, and the Treaty of Versailles, like other treaties, had gone into the limbo of forgotten and dishonoured things.[99]

On 19 March the French minister to Dublin, Pierre Guerlet, visited the departmental secretary at external affairs, Joe Walshe. Taking as his starting point the new French conscription law, Guerlet said it was not based on 'any bellicose intentions'. Rather, 'it was intended to fill in the gap caused by the low interwar French birth rate. But then Guerlet came to the central matter exercising his mind: certain indications of pro-German leanings in the Free State. He mentioned the editorial in the *Irish Press* of 18 March, which he considered 'indicated strong pro-German leanings' and he feared that the article's tone could create an impression in France that Ireland was anti-French.[1] Guerlet also objected to Seán MacEntee's comments relating to the German introduction of conscription. He asserted the article was 'the only instance of the formal approval by a minister of state of the action taken by Germany'. Guerlet specifically objected to MacEntee's statement about the vanquished of 1918 and the treaty of Versailles. This disparaged France as a 'conqueror' and labelled the treaty of Versailles as 'dishonourable'. Walshe weakly countered Guerlet's impression that the *Irish Press* and the minister for finance were anti-French by maintaining that the word 'conqueror' was not meant to imply 'that France had been out for conquests'. Apparently, Walshe believed that his lengthy

---

98 Ibid. The *Irish Times* adopted the opposite line to the *Irish Press* drawing attention to Hitler's covert rearmament ('rearming with the utmost possible speed'), before the Führer publicly announced it, as well as Hitler's deceptions (IT, 8 Mar. 1935). The world needed to be 'made safe for democracy' against rearming dictators who repeatedly defied Geneva (IT, 12 Mar. 1935). Germany's central position in Europe, her disruption of the Versailles peace with 'unlimited bilateral pacts', and 'Prussian militarism' gave Britain 'no reasonable alternative' but to consider improving her defence (IT, 15 Mar. 1935). Hitler's 'sheer boldness' in unilaterally renouncing Versailles (by brazenly announcing rearmament) simply reiterated the need for improved British defence (IT, 18 Mar. 1935). 99 IP, 19 Mar. 1935. 1 NAI, DFA 5/88B, Walshe memo, 19 Mar. 1935.

conversation with Guerlet had persuaded him that 'the Government were more Francophile than Germanophile',[2] but some external observers formed the opposite conclusion.

German and international public opinion would certainly have been given the impression that Ireland was pro-German from an article reporting MacEntee's speech in the *Kölnische Zeitung*. Under the heading of 'Ireland's understanding for the German situation', MacEntee's congratulatory remarks of 18 March on the announcement of German rearmament were cited fully.[3] Irish nationalists were, to a degree, sympathetic to the plight of Germany after the Great War, but perhaps never before had a member of the Irish government been so unequivocal in public. MacEntee, drawing on somewhat superficial parallels between the Irish and German postwar situations, said his government was struggling to roll back the Anglo-Irish Treaty in the same way that Germany appeared to be undoing the injustices of the imposed postwar settlement. But MacEntee's speech also implicitly criticized Nazism. He said the Irish people:

> might dislike the methods by which that unity of purpose had been achieved on the Continent. He himself disliked them intensely and believed that democratic government was, in the long run, the most effective system yet devised. Still, the unison and persistence with which the German people had sought their purpose had a lesson for us in Ireland.[4]

Such an ambivalent approach was also perceptible in de Valera's attitudes. Having been a qualified supporter of the League on coming to power after 1932, he was on record at the League Assembly as recently as 21 September 1934 criticizing the failure to implement Woodrow Wilson's idealistic new European order, an order based on recognizing the freedom and equality of all peoples, and their right to live in peace and security within nation states. He told the Assembly:

> it seems to us in Ireland that there is no greater source of war than that which arises from the existence of ... unsolved [national minority] problems. President Wilson used to protest against the cynical 'handing-over of peoples from sovereignty to sovereignty as though they were chattels,' and when we were looking at the Treaties that were being worked out at Versailles, some of us, at any rate, could not help thinking that protest had been completely lost sight of when the war was over ... At the end of the Great War, there were handed over to certain States minorities ... which were bound to be a perennial source of danger and a perpetual liability to the States concerned.[5]

---

2 Ibid.   3 *Kölnische Zeitung*, 20 Mar. 1935; NAI, DFA 5/88B, O'Donovan–Walshe, 26 Mar. 1935.   4 IP, 19 Mar. 1935.   5 De Valera, *Peace*, p. 28.

De Valera's prescription was that the inviolable rights of individuals (including the right to religious freedom) had to be guaranteed universally. Simultaneously, the minority problems created by the unsatisfactory postwar settlement needed to be addressed either through population transfers or by granting local autonomy.[6] De Valera's position on continental national and minority problems was implicitly linked to Irish nationalist claims on Northern Ireland. It was the perception in many Irish circles, including the government, that Germany and the Saorstát contended with the same residual problem that had originated with what both states considered to be imposed peace treaties.

Evidence of this perspective also emerged in de Valera's newspaper. For instance, the *Irish Press* had greeted the outcome of the Saar plebiscite positively, viewing it as a successful example of how the League effectively and fairly solved a minority and national problem.[7] The *Irish Press* expressed sympathy and admiration on behalf of the Irish people for the German 'rejoicing'. The editorial acknowledged that although socialists and Catholics in the Saarland were right to have reservations about rejoining 'Das Vaterland', it was nevertheless appropriate that they should succumb to German patriotism. In support of this argument the *Press* quoted Calvin Coolidge's dictum: 'Good Government is no alternative to Self-Government' and indicated the Irish people knew this from their own experience. The editorial drew a parallel between the Saarland and Northern Ireland regretting that the Northern Irish did not have an opportunity to vote in a similar plebiscite. The Saar result, the editorial optimistically commented, removed German resentment of France and '[b]y abolishing one of the storm centres of European politics it brings the world that much nearer to true peace.'[8]

EMERGING IRISH DISQUIET

On 25 April 1934 Dehn-Schmidt requested the department of justice to supply him with 'the names and addresses of the Marxist and Jewish organisations and, if possible, of the anti-communist, fascist, national socialist and anti-Semitic corporations in the Irish Free State'.[9] The official who received the request noted: 'Hitler is apparently not satisfied with driving the Jews out of Germany. He wants to keep his eye on them in all parts of the world.'[10] This was a foretaste of how the Nazis would use many basic fascist prerequisites, such as anti-Communism and race hatred, to increase their influence in the internal politics of other countries. The department of justice left the enquiry unanswered forcing the German legation to renew the request. Responsibility for the matter

6 Ibid., pp 29–31. 7 IP, 15 Jan. 1935. 8 IP, 16 Jan. 1935. 9 NAI, DFA 17/197, Dehn–Browne, 25 Apr. 1934. 10 Ibid., Browne–Roche, 2 May 1934.

was duly transferred to the department of external affairs. Seán Murphy, assistant secretary in that department, subsequently informed the German legation that the Irish government could not provide the information requested.[11] A democratic government could not communicate such delicate and confidential information relating to state security to a foreign government.

The circumstances surrounding the dismissal of Dehn-Schmidt, the first German envoy to the Saorstát, proved far more disturbing. Reputedly 'pro-British' and anti-Fianna Fáil, he had not initially appealed to de Valera[12] but his professional dedication to fulfilling his duties overcame de Valera's doubts. Dehn-Schmidt was recalled in November 1934 to take up a new appointment to Bucharest. De Valera's valediction said Dehn-Schmidt had earned 'the entire approbation and esteem of the Government of Saorstát Éireann' and he had been devoted 'to the maintenance and to the improvement' of Irish-German relations 'to which we attach the highest value'.[13] Unfortunately it was Dehn-Schmidt's attention to duty that was his undoing. Although a Protestant, Dehn-Schmidt cultivated Irish Catholic circles in deference to the Catholic beliefs of the majority population, and to the influence of the Catholic Church.[14] One of his final acts as German minister to Ireland was to pay a courtesy call on the papal nuncio, Dr Paschal Robinson. Dr Adolf Mahr, chief of the Nazi party organization in Ireland, the Auslandsorganisation,[15] ensured that a photograph of Dehn-Schmidt kissing the nuncio's ring later appeared in Julius Streicher's rabidly anti-Semitic and anti-Catholic paper, *Der Stürmer*.[16] Dehn-Schmidt was recalled from Bucharest and forcibly retired from the German diplomatic service. When Bewley in Berlin expressed concern about Dehn-Schmidt's dismissal, an official at the AA said:

> at a time when relations between Germany and the Holy See were strained the Minister's obsequiousness to the Nuncio amounted to a public criticism of the policy of the German Government; and that while, if he had been a Catholic it would have been quite proper, there could be no excuse for a Protestant behaving in such a way.[17]

---

11 Ibid., Minute by Murphy, 30 May 1934.   12 Duggan, *Neutral Ireland*, p. 21.   13 NAI, DFA 18/10, George R.I. [King] and Eamon de Valera to Hitler, n.d. (given to the Court of Buckingham Palace to be signed on 20 Nov. 1934).   14 NAI, DFA EA 231/4B, Binchy–Walshe, 21 Aug. 1930.   15 The Auslandsorganisation was 'in effect the foreign organisation of the Nazi party'. It fostered trade and ensured that German nationals abroad remained loyal to the Nazi party. Dr Adolf Mahr, the chief of the Auslandsorganisation in Ireland not only engineered the downfall of Dr Georg von Dehn-Schmidt, the first Irish German minister to Ireland, but he also contributed to that of the temporary representative of Herr Schroetter who represented Germany in Ireland while Dehn-Schmidt's successor, Herr von Kuhlmann, was on sick leave. See Duggan, *Neutral Ireland*, pp 14, 23, 262.   16 Ibid., p. 22.   17 NAI, DFA 18/10, Bewley–Walshe, 19 Feb. 1935.

The Irish government was offended by this cavalier treatment of the former German minister to Ireland, and by implication the Catholic Church. De Valera regretted 'very much that such a valuable servant of Germany should have been dismissed because he appeared to go too far in observing the local customs of this country'. Bewley was instructed to inform the German foreign minister, Constantin Freiherr von Neurath, that 'the custom of kissing a Bishop's ring is universal in this country', and Dehn-Schmidt felt obliged to pay deference to local customs. De Valera felt 'no other motive' could be attributed to Dehn-Schmidt other than that of 'desiring to do his country's work more efficiently'. De Valera and Walshe hoped Bewley could make 'friendly representations' to the AA to secure an alleviation of Dehn-Schmidt's punishment.[18]

Eventually, Dehn-Schmidt was allowed a pension and permitted to retain his official title of minister.[19] The incident served to demonstrate directly to the Irish government the practical effects of Nazi religious policies on Dehn-Schmidt and also on other innocent people in Germany, whether they were Catholic, Protestant or Jewish. Yet the Nazi government never considered the message that its actions against Dehn-Schmidt transmitted to Dublin. De Valera and Walshe never forgot the incident. When Dehn-Schmidt died a 'broken man' and 'a social outcast' in Germany in July 1937, de Valera wrote a letter of condolence to his son on behalf of the Saorstát. De Valera assured him that his father had 'worked with great success' in Dublin and that 'there was universal regret at his departure from Dublin' in 1934.[20]

As the totalitarian system under Hitler's charismatic rule developed and National Socialism consolidated its hold in Germany, de Valera and the department of external affairs increasingly disapproved of its domestic policies as unethical and immoral. The Irish government's concerns about the suppression of the German Catholic Church acted as the underlying motive for Ireland's failure to co-operate with several German requests. In April 1935, for example, Professor Ernst Schultze, a German scholar, contacted the Berlin legation to gain permission to conduct a series of lectures in the Saorstát. Bewley was instructed by Walshe to discourage him from coming 'in view of the general trend of things in Germany, especially the attitude of the State towards Christianity'. Schultze was provided with the official excuse that the German minister to the Saorstát usually arranged lectures.[21] The government line closely mirrored Irish clerical opinion. Although sections of the Catholic Church in Ireland evinced sympathy towards Mussolini, many distrusted Hitler's anti-clerical state. Evidence of this can be seen as early as 1934 in criticisms of Nazism in the *Irish Ecclesiastical Record*.[22]

18 Ibid., Walshe–Bewley, 26 Feb. 1935. 19 *Daily Express*, 23 July 1937. 20 NAI, DFA 18/10, De Valera–Dehn, 26 July 1937. 21 NAI, DFA, Berlin letterbook, Walshe–Bewley, 26 Apr. 1935. 22 W.F.P. Stockley, 'A Nazi on Nazi Germany', *Irish Ecclesiastical Record* (March 1934), pp 296–310; McGarry, *Irish politics*, pp 137–8.

The government was unhappy, too, about the difficulties encountered in its efforts to establish more equitable trade with Germany during 1934 and 1935. Bewley's recognition of undeniable German obsequiousness towards Britain in the interests of Anglo–German relations and at the cost of a fruitful Irish–German trading relationship, fed his instinctive dislike of Britain. He acknowledged that the AA was 'reluctant' to 'show itself to make any concession, which might be construed, as giving the slightest assistance to Ireland in the Economic War'.[23]

That Hjalmar Schacht, minister of economics and Reichsbank president, dismissively included the Saorstát in the British empire for trading calculations particularly annoyed Bewley. Hitler had given Schacht the task of ending Germany's foreign currency shortage and Schacht had 'near-dictatorial control over the economy' with the inauguration of his New Plan in September 1934.[24] In Schacht's efforts to justify the imposition of draconian foreign trade and foreign currency controls under the New Plan he alleged Germany's trading partners maintained unfair trading practices and impeded German exports through the use of quotas, tariffs and clearinghouse systems. Specifically, he complained about Germany's adverse trade balance with the British empire, presumably alluding to the imperial trade preference system. Bewley was disturbed:

> As regards Germany's economic relations with Saorstát Éireann, it is the reverse of the truth, as Saorstát Éireann has taken German goods and services to, relatively speaking, an enormous extent, and has by its tariff system actually favoured German imports. But, unfortunately, the German Government for practical economic purposes, and because it suits its particular argument, insists on treating the British Empire as a unit and complaining of its adverse balance with the Empire as a whole.[25]

For Bewley this was further evidence of either German misunderstanding of the status of the Saorstát. Schacht had the ultimate control of all Germany's international trade 'in order to hoard and enlarge Germany's fund of foreign currency'.[26] As John Weitz writes:

> Since no foreign debts could be paid directly, the 'blocked' currency left available for foreign dollar, pound, or franc creditors were in the form of scrip or one of the 'special' marks ... Certain weaker supplier nations, such as some Balkan and South American countries, got manhandled. Their

23 NAI, DFA, CRS 19/50, Bewley–Walshe, 8 Nov. 1934. 24 Kershaw, *Hubris*, p. 576. 25 NAI, DFA, CRS 19/50, Bewley–Walshe, 3 Sept. 1934. 26 J. Weitz, *Hitler's banker: Hjalmar Horace Greely Schacht* (London, 1999), p. 186.

shipments were credited to them totally in blocked German marks, which could be used only for the purchase of German goods.[27]

The Saorstát had already experienced tough German bargaining tactics and was in no mood to accept an imposed German economic arrangement. In 1934 the Irish adverse trade balance with Germany was the worst on record so far. According to Irish statistics, only £135,000-worth of goods was exported to Germany while £2.278 million-worth was imported. The Saorstát had exported only £1 of goods for every £17 imported from Germany.[28]

A number of factors combined to improve the situation by the end of 1934. As early as May that year Dehn-Schmidt, fearing a total rupture in trade relations, personally intervened. Pursuing an informal suggestion by Seán Lemass that a special compensation deal involving the export of cattle could help to redress the Irish trade deficit with Germany, Dehn-Schmidt travelled to Berlin. Rather than discussing Lemass' proposal with AA officials, whom Dehn-Schmidt mistrusted as excessively sensitive to British sensibilities, he bypassed them and discussed the matter with Hitler's economic adviser in the Reich chancellery, Wilhelm Keppler, and with Willuhn, leader of the trade department at the Reich chancellery. Eventually Keppler sanctioned discussions on a special compensation deal with the Saorstát for the latter months of 1934.[29] The German side was now also prepared to agree a currency clearing arrangement to ensure that Irish exporters could obtain prompt payment for their goods.[30]

So in October 1934, the new round of German-Irish negotiations opened in Berlin. An Irish trade delegation went to Berlin to open talks on a special coal-for-cattle pact to be in place for the end of 1934, whereby the Irish could purchase German products – mainly coal – to the value of £500,000, and Germany would purchase £117,000 worth of Irish cattle. Irish tariffs imposed on British coal made German coal more economical and 'an additional outlet for cattle would be much more valuable than an outlet for any other product', in the Irish view.[31] Increasing cattle exports was the primary objective of the Irish government because the beef industry was most badly affected by the tariffs used by Britain in the Economic War. In 1934 the Saorstát sold 100,000 fewer fat cattle on the British market than in 1933 and the resulting domestic glut led to the introduction of the infamous calf slaughter scheme.[32] The Irish delegation consisted of J.V. Fahy, from the department of external affairs, Bewley, and Joseph Brennan, chairman of the currency commission. Including Brennan in the Irish delegation indicated the importance attached by the Irish government to the

---

27 Ibid., p. 187. 28 NAI, DFA 314/10/6/3, German Saorstát trade agreement, n.d. 29 Dickel, *Aussenpolitik*, p. 38. 30 NAI, DFA 314/10/6/3, executive council: German negotiations, 2 Oct. 1934. 31 Ibid., Saorstát–German trade negotiations, 12 Oct. 1934. 32 McMahon, *Republicans*, p. 145.

negotiations and the centrality of currency arrangements. The special compensation negotiations commenced on 16 October 1934.

Despite the German concession that a one-off special compensation agreement could be negotiated, the Berlin negotiations proved testing.[33] The Irish delegation had arrived in Berlin prepared to discuss 1935 quotas for butter, eggs and cattle, as well as the special coal–for–cattle pact for 1934. The German delegation, led by Hemmen of the trade section of the AA, wanted only to discuss the projected special compensation agreement for October, November and December 1934. They said that they had not been authorized to negotiate an Irish-German trade deal for 1935, agreement on which could only be debated after decisions were made by the relevant German departments after 15 November.[34] In Dublin Dehn-Schmidt told Walshe he had informed him before the Irish delegation left for Berlin 'that about the future development of the German import of agricultural goods in the next year (1935) nothing definite could be said'.[35] Walshe's riposte was, 'if I had been aware of any such statement made by you, no delegation would have gone to Berlin'.[36] Nevertheless, the Irish delegation remained to discuss the special compensation agreement, periodically pressing Hemmen and his colleagues for information about the prospects for a 1935 general trade agreement.[37]

A number of other German actions irritated the Irish delegation including Hemmen's outrageous suggestion that a special compensation agreement of £10 million to £1 million should be concluded in Germany's favour. This was indicative of the power struggle between the AA and Wilhelm Keppler, Hitler's economic adviser at the Reich chancellery. Eventually, Hemmen retreated from this and proposed an agreement based on £1.5 million of German exports and £500,000 of Irish exports, instead of the £500,000 and £117,000 proposed before the Irish delegation had arrived in Berlin. The Irish refused to countenance such an alteration, because they regarded the offer as a 'red herring introduced for the purpose of prolonging the discussions' especially because every possible category of goods was involved in the latest German offer, not only cattle and coal.[38] Besides, the Irish side was worried that Germany lacked sufficient currency to be able to pay for this increase in trade. Next Hemmen raised another obstacle by claiming Germany preferred to export industrial goods rather than coal, although he knew Ireland needed coal. Faced with a demonstrable lack of co-operation, de Valera and the relevant ministers decided to adopt an unyielding position despite the urgent need to export cattle from the glutted Irish market. They were not prepared to negotiate any other types of compensation agreement than the provisional £500,000-worth of coal for

---

33 NAI, DFA 314/10/6/3, executive council: German negotiations, 2 Oct. 1934.   34 Ibid., 'Brief note on Saorstát–German trade negotiations', 10 Oct. 1934; ibid., 'Saorstát–German trade negotiations', 12 Oct. 1934.   35 Ibid., Dehn–Walshe, 19 Oct. 1934.   36 Ibid., Walshe–Dehn, 25 Oct. 1934.   37 Ibid.   38 Ibid., Walshe–de Valera, 19 Oct. 1934.

£117,000-worth of cattle initially agreed on. The year 1931 was designated as the base year for German-Irish trade for the purposes of the agreement and:

> If German offer of quotas for 1935, which will be known by mid-November, is unsatisfactory, immediate arrangements will then be made to exclude German coal except in so far as covered by the Compensation Agreement and drastic steps will be taken against other imports from Germany. If [the] compensation agreement on this basis [is] not accepted by Germany [the] delegation should return home immediately.[39]

But the German team wanted to establish 1934 as the base year for Irish-German trade and wanted to stabilize the ratio of trade between Germany and the Saorstát at the 1934 level. In 1934 the trade balance was 10 to 1 in Germany's favour according to German statistics, and 17 to 1 in Germany's favour according to Irish statistics. Germany refused to accept 1931 as the base year, and the Saorstát refused to accept otherwise.[40] The Irish government was determined not to repeat the mistake of November 1933 when Germany had been given a contract for sugar factory machinery without extra exports to Germany being secured as a *quid pro quo*. The talks were in jeopardy.[41]

The Germans' next move was to offer what the Irish believed to be £700,000-worth of coal or 1.2 million tons, for £117,000 worth of cattle as the special compensation deal for 1934. When it appeared that the Irish might withdraw from the negotiations because it was not the £500,000 to £117,000 compensation agreement that they had been sent to Berlin to finalize, the German delegation claimed the Irish had misinterpreted them and the offer was actually 700,000 tons of coal for £117,000 worth of cattle to be exchanged over the months of November and December. Hemmen said that 'he had always spoken in tons, as he did not understand pounds'. The 600,000 tons was equivalent to £500,000 worth of coal. The Germans wanted the Irish to take an extra 100,000 tons of coal for the months of November and December, but persisted in rejecting the Irish proposal that 1931 be the base year for future trade negotiations. At this stage the German negotiators had not even declared the number of cattle they were willing to import for £117,000.[42]

On 19 November 1934 the Irish delegation was ordered home immediately if the Germans persisted in refusing to accept 1931 as the base year, 'without informing [the] Germans whether any measures ... [were] to be taken against their imports in retaliation for their unreasonableness',[43] because 'there was no possibility of making an agreement without disproportionate concessions on

---

39 Ibid., Dublin–Berlin, tel. 48, 23 Oct. 1934.   40 Ibid., Bewley–Walshe, 2 Nov. 1934.
41 Ibid., Bewley–Walshe, 7 Nov. 1936.   42 Ibid., Bewley–Walshe, 9 Nov. 1934; ibid., Bewley–Walshe, 12 Nov. 1934.   43 Ibid., Dublin–Berlin, tel. 52, 19 Nov. 1934.

our side'.[44] A fruitless month had been spent in Berlin.[45] It was a tactic calculated to demonstrate to the Germans the Irish willingness to terminate
unfavourable trade talks. The Irish rationale was that Germany must understand the Saorstát was prepared to act on the threats it had made during the past
twelve months and Germany could not hope to take advantage of Ireland's weak
economic situation any longer. As the Berlin negotiations broke down, Hemmen
'expressed the hope that he would soon see our delegates in Berlin to discuss
quotas' for the 1935 Irish-German agreement, the Irish delegates 'expressed no
opinion on the subject'.[46] Instead it was the turn of Germany to adopt the role
of supplicant in an attempt to reverse the deterioration in Irish-German trade
negotiations.[47]

PLAYING THE GERMAN AND BRITISH CARDS

It is tempting to accept the later assertion by John Leydon, secretary of the
department of industry and commerce, that 'we were never able to make any
progress with the Germans until we showed them clearly that we were prepared
to take a firm line and stick to it'.[48] However matters were not so simple. A
German delegation went to Dublin in December 1934 to discuss the quotas for
a possible 1935 Irish-German trade agreement but the talks failed to reach
agreement because of the irreconcilable differences.[49] The prospects for future
Irish-German trade were bleak, yet in January 1935 there was a seemingly
miraculous turnaround.

The key stimulus impelling reconciliation between the Saorstát and
Germany on trade lay in their relations with Britain. Both states were involved
in parallel negotiations with Britain during late 1934. Both Irish and British del-
egations were in Berlin in late October 1934 negotiating with the German
authorities. An Anglo-German payments agreement, signed on 1 November
1934, was seen as an economic 'peace treaty' ending a conflict that had begun in
1933. This ran alongside Hitler's priority to improve Anglo-German political
relations. Nazism's protection of German 'peasants', in accordance with its ide-

---

44 Ibid., Walshe minute, 19 Nov. 1934; ibid., Bewley–Walshe, 23 Nov. 1934.   **45** Contrary
to Dickel's and McMahon's assertion that the Irish delegation remained in Berlin for only
three days (from 16 to 19 October), according to Irish government records the Irish representatives actually negotiated for over one month, they began to negotiate on 16 October and
continued to negotiate until ordered to terminate negotiations on 19 November. See
McMahon, *Republicans*, p. 151; NAI, DFA 314/10/6/3, statement made by Irish delegation
at opening meeting of Saorstát–German trade negotiations, 16 Oct. 1934; ibid., Dublin–
Berlin telegram, 19 Nov. 1934; ibid., Walshe minute, 19 Nov. 1934; ibid., Bewley–Walshe, 23
Nov. 1934.   **46** Ibid., Bewley–Walshe, 23 Nov. 1934.   **47** Ibid., Walshe–de Valera, 11 Dec.
1934.   **48** NAI, DFA 132/81, Leydon–minister, 28 Oct. 1938.   **49** NAI, DFA 314/10/6/3,
Walshe–president, 11 Dec. 1934.

ological belief that the German peasants were the soul of Aryan culture together with Germany's severe foreign currency difficulties, may have constrained the development of Irish-German trade but the dominant constraint was political. Hitler was concerned closer Irish-German trade ties could damage Anglo-German political relations.[50] If Germany took advantage of the Anglo-Irish Economic War to erode British economic influence in the Saorstát, the prospects for Anglo-German rapprochement in the international sphere might be damaged. Until an alleviation of the Anglo-Irish conflict could be achieved, Germany could not offer the Saorstát attractive terms. Simultaneously, of course, Germany could still benefit from the Saorstát desperation to obtain an alternative market.

German officials viewed de Valera as the actor in Dublin most decisive in his pursuit of a substantial alternative market in Germany. But Germany's failure to provide a substantial opening for Irish products weakened de Valera's position among his government colleagues. Powerful and interested ministers, such as Lemass and Ryan, viewed Irish trade diversification as a failed policy. The historian Dickel presents the Irish government as pursuing a Machiavellian two-level strategy in its attempts to play the British and the Germans off against one another for commercial benefit; this is neither a full nor accurate reflection of reality. Irish self-interest did dictate a certain degree of deception to derive the maximum possible benefit in the undesirable context of global economic meltdown, particularly when it was a weak pawn between Germany and Britain. But the Saorstát certainly had no monopoly on such devices. The mistrust and deceptions was reciprocal,[51] unlike the balance of trade between the two countries.

In addition, de Valera had staked considerable personal prestige on the strategy of seeking new markets to undermine British dominance in the Irish economy and to alleviate Ireland's dependence on Britain as an export market. As the Economic War proceeded, the department of industry and commerce and the department of agriculture became increasingly attracted to the idea of a compromise with their counterparts in London. But de Valera's commitment to pursuing the German trade option remained until late 1934, despite increasing dissent from within his own government.

On the British side of the equation calculations were also changing. The British board of trade feared that if the Economic War with Ireland continued for too long, a permanent trade relationship would develop between Ireland and Germany to Britain's cost.[52] The higher sulphur content of German coal was ill

---

50 Dickel, *Aussenpolitik*, p. 34.   51 Dickel's analysis of the Irish-German trade relationship is primarily dependent on German government documentation. Since Irish foreign policy documents were unavailable in large quantities until the 1990s this is understandable, and this documentary gap undoubtedly contributes to his alternative interpretation of events. 52 McMahon, *Republicans*, p. 69.

suited to Irish domestic and industrial appliances.[53] If Irish industry and Irish homes adjusted their appliances to suit German coal, English coal would be permanently excluded from the Irish market aggravating unemployment in the British mining industry.[54] As early as July 1934 the department of overseas trade in Britain worried, 'the longer the dispute continues and the more artificial barriers are imposed between the two countries the smaller will be the volume of trade which will be available for recovery if, and when, the dispute is ended'.[55] Other British exports to Ireland were also affected, especially cement, electrical goods, machinery and chemicals.[56]

J.W. Dulanty, the Irish high commissioner in London, realized the persistence of Economic War also caused anxiety among some British cabinet members who feared the diversion of Irish trade from Britain would become permanent. On 30 October 1934, he approached the dominions office in London with the news that the Saorstát was about to conclude a coal-for-cattle pact with Germany. His intention was to use the threat of a possible Irish-German agreement to secure a change of policy in London. De Valera was unenthusiastic but Lemass and Ryan were supportive.[57] Dulanty's intervention was judicious.[58] The British treasury and the dominions office welcomed the initiative as a means to 'prevent the Irish Free State from forming new and permanently close trade connections with Germany'.[59] The mines department was also anxious to keep the Irish market for its coal and protect the employment of 3,000 miners. It had concluded that the Saorstát was 'a better customer than New Zealand and Canada combined'.[60] As a result of Dulanty's initiative an Anglo-Irish coal–cattle pact was signed on 3 January 1935, three months after it was originally proposed.

This breakthrough in the Anglo-Irish Economic War prompted the Germans to offer a key concession and break the impasse in Irish-German trade negotiations[61] – the value of Saorstát products imported into Germany should be on a ratio of one to three in relation to the value of German goods imported into the Saorstát.[62] The advantageous £1 for £1 Anglo-Irish deal had prompted the German trade negotiators to offer a more attractive package if German coal was to retain its toehold in the Irish market. Furthermore, since Britain was repairing its trade relationship with the Saorstát, Germany could not be accused of trying to benefit from British misfortunes. The German concession also met the Irish demand that 1931 should be the base year for calculating the Irish-German balance of trade.[63] So the Irish-German trade agreement for the year 1935 was a marked improvement from the Irish perspective, the first time the Irish government achieved a reasonable understanding with Nazi Germany on trade matters. The cattle quota was increased from 6,000 head, to which Ireland was

53 Ibid., p. 148.   54 Ibid., pp 110–11, 148.   55 Ibid., p. 149.   56 Ibid., pp 148, 85.
57 Ibid., pp 151–2.   58 Ibid., p. 150.   59 Ibid., p. 151.   60 Ibid.   61 Ibid., p. 152.
62 NAI, DFA 232/1, Hemmen–Lemass, protocol 1, 28 Jan. 1935.   63 Ibid.

entitled to under her most-favoured-nation status, to 15,000 head;[64] and the Saorstát won the right to export goods to Germany worth £1 for every £3-worth imported while the Germans had to compete with other countries to gain an entrance into the Irish market.[65] In addition, the Irish exchequer gained because Irish goods commanded a higher price in Germany than in Britain.[66]

As a consequence of the deal Irish exports to Germany increased from a value of £163,828 in 1934 to £493,982 in 1935, while German exports to Ireland actually fell in value from £2.3 million to £1.4 million.[67] By the end of 1935 Germany was the second largest importer of Irish agricultural produce after Britain. After 1935 the Irish government continued to target the German market for further development although recognising the capacity for market expansion in Germany was limited.[68]

CONCLUSION

Bewley's reports, combined with those emanating from other Irish legations, proved helpful to the Irish government in assessing the changing international balance. But Irish foreign interests at first seemed largely untouched by central European political problems. Irish nationalists may initially have revelled at the precedent of Adolf Hitler overturning the Versailles treaty, attempted to ignore his methods, and drawn superficial comparisons with the Anglo-Irish relationship. But in the longer term it became apparent that Nazism was not a normal form of western European nationalism. Bewley's foreign policy analysis and the general newspaper reportage did not make comfortable reading for the Dublin government as they highlighted the destabilising impact of Nazi foreign policy tactics as well as the radical racial and *Lebensraum* ideas of Hitlerite ideology. Similarly Bewley's reports and Irish newspapers' coverage of Nazi domestic policy, in particular of Christianity and the Catholic Church, emphasized the radical and totalitarian nature of the Third Reich. At this stage the Saorstát's only direct interest in Irish-German relations lay in the fostering the growth of agricultural exports to alleviate the impact of the Anglo-Irish Economic War and reduce Ireland's precarious dependence on the British market. But the Germans were anxious not to upset Britain. There was no escaping the omnipresent Anglo-Irish connection in all aspects of Irish foreign policy in the 1930s, even in central Europe.

After mid-1935, however, the Saorstát also had other reasons to be concerned.

64 Ibid., Protocol No. 2. 65 NAI, DFA 314/10/6/3, Fahy minute, 'German-Saorstát trade agreement', n.d. 66 Ibid., Fahy note, 'Note on Saorstát–German trade position', 19 Feb. 1936. 67 NAI, DFA 232/1, statement issued by the Government Information Bureau, 3 Nov. 1938. 68 NAI, DFA 314/10/6/3, 'Note by the department of external affairs on forthcoming trade discussions with Germany', n.d.

Nazi Germany's transformation inaugurated a period of rapid international change and turmoil that fatally damaged the League of Nations. It could not be an effective tool of collective security, international peacekeeping and reconciliation on which much of Irish foreign policy was based. It was replaced by a pattern of unstable bilateral and multilateral alliances as power shifted from the democratic victors of the Great War (France and Britain) towards the new and revisionist fascist powers of Italy, Germany and Japan. As a parliamentary democracy the Saorstát would soon find it increasingly difficult to reconcile its nationalist conflict with a fellow democracy (Britain); its Catholic sympathies with the rebels against the Spanish republic; its instinctive anti-Communism; and its commercial need to export agricultural produce to Germany with its increasing discontent about the methods Hitler used to pursue superficially sincere nationalist goals. In this difficult foreign policy climate, Charles Bewley had a disturbing dispute with his political masters but there was also to be a convergence of sorts in Anglo–Irish relations.

6

International power politics,
September 1935–August 1937

'For myself I needed no argument to convince me that National Socialism whatever might be its defects, should be upheld by the Western Powers as the strongest, perhaps the only, force which could prevent the spread of the Communist Empire over half Europe ...'[1]

'[T]he official policy [of the Nazi party is] ... based on the knowledge that the masses without democratic ideas, leadership or organisation can always be controlled by a small fanatical and resolute body in the big positions. It is unnecessary to point out the resemblance to the Soviet system, to which the similarity in ultimate aim as well as in methods seems to be continually increasing.'[2]

By late 1935 a major conjuncture in interwar international relations restored the old balance of power system as the Versailles settlement collapsed. The grievances of revisionist or anti-status quo powers (Italy, Germany and Japan), nationalist ambitions and ideological conflict polarized Europe and the Far East. The League, already suffering progressive paralysis from institutional flaws, national self-interest and power politics, was humiliatingly proven ineffectual when it failed to prevent Mussolini's invasion of Abyssinia and foreign interventions in the Spanish Civil War. Hitler then openly remilitarized the Rhineland in contravention of the treaty of Versailles. Multilateralism declined as mistrust and realpolitik thrived, necessitating an adjustment in Irish foreign policy. This chapter places Irish-German relations in the context of these dramatic international shifts.

De Valera's initial reservations of 1932 concerning the League's efficacy were confirmed. Although he supported the League position during the Abyssinian crisis he began subsequently to distance the Free State from the League, strove for Irish neutrality, and urged a general European settlement to conciliate the aggrieved powers of continental Europe and avoid a general European conflict. The Spanish Civil War, in actuality a local internecine and domestic event, animated and divided an already ideologically riven Europe, offering a testing ground for a future war. These events transformed Irish and German foreign policy. A disillusioned de Valera redirected Irish foreign policy away from failed

---

1 Bewley, *Memoirs*, pp 124–5. 2 NAI, DFA, CRS 19/50A, Bewley–Walshe, 25 Apr. 1935.

multilateralism and collective security towards securing Irish freedom of manoeuvre vis-à-vis Britain as a precaution against entanglement in a European war. Ending British access to the Treaty ports and distancing the Free State constitutionally from the British Commonwealth was the ultimate objective.

Although the autarky, or striving for economic self-sufficiency, enforced by the Anglo-Irish Economic War had boosted industrialization and increased national self-reliance to some degree, it was cumulatively a costly failure. Both the Irish and British governments were now prepared to negotiate reconciliation on trade which, once achieved, diminished Irish interest in gaining access to German markets. De Valera's programme of constitutional detachment from the Commonwealth continued so that by 1937 he could complete the process with a new Irish constitution establishing an Irish republic in all but name. The British government, particularly under the guidance of Neville Chamberlain, proved conciliatory because it wanted to ensure the amiability of its western neighbour in case of a European war. In practice, the British search for a general settlement with Ireland paralleled its search for one with Germany. The general improvement in Anglo-Irish relations during the latter 1930s was driven by British political and strategic necessity.

Meanwhile, Bewley experienced Nazi Germany's new assertive foreign policy firsthand. His mentality altered in tandem with the fundamental shifts in European affairs. Previously Bewley had evinced unguarded admiration for Nazi Germany, rigid anti-Communism, fervent detestation of Britain, and a degree of religious or social anti-Semitism. Although his attitudes had sometimes coloured his perspective and his actions they had not attracted undue attention from his masters in Dublin. His were not unusual predispositions on the wider European (or even the Irish) stage. On the whole, his performance until late 1935 was deemed adequate, but quite unexceptional. There had been hints of unreliability and, on occasion, tension with Walshe.

By contrast, beginning with the Italo–Abyssinian war, his later conduct in Berlin was exceptional for entirely negative reasons. His anti-Communism and Anglophobia became amplified, distorting his interpretation of the general European situation and the Irish role within it. His reading of Irish national interests and his policy prescriptions for augmenting Irish independence internationally were now entirely predicated on those two axioms. Bewley wholeheartedly embraced the Nazi dictum that Nazism was the only reliable bulwark against the spread of Communism and resignedly accepted Nazism's persecution of Christianity. He also internalized the fascist critique of democracies as intrinsically weak-willed and decadent states infiltrated by left-wing and liberal ideologies. This merged with an extreme Anglophobic strain of Irish nationalism to which he had been prone since at least the early 1920s, and led him to view any defeat or sign of weakness emanating from London as beneficial to Dublin. He adopted a more extreme republican and assertive agenda for Irish foreign policy than did de Valera.

Bewley rejected the direction of de Valera's foreign policy that emphasized multilateralism in 1935 and during much of 1936 as a means to secure Irish international independence and establish Ireland as an international good citizen. He also disliked de Valera's drift towards neutrality after 1935, and the suggestion that Ireland accord 'special consideration' to Britain. Instead Bewley proposed a complete disassociation of Ireland from the British sphere of influence and condemned any hint of congruence between Irish and British foreign policy. His fear was that Ireland would be construed as pro-British by his German acquaintances in Berlin. So Bewley proposed that de Valera should reverse his policy of sanctions against Italy (during the Italo-Abyssinian war), intervene in Spain on the side of General Franco, and withdraw totally from what Bewley viewed as collaboration with Britain in the League. Bewley's progressively truculent recommendations to this effect did not accord with de Valera's foreign policy. In consequence, Bewley's relationship with headquarters deteriorated alongside the worsening international climate and as the Irish government grew more critical of Nazi domestic policies and Nazi activities in the Free State.

Despite these circumstances, in the period after the first Anglo-Irish coal–cattle pact was signed in 1935, Germany became entrenched as Ireland's second largest trading partner after Britain. Germany did not offer a very sizeable market but the Irish found that they could gain a more favourable balance of trade with Germany than with any country other than Britain. Irish attempts to develop the Belgian and US markets had failed to produce results. Thus a strong preference for trade diversification to Germany developed despite the Irish government's increasing doubts concerning the nature of Nazism. It was perhaps in the trade arena that Bewley maintained his strongest input into Irish policy at this time, although the AA's trade section did not take him seriously.

CHURCH–STATE RELATIONS

In deference to Irish interests, Bewley continued to keep a close watch on relations between the Nazi state and the Catholic Church. In October 1935 the Catholic bishop of Meissen was arrested suddenly on charges of currency smuggling. The relevant laws were exceedingly technical and complicated and had been generally disregarded, according to Bewley. But the authorities were now discovering their usefulness 'for the purpose of bringing charges against their political enemies'.[3] The following month saw the arrest of several other Catholic ecclesiastical dignitaries for unspecified reasons. Increasingly suggestions were being made that Catholics were in league with Communists. The

---

3 Ibid., 18 Oct. 1935.

University of Jena awarded a literature prize to an ex-Dominican for a scandalous book on his two years in the order.[4] Nonetheless, the hierarchy of the German Catholic Church continued to co-operate in the vain hope that the attack on Christianity and Catholicism as belief systems and institutions would be ameliorated.[5] Bewley recognized that, in particular, the treatment of Meissen's bishop was 'a clear breach of the concordat, but the Holy See would appear to have no remedy except at the cost of a total breach with the German government, which it is obviously anxious to avoid as long as possible'. A rupture at this particular point would simply feed Nazi anti-Catholic propaganda.[6]

The Protestant churches were under even more severe onslaughts at this time. The recently appointed minister for ecclesiastical affairs, Hans Kerrl, concentrated in the latter months of 1935 on consolidating the Protestant churches and imposing the Nazi view of 'positive Christianity' to transform them all into 'Deutsche Christen'.[7] Hitler was still exercising some restraint over his followers against conducting an overt *Kulturkampf*.[8] He was unwilling to launch a full frontal assault on religious institutions that still could depend on the allegiance of so many Germans.

THE NUREMBERG LAWS

Bewley did not extend his concern about religion to the fate of Jews during 1935 and 1936 when events in Nazi Germany gave him an opportunity to do so. On 15 September 1935 the Nuremberg laws further institutionalized the 'biological-racist anti-Semitism' of the Nazis under the Reichsburgergesetz ('The Reich Citizenship Act') and the Blutschutzgesetz ('The Blood Protection Act'). Respectively these denied German citizenship to Jews, and outlawed marriage or extra-marital relations between Jews and nationals of German or allied blood. The legislation continued the progressive exclusion of the Jewish minority from everyday German life. Jews were transformed into aliens with lesser rights than the rest of the population. Anti-Semitism was now codified in German law and discrimination was both legal and official.[9]

Bewley's reports on the Nuremberg laws proved to be perfidious. On the Reichsburgergesetz, he said: 'As the Chancellor pointed out, it amounts to the making of the Jews into a national minority; and as they themselves claim to be a separate race, they should have nothing to complain of.'[10] The Blutschutzgesetz's derogatory provision that Jews should not be allowed to give domestic employment to non-Jewesses under the age of 45 years found Bewley

4 Ibid., 4 Dec. 1935.   5 Lewy, *Catholic Church*, pp 129–30.   6 NAI, DFA CRS 19/50A, Bewley–Walshe, 4 Dec. 1935.   7 Ibid., 18 Oct. 1935 & 4 Dec. 1935.   8 Bracher, *German dictatorship*, p. 474.   9 H. Krausnick, 'The persecution of the Jews', in Krausnick & Broszat, *Anatomy*, pp 50–5.   10 NAI, DFA, CRS 19/50A, Bewley–Walshe, 17 Sept. 1935.

agreeing with the Nazi pretext that non-Jewess domestics were in very grave moral danger. To his mind a perusal of the criminal reports in the German press indicated there was indeed such a danger. He was effectively using the Nazi-inspired press propaganda to provide supporting evidence for Nazi party policy, yet in the same report he dismissed released German public finance figures as fabrications.[11] This inconsistent use of evidence by Bewley must be attributed to an anti-Semitic belief system. The *Irish Press* and *Irish Times*, although reliant on agency copy, provided a far more accurate and objective assessment of the Nuremberg laws than did Bewley.[12]

In November 1935, commenting on publication of the orders necessary to implement the Nuremberg laws, Bewley claimed they were 'somewhat milder than might have been expected'. He led Dublin to believe that one of the concessions made included the definition of Jewishness whereby 'One whose ancestry is half non-Jewish counts as a non-Jew'. Half non-Jewish was calculated on the basis of an individual having two non-Jewish grandparents. He suggested, too, that the lowering of the permitted age of non-Jewish female domestic servants in Jewish households from 45 years to 35 years was a concession. 'Whether this is later changed again will depend on whether the behaviour of Jewish householders towards their female servants is better in the future than it has been in the past'.[13] Bewley and the Irish government were soon to have the opportunity to assess the practical impact of these laws in a case closer to home.

In mid-November 1935 Professor Pokorny, who held the Kuno Meyer's chair of Indo-Germanic Philology and Celtic Studies at Berlin University, was again suspended from his position. He had already been suspended and then reinstated in 1933.[14] The move was not unexpected. In a letter to his old friend Dr Irvine Best of Ireland's National Library in October, Pokorny said he was pessimistic about retaining his chair: 'scientific considerations have nothing to do with it. It is merely a question of "blood and race"'. He suspected that Dr Ludwig Mühlhausen of Hamburg University who had tried to take advantage of his previous suspension in 1933 wanted his job, although his scholarly credentials were mediocre. Pokorny said, 'They [the Nazis] might just spare me, for diplomatic reasons, but I have no great hopes'.[15] Pokorny's letters captured the fear and intimidation that he and others labelled as 'non-Aryans' were subjected to in Germany. He implored Best to 'be careful in talking to friends – a little slip, and they have spies everywhere'.[16] Pokorny was suspicious that Dr Adolf Mahr, a fellow Austrian who was director of Ireland's National Museum in Dublin, was a Nazi. Pokorny's fears were justified because it later emerged that Mahr was the head of the Nazi Auslandsorganisation in Dublin and Ireland.[17]

---

11 Ibid. 12 Keogh, *Jews*, pp 102–3. 13 NAI, DFA, CRS 19/50A, Bewley–Walshe, 19 Nov. 1935. 14 NAI, DT, S. 8981, Gogan–McDunphy, 11 June 1936; NLI, Best papers, MS11003 (8), P [Pokorny]–B [Best], 21 Oct. 1935. 15 Ibid. 16 Ibid. 17 Keogh, *Jews*, pp 105–6.

Pokorny appealed for Irish diplomatic intervention because he considered informal Irish representations in 1933 had been instrumental in his reinstatement. The department instructed Bewley that de Valera had decided:

> that some démarche on the Professor's behalf is called for from the Saorstát Government. He fully recognises that an official démarche would be out of place, but he wishes you to make unofficial representations in the proper quarter – presumably the Foreign Office – on the following lines:
>
> The Chair of Celtic Philology in Berlin University that Professor Pokorny has filled with such distinction during the past fifteen years, is naturally of great interest and importance from the point of view of the Irish Government. In view of the Professor's long association with Celtic Studies and his close relations with Celtic scholars and students in this country, the Irish Government would regard it as a generous gesture if the German Government would see their way to allowing the Professor to retain his post.[18]

Pokorny, however, was suspended in late December.[19] Either de Valera's intervention was insufficient or Bewley had failed accurately to represent the views of the Irish government. Despite some further communications from Pokorny through unofficial channels, no further Irish action was taken on his behalf. Dr Ludwig Mühlhausen, Pokorny's old rival, was appointed to replace him at Berlin University.[20]

It was clear that Pokorny harboured the suspicion that Bewley had not been a strong or helpful advocate.[21] Incontrovertible evidence was soon to emerge of Bewley's deteriorating ability to accurately represent his government's nuanced views because of his own extremist views.

BEWLEY AND 'ENGLAND'

Bewley's attitude to Britain became central at this point, as Britain fruitlessly endeavoured to halt the deterioration in the international climate. Bewley's misgivings about Britain's influence in Berlin had long been transparent and the pragmatic pro-British sympathies of the Germans, and the AA in particular, served to inflame them.

The Nazis' racialist worldview reinforced Germany's pre-existing admiration of Britain. Aspirant nationalists within the British empire had to contend with British resistance, but also with incomprehension and even hostility from large

---

18 NAI, DFA, Berlin letterbooks, Walshe-Bewley, 16 Nov. 1935. **19** NLI, Best papers, MS 11003(8), P (Pokorny)–B (Best), 1 May 1936. **20** O'Donoghue, *Hitler's Irish voices*, p. xvi. **21** NAI, DT, S. 8981, P. Uinrighthe (Pokorny)–Gogan, 9 June 1936.

European states such as France and Germany. Britain was the dominant world power engaged in Europe given the isolationism of the powerful USA. Irish freedom of action was narrowed considerably. As early as 26 February 1934, the Nazi ideologue Rosenberg who was head of the party's foreign affairs department, told Bewley: 'England is our only possible ally: why should we run any risk for the sake of Ireland which is very remote from us?'[22]

It was not unusual for Bewley to refer to German anglophilia in his diplomatic reports.[23] On 8 November 1934, he had recorded that the German people, government and press were exceptionally 'obsequious' 'to everything English' to gain English sympathy. Bewley correctly judged that in such an environment it was extremely unlikely that the AA would grant Ireland trade concessions to ease the effects of the Anglo-Irish Economic War.[24] The most stable feature of German foreign policy, Bewley noted, was its concerted attempts to ingratiate itself with Britain.[25] Bewley's antipathy towards 'England' and 'Englishness' grew during 1935.

His frustration grew as the Nazi regime showed no sign of altering its cordial policy towards Britain although there was no sign of the long awaited Anglo-German 'special relationship'. Hitler's stubborn pursuit of Anglo-German understanding reduced Germany's interaction with Ireland to a simple calculus predicated on the Anglo-German relationship. By mid-1935, Bewley's inability to convince Berlin that Ireland should be treated independently of German diplomatic calculations concerning Britain maddened him. He concluded it was impossible to disabuse Nazism of its belief that Britain clandestinely fully supported Germany's foreign policies due to the doctrine of the common aims of the Aryan race, and the 'German psychology appears to be the slave to its own theories'.[26]

He attacked alleged British anti-Catholic tendencies, saying Britain would never intervene to aid German Catholics as it did for Protestants, Freemasons and Jews. The editor of the *Deutsche Allgemeine Zeitung* later told Bewley that 'England was so powerful that Germany could not afford to disregard any chance of obtaining her friendship'. Bewley responded 'that England has always in the past proved a treacherous ally and that her traditional policy had always been to support one European state against another, herself holding the balance of power'.[27] 'Perfidious Albion' was a central construct in his outlook.[28] His omnipresent distrust of Britain clouded his judgment.

Bewley's antipathy towards Britain became a problem particularly as Anglo-Irish relations began to improve, beginning with the coal and cattle pact in 1936. Bewley's boycott of the king's jubilee celebrations in 1935 antagonized the

22 NAI, DFA, CRS 19/50A, Bewley–Walshe, 26 Feb. 1934.   23 For example, NAI, DFA, CRS 19/50, Bewley–Walshe, 5 July 1934.   24 NAI, DFA, CRS 19/50, Bewley–Walshe, 8 Nov. 1934.   25 NAI, DFA, CRS 19/50A, Bewley–Walshe, 10 Jan. 1935.   26 Ibid., 2 May 1935.   27 Ibid., 28 Mar. 1936.   28 Ibid., 10 Mar. 1936.

foreign office in London.[29] Previously English relatives of Bewley's who occupied senior positions in the British civil service had sustained a relatively
positive image of him in London despite his political indiscretions.[30] But
Bewley's absence from the jubilee celebrations triggered a rapidly deteriorating
foreign office estimation of him.[31] It was ironic that his absence from the celebrations was in accordance with explicit instructions from Dublin to attend only
those functions at which members of the diplomatic corps other than the representatives of the states of the Commonwealth were present because de Valera
wanted some distance.[32]

The death of King George V on 20 January 1936 was the occasion for another
Irish effort to distinguish the Free State from other Commonwealth countries.
De Valera preferred that, as far as possible, the Free State should act as if it were
an ordinary independent state that had no special association with Britain. This
meant not attending Commonwealth gatherings that paid homage or respect to
the monarchy, while continuing to engage with the Commonwealth on many
practical matters.[33]

However, Bewley requested further clarification about attendance at official
diplomatic and social functions after a query from the AA protocol officer.
Walshe and de Valera wished to settle such potentially controversial issues 'in
the most non-committal way possible' and to be able to take the circumstances
of each case into account. If it seemed absolutely necessary to respect local
German tradition Bewley should inform the protocol officer that he would not
attend official engagements for four weeks and thus avoid functions within the
prescribed period of mourning in Germany for the death of a sovereign in a
state with which Germany had full diplomatic relations. Walshe said of de
Valera:

> The Minister is exceedingly anxious that our representatives abroad
> should, while observing the usual courtesies, abstain as far as possible
> from any appearance of solidarity with the British Embassy. He does not
> understand why there should be greater need in Berlin than elsewhere for
> a formal statement of mourning.[34]

The tenor of Bewley's request for instructions, and Dublin's response, indicate
Bewley was unimpressed by this low-key rejection of the British king as sovereign of the Free State.

29 Duggan, *Neutral Ireland*, p. 30.   30 J.P. Duggan, 'Foreword: The career of a sport' in
Bewley, *Memoirs*.   31 If, as Duggan suggests, the foreign office took until 1935 to real-
ize that Bewley was fundamentally anti-English this was extraordinary in light of his earlier
behaviour in Rome. 32 NAI, DFA Berlin letterbooks, Walshe–Bewley, 15 Apr. 1935;
McMahon, *Republicans*, p. 159.   33 McMahon, *Republicans*, pp 170–1.   34 NAI, DFA
Berlin letterbooks, Walshe–Bewley, 3 Feb. 1936.

Bewley in any case persisted in minimising his contact with the British embassy[35] as he had while in Rome. Bewley's simmering anti-Englishness, united with his intense anti-Communism and an extreme genre of Irish nationalism ultimately, led him to reject the course of de Valera's foreign policy.

THE LEAGUE'S 'FINAL TEST'

Nonetheless, Bewley presented a sound review of German geopolitical calculations until the end of 1935 following Mussolini's invasion of Abyssinia.[36] Despite Mussolini's estrangement from Hitler, Germany dissociated from League of Nations' sanctions against Italy and adopted a neutral public attitude to Mussolini's imperial adventure.[37] Italy's rupture with its Stresa Front allies was an encouraging development from Hitler's standpoint.[38]

As early as October 1935 Bewley had speculated about a rapprochement between Italy and Germany.[39] Hitler required an ally in case his policy of cultivating Britain failed. According to Bewley, 'the German Government wishes to keep a line of retreat, which would naturally take the form of an alliance with the discontented and revisionist countries of Europe, that is, Poland, Hungary, and Italy'.[40] German antipathy towards the League as an oppressive entangling alliance led by the Anglo-French victors of the Great War was another consideration.[41] Germany would benefit from providing vital military and fuel supplies to Italy undermining League sanctions and earning the gratitude of Mussolini.[42] Additionally, Bewley calculated 'if Italy succeeds in obtaining a colony by virtue of her over-population it would be a most valuable precedent for Germany, and therefore every effort has been made to do nothing which might in any way hamper Italy's policy'.[43] Thus during the Abyssinian crisis Bewley indicated Germany maintained a benevolent neutrality. Mussolini, grateful for Hitler's support in the face of international criticism and isolation, 'signalled ... he had nothing against Austria in effect becoming a satellite of Germany',[44] in January 1936. A new axis of diplomacy was emerging about which Bewley kept Dublin reasonably well informed.

According to his memoirs, it was during the Italo-Abyssinian crisis in 1935 that Bewley formed dissident perceptions of Irish foreign policy for the first time.[45] Indeed, the Italo-Abyssinian crisis proved to be a watershed for Bewley, de Valera's foreign policy and the League of Nations. After almost a year of aggressive Italian activity, Italian troops invaded Abyssinia on 3 October 1935. Two member nations of the League were now engaged in conflict that

35 Duggan, *Neutral Ireland*, p. 30. 36 NAI, DFA CRS 19/50A, Bewley–Walshe, 17 Sept. 1935 & 9 Oct. 1935. 37 Ibid., 17 Sept. 1935. 38 Ibid., 9 Oct. 1935 & 18 Oct. 1935. 39 Ibid., 9 Oct. 1935. 40 Ibid., 9 Oct. 1935. 41 Ibid., 18 Oct. 1935. 42 Ibid., 9 Oct. 1935. 43 Ibid., 17 Sept. 1935. 44 Kershaw, *Hubris*, p. 583. 45 Bewley, *Memoirs*, p. 166.

threatened the League's credibility. The League responded by trying to bargain with Mussolini and, when this failed, applied economic sanctions. The sanctions lacked strength because of the difficulty involved in winning a consensus between the many members of the League, some of whom were quite sympathetic to Mussolini.[46] The resultant weak sanctions and lack of unity of will among the League members caused limited damage to the Italian economy and war effort because crucial oil was not included in the embargo.[47]

Within seven months Mussolini was victorious in spite of the initial resistance offered by the basic Abyssinian army. Mussolini's imperialist victory and his ability to withstand the disapproval of the League legitimized the use of force as a tolerable tool in international politics by European fascist governments.

Throughout the crisis, de Valera was a stalwart of international morality and a supporter of the League. Although critical of the League, he considered it the only existing instrument capable of solving international disputes through 'reason and justice rather than force'.[48] He told the League Assembly in September 1935, when the Italian invasion appeared inevitable, that its conduct during the crisis would determine whether the League was 'worthy to survive'. The Covenant of the League which safeguarded the sovereignty and security of all of its members, including, Abyssinia, had to be upheld.[49] Otherwise the League would be defunct and international affairs would revert to the 'law of the jungle',[50] which would be injurious to virtually defenceless states such as Ireland.

Once the attempts to broker an agreement between Italy and Abyssinia failed and war broke out in October, de Valera supported the collective security principle. He supported the implementation of economic sanctions in the face of considerable domestic opposition. If sanctions failed to enforce Mussolini's withdrawal, de Valera publicly advocated the application of more rigorous measures including the use of collective force against Italy.[51] He cooperated closely with Britain at the League to garner support for the implementation of sanctions and Ireland duly implemented the sanctions against Mussolini's Italy.[52] The German press made limited mention of the Irish application of sanctions in a 'humorous article' under the heading of 'Ireland's harmless sanctions. Three elderly camels and an old cannon boat'. The article in question then proceeded to cite de Valera's statement that the sanctions would mean economic sacrifices for the Free State![53]

Initially, Bewley voiced no open dissent against de Valera's chosen course. Instead he cited the views of acquaintances in the diplomatic corps. It is curious that these views of critics of Ireland's Abyssinian policy were remarkably similar to ones he later voiced. In October 1935, for instance, Bewley reported the

46 R. Lamb, *Mussolini & the British* (London, 1997), p. 129.   **47** M. Gilbert, *Britain & Germany between the wars* (London, 1976, 2nd ed.), p. 32.   **48** De Valera, *Peace*, p. 43. **49** Ibid., p. 45.   **50** Ibid., p. 43.   **51** Ibid., pp 49–53.   **52** Keatinge, *Formulation*, pp 23–4. **53** NAI, DFA CRS 19/50A, Bewley–Walshe, 4 Dec. 1935.

views of the Italian ambassador in Berlin. The ambassador considered the anti-Italian attitude of the League a product of 'English influence' and that the League's secretariat was 'entirely under English and Masonic influence'.[54] The Italian was surprised that Ireland unconditionally supported the British policy on sanctions.[55] He was perplexed by the British refusal to accept Mussolini's declarations that Italian interests in Abyssinia would not harm British interests. Bewley continued:

> My own opinion is that Italians ascribe too much importance to purely material considerations in considering England's attitude, and not enough to the fact that England's policy is very largely dictated in addition to strategic considerations by the fundamentally anti-Catholic and Masonic character of the English philosophy.[56]

It was the Argentine minister in Berlin, Mr Labougle, who was the final catalyst in transforming Bewley's thinking in November 1935. Labougle had attended the sanctions debate at the League in 1935. He and other Latin Americans were unpleasantly surprised that Ireland concurred with the British policy of sanctions against Italy, when they were expecting a different point of view. Labougle, according to Bewley, said, 'Your prime minister showed himself more English than the English themselves'.[57] The Irish envoy reported the Argentinian's impressions, affecting 'some hesitation' in his role as a regretful but dutiful diplomat transmitting a message which could have grave implications for his state's foreign policy.[58] His memoirs state this was the occasion when he 'realized the value of de Valera to Great Britain' for the first time, and 'understood why the British Government had always treated him with indulgence in spite of the patriotic speeches which he delivered for the benefit of the Irish voter'.[59] Bewley's aversion to any impression that Ireland was Britain's lapdog during the Italo-Abyssinian crisis had a profound impact that ultimately transformed him into a trenchant critic of Irish foreign policy during 1936. On 11 November 1935, Seán Lester, League high commissioner in Danzig, noted in his diary that Bewley 'is more anti-English than pro-Irish. Also anti-League and even condemns de Valera for carrying out Ireland's obligations under the Covenant in the Abyssinian dispute'.[60]

54 Ibid., 9 Oct. 1935. **55** Ibid., 12 Nov. 1935. **56** Ibid., 9 Oct. 1935. **57** Bewley, *Memoirs*, p. 166. Argentina voted for the sanctions against Italy with no intention of imposing them, instead of stating its pro-Italian sentiments initially (NAI, DFA, CRS 19/50A, Bewley–Walshe, 27 Nov. 1935). **58** NAI, DFA, CRS 19/50A, Bewley–Walshe, 27 Nov. 1935. **59** Bewley, *Memoirs*, p. 166. **60** Seán Lester diary, 11 Nov. 1935 cited in Keogh, *Ireland & Europe*, p. 59. Lester was the League of Nations high commissioner in Danzig (1934–7) and the former Irish permanent delegate to the League. Bewley held a correspondingly low opinion of Lester because Lester not alone adopted an anti-Nazi stance but was supported by Britain in carrying it out in Danzig.

When the news leaked in December 1935 that the British and French foreign ministers, Hoare and Laval, had formed a pact to force Emperor Haile Selassie to cede part of his territory to Italy in return for Mussolini's cessation of hostilities, public opinion was shocked. The 'two-sided (not to say two-faced) policy'[61] pursued by Britain and France in the making of this pact reinforced Bewley's 'perfidious Albion' beliefs. Britain had provided leadership for the League's sanctions policy against Italy, but it also had in view the upcoming British general election and feared a possible retaliatory attack from Italy in the Mediterranean. Rewarding Mussolini for aggression, as the pact did, was not popular. Sir Samuel Hoare was forced to resign although the British cabinet as a whole had endorsed the peace plan. The infamous Anglo-French attempt to reconstitute the Stresa Front with Italy failed miserably, discrediting the European democracies in the process.[62] Hitler's benevolence towards Mussolini throughout the conquest of Abyssinia earned him the Italian dictator's gratitude.

The Hoare–Laval pact also served to quicken Bewley's transformation into an open critic of Irish foreign policy. By March 1936, as Mussolini's armies engaged in the conquest of Abyssinia, Bewley voiced his opinions openly, firstly in an interview with de Valera at the beginning of the month, and then in a diplomatic report.[63] He made the negative impact of Ireland's League policy (and its association with Britain) on German perceptions of Ireland the basis for his critique. From a racial and social point of view most Germans, Bewley claimed, experienced difficulty in accepting that Ireland did not want to remain a member of the 'British empire'. They could not believe that the Free State opposed, as Bewley termed it, 'English domination'. The similarity of Irish and British foreign policies towards the Italian invasion of Abyssinia reinforced the German 'impression' of Irish dependence on Britain. The Irish introduction of sanctions against Italy was seen as compliance with British wishes:

> Most unfortunately the fact that Saorstát Éireann acquiesced in the English programme of sanctions against Italy is assumed to be a confirmation of the German opinion that Ireland admits the rightness of English international policy and will always follow it in the long run. I am afraid that it will take a long time to live down this impression.[64]

Arising from his interaction with the Italian ambassador he believed there was also a prevalent view abroad that Ireland had voted for the League sanctions because it was intimidated by Britain.[65]

---

61 P.M.H. Bell, *The origins of the Second World War in Europe* (Harlow, 1997, 2nd ed.), p. 231.
62 Brendon, *Dark valley*, p. 275. See also Lamb, *Mussolini*, pp 129–54.   63 NAI, DFA, CRS 19/50A, Bewley–Walshe, 28 Mar. 1936.   64 Ibid.   65 Ibid.

REMILITARIZING THE RHINELAND

When Hitler ordered the successful, unilateral remilitarization of the Rhineland in March 1936, Bewley's interpretive powers finally and totally failed. Hitler took advantage of the destruction of the Stresa Front and the British preoccupation with Abyssinia to present this next brazen coup. Unfortunately, Bewley erroneously suggested that an Anglo-German cabal connived at the remilitarization.[66] He persisted in this fiction throughout April.[67] He even suggested Britain had precipitated the crisis by engineering the fall of the Laval government in France 'which was in favour of a rapprochement with Germany and Italy against the Soviet Pact'. Britain, he supposed, had brought Léon Blum's Popular Front government to power in France which immediately signed a pact with the Soviet Union.[68] On 8 April 1936 Bewley posited that 'it seems more and more clear that the occupation [remilitarization] was definitely connived at by the British Government'. Germany's return to the League of Nations, a possible Anglo-German air pact, and the ending of German demands for the return of its pre-Great War colonies were the price of British assistance to Germany, Bewley speculated.[69] Bewley's interpretive lapse would not have been so serious if his Irish counterpart in Paris, Art O'Brien, had been an effective analyst of the European situation and French foreign policy.[70] Bewley's misrepresentation of the causes of the Rhineland's remilitarization must be taken in tandem with events in Abyssinia.

IN THE WAKE OF ABYSSINIA

Bewley was by now effectively recommending a complete turnaround in Irish foreign policy. In this undertaking he impinged on the foreign policy formulation process that was jealously guarded by Walshe, as secretary of external affairs, and de Valera. Walshe considered this sphere of decisionmaking beyond the competence of diplomats in the field. Bewley prescribed a new Irish foreign policy whose aim was to rectify perceptions of Ireland in fascist Europe. Ireland should act solely on the basis of its own national interests, Bewley said, which should be defined as in opposition to Britain, irrespective of who was the guilty party in the Abyssinian crisis. International morality, justice and idealism had no place in Bewley's recommendations for Irish foreign policy. Nor did he consider that Abyssinia, like Ireland, was a small and vulnerable state. He said:

66 Ibid., Bewley–Walshe, 8 Apr. 1936. 67 Ibid. 68 Ibid., 18 Mar. 1936. 69 Ibid., 8 Apr. 1936. 70 R. Patterson, 'Ireland and France: an analysis of diplomatic relations, 1929–1950' (unpublished MA dissertation, UCC, 1993), p. 60.

Presumably in considering a question of this kind the only matter to be taken into consideration is the interest, material and moral, of Saorstát Éireann, and neither a belief in the justice of the Italian case nor sympathy for Abyssinia should be allowed to have any influence. Judged from this point of view I would suggest that Ireland is for once in a position to give a lead to the rest of the world, and to proclaim her independence of British policy in a dramatic way which would impress international public opinion more than years of propaganda; also to secure the lasting friendship of the one great Catholic power in the world at the present day.[71]

Bewley persisted in his calls for 'a definite and vigorous anti-English policy' throughout mid-1936 to correct Germany's misinterpretation of Irish foreign policy as pro-British.[72] In April 1936, he highlighted the export of agricultural products and livestock from Germany to Italy, adding an economic dimension to his anti-sanctionist convictions: 'it would seem to follow that the only practical effect of the "sanctions" imposed by Saorstát Éireann has been to deprive the Irish farmer of his legitimate profits and to transfer them to the German Government'. Bewley also criticized an Irish doctor who was allegedly employed in anti-Italian propaganda activities at the British foreign office, according to the German press. He warned 'unpatriotic action on their part renders it almost inevitable that the Irish Free State should be regarded as a supporter of English imperial policy'.[73]

Eventually, with the 'Italian victory in Abyssinia' in May 1936, Bewley told his superiors that European affairs had been 'so completely changed' as to 'necessitate a reconsideration of policy by all the states of Europe'. On 18 May he prepared a 'review of the facts' for the minister.[74] He had noticed on a visit to Dublin in February that 'even the most nationalistic sections of the public had apparently swallowed English propaganda wholesale on the political situation in Europe'. He suggested:

it is not realized even by official circles in Ireland to what an extent the picture of events as seen by the average man throughout Europe and reflected in the international press differs from that seen in the distorting mirror of Geneva and placed before the Irish public by the English agencies.[75]

---

71 NAI, DFA, CRS 19/50A, 28 March 1936. **72** Ibid., Bewley–Walshe, 1 Apr. 1936. **73** Ibid., 20 Apr. 1936. At least three Irish doctors travelled to Abyssinia to offer their services to the emperor (IP, 26 Sept. 1935). **74** NAI, DFA, CRS 19/50A, Bewley–Walshe, 18 May 1936. **75** Ibid.

He savaged the 'official theory of the League of Nations' that it had acted against an aggressor (Italy) who broke the League's Covenant in order to maintain collective security as propagandistic and simplistic.[76]

To demonstrate how misinformed the Irish public was on the matter he described the general opinion in Germany. Such opinion considered three forces – British imperial interests, international freemasonry, and international Communism – controlled the League. This meant that Germans dismissed the League as incapable of objective mediation in the Italo-Abyssinian crisis. In Germany, the crisis was perceived simply as a great power struggle between Britain and Italy and led to 'no moral indignation whatever against Italy in any quarter, such as prevails in England and apparently in Saorstát Éireann'. In Bewley's opinion the rupture of the Stresa Front by Britain and sanctions against Italy weakened Mussolini's ability to defend Austria from a German invasion, and thereby destabilized the entire European situation.[77]

Irish policy at the League in Geneva, he argued, had 'a most unfortunate result on our international reputation'. France, Germany and Italy regarded Ireland simply as an extension of Britain adhering to the metropolitan power's wishes.[78] To them the Irish were simply a 'backward and uncultivated variety of the English race' and they did not understand Irish policy towards Britain. Contrary to its goal of achieving independence, the Irish Free State collaborated with its ex-colonizers at Geneva despite the existence of an economic war between the two countries. Why did Ireland impose sanctions on Italy, a country that had never interfered in Irish affairs? And why should the Irish Free State ally with Britain against Germany, a nation which the pope had recently described as a 'great and good people in their joy and triumph at a peace which will be an efficacious factor and a prelude to true peace in Europe and the world'? Bewley concluded:

> It is impossible to convince either German or other non-English public opinion that the Irish desire for complete independence is genuine or deep-rooted if Irish policy at Geneva coincides with English policy in matters affecting England's vital interests.[79]

His memoirs leave no doubt that this was his attitude as well as the one he ascribed to the German people.[80]

De Valera, and particularly Walshe, perceived a professional diplomat discarding his objectivity to sympathize with views from the ranks of the opposition (ex-Blueshirts, radical right-wingers, extreme republicans, Cumann na nGaedheal). According to writer Sean O'Faolain, such a person as Bewley 'automatically looks to see what Great Britain is doing in any given situation and

76 Ibid.   77 Ibid.   78 Ibid.   79 Ibid.   80 Bewley, *Memoirs*, p. 166.

without a thought ... does the opposite'.[81] Thus, observing that Britain favoured
sanctions against Italy, a discomfited Bewley sought to use the situation for narrow Irish nationalist objectives, exhibiting 'bad morality', as Frank MacDermott
would later term such behaviour.[82] Anglo-Irish political considerations for
Bewley over-determined his view of the most appropriate policy line. Nor did
Bewley share his superiors' concern for international morality and justice.

Bewley was not alone. There was widespread public and international confusion about whether the Free State supported Britain or the League during the
Abyssinian crisis. This perplexity arose because 'Ireland was, for once, in the
same boat as Great Britain', in the apt words of the Robert Brennan, secretary
of the Irish legation in Washington.[83] In domestic Irish politics, sympathy for
Italy, rather than Abyssinia, was prevalent outside and even within government
circles. The civilising force of a Catholic European power was contrasted sim-
plistically and favourably with the perceived backwardness of an African state.
William Cosgrave, leader of Fine Gael, advocated a similar policy to Bewley's.
Ireland should only implement sanctions if Britain awarded concessions to it in
the trade war, he suggested.[84] The *Irish Independent* was critical of the League's
sanctions policy and Irish support for it. De Valera's entire pro-sanctions line
was a 'stupendous and futile blunder'.[85] Eoin O'Duffy, leader of the new but ill-
fated National Corporate Party, considered dispatching Blueshirts to aid Italy.[86]
Bewley's views coincided with significant sections of right-wing Catholic and
extremist republican opinion in the Free State.[87]

In contrast to de Valera and Walshe, Bewley refused to see the League as an
arena in which to assert Irish independence through constructive engagement.
De Valera envisaged League participation as enhancing the security of small
states such as Ireland and, potentially, replacing force as an arbiter between
states by nurturing a sense of international justice and collective security. For
the League to function properly he knew all states had to sacrifice immediate
advantage to 'the distant goal and the ultimate good', contrary to Bewley's
advice.[88]

De Valera had responded to domestic criticism in a speech at Ennis in
October 1935:

> Now I know that there are a number of people who think that because
> British interest is in a certain direction in this dispute we should act in
> quite the contrary manner. My view is this: If I am on the road to heaven

81 P.F. O'Malley, 'The origins of Irish Neutrality in World War II, 1932–1938', p. 344.   82
Ibid., p. 357.   83 NAI, DFA 26/94, Brennan–Walshe, 18 Sept. 1935 cited in Kennedy,
Ireland, p. 210.   84 Keogh, *Twentieth-century Ireland*, p. 88.   85 II, 4 May 1936.   86 IP,
18 & 19 Sept. 1936; McGarry, *Irish politics*, p. 23.   87 See Keogh, *Ireland & Europe*, pp
58–60; Kennedy, *Ireland*, p. 205.   88 De Valera, *Peace*, p. 51.

I am not going to go the other way because there is somebody going in the same direction that I have certain doubts about.

We are in this as a matter of duty and because we are in it as a matter of duty I want to see for our own good and the good of humanity the Covenant of the League maintained. We cannot bargain about it.[89]

De Valera's desire for cordial relations with Britain on matters of common interest outside the traditional Anglo-Irish conflict did not imply an abandonment of the claims of the Free State against the Britain,[90] he said. 'The fact that we may suspect the motives of some founders [of the League] should not influence us too far'.[91]

De Valera accepted Germany had valid nationalist grievances that should be dealt with through peaceful international arbitration.[92] But the failure of the League to protect Abyssinia discredited it as an international actor and left deValera disillusioned. Instead, realpolitik, alliance politics and aggressive foreign forays became standard practice reducing the League to an impotent discursive gathering of states, lacking consensus and failing to represent all states. The US, Japan, Germany and soon Italy were no longer members but were crucial actors in the international conundrum. De Valera became increasingly detached from the League and moved towards a neutralist line on international affairs, a line whose origins lay in 1935. The Spanish Civil War accelerated de Valera's retreat from conditional idealism towards hardheaded realism.

POPULAR FRONTS AND THE OUTBREAK OF THE SPANISH CIVIL WAR

Bewley, Ireland and Germany all felt the impact of the left-right polarization of politics during 1936. Right-wing governments in Spain and France had failed to tackle the problems facing their countries between 1934 and 1936, and were replaced in early 1936 by broad left-wing coalition governments united against fascism and right-wing extremism. The rapid success of this 'Popular Front' tactic, uniting the fragmented left, frightened the right not only in Spain and France but elsewhere. The anti-clericalism and social radicalism of the Popular Fronts was inimical to the traditional right and to the Catholic Church. The inclusion of radical left-wingers including anarchists and Communists in the Popular Front governments accentuated this concern among traditional conservatives. Rabidly anti-Communist extreme right-wingers and fascists, who

---

89 IP, 7 Oct. 1935. 90 O'Malley, 'The origins of Irish neutrality', p. 352. 91 De Valera, *Peace*, p. 43. 92 For a more detailed exposition of this mode of thought see the IP editorials of 10 & 11 Mar. 1936.

normally conflated moderate socialism (Social Democracy) with Marxist–Leninist Communism, were horrified. Of specific concern was the involvement of Stalinist-controlled communist parties in the Popular Fronts. This reversed Stalin's earlier failed policy of non-cooperation and opposition to what he termed 'social fascists' (Social Democrats). Many in Ireland were opposed to Popular Fronts on instinctive anti-Communist and Catholic grounds.[93] Even Joe Walshe and the Irish minister in Paris, Art O'Brien, succumbed[94] despite the lack of any perceptible Communist threat in Ireland.

When the Spanish Civil War broke out in July 1936 this ideological polarization and division of the European continent was superimposed on the Iberian peninsula. However, the Spanish Civil War's origins were primarily endogenous. Spain was less a nation and more a simple 'geographical expression'.[95] Lack of centripetal state strength, combined with enormous diversity, strong regional and institutional vested interests and gross inequalities, contributed to extremism, factionalism and national disintegration. The causes of its civil war lay in the domestic political instability and division which simmered for decades as governments alternated dangerously and the left and right wings polarized. It was the reaction against a divided left-wing government seeking the creation of a unitary, liberal, secular republic that initiated the Civil War.

When the Spanish Civil War finally became a 'hot' war in July 1936 outsiders interpreted the 'Spanish ulcer' as a war of modern ideology between fascism and communism. The fact that as the Civil War progressed the belligerents adopted this ideological language to acquire external aid exacerbated this falsehood. The rebel Nationalists began to adopt fascist rhetoric to gain aid from Italy and Germany, while the republican government spoke of democracy and social justice. Abroad fascists and Communists began to see it as the opening salvo in their great ideological war.[96] Many Irish people perceived it as a war between Communism and Catholicism.

On 23 August 1936 the Irish government adopted the principle of non-intervention in line with Anglo-French policy.[97] The government's justification for its stance was that, while it sympathized with the suffering of the Spanish people, 'diplomatic relations are primarily between States rather than between Governments, and ... the severance of diplomatic relations between the two countries would serve no useful purpose'. Non-intervention would 'best serve the cause of European peace'.[98]

In actuality, the Fianna Fáil government and party were appalled by the Spanish tragedy and de Valera 'hinted' in Dáil debates that he was outraged by reports of anti-clerical atrocities.[99] However, the conduct of foreign policy was

---

93 McGarry, *Irish politics*, p. 7.   94 Keogh, *Ireland & Europe*, p. 65; Patterson, 'Ireland and France', pp 65–7.   95 Brendon, *Dark valley*, p. 308.   96 Ibid., p. 318.   97 Keogh, *Ireland & Europe*, p. 67.   98 NAI, DFA 227/4, copy of government statement, 25 Aug. 1936.   99 McGarry, *Irish politics*, pp 199–200, 210.

guided by national security considerations and self-interest rather than emotion.[1] De Valera's sympathies may have been with Franco's Nationalist forces, but he pointed out the incongruity of joining a war that Ireland thought was between God and Communism, when most other states intervening in the conflict clearly did not perceive traditional religion as an issue; rather it was the new religion of ideology that motivated them.[2] Intervention would add to the already heightened tensions surrounding the revisionist Italian and German powers and had the potential to tip over into a European-wide civil war. During 1936 and 1937, de Valera emphasized that the Spanish Nationalists lacked the standard international prerequisites for diplomatic recognition: that was, political control of the whole of the country. So the republican government remained the legitimate government of the Spanish state.

While de Valera endeavoured to maintain a neutralist foreign policy he faced a domestic political crisis. The opposition and the newly formed populist Irish Christian Front wanted the Irish state to recognize Franco's Nationalists. The Fianna Fáil government was vulnerable during the winter of 1936–7 because a general election was due in mid-1937.[3] The Front, consciously founded as a countermovement to the left-wing continental Popular Fronts, saw the Spanish Civil War as a 'holy war' against atheism and Communism.[4] De Valera's refusal to reverse the non-interventionist policy led Paddy Belton of the Irish Christian Front to label the Irish government as 'Red' implying it harboured sympathies for the Spanish Republic.[5] The public hysteria generated about the possible advance of Communism concerned de Valera. On 27 November 1936, he pointedly reminded the Dáil that a 'Red Scare' had engulfed the country in 1932 as Fianna Fáil took power but was subsequently demonstrated to be absolutely groundless.[6]

A DIPLOMATIC MAVERICK

As the Irish government experienced these foreign policy challenges, the unsettling demeanour of their representative in Berlin worsened. Bewley moved in the margins of Berlin and Nazi social circles, enjoyed observing the intrigues in the top echelons of Nazi life and became preoccupied with endless diplomatic engagements and social functions. In January 1935 he asked to move the Irish legation to larger premises for entertainment purposes. Initially de Valera was reluctant to sanction this extravagance finding 'it difficult to see how the present premises which were considered suitable by your predecessor and in which he was able to entertain, should not be regarded as impossible'.[7] However,

1 Keogh, *Ireland & Europe*, p. 68. 2 *Dáil Debates*, vol. 65, col. 605, 18 Feb. 1937. 3 Keogh, *Ireland & Europe*, pp 67, 69, 77. 4 Ibid., p. 68. 5 McGarry, *Irish politics*, p. 130. 6 *Dáil Debates*, vol. 64, col. 1218, 27 Nov. 1936. 7 NAI, DFA Berlin letterbooks,

Bewley proved persuasive and on 1 January 1936 the legation moved to 3 Drakestrasse.[8] Bewley enjoyed the diplomatic cocktail circuit but never gained an influential role within it or with the Nazi government, although he was on personal terms with Hermann Göring, the second man of the Third Reich, and in the post-World War II period he wrote an apologist biography of him.[9]

The environment permitted Bewley to indulge uncritically in his unbalanced views. Bewley's anti-Communism in particular became extreme in response to European political developments during 1936. As early as January 1936, he was convinced 'the real driving force behind National Socialism is its hatred and distrust of Communism'.[10] He repeatedly criticized Irish newspapers for naiveté about the Soviet Union and the 'Red' threat,[11] and he was convinced their coverage was anti-Nazi.[12]

Increased prominence accorded to the Communist threat in Bewley's reports during the first six months of 1936 reflected the success of the Popular Front strategy in Spain and France, as well as the Nazi tendency to highlight the Communist menace in its propaganda. In May, Bewley argued that events in Spain, Greece and South American countries were 'evidence of the work of Communism in the various countries of the world, controlled and financed by Moscow'.[13] After the outbreak of the Spanish Civil War in July, Bewley adhered to the Nazi anti-Communist line. The Irish envoy accepted the anti-Czech and anti-Soviet tenet of German propaganda to such an extent that he admitted, 'I do not think that it is possible to form a reasonable view of events and policy in central Europe at the present time without taking into account the (at least potential) menace of Moscow and Prague.'[14]

By August 1936 Bewley was almost totally under the Nazi spell. Like other commentators he was impressed by the success of the Berlin Olympic Games. In his estimation they were a triumph and the regime's calculation that they were 'likely to dispel many of the false impressions about Germany which have been spread by enemies of the regime' was correct. He considered there was substance in the allegations that the US was hypocritical in its criticisms of Nazi Germany not allowing Jews to compete for Germany, while American policy was to win Olympic events using 'coloured competitors and inviting only the white competitors to official American receptions'.[15] Bewley also accepted

Walshe–Bewley, 10 Jan. 35.   8 Ibid., Murphy–Bewley, 20 Dec. 35.   9 C. Bewley, *Hermann Goering & the Third Reich* (New York, 1962), p. x.   10 NAI, DFA CRS 19/50A, Bewley–Walshe, 22 Jan. 1936.   11 Ibid., 10 Mar. 1936.   12 Ibid., 25 May 1936. A reading of both the *Irish Times* and the *Irish Press* for 13 May 1936 reveals Bewley's allegations were largely unsubstantiated.   13 NAI, DFA CRS 19/50A, Bewley–Walshe, 25 May 1936.   14 Ibid., 15 July 1936.   15 Ibid., 18 Aug. 1936. He was concerned that the Saorstát was not represented at the games. It might create a false impression that a quarrel existed between Ireland and Germany leading to the drawing of parallels between the Saorstát's position and that of the Soviet Union and Lithuania who did not attend for 'political reasons, or else that the British team represented the Free State'. A dispute between the Irish National Athletic

uncritically the 'considerable justice' of the assertion of the 'semi-official' *Deutsche diplomatisch–politische Korrespondenz* that 'the molestation of a Jew or the imprisonment of a priest in Germany is apparently considered a greater crime than the wholesale massacres which are taking place in Spain'. He thought Europe was dividing into two camps – anti-Communist and pro-communist liberal – and that 'the former would enjoy at least the partial support of the Vatican'.[16]

Curiously Bewley considered the sacrifice of his co-religionists in Germany (never mind Christians of other denominations or members of other religions) as a necessary price for Nazi anti-communism.[17] He believed the Holy See was 'much less apprehensive of Nazism than of Bolshevism', and that all Catholics with 'a reasonable knowledge of the facts' would ultimately reach the same conclusion. The troubles of the Catholic Church in Germany, he asserted, were caused by the unwise actions of ecclesiastical authorities in Germany.[18] It was his firmly held view that in the early 1930s the German Catholic Church had ill advisedly allied with the SPD against the Nazis at the end of the Weimar Republic. The Holy See had then acquired a prejudiced view of National Socialism from the German episcopate and failed to moderate 'the action of the more politically-minded members of the German Episcopate' after the Nazis gained power. Unconvincingly Bewley reported:

> I am not of course attempting to palliate or excuse in any way the conduct of the present regime towards the Church: it has undoubtedly broken the Concordat both in the letter and the spirit, and is taking every possible step to discredit the Church in the eyes of the German people. But I also believe that matters would never have come to their present state, and that Hitler himself would probably not have given a free hand to the anti-Christian wing of the Party if the same policy had been pursued in Germany as in Italy by the Episcopate.[19]

Responsibility for the regime's mistreatment of the Catholic Church rested on the German hierarchy's failure to implement an appeasement policy on the Italian model. Bewley's transformation into a relatively uncritical defender of the Nazi regime was virtually complete.

Further evidence that Bewley had by now been fully ensnared by the lure of Nazism occurred after he went to the annual Nuremberg rally in September 1936. The theme was 'the necessity to unite against Bolshevism in defence of European civilisation'. Bewley reported to Dublin that the rallying cry should

---

and Cycling Association and the International Amateur Athletics Federation had prevented an Irish team from participating (NAI, DFA, Berlin letterbooks, Walshe–Bewley, 7 May 1935). **16** NAI, DFA, CRS 19/50A, Bewley–Walshe, 18 Aug. 1936. **17** Bewley, *Memoirs*, p. 125. **18** NAI, DFA, CRS 19/50A, Bewley–Walshe, 24 Aug. 1936. **19** Ibid.

'be taken at its face value as an effort to awaken the conscience of the world against Communism'. He considered the rally an unqualified triumph for Hitler, not least because 'numerous countries whose representatives had previously declined to attend were this time represented – a striking proof of the increased prestige of Germany in the last year'.[20] Neither the British nor US ambassadors attended because the rally was the affair of the Nazi party and not the German state.

By the late summer of 1936 Bewley's anti-Communist framework of analysis, his admiration of Nazism and his belief that the interests of Catholicism were best served by Franco in Spain led him to adopt a very partial perspective on the Spanish Civil War. The impression he formed was the Vatican was more anti-Communist than anti-fascist or anti-Nazi.[21] Interestingly, the German Catholic hierarchy was similarly animated by atrocity stories relating to republican Spain and adopted the Nazi analysis of the Spanish Civil War as a conflict between God and anti-God.[22] Bewley was impressed by the German episcopate's joint pastoral letter of August 1936 which fulminated against the danger of Communism,[23] and alluded to the belief that 'a special emissary of the Vatican assisted in its composition'.[24]

Bewley hoped for a rapprochement in German church–state relations based on their mutual anti-Communism. Signs of increasing intimacy between Italy and Germany also appeared to confirm, in Bewley's mind, the rightness of the nationalist cause in Spain. Italy and Germany had by this stage begun military intervention in the Spanish Civil War supporting General Franco's armies. Bewley commented:

> the strength and determination of the Italian Government have naturally exercised on Germany a greater attraction than the vacillation of the English Government and the pusillanimous pacifism of the English people. But no doubt the final determinant has been the obvious wish of England to see a Red Government established in Spain rather than an authoritative Government which would certainly drift out of the British sphere of influence.[25]

This Italian-German co-operation contributed to the formation of the Rome–Berlin Axis in October, and anti-Communism provided the cover for the anti-Comintern German-Japanese pact in November.

By late 1936 Bewley detected a new Nazi contempt towards Britain in Hitler's utterances and in the press. Britain was increasingly regarded as one of the chief supporters of Soviet Russia, pacifistic, and preferring Bolshevism to

20 Ibid., 16 Sept. 1936.   21 Ibid., 24 Aug. 1936.   22 Lewy, *Catholic Church*, pp 205–6.
23 NAI, DFA, CRS 19/50A, Bewley–Walshe, 3 Sept. 1936.   24 Ibid.   25 Ibid.

fascism.[26] He did point out that as far as possible Germany would continue to seek conciliation with Britain.[27]

When he began to detect a growing German aloofness to Britain it was axiomatic that Ireland should take advantage and develop closer relations with Germany. He was, therefore, annoyed about anything which substantiated the prevalent Nazi impression that Irish foreign policy was subordinated to that of Britain.[28] It was inappropriate that German misperceptions should continue, particularly at a time when Anglo-German relations were under apparent strain and Ireland had an opportunity to differentiate itself. Walshe requested him to account for such false German perceptions and Bewley responded on 6 November 1936.[29]

Bewley again reported the German belief that the Free State was 'acting under English influence' at the League. The fact that the Free State's position coincided with Britain's policies in the League suggested to Germans that the Free State was voting in accordance with English instructions.[30] Germans approved of Blueshirt leader Eoin O'Duffy raising an Irish brigade to support the Spanish Nationalists in the Civil War, but were aghast that the Irish government had not declared its sympathy with the Spanish Nationalists and Catholics. Ordinary Germans could not comprehend his explication of the Irish position.[31] Indeed, it seemed to be Bewley's view that de Valera's government was absconding from its Catholic duties as well as creating a negative international image of the state.

Irish nationals' dependence on British consular facilities in Germany and in other European countries was another negative factor, making it impossible to convince the German public 'that Ireland is anything but a somewhat backward English province' and that Ireland did indeed want total separation from the British empire. Bewley had repeatedly recommended the appointment of honorary Irish consuls in Germany ever since 1933.[32] However, the department of external affairs was opposed in principle to the appointment of such honorary consuls because its experience of such consular officers in Dublin indicated 'these gentlemen invariably use their positions for personal aggrandizement and are quite useless as representatives of the country from whom they hold their appointment'.[33] Bewley, however, considered it was a simple matter of Irish national prestige and of assistance to Irish nationals who should not be forced to rely on British consular assistance. A British consul placing Irish citizens on their register as British subjects 'naturally tends to assimilate them more and more to the English colony', reinforcing popular German perceptions of the Irish as English provincials.[34]

---

26 Ibid.; ibid., 16 Mar. 1936; ibid., 26 Oct. 1936. 27 Ibid., 26 Oct. 1936. 28 Ibid., 6 Nov. 1936. 29 Ibid. 30 Ibid. 31 Ibid. 32 NAI, DFA 17/160, Bewley–Walshe, 21 Nov. 1933; ibid., Pritschow–Bewley, 17 Nov. 1933; ibid., Fahy–assistant secretary, 6 Dec. 1933; ibid., Briscoe–Walshe, 11 Apr. 1934. 33 NAI, DFA 17/238, Murphy–Bewley, 26 Sept. 1936. 34 Ibid., Bewley–Walshe, 5 Nov. 1936.

Bewley also took the opportunity in his response to Walshe to expand on another theme that had exercised him since 1933: the manner in which Irish newspapers reported on 'foreign affairs in general, and on German affairs in particular' was 'not calculated to increase our reputation for mental independence in a national sense'.[35] In Bewley's estimation the few Germans who read Irish newspapers were AA officials or Germans 'interested in or sympathetic to Ireland'. Consequently, critical Irish press coverage of Nazi Germany alienated the Germans who mattered, Bewley argued.[36] On 6 November 1936 he wrote:

> I am of course aware that the Irish Government cannot be held responsible for anything written in the organs of the Opposition, and also that it is its policy not to interfere even with those which support the Government. Unfortunately this is a point of view which the German Government and German opinion in general absolutely refuse to accept.[37]

Bewley advised that the government should directly control the editorial policy of the *Irish Press* as it was considered the official organ of the government. De Valera defended the editorial freedom of the *Irish Press* believing there was a need for 'a real live paper' independent of politics in Ireland. Bewley believed that the pretext of the 'freedom of the press gave de Valera the possibility of putting forward in his organ views for which he did not wish to be held personally responsible'.[38]

One specific area of Irish press coverage Bewley highlighted was German church–state relations. He regretted Irish newspapers seemed to take views on Catholic subjects from non-Irish and non-Catholic sources and failed to highlight the numerous signs of reconciliation between the German state and the churches.[39] Bewley himself, however, failed to mention that the Nazis had rejected a recent Vatican overture proposing a common front with Germany against Communism (especially in Spain). The Vatican in response composed the encyclical *Mit brennender Sorge,* that censured the Nazis' treatment of the church and the German bishops read it on Palm Sunday, March 1937.[40]

Bewley continued to entertain the hope that Ireland would join the European-wide, German-led anti-Communist coalition he believed was forming during late 1936.[41] His prescription for Irish foreign policy had such an unbalanced Germanocentric focus that he completely failed to recognize the Free State had vested interests with other states and international bodies. Then, to

35 NAI, DFA, CRS 19/50A, Bewley–Walshe, 6 Nov. 1936.   36 Ibid.   37 Ibid.
38 Bewley, *Memoirs*, p. 161.   39 NAI, DFA, CRS 19/50A, Bewley–Walshe, 26 Oct. 1936.
40 A. Rhodes, *The Vatican in the age of dictators, 1922–1945* (London, 1973), pp 202–4.
41 NAI, DFA, CRS, 19/50A, Bewley–Walshe, 26 Oct. 1936 & 9 Nov. 1936.

the acute embarrassment of Dublin, in early 1937 Bewley publicly declared his Nazi sympathies. In April he told a Berlin newspaper, *12 Uhr Mittag*, that the Irish government would persist in promoting good relations with Germany, ominously adding 'our growing patriotism helps us to find recognition in countries where people are willing to stake their lives for liberty and honour. That your Reich and its leaders have many admirers among our youth is a well-known fact'. His comments prompted the *Irish Times* to wonder how 'a democratic state ... which has made no secret of its abhorrence of dictatorship ... could approve the German system, which, for all its admirable elements is based upon dictatorship and the negation of liberty'. The controversy generated by Bewley's remarks provoked an attack on de Valera in the Dáil, in which the taoiseach was forced to deflect the question and avoid answering. Bewley's gaffe ensured his tenure in Berlin was now certainly in question, if it had not already been so.[42]

De Valera did not immediately remove Bewley from Berlin because it would have generated further controversy in Ireland and could have threatened relations with Nazi Germany. Bewley's recall would amount to a capitulation to the domestic opposition. Besides, finding a suitable replacement trained in diplomacy and linguistically competent was a further problem. Bewley remained in his post in Berlin but came under closer scrutiny from his superiors.

A MEETING OF MINDS

Bewley had clearly failed to comprehend the premises of de Valera's foreign policy, particularly in relation to Britain. De Valera's activity in the League of Nations between 1932 and 1936 was based on a degree of international idealism and also served to distance Ireland from the British Commonwealth. It should be contrasted with de Valera's reluctance[43] to permit Irish representatives to attend commonwealth gatherings.[44] Ireland's League activity was intended to increase its international profile and to assert its autonomy. Conversely, this did not prevent the Free State from making common cause with British representatives. 'In a climate of antagonistic Anglo-Irish relations, the League provided the two states with their only neutral meeting-place.'[45] The exclusion of bilateral differences permitted a greater, but largely unpublicized, alignment of interests. The Free State and Britain held similar attitudes to many international issues, arising from their common adherence to democratic mores, a parallel desire for peace and stability, and their belief in the efficacy of conciliation on European matters. In September 1937 the British delegation to the League helped to elect de Valera as vice-president of the League Assembly.[46]

---

42 IT, 6 Apr. 1937; Keogh, *Ireland & Europe*, pp 56–7; see also Dickel, *Aussenpolitik*, p. 73.
43 McMahon, *Republicans*, p. 159. 44 Ibid., p. 158. 45 Kennedy, 'Prologue', p. 423.
46 McMahon, *Republicans*, p. 222.

Admittedly, de Valera and his government were more inclined to co-operate with Britain when that co-operation was concealed from a sensitive Irish public,[47] but it was difficult to camouflage this strong Anglo-Irish congruence on issues such as Abyssinia and Spain.

Bewley's unhelpful construct was that Ireland was 'standing behind' Britain, rather than 'alongside' her, on the major issues faced by the League between 1935 and 1937. That view mirrored widespread Irish and international confusion about Ireland's relationship to Britain.[48] That the Germans failed to appoint a relatively longstanding or well informed minister to Dublin had exacerbated the problems caused by Bewley's unreliability as an accurate representative of Irish interests in Berlin.

But Anglo-Irish convergence on some international issues did not prevent de Valera pursuing his nationalist agenda in bilateral relations with Britain. He progressively remoulded the Anglo-Irish connection culminating in the 1937 Irish constitution.

THE DEPARTMENTAL PERSPECTIVE

Walshe, initially impressed by Nazism, had by 1936 developed a loathing of it because of its religious policies.[49] Bewley's benign assessment of Nazi policy towards the Catholic Church's position was not in accordance with the views of de Valera, Walshe or Irish public opinion as Irish newspaper coverage showed.

The prominent Catholic periodical, the *Irish Ecclesiastical Record*, had made it clear that its sympathy towards Mussolini's Italy did not extend to Hitler's Germany because of Nazi anti-Catholic practices.[50] In 1937 it launched a scathing attack on the insidious methods adopted by the Nazis to annihilate Christianity.[51] National Socialism 'assumed the character of a religion as radically opposed to Christianity as Bolshevism',[52] except it was less open and more dishonest in its deChristianising aspirations than Soviet Communism: 'There is more method, more vision, more careful adaptation of means to the end in the German process; there is no material destruction, but who will say it is less diabolic?'[53]

Walshe and de Valera subscribed to a similar view as was confirmed in June 1937 when Walshe told Bewley that, until the religious question in Germany became less acute, de Valera would not allow officials to supply information on Ireland to the German press.[54] This underlined the extent to which by 1936 and

---

47 Ibid., p. 160.   48 In this he was similar to the Irish newspapers.   49 Keogh, 'Profile of Joseph Walshe', p. 74.   50 McGarry, *Irish politics*, p. 136–8.   51 Anonymous, 'Whither Germany?', *Irish Ecclesiastical Record*, fifth series, 49 (Jan.–June 1937), p. 453.   52 Ibid., p. 611.   53 Ibid.   54 NAI, DFA, Berlin letterbook 1936–7, Walshe–Bewley, 30 June 1937.

1937 any initial sympathy for Hitler and Nazism within Irish official circles in Dublin[55] had disappeared. Many Irish people, even in government, maintained their initial preference for Mussolini's Italy, judged it to be in accord with Catholic social teaching and vocationalism, unlike the anti-clerical positions which infused Nazism.

Anti-Nazi sentiment had been apparent since 1934 or 1935 in the higher echelons of the department of external affairs. The Irish government had limited direct dealings with Germany and the government avoided direct, public condemnation of Nazi domestic activities. But policy inferences could be drawn from repeated Irish refusals to cooperate with Nazi Germany on a number of matters. In March 1937, for instance, the departments of post and telegraphs, and external affairs refused a request for de Valera to contribute to an anti-communist German publication, *Frankfurter Volksblatt*.[56]

In the autumn of that year Walshe and de Valera explicitly aired their critical views on Hitler's Germany. The two made their comments following an exchange with Bewley about a controversy sparked by an article in the *Irish Press*. On 10 September 1937 the paper criticized an exhibition mounted at that year's Nuremberg rally which depicted Ireland in red, along with the USSR. Bewley condemned the article as the work of a semi-educated person and it was left to Walshe to explain to a German diplomat:

> If official Germany chooses to brand Ireland as a country which is indifferent to the growth of Communism, she must expect some retort ... at least so long as her zeal to keep Communism out of Europe is accompanied by a teaching which retains the very worst element in that creed.[57]

In response, the German authorities maintained the anti-Communist display had been designed only to depict in which countries of the world Communist parties and groups existed.[58] It was not intended to indicate the governments of those countries were pro-Communist or Communist. An exasperated Walshe, unhappy about Bewley's reluctance to deal with the problem, told the Irish envoy:

> The *Irish Press*, in condemning this particular pictorial representation of Ireland's attitude towards Communism, was reflecting the views of the vast majority of the people of the country. It would be unfortunate if a paper which is known to have affiliations with the political party in power could give expression to no views about foreign countries which might be unpalatable to their rulers.

---

55 Elsasser, *Germany & Ireland*, p. 48. **56** NAI, DFA 116/64. **57** NAI, DFA, Berlin letterbook, Walshe–Bewley, 23 Sept. 1937. **58** PA, AA, R122531, Stumm–Dublin, 12 Sept. 1937.

Walshe justified the *Irish Press*' critical attitude on the basis of Germany's 'persecution of Christians and Jews'. Walshe said it was the 'fundamental duty' of 'the world press' to inform 'the average man' of Nazi abuses. Walshe pointed out to Bewley:

> the actions or views of newspapers or the Government of this country should not be represented as ipso facto wrong because they happen to be in conformity with opinion in the neighbouring country and the Minister is still at a loss to understand how this frequent community of views in international relations between this country and Great Britain can in any way prevent our Ministers abroad from pursuing their task of obtaining the fullest recognition for Irish nationality.

By now Bewley appeared to be representing the views of Berlin rather than Dublin. Walshe informed him: 'If official Germany continues to insult actively the most sacred beliefs of the people of this and other Christian countries of the world, there may easily be a movement here in favour of closing down our Mission in Berlin.'[59]

The relationship between Bewley and Walshe had become extremely strained, if not unworkable, by this time. De Valera, too, recognized Bewley was a serious problem. Walshe told Bewley 'the Minister would be glad to have some constructive suggestions from you as to what really should be your work in Germany in order to promote our interests in other than purely commercial circles'.[60]

Irish officials harboured apprehensions about the Nazi conduct of diplomacy and the Nazi movement's organisation of Germans in Ireland. A total of 125 German aliens were in residence, dropping to approximately 95 as at 1 June 1937, together with a small number of Germans who had been granted naturalization.[61] While these figures were minuscule there were, in addition, up to 23 Austrians resident in the Free State.[62] Many of the Austro–German community occupied important positions in Irish semi–state sector (particularly in the ESB and sugar factories) or state sector, because of their particular expertise or skills. Some were Nazi Party members and members of the Nazi Auslandsorganisation.[63]

The Auslandsorganisation (AO) was the extension of the Nazi *Gleichschaltung* policy to all Germans living overseas. The AO was the Nazi party abroad, responsible for promoting German and Nazi interests, collecting information and Nazifying Germans overseas. The most senior Nazi in Saorstát during the later 1930s was the prominent Austrian archaeologist Dr Adolf Mahr

---

59 Ibid. **60** Ibid. **61** NAI, DFA 102/130. **62** Under the Aliens Order British and Commonwealth citizens were not regarded as aliens. **63** NAI, DFA 102/130; O'Donoghue, *Hitler's Irish voices*, p. 4–32, 219–20.

who held the position of Ortsgruppenleiter of the AO in Ireland. After 1934 he was also the director of Ireland's National Museum and, as a senior member of the German community, attended the coronation of George VI in Westminster in May 1937.[64] Although there was a potential conflict between Mahr's role as an official in the Irish state and his role as group leader in the AO, his activities for much of the 1930s appeared superficially harmless and included the promotion of trade and the arrangement of recreational events for the German community such as an annual Christmas party.[65] The government and Irish officials were aware of Mahr's dual allegiances but he only came under close surveillance with the approach of war in the later 1930s. Nevertheless a pattern emerged during the mid-1930s when the Irish section of the AO, under Mahr's leadership took an interventionist line in German-Irish trade and diplomacy complicating Irish-German relations. German AA officials were annoyed, in particular, by the Dublin AO's activities to promote German exports to Ireland during difficult trade negotiations.[66]

Officials at the department of external affairs in Dublin were also displeased with AO interference. Walshe complained on numerous occasions about the Nazi organisation in Dublin to the German chargé d'affaires, Dr Erich Schrötter, and to the subsequent German minister, Dr Eduard Hempel.[67] The Irish authorities knew the AO had been responsible for the dismissal of a previous German minister to Ireland (Dehn-Schmidt) from his post in Bucharest. They might have been aware (or suspected) that the AO had prevented Schrötter's promotion to the position of German minister in Dublin during 1937 following the death of the incumbent, von Kuhlmann.[68]

De Valera and the Irish government 'let it be known that it did not favour the appointment of a Nazi party member as the new German minister in Dublin'.[69] Dr Eduard Hempel presented his credentials as new German minister to de Valera on 28 July 1937 expressing the ritual pleasantries concerning the fostering and deepening of friendly relations.[70] When Hempel, a shrewd and even-tempered career diplomat, became German minister to the Free State he was not a member of the Nazi party but almost exactly one year later (1 July 1938) he joined.[71] Despite Irish concerns about Nazism, Hempel's professional execution of his diplomatic role and continuing Irish interest in Germany as an export market smoothed his way.

---

64 O'Donoghue, *Hitler's Irish voices*, p. 20.   65 Ibid., p. 19–23; M. Hull, 'German military intelligence operations in Ireland, 1939–1945' (Phd thesis, UCC, 2000), pp 57–9. 66 Dickel, *Aussenpolitik*, pp 69, 71.   67 O'Donoghue, *Hitler's Irish voices*, p. 21, 24, 26–7. 68 NAI, DFA 118/16, Schrötter–de Valera, 18 Jan. 1937; ibid., Bewley–Walshe, 21 Jan. 1937; and ibid., Bewley–Walshe 22 Jan. 1937; PA, AA R 27203, Ruberg–Mahr, 6 July 1937. 69 *Sunday Press*, 17 Nov. 1963.   70 NAI, DFA 318/6, Address by Hempel, 28 July 1937. 71 O'Donoghue, *Hitler's Irish voices*, p. 219; see Hull, 'German military intelligence', p. 66 f. 98 for a discussion of the controversy surrounding the mistaken assumption that Hempel was not a Nazi.

NEGOTIATING THE 1936 TRADE AGREEMENT

By 1936, previously fraught Irish–German trade negotiations had settled into a more normal pattern with the smooth operation of the 1935 Irish–German agreement. The 1935 agreement had improved the Irish balance of trade with Germany.[72] Irish ministers were now 'particularly interested' in the prospect of placing trade with Germany 'on a more permanent footing'.[73] In February 1936, relevant Irish government departments assessed the existing trade agreement in readiness for the forthcoming trade negotiations. John V. Fahy of the department of external affairs' trade section believed the bilateral trade agreement for 1935 had proved valuable for Ireland. Prices for most agricultural produce were considerably higher in Germany than the prices prevailing on the British market. The study found the diversion of surplus supplies of cattle, eggs and butter to Germany also had the effect of raising prices on the British market as Irish goods became scarcer. In particular, the 15,000 head of fat cattle that were excess to demand both in Britain and the domestic Irish market could be sent to Germany and secure a profit of more than £3 per head over British prices. The Irish government did not have to pay farmers export bounty payments to overcome the tariff penalties applicable to the British market. As a result, the exchequer saved approximately £87,000 by exporting £433,000 of Irish agricultural product to Germany rather than to Britain during 1935. The Irish concluded 'a permanent remunerative trade to Germany in eggs and butter' also appeared practicable. The government's objective was to maintain 1935 as a framework for subsequent trade agreements but to seek parity in Ireland's trade with Germany. The previously agreed monetary ratio of 1:3 in favour of Germany was no longer acceptable. Information emanating from Berlin in early 1936 led the department of external affairs to conclude that 'the bigger the imports of German goods the bigger will be our exports and the better the ratio, and probably also better the prices'.[74]

The Irish cabinet maintained a strong interest in the Irish–German negotiations.[75] Although Germany's existing proportion of Irish export trade was still small in absolute terms, internal department of external affairs memoranda revealed that Germany continued to occupy a central place in Irish government export calculations:

---

72 NAI, DFA 232/1, Protocol No. 1, Lemass–Hemmen, Saorstát–German trade agreement, 28 Jan. 35.   73 NAI, DFA 314/10/6/3, Walshe conversation with Hemmen, 14 Oct. 36. 74 Ibid., Fahy: Saorstát–German trade position, 19 Feb. 36. See also DFA 314/10/6/3, Fahy: export of eggs to Germany, 22 May 1935; DFA 314/10/6/3, note by department of external affairs on forthcoming trade discussions with Germany, n.d. (c.early 1936).   75 See NAI, DT S. 8684.

> After Great Britain, Germany is the largest importer of agricultural prod-
> ucts, and her imports of eggs and butter particularly, and cattle to a lesser
> extent, are not inconsiderable compared with Great Britain's imports.
> Furthermore, Germany's imports in these products are large relative to
> the Saorstát's total exports.[76]

The internal assessment added that apart from Britain and Germany, the two
largest importers in Europe, the prospects of finding a market for Saorstát agricultural products were extremely poor. 'Therefore, if any development is to take
place outside the British market, Germany stands out as the second in line for
any development, although it must be recognized that the development will be
small relatively.'[77]

The priority then was to divert Irish imports away from countries not prepared to take substantial quantities of Irish exports.[78] The existing
Irish-German trade ratio, while not perfect, was preferable to the imbalances
with other countries. Nazi efforts to make Germany agriculturally self-sufficient
were a failure, and the regime was forced to import the shortfall to meet its
domestic needs. This had led to annualized bargaining and agreements with
chosen supplier countries to ensure Germany, which was suffering from severe
foreign currency problems, had sufficient currency in reserve to pay for imports.
The German strategy was to lobby for explicit barter agreements, if necessary
on a 1:1 ratio as a means to overcome its shortage of foreign currency.[79]

Dr Hans R. Hemmen, German trade negotiating leader, was anxious to negotiate an Irish-German trade deal in early 1936 when he became aware of the
concurrent Anglo-Irish trade negotiations. Hemmen revealed that 'if Germany
is to have any hope of making a Treaty satisfactory from her own point of view'
advantageous proposals should be put to the Irish before the Anglo-Irish agreement was concluded. Referring to the events of early 1935 when an Anglo-Irish
trade deal was sealed forcing Germany to come to better terms with Ireland,
Hemmen told the industry and commerce department secretary, John Leydon,
'he was proceeding on the principle "once bitten twice shy"'.[80] Hemmen's experience had taught him that Anglo-Irish and Irish-German trade negotiations
were intrinsically linked. By making the Irish aware of what he was prepared to
offer, he hoped to avoid undue intricacies in the trilateral trade web.[81]

Hemmen knew he also needed to secure an agreement with Ireland before
commencing negotiations with Germany's neighbours if he was to ensure that
he could find markets for large quantities of agricultural produce from Ireland.
The Germans were clearly satisfied that Irish produce was of the 'highest

---

76 NAI, DFA 314/10/6/3, Note by department of external affairs on forthcoming trade
discussions with Germany, n.d.   77 Ibid.   78 Ibid.   79 NAI, DFA 314/10/6/3,
Germany's trade policy, 20 Feb. 1936.   80 Ibid., Saorstát–German trade, Leydon, 10 Jan.
1936.   81 Ibid., Walshe memo of conversation with Hemmen, 14 Oct. 36.

quality' but they were also driven by a new German policy to restrict imports from countries such as the US because Germany was in no position to sell goods in return.[82] The initial German offer for 1936 was to renew the 3:1 ratio of the 1935 trade agreement for a further year. Hemmen's opening negotiating tactic was to tempt Irish negotiators with the promise that Germany might be prepared to offer a 1:1 agreement for 1937 if the 1936 agreement worked well. In addition he held out the alluring prospect of a slight improvement in the 1936 agreement in comparison to the previous year. The Irish could have a special barter arrangement on a 1:1 ratio for orders of machinery. Hemmen argued 'the only practical limitation on our exports under the barter agreement would be the limitation imposed by ourselves in restricting our imports from Germany'. The Germans were evidently eager that the Irish continue importing German coal and machinery.[83]

Irish officials, particularly in the department of industry and commerce, raised objections and felt they could not commit to Germany until the British offers were available. De Valera and Lemass, minister for industry and commerce, agreed with the officials' advice. Besides the Irish found the continuance of the 1:3 trade ratio in favour of Germany repugnant although additional trade in excess of 1935 could be taken on a 1:1 barter basis.[84] The Irish cabinet explicitly authorized Lemass to inform the German negotiators that the Saorstát would not consider any proposals that would involve the continuance of the ratio of trade' agreed to in 1935.[85]

The department of agriculture also disliked the precarious annual agreements with Germany and sought longer-term arrangements and a reliable, permanent trade since it took time for agriculture to meet German consumer requirements.[86] Furthermore, Lemass and the department of industry and commerce were hostile to the concept of barter arrangements, which Hemmen considered as a means to overcome the strain on German sterling reserves.[87]

The Irish 'reluctantly' accepted the German offer of an extension of the existing 1935 trade agreement for a year from 1 April 1936 although they did not gain trade parity they had demanded in principle. Instead, while the general framework of the 1935 agreement remained in place, the trade ratio was changed from 1:3 to 1:2 in Germany's favour for the value of German goods imported into Ireland. This meant that if German imports remained at the same level as in 1935, Ireland would be able to increase its exports to Germany to the value of £700,000. The attendant advantage was that the exchequer would be

82 Ibid., Saorstát–German trade, Leydon, 10 Jan. 1936.   83 Ibid.   84 Ibid., Saorstát–German trade, Leydon, 14 Jan. 1936.   85 NAI, DT, S. 8684, Cab 7/299, 26 Feb. 1936.   86 NAI, DFA 314/10/6/3, Saorstát–German trade, Leydon, 14 Jan. 1936. 87 Ibid., Leydon memo, 28 Feb. 1936.

liable for fewer export bounty payments since Irish produce had free entry into Germany, unlike Britain.[88]

An intrinsic element of the 1935 agreement, extended in full for 1936, was the Irish-German understanding contained in the protocols attached to the trade agreement. Under these the Irish government undertook to use their own orders and their influence with institutions established under statutory authority, and generally, to increase trade with Germany particularly in industrial and manufactured items. Ireland also promised to divert trade to Germany from countries that offered a less favourable balance of trade to the Saorstát. Germany, in return, pledged to maintain due regard to Saorstát export interests in agricultural products particularly cattle, eggs, butter, wool, hides and skins.[89]

Since 1933 the Irish government had adhered to a policy of using state-controlled contracts as a tool to maximize Irish exports. Departments were required to inform the department of industry and commerce when it was proposed to place any contract outside the Saorstát for goods exceeding a value of £1,000. The Foreign Trade Committee then had to recommend in which country the contract should be placed, taking Irish export interests into account.[90] Since 1933, but more especially after the normalization of Irish-German trade relations under the 1935 agreement, most of the contract diversions had been made to Germany and Britain because of the reciprocal export advantages.

THE 1937 TRADE AGREEMENT

Anglo-Irish trade, unlike that with Germany, was not regulated by a formalized trade ratio. But the Irish, even in the midst of the Economic War thought it wise to divert trade to Britain 'at the expense of countries other than Germany in the expectation that that country would give a quid pro quo subsequently and because no worthwhile quid pro quo could be procured from the country of the lowest tender'.[91] The Foreign Trade Committee's deliberations surrounding the placing of state and semi-state contracts therefore acquired significant political and economic importance. The government had the means to place pressure on other states to increase their imports of Irish produce. British and German firms often found themselves in competition, particularly for machinery and equipment contracts offered by semi-state bodies such as the ESB or private firms attracted to Ireland by the government's industrialization drive. One such

88 Ibid., Memo: Saorstát trade agreement with Germany, 16 Apr. 1936; ibid., Köster–de Valera, 26 Mar. 1936; ibid., Walshe–Köster, 27 Mar. 1936; ibid., aide mémoire (to Germany), 3 Apr. 1936.   89 NAI, DFA 232/1, Protocol No. 1, Hemmen–Lemass, Saorstát–German trade agreement, 28 Jan. 1935.   90 NAI, DFA 107/115, Memo: Placing of contracts outside of the Saorstát, DFA–industry and commerce, 30 Nov. 1937.   91 Ibid., memo: Placing of contracts in outside countries, department of external affairs, 9 Dec. 1937.

order was to complicate negotiations on a new Irish-German trade agreement for 1937.

Saorstát Oil Refineries Ltd had placed an order for approximately £1 million-worth of oil tankers in Germany prior to Irish-German trade discussions. The Irish government hoped to get the special 1: 1 barter agreement to facilitate an increase in Irish agricultural exports, as agreed in the 1936 trade deal. It also wanted agreement on an improved monetary ratio of 2:3 for 1937 rather than the 1:2 ratio of the 1936 agreement.[92] The Germans, before they knew that the oil tanker contract had already been signed, agreed to the special barter arrangement but wanted to deduct the cost of any imported raw materials. In late October 1936 when an Irish trade delegation went to Berlin to discuss trade matters, the Germans discovered the oil tanker order had been placed before negotiations had opened and maintained it was old business.[93] Furthermore, Crusader Petroleum Industries of London, an English firm that was constructing the oil refinery in Dublin, had originally placed the order for the oil tankers, so the German trade authorities had treated it as an order from England. The Germans did eventually accept the arguments of the Irish side that 'Irish money would ultimately, in fact, pay for the tankers', that the order was a result of the Saorstát government's economic development policy and that the English oil company was in effect an intermediary for the Irish government. The negotiators, by way of some compensation, offered a new Irish-German trade agreement for 1937 and for 1938 based on a monetary trade ratio of 3:2 instead of 2:1, conditional on the exclusion of the tankers from calculations of Germany's Irish import values for the purposes of the agreement.[94] Inclusion of the tanker order would have increased by £500,000 Germany's commitment to take Irish imports.

The Irish trade delegation[95] and Bewley[96] recommended this offer should be accepted and the three Irish departments concerned (external affairs, industry and commerce, and agriculture) eventually jointly decided to agree to the German proposal.[97] The 2:3 ratio was, in fact, probably closer to parity because the Irish method of calculating the value of trade with Germany failed to factor in that approximately 70 per cent of Irish-German trade was transported in Irish registered ships to the benefit of the Saorstát. Consequently, in December 1936, the trade section of the department of external affairs calculated that 'it is not improbable that an exchange of goods on a 3 to 2 ratio *calculated on the value of German goods at the Saorstát port of entry* is not much less favourable to the Saorstát than a 1:1 ratio *calculated on the actual foreign exchange accruing to Germany*' since much of the German manufactured goods imported into

---

92 NAI, DFA 132/81, Foreign Trade Committee meeting held on 6 Oct. 1936.   **93** Ibid., Ferguson, Fahy & McGrath memo, 24 Oct. 1936.   **94** Ibid.; ibid., DFA memo: Proposed new trade agreement with Germany, 11 Dec. 1936.   **95** Ibid., Ferguson, Fahy & McGrath memo, 24 Oct. 1936.   **96** NAI, DFA 132/81, Bewley–Walshe, 24 Oct. 1936.   **97** Ibid., Leydon–Lemass, 28 Oct. 1938; unknown–de Valera, 4 Nov. 1936.

Ireland were heavily dependent on raw material imports to Germany. The department recognized, too, that: 'Owing to existing German economic circumstances, Germany's foreign trade policy is based primarily on importing and paying for goods from any country out of the proceeds of foreign exchange accruing to Germany from exports to that country'. Ireland could not expect to gain more from the Germans than it had now achieved.[98]

In March 1937 after the new trade agreement came into force, Bewley submitted a persuasive proposal to the relevant government departments advocating a renewed diversion of Irish purchases from other markets to Germany. After highlighting the failure of de Valera's policy of seeking alternative markets to Britain thus far (92 per cent of Irish exports were still destined for Britain according to Irish trade statistics for 1936) he argued against the dangers of 'putting all our eggs in one basket'. He feared Britain still had the power to implement reprisals against Irish products. Since Germany was the only country outside Britain in a position to take substantial quantities of Irish produce, and it was one of the few countries with which Ireland had a relatively equitable trade balance (if the use of Irish ships in Irish-German trade was factored in), then the Irish government should seek to encourage Irish exporters and importers to pursue trade options with Germany. The government was already ensuring that many purchases by state and semi-state bodies were made in Germany. Private enterprise in Ireland had to be persuaded to consider the possibilities, too.[99]

The Foreign Trade Committee, comprised of relevant officials from the departments of external affairs, agriculture, and industry and commerce and responsible for placing external contracts, 'recommended that a detailed examination should be made as to the practicability of purchasing in Germany and other countries from which adequate reciprocal trade might be obtained, goods which are at present imported from countries with which the balance of trade is unfavourable'.[99] The introduction of tariffs against countries that failed to maintain a favourable balance of trade was suggested to prevent a drain on the Ireland's foreign currency position. An analysis of 1936 foreign trade figures revealed Ireland imported £17.282 million-worth of goods and materials from all countries other than the Britain and Germany, but had exported only £1.256 million-worth.[1]

In late summer 1937 Bewley reported a conversation with the chief of the trade section of the AA. The German official stated Irish products were ones 'which Germany would always be obliged to import'. He regretted that Irish purchases of German goods had not increased despite the improved trade ratio. Bewley regarded these as 'official' opinions.[2] Bewley warned Berlin was dissat-

---

98 Ibid., proposed new trade agreement with Germany, 11 Dec. 1936. 99 Ibid., Bewley–Walshe, 22 Mar. 1937. 99 Ibid., Foreign Trade Committee meeting of 6 Apr. 1937. 1 Ibid., memo: Trade with US, Belgium and Germany, 6 Apr. 1937. 2 Ibid., Bewley–Walshe, 30 Aug. 1937.

isfied that the volume of trade with Ireland had not increased despite the advantageous trading relationship. Irish imports of German goods had not grown; rather, they had declined.

The bargaining of state controlled contracts for export advantage in Germany proved more arduous and complicated to implement than anticipated. The policy caused intra-government controversy and introduced substantial complications in Ireland's relationship with Germany. One incident involving National Oil Refineries Ltd and its English parent company (Crusader Oil Ltd) in 1937 illustrates this.[3] There were discussions about the machinery and tanks necessary for building a Dublin oil refinery and whether they should be ordered from Britain or Germany under the Irish–German trade agreement for 1937. There followed a complex series of negotiations between the German and Irish governments, and the private companies concerned, about possible direct barter deals and about whether orders placed for German supplied equipment would allow Ireland to increase its agricultural exports to Germany.

A second incident involving the supply of equipment to semi-state bodies (the ESB, Turf Board and so on) provoked arguments among Irish officials as to how Germany should be treated as a special trading partner. Should government external contracts be awarded to the lowest tender or to a more expensive German tender which could bring valuable export opportunities for Ireland? In at least one case, relating to a contract for rails for the Turf Board (Bord na Móna), the German government had been asked to seek a reduction of a German firm's higher tender. There was no reduction and the department of industry and commerce granted the contract to a Dutch firm although it was later proved that 'had the contract been given to the German firm at the original tender figure, the profit which would have been made for the Exchequer by the export of additional quantities of agricultural goods to Germany would have been at least equivalent to the difference between the German tender and the Dutch tender'.[4] Together the departments of agriculture and external affairs overcame the department of industry and commerce's objections on tendering issues and Germany continued to receive special consideration into 1938 and 1939.[5]

3 NAI, DFA 107/123, Leydon note, 4 Jan. 1938. Crusader Oil Ltd was a subsidiary of Parent Petroleum Interests Ltd, which was controlled by Lord Inverforth, Mr T. C. Burgess and Mr Davis. Parent Petroleum was 'financing Irish National Refineries Ltd pending the raising of the necessary capital by an issue of shares'. 4 NAI, DFA 107/115, Fahy–Walshe, 17 Nov. 1937. 5 Ibid., Fahy–Bewley, 29 Nov. 1937.

CONCLUSION: A TURNING POINT?

George Orwell's observation that 'History stopped in 1936' is instructive.[6] Propaganda and ideology became the animators of popular emotions especially in fascist states but also in the democracies. In Ireland a significant level of popular support emerged for Mussolini's conquest of Abyssinia and Franco's rebellion against the Spanish Republic based on a simplistic analysis of those situations. However, the Irish government chose an alternative course recognizing the complexity of those situations and realizing the wider unsettling implications for European peace.

As for Bewley, even in the aftermath of the Abyssinian crisis, he offered some valuable insights on developments in Nazi Germany and in Europe. In the international field, he recognized, that the face of European politics was transformed by Mussolini's defiance of the League and Britain.[7] He reported that Germans viewed Mussolini's success as a British defeat. British unwillingness to act decisively or to intervene was interpreted as a sign of weakness.[8] The Nazi regime no longer attached much importance to the League and, in any case, it was viewed as the creation of vested interests.[9] Bewley told Dublin as early as May 1936 that Hitler's regime sensed it was free to act unilaterally in defiance of the treaty of Versailles as a way to satisfy its national grievances with regard to Danzig, Memel and Austria.[10] Bewley also predicted the signing of an Austro-German agreement in July 1936 that he subsequently accurately assessed as a great deal for Germany. It eased tensions and held out the prospect of cooperation with Italy and many eastern European countries.[11] The agreement meant that Austrian Nazis were given a role in the Austrian government and began to penetrate the administration of the country establishing what would later be a valuable fifth column. Then in the months leading up to the formation of the Rome–Berlin Axis on 25 October 1936 he drew attention to many signs and rumours of increasing intimacy between Germany and Italy.[12]

Bewley highlighted other developments from his vantage point in Berlin. In May he noted the increasingly anti-Communist posture of the German government and diplomatic corps in response to the breakdown in public order under the recently formed Popular Front government of Léon Blum in France. Continuing military cooperation between the Czechs and the Soviets under the 1935 Czech–Soviet mutual defence security pact was also cited as further evidence of a growing Communist menace.[13] For Bewley Communism was the key cleavage in European politics and international alliance systems. Bewley argued, however, that the use of anti-Communism by the Nazi government was to an

6 Brendon, *Dark valley*, p. 341.   7 NAI, DFA, CRS 19/50A, Bewley–Walshe, 18 May 1936. 8 Ibid., 20 Apr. 1936 & 22 June 1936.   9 Ibid., 22 June 1936 & 26 June 1936.   10 Ibid., 6 May 1936.   11 Ibid., 10 July 1936, 13 July 1936 & 15 July 1936.   12 Ibid., 6 May 1936, 16 June 1936 & 3 Sept. 1936.   13 Ibid., 25 May 1936.

extent opportunistic; he admitted that the government used any justification it could to further the rearmament programme of which he saw increasing evidence. The regime was using the possibility of war between Nazism and Communism to justify authoritarian and 'strong' government.[14] Germans now believed, according to Bewley, that Communism had weakened many governments and were now thankful that Germany had a strong man to resist the industrial strife widespread under the French Popular Front government.[15] Reports emerging from Madrid and Barcelona 'united the people round Hitler as their saviour from Communism,'[16] Bewley noted, drawing Dublin's attention to the interdependence of Nazi domestic and foreign policies. The alleged progress of Communism abroad and the turmoil it produced was used to justify Nazi foreign policy and rearmament. It also served to legitimate the regime, while Hitler's foreign successes were significant in boosting domestic support for the Nazis.[17]

Bewley even noted striking organisational parallels between the Nazi and Soviet political systems. In April 1936, he pointed out both systems had a fundamental dislike of democracy, used the 'Party' (Nazi or Bolshevik) to mobilize and discipline the population, and adhered to the principle that a fanatical vanguard or party elite should control the state.[18] Both also used state youth organisations to indoctrinate the young.

But Bewley was radicalized by the Italo-Abyssinian crisis and the Spanish Civil War. His pre-existing conspiratorial beliefs about Britain, Jews and Freemasonry, together with his anti-Communism, transformed him into a harsh critic of Irish foreign policy. This, in turn, badly affected his ability to present a balanced account of events in Germany and internationally during late 1935 and 1936. His public pro-Nazi utterances in the German press in April 1937 embarrassed the Irish government and compromised his position. In tandem with his active campaign to reorient Irish foreign policy to be more explicitly anti-English and pro-German since 1935, it was apparent that the longer Bewley remained in Berlin the more he presented a problem to Walshe and de Valera. By April 1937 his Nazi preferences were public knowledge and by late 1937 relations between Bewley and his home department were at their lowest ebb.

Meanwhile de Valera persisted with a pragmatic foreign policy although the importance of the Saorstát to British defence, by virtue of geopolitics, suggested that a truly independent course would be difficult to follow. It depended on treading a narrow line between fulfilling Irish nationalist expectations and meeting British defence concerns, at least at a minimal level. De Valera would later acknowledge the Saorstát was fortunate that it had to deal with Britain as a powerful neighbour rather than Nazi Germany. On the international stage, a

14 Ibid., 6 June 1936.   15 Ibid., 22 June 1936.   16 Ibid., 18 Aug. 1936.   17 Ibid., 24 Mar. 1936.   18 Ibid., 25 Apr. 1935.

distinction was already being drawn between the legitimacy of German irredentism and the internal excesses of the Nazi regime. In the next two years the
nature of Nazism was to become clearer and to play an influential role in the
renegotiation of Anglo-Irish relations.

7

The appeasement triangle,
September 1937–September 1938

'If we held the whole of territory, there is no doubt whatever ... our attitude would be ... that we have no aggressive designs against any other people. We would strengthen ourselves so as to maintain our neutrality. We would strengthen ourselves so that we might resist any attempt to make use of our territory for attack upon any other nation'[1] (de Valera).

Ireland was an indirect beneficiary of Nazi fait accomplis beginning with the reoccupation of the Rhineland from March 1936 onwards. Nazi foreign policy initiatives destabilized the international situation triggering a deterioration in international relations as crisis succeeded crisis and nations rearmed in earnest. The British administration and the Irish government became more flexible and amenable to reconciliation in this atmosphere. Intransigence on both sides declined as the advantages of a pragmatic and workmanlike relationship in an increasingly violent environment became obvious. By this time, de Valera had remoulded the constitutional Anglo-Irish connection, a process culminating in the 1937 constitution. The British prime minister, Sir Neville Chamberlain, adopted a parallel appeasement policy towards both Éire and Germany, in part to secure his flank in case his pacification of Germany eventually failed. As Hitler grew more expansionist during 1938, de Valera's and Chamberlain's policies converged. De Valera and Walshe supported London's desperate conciliation measures in the hope of preventing a general European war that neither Britain nor Éire desired or considered to be in their best interests.

Meanwhile, Irish-German bilateral relations continued. The development of formal Irish-German trade relations during the early 1930s had prompted Britain to ameliorate the Anglo-Irish trade conflict and to safeguard Irish markets for its exports in the long-term. It is ironic that it was the Anglo-Irish Economic War that had originally motivated Ireland to develop Germany as an alternative market for Irish agricultural produce especially cattle. In this sense Irish-German trade, despite its limited economic value, served a larger purpose as a means to apply pressure on Britain.

1 M. Moynihan (ed.), *Speeches and statements by Eamon de Valera, 1917–73* (Dublin, 1980), p. 276.

CONSTITUTIONAL REVOLUTION

Anglo-Irish trade differences had eased as a result of the coal–cattle pact of 1936, but those differences remained substantial and, more importantly, the constitutional quarrel remained unresolved. De Valera took the opportunity of King Edward VIII's abdication to continue his revision of the relationship. The resulting External Relations Act (December 1936) completed the elimination of the British crown from Irish domestic affairs and strictly limited its role in external affairs to rubberstamping consular and diplomatic appointments, without even admitting Irish allegiance.

Following de Valera's republican labours since 1932, the original spirit of Free State Constitution of 1922 was dead. De Valera's constitutional revolution, which admittedly exploited the advances made by the previous Cumann na nGaedheal governments (particularly in regard to the treaty of Westminster), was both symbolically and legislatively copperfastened with the advent of a new constitution on 29 December 1937. It was endorsed by a referendum of the Irish electorate. To all intents and purposes, de Valera had transformed the Saorstát into a republic 'in all but name'. The state was retitled Éire (Ireland). The British government resisted the temptation to challenge these developments during 1937 because not only were de Valera's initiatives within the bounds of Commonwealth rules but, ultimately, Éire remained however tenuously a member of the British Commonwealth. This meant it indirectly accepted the crown as part of the Commonwealth package without admitting Irish allegiance to the crown in the External Relations Act or the 1937 constitution.[2]

TOWARDS ANGLO-IRISH RECONCILIATION

Irish nationalist sentiment still insisted on the return of the Treaty ports and the termination of partition, in addition to a general economic settlement. These were the substantive issues remaining, and de Valera could not deliver these by his usual opportunist and unilateralist tactics. Nor was a military solution practical or desirable, and it was not even considered as a means to achieve unification and repossession of the treaty ports. The only feasible means by which de Valera could achieve his objectives was through negotiation with Britain. Despite a fraught atmosphere in Anglo-Irish relations, considerable

---

2 It should also be noted that the 1937 constitution was significant in another way. The inclusive Article 44 specifically recognized the right of people to practise Judaism and recognized Jewish congregations' rights, in addition to many other religious denominations existing in Éire at the time of the implementation of the constitution. This represented a repudiation of the intolerant policies of Nazi Germany, many states of eastern Europe and the Soviet Union.

goodwill remained on both sides. To a large extent this was a product of some of the personalities involved in the conduct of Anglo-Irish relations such as Joseph Walshe, John W. Dulanty, Malcolm MacDonald and Neville Chamberlain.

MacDonald, in particular, was vital. A member of a new British political generation, he had not formed negative preconceptions as a result of the Anglo-Irish conflict during and after Irish independence and he was prepared to discuss Anglo-Irish differences with more even-handedness and sensitivity than most of his more senior cabinet colleagues.[3] He was the first British minister to recognize and accept that the Anglo-Irish Treaty (1921) was a dead letter[4] and he was enthusiastic about a British commonwealth of independent states rather than the traditional idea of a British empire.[5] In his conception of the Commonwealth as 'a gentlemanly club of ex-colonial states' he believed Ireland had a role. Between 1936 and 1938 he used his undoubted persuasive powers to overcome the objections of cabinet colleagues and officials to reaching an accommodation with de Valera. MacDonald tended to emphasize the positive elements of de Valera's position.[6] His minimal definition of Commonwealth membership, his political realism and his patience permitted him to develop a rapport with de Valera that had been lacking among his predecessors.

Chamberlain, one of the most powerful British prime ministers of the 20th century,[7] played a decisive role in achieving the Anglo-Irish Treaty of 1938. The British policy of conciliation, to earn the label of appeasement, emerged in relation to Ireland, Italy and Germany as early as 1936. The fundamental presumption underlying this policy was that it would lead to new trusting relationships.[8] Although Chamberlain in particular became identified with the policy of appeasement after he became prime minister in May 1937, it originated earlier and had wide popular and political support. The policy of conciliation or appeasement was intended as a constructive policy towards all states with grievances. As Sir Samuel Hoare recorded: 'appeasement did not mean surrender, nor was it a policy only to be used towards dictators. To Chamberlain it meant the methodical removal of the principal causes of friction in the world'.[9]

Chamberlain's impression of Hitler in part paralleled his view of de Valera during darker moments, and his attitude towards the 'Irish question' was identical in many respects to his views on the 'German question'. He found both men extremely difficult to negotiate with. This parallel in British policy was explicitly extended by Chamberlain on at least one occasion when the prime

---

3 J. Bowman, *De Valera and the Ulster question, 1917–1973* (Oxford, 1982), p. 137. 4 McMahon, *Republicans*, p. 175. 5 Ibid., p. 166. 6 Ibid., p. 205. Although the Irish government was 'fortunate' in MacDonald's appointment, MacDonald's motives were not entirely 'altruistic' (see Fisk, *In time of war*, p. 30). 7 McMahon, *Republicans*, p. 218. 8 Fisk, *In time of war*, p. 32. 9 Cited in McMahon, *Republicans*, p. 218.

minister, exasperated by de Valera's obstinacy as a negotiator, informed his cabinet colleagues that he feared de Valera's 'mentality was in some ways like Herr Hitler's. It was no use employing with them the arguments which appealed to the ordinary reasonable man'.[10]

On the Irish side, de Valera remained faithful to his republican agenda and worked towards attaining his sacred cow of external association. He supposed this option sufficiently finessed the ambivalences of Anglo-Irish relations and Irish membership of the Commonwealth to placate Irish democratic nationalist and republican opinion, and meet the minimum British requirements. It also had the advantage, in his mind, of extending a fig leaf to the northern unionist population should they consent to unification with the south. No matter how flawed his analysis, on the whole it had the advantage of satisfying, at least in the medium term, the majority of the southern electorate. De Valera was single-minded in pursuing his constitutional revolution and repeatedly stated that a truly sovereign and independent Ireland, and on occasion a neutral Ireland, would not undermine Britain's vital national security interests, but rather would strengthen them.

THE INTERNATIONAL FACTOR

From late 1937 the deteriorating international environment accelerated an Anglo-Irish settlement. Potential external threats to security created a temporary Anglo-Irish convergence facilitating agreement in early 1938. National self-interest on both sides dictated pragmatism since the security of one island was closely linked to the security of the other island. Despite de Valera's denial, it could be argued he used Britain's strategic weaknesses on the European continent and in the Far East to his advantage.[11] However, he did so peacefully in contrast to the European dictators. MacDonald as early as mid 1936 considered the lack of a settlement between Britain and the then Free State as the most serious aspect of inter-imperial relations that tended 'to weaken the moral authority of the British Commonwealth of Nations in world affairs'.[12] By late 1937 and early 1938 with Nazi Germany in the ascendant and Hitler eyeing Austria and Czechoslovakia, a general European conflict was possible. Hitler, Mussolini, Chamberlain and de Valera were caught in an interconnected web of international relations.

The beginning of the conciliation process with Ireland was aided by the fact that, despite Anglo-Irish disagreements throughout the 1930s, at the multilateral level both countries had sought the stabilization of the international situation and adopted complementary stances and policies on many issues. De

10 Cited in Bowman, *De Valera*, p. 162. 11 McMahon, *Republicans*, p. 223. 12 PRO, CAB 24/262, MacDonald memo, July 1936.

Valera and his government were inclined to co-operate with Britain when such exchanges were shielded from the Irish public.[13] A strong congruence already existed between British and Irish foreign policies on many European matters. Unlike Bewley and much of the British and Irish publics, de Valera had adopted (admittedly in retrospect) a 'remarkably understanding' attitude towards the Hoare–Laval pact of 1935. He believed the Free State government could:

> quite understand why Sir Samuel Hoare should be shown to advocate a policy which might involve the people of Great Britain in armed conflict with Italy. They also feel that most countries would not be prepared ... to take military sanctions against Italy. Consequently they appreciate that Sir Samuel Hoare had to act with great care as in the event of a situation developing so as to call for naval or military action the Powers immediately concerned ... would be Great Britain and France.[14]

Eventually, the inability of the League of Nations to transform itself into an effective, international arbiter in the face of the crumbling Versailles treaty edifice disillusioned de Valera. In May 1937 de Valera hinted in the Dáil about Ireland's possible withdrawal, causing consternation in the European press.[15] During the summer of 1937 continental speculation presumed Ireland was preparing to leave the League and retreat into isolationism. It did not because, although Irish policymakers were dissatisfied with the League's performance, it still retained a useful residual function as an independent multilateral forum. However, as if to underline its irrelevance in international affairs, Italy withdrew from the League on 11 December 1937.[16] Walshe nonetheless considered the League served a purpose and should be maintained, but that it needed to be detached from the Versailles treaty.[17]

The deterioration in international events eventually prompted de Valera to propose Anglo-Irish ministerial negotiations after two years of failing to respond to MacDonald's frequent peace feelers. De Valera had evinced concern about European developments since 1936 but only engaged in secret discussions with MacDonald about a general Anglo-Irish settlement in November 1937. Chamberlain, who had replaced Baldwin as prime minister, was actively engaged in appeasing the fascist dictators of Italy and Germany. Chamberlain's search for a peaceful solution to Germany's grievances began in earnest when Lord Halifax visited Hitler at his Bavarian retreat at Berchtesgaden in October 1937.[18] Simultaneously Italy acceded to the German-Japanese anti-Comintern pact.

It was in this context that de Valera informed MacDonald on 24 November

---

13 McMahon, *Republicans*, pp 160–1. 14 Cited in McMahon, *Republicans*, p. 161.
15 Kennedy, *Ireland*, p. 229. 16 Lamb, *Mussolini*, p. 294. 17 PA, AAI, R 102387, Hempel–AA, 19 Jan. 1938. 18 Parker, *Churchill*, pp 126–8.

1937 of his willingness to undertake full-scale negotiations. He claimed he was undertaking this initiative because of his government's apprehension concerning 'how best to protect the people of this country from the dangers to which they will be exposed in the event of the outbreak of another war'.[19] De Valera told the Dáil, after the successful outcome of the negotiations, that the threat of another European war had impelled him to enter the negotiations.[20] The prospect of a satisfactory Anglo-Irish treaty suited Chamberlain's general programme of appeasement, as he informed Lord Craigavon, prime minister of Northern Ireland's Stormont government:

> In my anxieties over the international situation it has become almost essential for me to show some evidence that the policy of peace by negotiation can be successful. I have good hopes that I shall be able to bring forward an Anglo-Italian agreement as evidence of this, but if I can accompany that with an Anglo-Irish agreement it would greatly add to the impression made upon the world. And it is very necessary that an impression of solidarity here should be made, and not least in Berlin.[21]

Chamberlain's appeasement of Éire did not produce the ultimate result – an Irish ally in a potential future war – but it did considerably placate the western flank of Britain. De Valera told the Dáil in May 1936 of his wish that Éire should be neutral in any future conflict.[22] Nonetheless in a tactful intimation to MacDonald in January 1937, 'he personally thought that if we [Britain] were involved in war we should get the use of the [Treaty] ports', but the British could get no guarantee if they insisted on it, they had to rely on the goodwill of the Irish people and the freedom of the Dáil to grant use of the ports in a war situation.[23]

Thus mixed signals were emerging from Dublin and in particular from de Valera before and during the Anglo-Irish negotiations of early 1938. De Valera's ambitious goal was the acquisition of sufficient Irish independence to ensure neutrality in the case of a European war. However, there was doubt in Irish government and official circles that Éire could achieve this necessary freedom of manoeuvre or to muster sufficient resources to ensure Irish neutrality had international credibility in event of war. It was, however, tactically useful in negotiations that the Irish government retained the option to intimate that if all Irish nationalist demands were met, including the return of the Treaty ports

---

19 Cited in McMahon, *Republicans*, p. 226. **20** *Dáil Debates*, vol. 72, cols. 639–716, 13 July 1938. **21** McMahon, *Republicans*, p. 279. **22** Moynihan, *Speeches*, p. 276. The German legation reported de Valera's speech in depth to Berlin (PA, AAI, R102387, Köster–AA, 24 June 1936). **23** But de Valera appended an 'extraordinary request' to his conversations with MacDonald: to conceal the substance of his views from the British cabinet (McMahon, *Republicans*, pp 203–5).

and the ending of partition, a benevolent Éire might enter into a mutual defence agreement with Britain. By early 1938, when it became apparent that the return of the Treaty ports was probable, de Valera used the existence of partition to argue that Irish neutrality was the only acceptable and popular policy for Éire. A mutual defence agreement between Éire and Britain was unacceptable. But how did vested interests in Germany view Ireland's changed relations with Britain?

GERMAN ASSESSMENTS

For Nazi Germany the 'Irish question' remained a subservient part of the Anglo–German equation.[24] Nazi foreign policy remained predicated on the belief that British maritime global–imperial interests were complementary to Germany's self-characterized limited continentalist ambitions in east-central Europe. However, by 1938, the British failure to respond to such a proposed generous division of spheres of interest led to growing frustration in Berlin. Nonetheless Nazi Germany persisted in largely avoiding interference in Britain's sphere of influence and hoped an amicable relationship could be maintained so that Britain would remain neutral in the event of German expansion.[25]

Germany sustained a benevolent or neutral line on Anglo–Irish relations, and made positive noises about the possibility of a general Anglo–Irish settlement. Thus the Goebbels' directed German newspaper coverage of Anglo–Irish relations between 1936 and 1938, although sympathetic to Irish nationalist aspirations and applauding de Valera as a moderate seeking accommodation with Britain, portrayed Ireland as inescapably linked to Britain because of geopolitics and commercial dependency. German newspaper reports expressed concern that the 1937 Irish constitution fundamentally weakened the British commonwealth. Conversely, when the Anglo–Irish negotiations commenced in early 1938, they were applauded as strengthening the British empire. The 1938 Anglo–Irish treaty was greeted warmly by German newspaper plaudits. German media coverage of the Irish question was officially coordinated to accord with the Nazi leadership's strategic anglocentric conceptions.[26] German policymakers remained largely disinterested in Anglo–Irish relations until the negotiations to reach a general settlement commenced in spring 1938 and when Hitler became increasingly agitated by perceived British interference in the German sphere of influence. Then the security implications of the Anglo–Irish feud became of interest to German commentators.

24 Dickel, *Aussenpolitik*, p. 54.   25 Ibid., p. 58.   26 Ibid., p. 56.

Until then the only dedicated, knowledgeable and balanced German observer of Ireland was the new German minister in Dublin, Eduard Hempel, who had gained the trust of both de Valera and Walshe. This 'old school' diplomat demonstrated admirable control of his brief in his numerous reports to superiors following his arrival in July 1937. His assessment of the impact of 1937 constitution on Ireland's situation proved insightful. He realized that the constitution was important symbolically as a wholly Irish creation unlike the Free State Constitution. Practically, however, it contained no change in Anglo-Irish relations or in Irish Commonwealth membership. It simply systematized de Valera's *ad hoc* changes in these relationships since 1932.

As a result, Hempel noted the most significant aspect of the new constitution was that de Valera had not declared a republic, although this had angered elements within Fianna Fáil and extreme republicanism. Thus the constitution had not damaged British interests, but indications were that de Valera still sought national unity and wished to sever Commonwealth links totally by simply withdrawing the External Relations Act. Hempel's evaluation was that the Anglo-Irish power–political relationship remained exactly the same as it had prior to the new constitution because Britain still retained Northern Ireland and the Treaty ports. Éire's strategic location and its importance as a food supplier were of vital interest to Britain; it would not permit Irish neutrality in a future conflict in which it was involved. Hempel did not foresee any solution to partition because of the steadfastness of unionism. Correctly, he observed that both countries were now beginning to realize that their fates were linked and some communication and accommodation was necessary. The German representative believed their common experience of democracy created a bond that was reinforced by the uncertain European situation.[27] However, Hempel underestimated the extent of the concessions Chamberlain was prepared to offer de Valera to ensure Irish benevolence in any war in which Britain was involved. Hempel discounted Irish neutrality as a viable option 'in time of war'.[28]

Hempel met de Valera on 8 February 1938, immediately before the second round of the Anglo-Irish negotiations was to be held in London, and just as the Anschluss crisis was beginning. Hempel formed the impression de Valera would moderate his desire for neutrality because of his pessimistic evaluation of the general European situation and the possibility of a future war. De Valera told Hempel that Éire had an interest in being protected against an invasion from a third power. Partition was the stumbling block to an Anglo-Irish defence compact. Hempel concluded that a completely independent and united Ireland could make a defence pact with Britain, but a divided Ireland could not.[29] Hempel (and most other German commentators such as Woermann and Theo Kordt) presumed Britain could not afford for military–strategic reasons to give

27 PA, AA II, R 102796, Hempel–AA, 20 Dec. 1937. 28 Dickel, *Aussenpolitik*, p. 60.
29 PA, AA II, R 102796, Hempel–AA, 9 Feb. 1938.

up rights to the Irish Treaty ports, a presumption confounded in April 1938 by the unconditional British agreement to return the Treaty ports to Irish control. Hempel also persisted in his belief that de Valera could not maintain Irish neutrality in the event of a war. Joint defence interests, a new spirit of cooperation and Irish defencelessness would propel Éire to join a British war effort. Throughout 1938 German civil and military analysts in the Dublin legation, London embassy, the Wehrmacht, and the AA persisted in their apparently unshakeable belief that geostrategic reality and military–security weakness would convince Éire that an Anglo-Irish defence arrangement was the only credible security posture.[30]

WALSHE

The secretary of the department of external affairs, Walshe, held views not dissimilar from these and at variance with his political master's neutralist thinking. He doubted whether Irish neutrality was either a feasible or credible policy. Walshe considered Éire incapable of maintaining a neutral policy because of Ireland's central role in British security.[31] Walshe's analysis of the Anglo-Irish relationship during 1937 and early 1938 was congruent in many respects to the views expressed by Hempel during this period. He acknowledged the impossibility of achieving all island unity in the Anglo-Irish negotiations of 1938 and advocated a defence agreement with Britain. He saw such cooperation as 'a dynamic thing' believing progress in Anglo-Irish understanding and unity was an evolutionary process.[32] At one point in the midst of the negotiations in London he advised de Valera to make a defence agreement to ensure the return of the Treaty ports:

> I should be ready to make real sacrifices ... The sacrifices we are asked to make in defence is more apparent than real, because it is the only means of preventing the possible permanent loss of our independence in the almost certain crisis of a great war.[33]

Hitler, too, maintained a similar prognosis of the intrinsic Anglo-Irish linkage. Hempel records how Hitler divulged to him in mid-1937 that although Ireland was adopting an assertive line independent of Britain and the Commonwealth, the economic and political realities were that it remained dependent on Britain.[34] Hitler drew the false conclusion that Britain's preoccu-

---

30 Dickel, *Aussenpolitik*, p. 62–65. **31** Nolan, 'Walshe', pp 85–6. **32** Ibid., pp 91–3.
33 Franciscan Archives, Killiney, de Valera papers, 953, Walshe to de Valera, n.d. (*c.*February 1938) cited in Nolan, p. 91. The de Valera papers have since been moved to UCD Archives.
34 *Sunday Press*, 12 Jan. 1964.

pation with the Irish question and other serious Commonwealth problems weakened and prevented it from interfering in Europe, thus increasing his freedom of action.[35] The Nazi dictator and other senior Nazis such as Göring, an acquaintance of Bewley, continued to use crude parallels between the Anglo-Irish situation and German post-Versailles revisionism in central Europe until March 1939 to bolster German demands. Göring, for instance, pointedly asked Lord Lothian in May 1937 what Britain would do if Ireland suppressed 3.5 million Englishmen like the Prague government was doing to Sudeten Germans. Yet that same month to the same English lord, Hitler contrasted his own pacific methods of achieving valid German nationalist aims in east–central Europe with what he characterized as traditional English military coercion, or the 'Ulster method', to control neighbouring weaker nations. Hitler may have harboured sympathy for Irish nationalism because he later informed the Aga Khan that the Sudetenland was entitled to similar autonomy as that of Ireland. But wherever his sentiments really lay, the Irish analogy served as a tactical tool to deflect criticism from Germany.[36]

ANGLO–IRISH AGREEMENT

The threat of European war was the main catalyst in the eventual success of Anglo-Irish negotiations of 1938.[37] The negotiations of January to April 1938 were reminiscent of those in October 1921: 'War ... was once again in the air, but this time there was no question of hostilities between England and Ireland. War, if it came, would come from an external aggressor. It would be of a kind to jeopardize the very existence of Britain and, it might well be, of Ireland.'[38] That Germany was increasingly viewed as the likely aggressor was underscored by the Anschluss when Hitler used intimidation and deception to unite Austria with Germany by marching into Vienna on 12 March 1938.[39]

Walshe considered the more fearful Britain was of international developments then the more it would offer in return for a defence arrangement.[40] Until the Anschluss, de Valera and the Irish cabinet had been disinclined to accept the latest British offers and on 14 March de Valera informed Cudahy, the US minister to Éire, that negotiations had collapsed and he would not return to London.[41] However the Anschluss forced him to reconsider breaking off negotiations on the issue of partition. He told Cudahy that 'Ireland on the continent would suffer a fate similar to Austria' implying gratitude for Ireland's peripheral location and the fact that Britain, rather than Germany, was Ireland's neighbour. De Valera also recognized an undeniable degree of Anglo-Irish

35 Dickel, *Aussenpolitik*, p. 66. 36 Ibid., p. 67. 37 Bowman, *De Valera*, p. 136.
38 Longford and O'Neill, *De Valera*, p. 313. 39 McMahon, *Republicans*, p. 276.
40 Nolan, 'Walshe', pp 91–2. 41 McMahon, *Republicans.*, p. 275.

convergence on international affairs as he admitted to Cudahy that his only concern was that Irish racial and cultural identity *vis-à-vis* the English could be
safeguarded.[42]

Chamberlain for his part wished for a gentleman's agreement to settle all
aspects of the Anglo-Irish feud. Unable to persuade the Ulster unionists to
unite with Éire, he was prepared to come to terms with de Valera to ensure he
had a benevolent neutral, rather than an enemy, in the event of a war with
Germany. Chamberlain continued to harbour the hope that Éire would reconsider neutrality if faced with a general European war and instead ally with
Britain. So de Valera benefited from appeasement while supporting
Chamberlain's conciliation of Nazi Germany, and Germany was supportive of
Britain's appeasement of Ireland.

AFTER ANSCHLUSS

The increasing power of Germany in particular, and of the revisionist states
(Germany, Italy, Japan) in general, prompted the Irish, too, to adopt a policy of
appeasement not least in the interests of Irish security. In mid-November 1937
Walshe told Hempel, that Germany was in a favourable international situation
to attain its revisionist or irredentist demands. Britain, by comparison, had not
occupied such a difficult situation for centuries, especially since its
Mediterranean and Asian interests were threatened. Walshe supposed Britain
should now come to an accommodation with Germany and Germany could
regain its lost colonies and seek a solution to the Sudeten–German question.
Walshe encouraged Hempel and the AA to engage with Chamberlain's efforts at
conciliation. Most interestingly he also revealed his hope that improved Anglo-
German relations would be a positive influence on settling the Anglo-Irish
quarrel. Hempel noted the Irish press voiced similar sentiments, most notably
that enlargement of the anti-Comintern pact to include Italy as well as Japan,
improved Germany's chances of gaining the return of its lost colonies.[43]

Walshe also favoured a conciliatory policy towards Mussolini's Italy. He lobbied for the appointment of an Irish minister to the Quirinal in Rome in late
1937 although the Free State had opposed Mussolini's conquest of Abyssinia
and maintained a strict non-intervention policy in the Spanish Civil War. Such
an Irish minister would be accredited to the king of Italy, the self-styled emperor
of Abyssinia, at a time when Britain and the remainder of the Commonwealth
refused to accept the legitimacy of Italian rule over Abyssinia. Walshe's proposal
caused Anglo-Irish controversy which 'rather peeved' de Valera who decided to
delay the accreditation of the Irish minister to Italy until April 1938 after an

---

42 Ibid., pp 275–6.   43 PA, AA II, R 102796, Hempel–AA, 17 Nov. 1937.

Anglo-Italian agreement to recognize the king of Italy's new title.[44] Whether for sentimental reasons or for pragmatic defensive calculations, in late 1937 and early 1938 Walshe and de Valera adopted an active appeasement policy towards the fascist powers and correspondingly supported Chamberlain's efforts.

The Irish government extended recognition of the incorporation of Austria into Germany in March 1938 despite Article 30 of the treaty of Versailles, Article 88 of the treaty of St Germain and subsequent agreements between the major European powers to protect the independence of Austria.[45] It did so after the German legation in Dublin formally notified de Valera on 15 March of the absorption of Austria into Germany. De Valera's formal response of reimposing visa requirements for holders of German and Austrian passports'[46] was an act of recognition by the Irish government of the Anschluss.[47] The Irish government also acceded to Hempel's request that German residents be able to vote in the plebiscite held throughout the Reich (including Austria) on 14 April to retrospectively affirm the Anschluss.[48] Almost 100 per cent of the German and Austrian electorate duly assented to the 'Reunion of Austria with the German Reich'.[49]

Then a month later on 14 June 1938, the Foreign Trade Committee recommended Austria should be regarded as part of Germany for the purposes of the Irish-German trade agreement.[50] De Valera approved and instructed the German authorities be formally notified of the action.[51] The 1930 treaty of commerce and navigation was extended to the territory of the former Austrian state 'from the day of the removal of the customs frontier between the former Austria and the rest of Germany'[52] on 31 March 1939.[53]

Despite this *de facto* and *de jure* recognition of the Anschluss there was considerable unease in Ireland about Germany's action. The *Irish Press*, for instance, considered the annexation both alarming and ominous: 'It is evident

---

44 McMahon, *Republicans*, p. 223. Hempel accurately predicted de Valera would not appoint an Irish minister to Rome in these circumstances because it would needlessly annoy London (PA, AA II, R 102796, Hempel–AA, 18 Dec. 1937). He argued there had been no case relating to European matters in which Irish and British interests conflicted. Therefore, he followed the standard German line of thought that angered Bewley, i.e. Britain always catered for her political interests in continental and international affairs, but Éire as a small country was disinterested and tended to follow the British line in foreign affairs. However, Hempel recognized that the Commonwealth was not unitary and there was certainly diversity of opinion within it. Thus he did not rule out the possibility of Ireland taking an independent line since it had the legal right to do so (PA, AA II, R 102796, Hempel–AA, 20 Dec. 1937). **45** The treaty of St Germain-en-Laye, signed on 10 September 1919 by the Allies and Austria, was the Austrian equivalent of the treaty of Versailles. MAI, MIS 25, 1 Jan. 1938–31 Mar. 1938. **46** NAI, DFA 207/10, Rynne–Leydon, 4 June 1938. **47** Ibid. **48** NAI, DJ 12/38, Roche–Garda commissioner, 1 Apr. 1938. **49** Kershaw, *Nemesis*, p. 82. **50** NAI, DFA 207/10, Foreign Trade Committee meeting held on 14 June 1938. **51** Ibid., Egan–Murphy, 15 June 1938; ibid, Walshe annotation, 16 June 1938. **52** Ibid., Hempel–de Valera, 3 Jan. 1939. **53** Ibid., Thomsen–de Valera, 23 Mar. 1939.

that the whole thing was carefully and systematically arranged beforehand'.[54] Hitler had destabilized the whole European situation, and 'all feelings of confidence in Europe' had been destroyed.[55] German minorities resided throughout central Europe. Hitler could apply the same methods to incorporate them in the Third Reich as with Austria, and this could lead to war. The *Irish Press*, therefore, did not approve of Hitler's wiping 'from the map a nation with a history going back more than a thousand years'.[56] Nazi treatment of the Catholic Church in Austria was also criticized in the Irish press[57] and similar but more forceful antipathy was expressed in a small protest against the Anschluss outside the German legation in Dublin on the evening of 16 March 1938. Although the German minister and legation officials were absent at the time three young men left a written protest 'on behalf of the citizens of Dublin' for Hempel 'against the brutal invasion by your Fascist Government of Austria and the destruction of its independence'. It stated:

> We protest as Irishmen because our nation has always fought against national enslavement and imperialistic invasions. We protest as democrats because of your fascist government is the brutal enemy of all freedom – national, individual and social. Your government is the enemy of every small and weak nation struggling for its rights. We protest as Christians because your fascist government is the deadly foe and persecutor of all Churches and the enemy of religious freedom. We protest your abuse of diplomatic privilege here to propagate the doctrine of Hitler's fascists ...

It was a peaceful anti-fascist demonstration but as a result 'special police supervision' for legation premises and the residence of the Dr Hempel in Dun Laoghaire was arranged.[58]

Irish Military Intelligence (G2) noted: 'Hardly had Europe accepted the changed situation than the dying echoes of anti-Austrian propaganda changed to a rising crescendo of anti-Czech propaganda.'[59] The Anschluss initiated an unprecedented period of upheaval and readjustment in European diplomacy and politics. The birth of Greater Germany required every European nation to reassess its interests, alliances and treaties.[60]

---

54 IP, 15 Mar. 1938.   **55** IP, 14 Mar. 1938.   **56** Ibid.   **57** PA, AA, R122531, Hempel–AA, 19 July 1938.   **58** NAI, DJ D.17/37, see annotations to R. Wolfe memo 'German legation visited by three men who made anti-fascist representations', 17 Mar. 1938.   **59** MAI, MIS 27, 1 July 1938–30 Sept. 1938.   **60** Ibid.

STRATEGIC REVOLUTION

Following the Anschluss, Hitler turned his attention to the ethnic or Sudeten Germans in the multi-ethnic, unitary and democratic state of Czechoslovakia. It was the last surviving democracy of those created by Versailles in east–central Europe. Despite its ethno-linguistic diversity and economic inequalities, the longstanding premier T.G. Masaryk advocated principles of democracy and full civil and human rights for all, including minorities. Unlike most other eastern European states, therefore, Czechoslovakia maintained its international commitments to minorities and, in that sense, provided an effective democratic alternative to the fascist, totalitarian and authoritarian options pursued by its neighbours. However, the resurgence of Germany isolated the country internationally and exacerbated its internal divisions.

Again Military Intelligence's (G2) summaries, forecasts and analyses of the international situation provided a solid overview of the developing situation in 1938 and were less value-laden than assessments submitted to Dublin from Bewley in Berlin. The German annexation of Austria, G2 bluntly concluded, was a strategic revolution. Its analysis of the formation of Greater Germany was explicitly informed by Winston Churchill's speech in the house of commons on 14 March to the effect that: 'This mastery of Vienna gives Nazi Germany military and economic control of the whole communications of south-eastern Europe by road, by river and by rail.'[61] Vienna was the centre of communications of the old Austro–Hungarian empire and Nazi domination of Vienna endowed it with strategic and economic control of the whole of south-eastern Europe.[62] The previous strategic calculations of Italy, Switzerland, Hungary, Yugoslavia and Czechoslovakia had been destroyed. G2 officers pointed to Czechoslovakia as the state most affected by the termination of Austria's independence. Czechoslovakia was primarily populated by non-Germanic peoples but its western and southern margins, or the Sudetenland, were home to more than three million ethnic Germans. The Irish intelligence officers recognized that Czechoslovakia was in a precarious position by virtue of geography alone:

A glance at the map will show vividly the peril of her position and shows too, from Germany's point of view, how inconvenient it is that a non-German state – except for a comparatively small German minority – should be thrust deep into her side. Moreover, the German population of Czechoslovakia mostly inherit the belt bordering on the new Germany along the entire border from Eastern Silesia to Eastern Austria.

61 MAI, MIS 26, 1 Apr. 1938–30 June 1938.   62 Ibid., 1 July 1938–30 Sept. 1938.

Hitler's comments in February 1938 had suggested Czechoslovakia was the next target for Nazi penetration and the orchestration of German irredentist feelings. Hitler's expressed intentions, together with the Anschluss, placed Czechoslovakia and its military allies, France, the Soviet Union, Romania and Yugoslavia, on defensive alert in the spring of 1938. Britain had no alliance commitment to Czechoslovakia.[63]

G2 recognized Czechoslovakia's strategic isolation. The Czechs possessed 'the best equipped and trained army in central Europe [but] their strategic position was such that they could be surrounded and crushed before any ally – Romania excepted – could aid them'.[64] Hitler sought to exploit concern for the welfare of the German speakers inhabiting the Sudetenland through his influence over Konrad Henlein and the Nazi Sudeten German party, the Heimatsfront. A 'war of nerves' ensued following the Anschluss. There is some evidence that Hitler wanted a full-scale conflict with Czechoslovakia in 1938. However Prague, during April and May 1938 with Anglo-French prodding, met most of Henlein's demands, undermining Nazi efforts to represent Sudeten Germans as the injured parties.

German troop movements on 19 May provoked a war scare and Czech mobilization. The British and French governments continued to accept the legitimacy of German nationalist demands and yet again interceded with the Czechs urging them to prevent frontier incidents and internal ethnic clashes, and 'to reach an early and comprehensive settlement with the Sudeten Germans'.[65] They also lobbied Hitler to demonstrate forbearance and understanding. France, publicly stated it would support Czechoslovakia in a crisis while Halifax reiterated Chamberlain's earlier warning that Germany could 'not count upon this country being able to stand aside' since 'if once war should start in central Europe it was quite impossible to say where it might not end, and who might not become involved'.[66] War was avoided but the ramifications were ominous. Hitler, infuriated by British intervention in the self-ascribed German sphere and humiliated by the perception that he had capitulated to such pressure, resolved to 'smash Czechoslovakia by military action in the near future'.[67] Bitter German press comment on the British intervention credited the British initiative as mainly responsible for avoiding a violent degeneration in the situation in May.[68]

---

63 MAI, MIS 25, 1 Jan. 1938–31 Mar. 1938.   64 MAI, MIS 27, 1 July 1938–30 Sept. 1938.
65 MAI, MIS 26, 1 Apr. 1938–30 June 1938.   66 Graham Stewart, *Burying Caesar: Churchill, Chamberlain and the battle for the Tory party* (London, 1999), p. 294.   67 Bell, *Origins*, pp 268–9.   68 MAI, MIS 26, 1 Apr. 1938–30 June 1938.

SUDETENLAND

Éire had no direct involvement in the 'May scare' although it did have a direct interest in the outcome. If a European war erupted at this stage, de Valera's preferred policy of neutrality might not be implemented as the Anglo-Irish treaty had only just been signed (on 25 April) and the Treaty ports had not yet been returned. The British forces left Spike Island, Cobh, only on 11 July 1938. Irish apprehension that the deal would not be honoured increased with the nearly two-week delay in the handover.[69] The other two Treaty ports, Berehaven and Lough Swilly, were not scheduled for return until September. De Valera had regarded the Treaty ports as primarily a political issue,[70] but the threat of war over the Sudetenland made him aware 'that Irish possession of the ports was not just a symbol but an essential physical requirement of an independent foreign policy in a European war'.[71] The Irish authorities began to doubt their return because of the ports strategic, naval and potentially aeronautical importance to Britain. Thus, as the European situation evolved, Anglo-Irish relations and defence concerns were once again inherently linked.

Irish policy largely paralleled British policy towards Czechoslovakia. It was the culmination of Irish policy towards the Versailles treaty. Czechoslovakia was a modern practicing democracy and one of the most modern industrial states in Europe, but to Irish eyes it appeared to be an unnatural polyglot state. Irish adherence to the nationalist principle as the basis for state formation and statebuilding permitted Irish policymakers, like many others, to accept uncritically Hitler's case for the incorporation of the Sudetenland into the Greater Germany. Czech arguments against such an action received little consideration in Ireland or Britain. The Sudetendeutsch had never been part of Germany historically. They had occupied a relatively fortunate position in the former Austro–Hungarian empire and, while absorption into Czechoslovakia in the post-war settlement may have 'reduced their circumstances', they were probably one of most benevolently treated minorities in Europe in the 1930s.[72] In the interests of international peace, however, and fearing that Czechoslovakia was 'strategically and racially ill composed' many considered 'it was not worth fighting for'.[73] This view was prevalent in Dublin as well as in London.

Hitler continued to foment Sudeten resentment and intensified the Czechoslovak political crisis during the summer. The Sudeten Nazi leader, Henlein, broke off talks with the Czech government in early September 1938 ostensibly because the Beneš government was prepared to meet nearly all of his demands.[74] Henlein's position, as masterminded by Hitler, was 'We must always demand so much that we can never be satisfied'.[75] Beneš was prepared to meet

69 Fisk, *In time of war*, p. 1. **70** Ibid., p. 40. **71** Ibid., p. 41. **72** Stewart, *Burying Caesar*, pp 294–5. **73** Ibid., p. 295. **74** Bell, *Origins*, p. 270. **75** *DGFP*, series D, vol. 2, doc. 107.

most of Henlein's demands and grant Sudetenland autonomy. The Nazis' goal, however, was to incorporate Sudetenland into the Greater Germany. In addition Hitler had strategic reasons for wanting to extract the Czech geographical 'thorn' from Germany's side. He also loathed the Czechs, holding Czech nationalists responsible for breaking up the Austro–Hungarian empire which had been dominated by German peoples and character.[76] He resolved 'to smash Czechoslovakia by military action'.[77] Playing on a minor local incident Hitler used the annual Nazi party Nuremberg rally in mid-September 1938 to rage about alleged injustices against the oppressed Sudetens and to create a possible pretext for intervention. This was the cue for Henlein's followers to launch an uprising against their 'oppressors' and for Hitler to intervene with military force. Hitler was allegedly defending Sudeten Germans against the superior force of the Czech state but, in reality, intended to dismember that state. However, at this point Chamberlain personally intervened and Czech forces promptly suppressed the Sudeten rebellion – in actuality Nazi orchestrated riots.[78] Chamberlain misread the situation believing Hitler genuinely wanted a general settlement, so he intervened personally on 15 September to mediate between Berlin and Prague.

Throughout September the British dominions office kept the Irish government informed of the latest developments and J.W. Dulanty, the Irish high commissioner to London, attended daily dominions office briefings for the London-based Commonwealth high commissioners.[79] De Valera, Walshe and Dulanty encouraged Chamberlain in his initiatives to secure peace through concession.[80] Dominion status accentuated Irish influence over Chamberlain and British policy during what came to be known as the Munich crisis. Chamberlain's preoccupation with British frailty in the face of German, Japanese and Italian threats made him keen to secure the united support of the dominions for his actions and policies.[81] Ironically, Éire as a dominion exercised more influence through its Commonwealth membership than by means of its League membership despite de Valera's election as president of the League Assembly on 12 September.[82] The League, however, was a much-reduced remnant of former aspirations. De Valera and Cremins, the Irish representative to the League, thought it was of little use in resolving the conflict particularly since Germany and Italy had left. For de Valera to prompt League to take a formal position was deemed undesirable in light of the League's weakness, and also because de Valera considered such a move would contravene his espoused wish to maintain Irish neutrality.[83]

Éire like other League members retreated from its collective security obliga-

76 Carr, *Arms*, p. 86.   77 Ibid., p. 89.   78 Bell, *Origins*, p. 270.   79 See D. McMahon, 'Ireland, the dominions and the Munich crisis', ISIA, 1: 1 (1979).   80 Ibid., p. 30. 81 Canning, *British policy*, p. 229.   82 McMahon, 'Ireland', p. 30.   83 Kennedy, *Ireland*, pp 234–7.

tions under the League's founding covenant. John Hearne, the legal adviser to the department of external affairs, said as much to Hempel, the German representative in Dublin, in late September 1938. Hearne revealed the Irish government would not feel committed to League of Nations' common action or sanctions. Hempel advised the AA that de Valera had frequently expressed the view that the League required urgent revision and would not support the implementation of collective security.[84] Instead de Valera made use of the Anglo-Irish and Commonwealth connections to support Chamberlain's appeasement policy throughout the crisis. He especially relied on the intimacy that had been created between the two leaders during the Anglo-Irish negotiations earlier that year.

On 15 September de Valera wrote to Chamberlain before the British prime minister was due to meet with Hitler at Berchtesgaden and informed him that 'one person at least is completely satisfied that you are doing the right thing no matter what the result'.[85] Dulanty, throughout September, added his voice to the other dominions to support the British government's continued efforts to appease Hitler.[86] Later, on 27 September, de Valera personally sent a telegram to Chamberlain imploring him 'to let nothing daunt you or deflect you in your effort to secure peace'.[87] Walshe told Hempel that the Irish government had been in constant contact with the British government during the crisis and 'had done all in their power to achieve in London the speedy intervention of the British government for the achieving of a peaceful solution'. Walshe told Hempel on a number of occasions, 'that the Irish government understood the necessity of obtaining full rights of self-determination for the Sudeten Germans'. Walshe even proffered the opinion that Britain was opposed to joining in a European war arising from the crisis and it might even be willing to accept a German statement that it would confine itself to measures in defense of German territory *vis-à-vis* France.[88] Walshe presumed the only alternative was a war for which Éire was unprepared.

De Valera made a public statement on the crisis on 25 September in a broadcast to the US from Geneva. Chamberlain had by this stage persuaded the Czechs to transfer the Sudeten territory to Germany. But on 23 September Hitler again increased his demands, assuming the role of advocate for other nationalities. Not only should the Sudetenland be transferred to Germany immediately, but Polish and Hungarian claims on Czechoslovakia should also be met and Slovakia made autonomous. In this rapidly changing context, de Valera advised his audience:

---

84 PA, AAI, R102387, Hempel–AA, 27 Sept. 1938; see also IT, 24 Sept. 1938 & 27 Sept. 1938. 85 McMahon, 'Ireland', p. 31. 86 Ibid., passim. 87 NAI, DFA 126/73, de Valera–Chamberlain, 27 Sept. 1938. 88 DGFP, Series D, vol. 2, doc. 483, Hempel-AA, 15 Sept. 1938.

The war of sheer aggression ... is not the war that we need to fear the most. The most dangerous war is that which has its origin in just claims denied or in a clash of opposing rights – and not merely opposing interests – when each side can see no reason in justice why it should yield its claim to the other. If by conceding the claims of justice or by reasonable compromise in the spirit of fair play we take steps to avoid the latter kind of war, we can face the possibility of the other kind with relative equanimity.[89]

De Valera's advice was, in effect, to concede supposedly legitimate national claims to Hitler. If he then presented the world with an unjust demand or a fait accompli his true character would be revealed after the expiration of every reasonable effort to pacify him. De Valera continued: 'To allow fears for the future to intervene and make us halt in rendering justice in the present, is not to be wise but to be foolish.'[90]

On 25 September, Chamberlain's cabinet rebelled against continued conciliation of Hitler and the following day British naval mobilization was announced. France also mobilized its army; the Czechs had mobilized much earlier. War appeared imminent but on 28 September Hitler finally agreed to Mussolini's facesaving suggestion to convene the Munich conference at which Italy, Germany, Britain, and France would decide the fate of the Sudetenland in the absence of Czechoslovakian representation. Hitler's concern was that the pacific nature of the German masses would undermine his preferred military solution. In any case, the element of surprise for an attack on Czechoslovakia had disappeared. Hitler was evidently irked by 'that fellow', his description of Chamberlain, whose efforts to prevent war had 'spoiled my entry to Prague'.[91] Chamberlain had prevented Hitler from presenting the Sudeten Germans as a *casus belli* and Germany began its occupation of the Sudetenland on 1 October. The Polish and Hungarian ethnic questions were to be settled within a prescribed timeframe.[92] Nonetheless, Hitler regretted that his 'capitulation' had prevented him from imposing a military solution.[93]

De Valera had considered an appeal as taoiseach directly to Hitler and Mussolini in an effort to preserve peace before Chamberlain's first meeting with Hitler.[94] When war was avoided, the Irish government granted recognition to Germany's absorption of the Sudetenland. On 3 November 1938, the Irish Government's Information Bureau announced the renewal of the Irish trade agreement with Germany, emphasizing that both Austria and the Sudetenland were included in the agreement with the German Reich.[95]

---

89 De Valera, *Peace and war*, p. 72. 90 Ibid., p. 73. 91 Carr, *Arms*, p. 102. 92 Bell, *Origins*, p. 272. 93 Carr, *Arms*, p. 102. 94 DGFP, Series D, vol. 4, doc. 285, Hempel–AA, 3 Jan. 1939. 95 NAI, DFA 232/1, statement issued by Government Information Bureau, 3 Nov. 1938.

Hempel's retrospective report in October on Irish opinion during the September crisis identified a manifest desperation to maintain international peace. He said the Irish tended to favour the transfer of the Sudetenland to Germany and failed to view the crisis more deeply as a matter of German nationalism. Hempel noted, too, that the Anglo-Irish section of society adhered closely to Britain's stance throughout the crisis. But Irish nationalist opinion was more reserved and displayed an instinctive distrust of Britain for historical reasons. Anti-English sentiment was expressed vehemently in revolutionary nationalist circles. As the crisis progressed he sensed that average Irish opinion was attempting to maintain an impartial attitude and often heard the view expressed that the September crisis was caused by great power politics between Britain and Germany, and thus had no direct interest for Ireland.[96]

Irish Press editorials during September illustrate the difficulties and ambiguities. Supportive of appeasement, it was less than approving of Hitler's actions, but broadly followed de Valera's foreign policy line. The Sudetenland was only the occasion, not the cause, of the crisis, the paper said.[97] While reiterating the familiar Irish theme that 'the evil work of Versailles has brought its own nemesis', it said the Czechoslovakian state established by Versailles 'had made good' and was 'a credit to the men who founded it'. It had been 'a stronghold of democracy'.[98] (As the *Irish Press* wrote in October: 'the impartial observer in a neutral country is not easily convinced that the Sudeten Germans were badly treated' but the 'magnetism of race' had been too powerful.)[99] The *Press* believed the cause of the crisis was the old problem of the European balance of power, and whether France and Britain would allow Germany to establish hegemony over Europe. Like de Valera, the paper supported reform of the peace treaties and the League of Nations.[1] In a strongly worded editorial on 17 September the *Press* called for a new peace conference in Europe to draw up new treaties agreed upon by all and not imposed by any.[2] (Even the *Irish Times* of 19 September pointed to the possibility of a voluntary agreement between Czechoslovakia and Germany as a solution,[3] an idea that had been expressed in Irish official circles in former times as the basis of a solution for the Czechoslovakian question.)[4]

Therefore, the *Irish Press* reasoned that self-determination was a justified end, but the use of coercion, threats and crises, the adoption of 'passion' over 'reason', and the use of press propaganda to influence public opinion was unjustified: 'Such methods are neither sane nor civilized. They are a world removed both from the principles of international law and the principles of Christianity'.[5] If, however, the principle of self-determination was admitted in the Sudetenland there was a better case for it in Ireland in relation to Northern

96 PA, AA I, R 102387, Hempel–AA, 17 Oct. 1938. 97 IP, 14 Sept. 1938. 98 IP, 23 Sept. 1938. 99 IP, 4 Oct. 1938. 1 IP, 14 Sept. 1938. 2 IP, 17 Sept. 1938. 3 IT, 19 Sept. 1938. 4 PA, AA, R122531, Hempel–AA, 20 Sept. 1938. 5 IP, 22 Sept. 1938.

Ireland,[6] because the island of Ireland was a geographic unit artificially divided into two political units.[7] It did betray a suspicion that the Sudeten German issue was to a great degree orchestrated, but argued that valid calls for national self-determination could not be denied easily. That Chamberlain's efforts were sufficient to prevent Hitler from deploying force (if only temporarily) suited pacific and neutralist Irish opinion.

NEGOTIATING A TRADE EXTENSION

By the late 1930s Irish state and semi-state bodies such as the ESB, the Turf Development Board,[8] and the department of post and telegraphs purchased much of their requirements for electrical, other plant machinery and industrial products from Germany, not least because of German expertise in such sectors. In the case of the ESB, this was based on the special relationship established with Siemens-Schuckert during the construction of the Shannon hydroelectric project in the late 1920s. The 1936 Irish-German trade agreement was scheduled to expire on 31 December 1938 and the omens for a renewal of the treaty were not promising, despite the best efforts of Irish officials especially in the department of external affairs to ensure the maintenance of good trade relations with Germany.[9]

By this time there were increasing difficulties when the Irish approached their German counterparts to secure special trade compensation deals for large public contracts which were not included as part of normal Irish-German trade but as special compensation deals provided for under the 1936 agreement.[10]

The Germans sought to impose a new valuation system for German exports to Ireland as part of any special trade compensation deals. The existing CIF (cost, insurance and freight included in the price quoted) system held that the 'value of imports of either country which are the produce or manufacture of the other shall be the figure representing the *total* [author's italics] cost to the importer, including freight, insurance, and all other charges arising in respect of the goods up to the time of landing at the port or place of entry into the importing country'.[11] Germany wanted to revise the CIF system because it was experiencing a haemorrhage of foreign currency (*Devisen*). By 1938 international free trade had halted. Germany needed to import large quantities of raw materials for its rearmament programme and required large amounts of foreign currency to do so. It also needed to import considerable quantities of raw materials, from outside the German currency area, to manufacture goods it exported

6 IP, 20 Sept. 1938.   7 IP, 4 Oct. 1938.   8 NAI, DFA 115/360 contains details of Irish consultation with German and Soviet firms regarding mechanized turf production.   9 NAI, DFA 107/123, Fahy memo: Proposed compensation agreement with Germany, 24 Dec. 37. 10 NAI, DFA 107/115, Fahy–Leydon, 13 May 1938.   11 NAI, DFA 232/1, Protocol no. 2, Saorstát–German trade agreement, 28 Jan. 1935.

to countries such as Ireland and thus drained valuable foreign currency reserves in meeting Irish needs. German trade officials requested that the cost of imported raw materials imported for manufactures subsequently exported to Ireland be excluded in trade compensation deals with Ireland.[12] This proposed *export valuta* system was intended to limit the German loss of foreign exchange.

The Irish objected on principle. There were 'no grounds for the contention that the cost of raw materials should be deducted'.[13] As Seán Murphy of the department of external affairs argued 'there are considerable implications in admitting in any way Germany's raw material argument, as they could easily have very awkward repercussions in future trade discussions'[14] for the renewal of the 1936 Irish-German trade agreement at the end of 1938.[15] He was correct. The Reichsbank and firms such as Siemens, which were experiencing net foreign currency losses, were anxious to prevent the extension of the Irish-German trade agreement on the existing model of a 3:2 ratio in trade to the German advantage. They wanted a new framework based on the so-called *export valuta* system.[16] But the Irish, too, were concerned about currency issues evidenced by a serious decline in Irish banks' sterling assets and rising public indebtedness.[17] Officials from the AA argued Germany had given more advantageous trade terms to the Free State in 1936 than to any other country on the understanding that the volume of their trade would increase.[18] They maintained the volume had instead decreased.

Bewley added to the Irish negotiators' problems by agreeing with German officials' assumptions that Irish departments did not really want to increase imports from Germany and were not serious about finding alternative markets to Britain.[19] Bewley reported to Dublin that one German informant had said the diminution in Irish imports of German produce was proof that Ireland had 'no interests outside of England'.[20] He also indicated that 'I regret to state that from numerous conversations which I have had I can have no doubt that Ireland has come to be regarded in Germany as to a great extent identified with British imperialistic and anti-Fascist policy' and thus the Germans were against granting 'Ireland favourable terms in a new trade agreement on political grounds'.[21] Dr. Rüter, the AA official in charge of overseeing Irish-German trade, told Bewley that he thought since Ireland had settled its differences with Britain in the recent Anglo-Irish agreement 'the Irish authorities had no longer so much

12 NAI, DFA 107/115, Leydon note, 4 May 1938. **13** Ibid., Murphy–Hempel, 28 Jan. 1938. **14** Ibid., Murphy–Leydon, 15 Jan. 1938. **15** Similarly, suggestions by Germany that special barter deals involving Irish agricultural produce being traded directly for German manufactures without the exchange of currency to reduce pressure on German sterling stocks were not acceptable to the Irish side. **16** Dickel, *Aussenpolitik*, p. 71. **17** McMahon, *Republicans*, p. 226. **18** NAI, DFA 232/1, Bewley–Walshe, 15 July 1938. **19** Ibid., 15 Aug. 1938. **20** Ibid., 15 July 1938. **21** Ibid., 15 Aug. 1938.

interest in trade with Germany'.[22] Bewley contributed to Rüter's speculations by implying that, in his view, Irish trade interests were now totally focused on the British market, thereby undermining the interests of his own government.[23] The impression created was that Éire was no longer seriously interested in Irish-German trade. In late 1938, Hempel was instructed by his superiors to ascertain whether 'there was sufficient interest on the Irish side to justify Germany sending a delegation to Dublin' to negotiate an Irish-German trade agreement for 1939. Fortunately, Hempel was 'satisfied that the Irish Government had an interest in continuing trade to Germany'.[24]

The Irish government did have a number of problems with the conduct of Irish-German trade during 1937 and 1938 although it did favour a renewal of the 1936 deal. First, it objected in principle to the proposal that German imports into Ireland should be calculated on the *export valuta* basis. Second, the Anglo-Irish trade reconciliation had negative repercussions for Irish agricultural producers selling to Germany. The end of penal tariffs meant British net prices for the three main Irish agricultural commodities (cattle, eggs and butter) were now higher than German prices[25] if the costs of shipping and the absence of Irish exchequer export bounty payments were included. As a result Irish exporters lost money on the contract prices for butter and cattle they received from Germany during 1937 and 1938.[26] Third, Irish officialdom also had reason to question the accuracy of the German official assertion that German imports into Ireland had decreased in 1937 and 1938.[27]

The inter-departmental Foreign Trade Committee recommended that the Irish delegation should seek a renewal of the 1936 Irish-German agreement on the existing 2:3 monetary ratio recognizing that, although the German government might accede to a 1:1 ratio under an *export valuta* system this would probably be a worse deal. Their negotiating position was to improve the prices Irish producers received rather than to seek an improved volume of Irish exports to Germany. It was counterproductive to increase Irish export volumes to Germany if it was less profitable than the British market.[28] The new Irish-German trade agreement was signed on 3 November 1938. Under the deal German buyers would purchase agricultural products on the open market in

22 Ibid., 31 Aug. 1938. **23** Dickel, *Aussenpolitik*, p. 70. **24** NAI, DFA 232/1, unsigned memo, 15 Oct. 1938. **25** NAI, DFA 107/115, Fahy–Murphy, 2 May 1938. **26** NAI, DFA 232/1, Leydon, 23 Sept. 1938. **27** NAI, DFA 232/1, Foreign Trade Committee meeting, 3 Aug. 1938. According to Irish statistics Irish imports from Germany increased by £52,000 from 1936 to 1937. On the basis of Irish trade statistics for the first six months of 1938, trade had increased by £81,000 over the first six months of 1937. Interestingly, German trade statistics demonstrate a major increase in German exports to Ireland as a result of the sale of seven oil tankers to the National Oil Refineries Co. Thus German trade statistics demonstrate that her exports to Ireland in 1938 amounted to 29.1 million RM while it imported only 11.2 million RM from Ireland. See Dickel, *Aussenpolitik*, p. 72. **28** NAI, DFA 232/1, Foreign Trade Committee meeting, 3 Aug. 1938.

Ireland from 1 January 1939 'obviating the necessity for special price arrangements between the Governments and eliminating any risk of loss to the Irish Government'.[29] The November 1938 agreement simply extended the general framework trade agreement of January 1935 and the subsidiary revisions of 1936 for one year from 1 January 1939.

CONCLUSION

Declining Irish interest in trade with Germany, arising from primarily commercial considerations, mirrored official Ireland's disenchantment with the Nazi regime. While it could be readily recognized that Germany had some legitimate national claims regarding the expansion of its borders, the nature of the regime was unavoidably odious to democratic eyes while the coercive methods it ever more employed to achieve a Greater Germany of all German peoples in central Europe were in themselves ominous and threatened to finally and irrevocably destroy the unsettled European peace. Thus Irish policy remained cautiously ambivalent towards Nazi Germany seeing little reason to antagonize Nazi Germany unduly since the independent Irish state had no influence over German actions. In this situation of impotence it was preferable apparently in Dublin's viewpoint to appease in the hope of pacifying Hitler. If appeasement failed it might at least purchase additional time for an otherwise ill-prepared Éire to prepare itself and undertake contingency planning for a possible international conflagration. The next several months clarified Hitler's intentions.

29 Ibid., Government Information Bureau statement, 3 Nov. 1938.

8

Perception, reality and neutrality,
October 1938–September 1939

'[I]n spite of the Irish Government's sincere desire to observe neutrality equally towards both belligerents, Ireland's dependence on Britain for trade vital to Ireland on the one hand, and on the other the possibility of intervention by Britain if the independence of Ireland involved an immediate danger to Great Britain, rendered it inevitable for the Irish Government to show a certain consideration for Britain, which in similar circumstances they would also show to Germany'[1] (de Valera).

Munich completed the transformation of Nazi Germany. Germany was now completely reinvigorated and all European relations revolved around the question of Hitler's future intentions. Although the Irish and British authorities hoped that Hitler's nationalist grievances were now satisfied, there remained unresolved issues such as the Free City of Danzig, the Polish corridor and Memel, which were separated from Germany by the treaty of Versailles. Hitler's use of threats, coercion and subversion during the Munich crisis provoked anxiety. Would a resurgent Nazi Germany which perceived Britain, France and all democracies as weak-willed abide by international arbitration? Would the rearming allies of the Great War (France and Britain) accept future *fait accomplis*? When Nazi Germany unceremoniously seized the rump Czechoslovakia (Bohemia and Moravia) and quickly acquired Memel from Lithuania in March 1939, appeasement had demonstrably failed. Nazi Germany was now increasingly viewed as an implacable and unreasonable power threatening to dominate Europe prompting Chamberlain to extend his security guarantee to Poland. As the Great Powers prepared for war, the Irish government had to consider its options. As a defenceless small power distant from the likely battlefields on the mainland continent it chose to distance itself diplomatically as a neutral. But neutrality would not be an easy policy to implement successfully.

The period was a watershed in Irish-German relations because of Hitler's disillusionment with and misreading of Britain. As the differences between Britain and Germany became irreconcilable, Nazi Germany's attitude towards Éire altered. Éire's military–strategic position could no longer be ignored. Was it inevitable that Éire as a Commonwealth member would join on the side of

---

1 DGFP, Series D, vol. 7, doc. 484, Hempel-AA, 31. Aug. 1939.

Britain? De Valera's public rhetoric was that Éire would be neutral – how was this information transmitted and interpreted in German circles? De Valera, as taoiseach and minister of external affairs, and Joe Walshe, as secretary of external affairs, now occupied the central roles in dealings with Nazi Germany and, in particular, with the Dublin-based German minister Hempel to ensure that Irish neutralist signals were communicated to best effect. Bewley's relationship with his superiors completely disintegrated and they considered him a dangerous liability in Berlin. His acrimonious departure was an unwelcome distraction for an overworked and understaffed department of external affairs coping with the repercussions of an impending international catastrophe.

It is not intended to discuss in detail the international developments between October 1938 and September 1939, nor to examine in detail Irish defence preparations, German espionage, Anglo-Irish relations, and Irish counterespionage since these aspects of Irish policy have been dealt with adequately by other authors. Instead the objective is to focus on the formal Irish-German government-to-government diplomatic and political dialogue in this final period of peace.

DEFENCE QUESTIONS

The Sudetenland crisis acted as a major warning to the Irish government. Years of government and financial neglect limited the Irish defensive ability to repel potential invasion from any quarter, constrained Irish foreign policy choices and stretched the international credibility of Éire's neutral stance. The Irish defence forces had been severely underfunded since 1924 by successive cash-strapped governments desirous of a docile army following the attempted army mutiny in March 1924. This military incapacity continued despite warnings from the army general staff throughout the interwar period. In particular, despite warnings from Colonel Dan Bryan, second-in-command of G2, as far back as 1936 that the state should prepare actively for a probable future war; a war he predicted would break out during 1938 or 1939. At the time he argued the principal duty of an independent state was 'to provide for its national defence' – thus while Ireland was 'sovereignty conscious' it was not 'security conscious'. He went further stating: 'Actually the Saorstát may be said to be not relatively but absolutely disarmed' and argued the guardians of the Irish state were 'largely ignorant' of national defence matters.[2] Nonetheless despite such a bold indictment defence expenditure remained stagnant at the insistence of a parsimonious department of finance which persisted in its complacent belief that the island's geographical location meant it was untouchable and in any case Britain would prevent any other power from invading. Though this was ulti-

---

2 MAI, G2/0057, Fundamental factors affecting Irish defence, May 1936.

mately proven to be the case, it was nevertheless a foolhardy risk which created the beginnings of a 'free rider' Irish neutrality mentality.

Thus Éire ('the republic in all but name') was in September 1938 to all intents and purposes defenceless with no navy, an air force consisting primarily of training aircraft, an undermanned and an underequipped army of about 20,000 troops of which only approximately 6,000 were regulars (the remainder were reservists or members of the Volunteer Force). Earlier grandiose plans for a munitions factory and a four brigade regular army had not materialized. It was doubtful whether the Irish defence forces could, at a minimum, defend the recently returned treaty ports. Without adequate war stores and armaments (such as anti-aircraft guns, tanks, armoured cars), the small regular army was not an effective fighting force. No arrangements had been made to ensure the security of military supplies from overseas in the event of a war.[3] Thus in terms of military resources (manpower, finance, equipment, planning) the situation was grim.[4]

However, the Sudetenland crisis focused the de Valera government on defence, the first time any Irish government had made it a priority since the end of the Irish civil war. During the climax of the Munich crisis in late September, the army general staff warned that the defence forces were fit only for internal security purposes. On October 19, de Valera finally spearheaded a decision in the Defence Council to reorganize, modernize and re-equip the defence forces. The department of finance, however, fought a rearguard action against increased defence expenditure and repeatedly attacked the idea of a continental style land army. Nonetheless in January 1939 de Valera and his government sanctioned a military modernization programme.[5] But Irish preparations had begun too late. There were plans to build a munitions factory, purchase fighter aircraft and anti-aircraft artillery as well as tanks. The government discovered it was impossible to purchase its requirements from the British, busily rearming for their own defence and unwilling to divert some of their national armaments production to meet Irish defence needs, particularly when the Irish government was unwilling to enter into a defence arrangement with Britain. Moreover the US would not meet Irish military supply needs without British sanction. So the Irish external military defence position remained extremely weak with the Irish government forced to survive primarily on its own limited resources.

Hempel reported this new Irish interest in matters military to his superiors in Berlin, noting it had arisen partly as a result of the Anglo-Irish agreement of April 1938 when de Valera promised Britain that Éire would endeavour to defend itself sufficiently to preclude it becoming a base of attack against Britain.

---

3 The appalling state of Irish defence planning and preparation is captured in O'Halpin, *Defending*, pp 45–53, 82–93, 133–50; Duggan, *Irish army*, pp 138–77.   4 MAI, G2/0057, Fundamental factors, May 1936.   5 O'Halpin, *Defending*, pp 142–4; Duggan, *Irish army*, pp 172–6.

He also correctly noted the Sudetenland crisis had provoked more interest in the Irish defence question.[6] He doubted Éire had the military resources necessary to defend itself independently and maintained this belief into 1939.[7]

THE JEWISH DILEMMA

While the Irish government attempted to improve its defensive capabilities it was distracted by another international crisis of Nazi Germany's making. As the historian Piers Brendon has noted, 'Nothing shocked world opinion more than the dawning appreciation that Hitler's anti-Semitism was not rhetoric but reality.'[8] By 1938 Jews in the Third Reich were desperate. Discrimination, boycott, professional prohibitions, legislation and local initiatives left the vast majority of Jews unable to make a living.[9] Successive expansions of the Third Reich to include Austria and the Sudetenland radicalized Nazi anti-Semitism by increasing the Jewish population of the Third Reich. The Anschluss led to a merciless extension of Nazi anti-Semitic practices to the new territories whence many Jews had earlier fled the Nazis. This had profound international repercussions. Irish refugee policy, however, remained stubbornly restrictive as thousands of people arbitrarily labelled Jewish by the Nazis tried to flee from the former Austria.

In 1936 Walshe, prompted by the impact of the Nuremberg laws and anticipating an influx of Jewish refugee visa applications from Germany, wanted to ascertain how many Jews were in Ireland. Statistics revealed only 0.13 per cent of the Irish population was Jewish and that the Irish Jewish population had grown by only 1.7 per cent between 1926 and 1936.[10] Walshe advised against a sudden increase in the Jewish population in the then Saorstát. It was only after Nazi Germany had annexed Austria that Ireland saw a perceptible increase in Jewish refugee entry applications.

Until November 1938 refugees applying to Ireland for sanctuary from Nazism faced a cumbersome and unsympathetic bureaucracy. Only a handful of individuals successfully overcame the culling process.[11] Most were registered initially at an Irish legation, especially Berlin, and then forwarded to the department of justice in Dublin. The department of industry and commerce often became involved as applicants offered professional, technical, or entrepreneurial skills to strengthen their cases. Both departments were hostile to admitting aliens. Justice insisted on two requirements. First, 'whether the applicant is Jewish, or for any other reason is unlikely to be allowed to return to Germany'.[12]

---

6 PA, AA, R102797, Hempel–AA, 12 Dec. 1938.   7 Duggan, *Neutral Ireland*, p. 44.
8 Brendon, *Dark valley*, p. 465.   9 Krausnick, 'The persecution of the Jews', p. 55.   10 NAI, DFA 102/510, Lyon–Walshe, 29 Oct. 1938.   11 See K. Goldstone, 'Benevolent helpfulness?', pp 74–95.   12 NAI, DFA 102/575, Duff–Walshe, 24 Nov. 1938.

It did not want to grant short-term visas (for holidays or business) if the applicant would not be accepted back by the Third Reich. Second, applicants should
be able to support themselves without becoming a burden on the state or competing for scarce employment. It was apparently feared that if many refugee
applications were granted, indigenous anti-Semitism would increase. G2 was
concerned that visas given to applicants from the Third Reich were a means of
Nazi infiltration and could form a fifth column within the state.[13]

A successful applicant in 1938 was typically wealthy, middle-aged or elderly,
single, from Austria, Roman Catholic and desiring to retire in peace to Ireland
and not engage in employment. Only a few Viennese bankers and industrialists
met the strict criteria of being Catholic, although possibly of Jewish descent,
capable of supporting themselves comfortably without involvement in the economic life of the country.[14] Jewish intellectuals also tended to have a better
chance of gaining entry due to Irish academic connections with German and
Austrian universities, particularly in the field of linguistics. Occasionally, when
an applicant was on the margin of meeting the necessary criteria, the recommendation of the relevant Irish legation was taken into account.

This policy was primarily justified by reference to Ireland's 'backward' economy. The attitudes of some officials and parts of Irish society were tainted by
traditional European Christian anti-Semitism. At the Inter-Governmental
Committee on Refugees Conference at Evians-les-Bains in July 1938 the Irish
delegation put forward its well-rehearsed economic excuses for an illiberal
refugee policy.[15] Although overt anti-Semitism was untypical, the Irish were
indifferent to Nazi persecution of Jews and those fleeing the Third Reich. Then
the Goebbels-devised anti-Semitic pogrom of the night of 9–10 November 1938
(Kristallnacht) seemed to indicate indifference was no longer an option.

KRISTALLNACHT

The pretext for the pogrom, which left at least 100 Jews dead, was the assassination of Ernst von Rath, secretary at the German embassy in Paris, by a 17-
year-old Jew angered at the forced deportation of his family from Hanover to
Poland.[16] Virtually all synagogues in Germany and about 7,000 Jewish shops
were destroyed. The Nazi regime blamed the Jewish population for provoking
the devastation, levied a collective fine of one billion marks on Jews and confiscated their rightful compensation from insurance companies.[17] Furthermore, in
the aftermath, the Nazi state issued arrest orders for 40,000 Jews and non-

---

13 Keogh, *Ireland & Europe*, pp 110–11. **14** See: NAI, DFA 102/495; NAI, DFA 102/496;
NAI, DFA 102/487. **15** Keogh, *Ireland & Europe*, p. 106. **16** Kershaw, *Nemesis*, p. 136.
17 Bracher, *German dictatorship*, p. 456.

Aryans, notably 'intellectuals'. Professor Julius Pokorny had been warned of the planned arrests and 'had gone away for a few weeks'. Pokorny's dilemma mirrored thousands of others in Germany. He wrote:

> I still have not given up hope and shall try to remain in Germany as long as possible. But, I am afraid, the chances grow worse from day to day, and in the end I shall be probably obliged to leave the country as a scoláire bocht [poor scholar]![18]

Although external commentators rarely appreciated the personal tragedies, international and Irish public opinion was shocked by Kristallnacht. While many in the Irish population retained anti-Semitic attitudes, the Nazi persecution of the Jews was perceived as immoral and inhumane. A sample of Irish national daily newspapers can be taken as an indicator.[19] Both the *Irish Press* and the *Irish Times* held that the Nazis had excited the German people with their vitriolic anti-Semitism, and then sanctioned violence against Jews and their property on 9 and 10 November 1938.[20] According to the *Times* the Third Reich no longer ranked as a 'civilised country'.[21] Later the *Press* alleged that Aryanism was 'the laughing stock of the scientific world' and the 'racial purity' policies of totalitarian countries such as Germany and Italy were responsible for bringing 'more discredit' on their internal policies than anything else.[22]

Even Hempel reporting back to Berlin was unable to conceal widespread Irish disapproval of the Nazi purge against the Jews.[23] But he recognized this did not imply a sensitive Irish attitude towards Jewish immigration. Nonetheless, the Irish government was forced to rethink the cumbersome mechanics of processing visas as a result of the continuing influx of Austrian applications (now joined by those from the Sudetenland); public outrage at Kristallnacht; and the expected upsurge in applications from German Jews. In November 1938 the Irish Coordinating Committee for Refugees (ICCR) was established to monitor and process applications. The committee included many interested and knowledgeable Irish academics with Professor T.W.T. Dillon of UCD as its secretary.[24] But the stereotype persisted of Jews as a wealthy, influential, non-assimilative caucus – 'a sort of colony of a world-wide community' – who would awaken anti-Semitism in Irish society.[25] De Valera supported establishing the voluntary ICCR as a means to moderate the powers of the departments of justice and of industry and commerce in processing European refugee applications. Although responsible for facilitating the settlement of German and Austrian refugees in Ireland, the ICCR ruled practising Jews ineligible for aid

18 NLI, Best Papers, MS 11003 (8), Pokorny–Best, 1939.   19 IT, 14 Nov. 1936.   20 IP, 17 Nov. 1938; IP, 14 Nov. 1938; IT, 14 Nov. 1938; IT, 12 Nov. 1938.   21 IT 12 Nov. 1938. 22 IP, 17 Nov. 1938. 23 PA, AA, R122531, Hempel–AA, 12 Nov. 1938. 24 Keogh, *Ireland & Europe*, p. 107.   25 Ibid., pp 110–11.

from Ireland. The rationale was that Jewish communities abroad had sufficient resources to cope with Jewish refugees. In practice Jewish converts to Christianity, especially Catholicism, were favoured; a policy which betrayed an underlying religious hostility to Judaism.[26]

Hempel underlined the illiberal government policy towards refugees from the Germany, Austria and in its turn Czechoslovakia. While he was, to a certain extent, catering for the prejudices of his superiors in Berlin, his reports ring true. He reported Irish officialdom was hostile to Jewish immigration and that the Irish in general had a disapproving, if rather uninformed, attitude towards Jews. The temporary flight to Ireland of some Jews from Britain during the Munich crisis had created a poor public impression, although most returned after the threat of war receded. Government policy prevented permanent settlement of Jews in Ireland, although temporary residence visas were granted to refugees in transit to permanent resettlement elsewhere.[27] De Valera, however, favoured a more liberal refugee policy, adopting an understanding approach to the few cases brought to his personal attention such as the Austrian students who required visas to attend UCD.[28] Walshe, adhering to the strict anti-immigration line of the justice department, established that such leniency should not become a precedent for liberalising immigration policy and stated, 'we can avoid the consequences of having established these precedents by examining all the cases we get on their merits'. Consequently, just prior to Kristallnacht in September 1938, Walshe instructed Bewley 'to report very fully' on all those applying to the Berlin legation for visas.[29] Bewley had the power to recommend visas, at least until the ICCR was established. He was often asked to verify or seek further information on certain applicants, or to certify that everything was in order before granting a visa. Bewley was given ample opportunity to indulge 'his fashionable' attitude towards Jewish applicants.[30] His rationale was similar to that of the departments of justice, and industry and commerce. He was unsympathetic to the plight of religious, racial and political minorities in Germany.

The foundation of the ICCR in November 1938 to some extent ameliorated the system's inflexibility and diminished Bewley's role in monitoring and processing applications. This change occurred as the number of applications to Ireland grew steadily in the aftermath of Kristallnacht. The ICCR was less reliant on Irish diplomats abroad for information concerning each applicant's case and was in contact with, for example, the Jewish Refugee Committee which had relevant information about Jewish and other refugees recommended for visas.[31] Except for the foundation of the ICCR and a few individual cases in

26 Ibid., pp 108–9.   27 PA, AA, R102282, Hempel–AA, 7 Dec. 1938.   28 NAI, DFA 102/438, Roche–Walshe, 29 Aug. 1938.   29 Ibid., Walshe–Roche, 7 Sept. 1938.   30 Keogh, *Ireland & Europe*, p. 101.   31 NAI, DFA 102/642, Belton–Walshe, 6 Feb. 1939.

which he had a personal interest, de Valera was content to allow the relevant authorities to deal with such applications.

BEWLEY'S KRISTALLNACHT

In the aftermath of Kristallnacht, Walshe asked Bewley to report on German anti-Semitism.[32] He was to be shocked by his analysis which adopted an overtly anti-Semitic interpretation of events. Anti-Semitic comments and assumptions had appeared in Bewley's reports before.[33] But his main commentary on the Jewish question in Germany was produced on 9 December 1938.[34] The governments of Germany, Italy, Czechoslovakia, Hungary and Poland had adopted 'discriminatory measures in respect of Jews', Bewley reported, repeating Nazi justifications for anti-Semitic policies without qualification. He used terminology such as: 'This is, of course, obvious'; 'Anyone ... will feel inclined to adopt the German view'; 'It is a notorious fact ...' Thus he endorsed the views he presented. As Bewley stated: 'I desire ... to point out that the facts here stated are well known to everyone who has lived in Central Europe, or who has taken the trouble to make inquiries from non-Jewish sources into the situation as it really is.'[35]

Jews were unpatriotic, 'invariably sacrifice the interests of the country of their birth to Jewish interests', and organisers or supporters of Communism. Bewley alleged the Bolshevik movement was Jewish led, and this 'is a fact so well known as to need no emphasis', quoting the pamphlet, *The Rulers of Russia*, which was written by the anti-Semitic, conspiratorial minded Holy Ghost father, Denis Fahey.[36] To further confirm his theory, Bewley said the vast majority of those arrested and found guilty of illegal Communist activities in central Europe were Jews. He suggested naively that 'a perusal of the reports of trials of Communists' in central European countries was sufficient proof for this premise.[37]

As for the common Nazi claim that Jews monopolized international finance, universities, public policy, public opinion and governments, Bewley said: 'Anyone who knew Germany before 1933, whatever be his political opinions, must admit the truth of this particular claim.'[38] He contended: 'The whole press, theatre, cinema, stock-exchange, the banks were completely under Jewish control'.[39] He added: 'This situation of course no longer exists in Germany; it exists at the present day in Warsaw, Budapest and Prague, although measures are being adopted to alter it in these countries also.'[40]

32 NAI, DFA 202/63, Bewley–Walshe, 9 Dec. 1938. 33 NAI, DFA, CRS 19/50A, Bewley–Walshe, 12 Nov. 1935 & 18 Aug. 1936. 34 NAI, DFA 202/63, Bewley–Walshe, 9 Dec. 1938. 35 Ibid. 36 Ibid. 37 Ibid. 38 Ibid. 39 Ibid. 40 Ibid.

Bewley cited another 'cause' of special anti-Jewish legislation as the 'fact' that Jews avoided occupations involving manual labour and concentrated on finance, commerce and trade: 'This is, of course, obvious whether in Germany, America or Ireland.'[41] As regards the claims made in Germany and elsewhere that a Jew always avoided defending 'the state in which he resides',[42] he said:

> Anyone who witnessed the immigration into Ireland of English Jews after the introduction of conscription in England [during the Great War] will feel inclined to adopt the German view. When it was found in Germany, as in many other countries, that the Jews had not only succeeded in avoiding military service but also in enriching himself during the agony of the country, it is comprehensible that popular feeling has tended to become anti-Semitic.[43]

Bewley argued Jews demoralized and corrupted their host societies and controlled the international white slave traffic. No one who had even a superficial knowledge of Germany could be ignorant that its moral degradation before 1933 was, if not caused, at least exploited by Jews, he said. Jews were responsible for indecency on the German stage, the production of pornographic papers and the legalisation of abortion in Germany. He added that Jewish emigrants infected and corrupted every country they entered.[44] He accepted Nazi police statistics which conveniently corroborated Nazi allegations that Jews were more criminally inclined than non-Jews.[45]

Finally referring to the von Rath murder in Paris, Bewley believed 'this is one of a series of murders committed by Jews against persons whom they considered enemies of their race'. Concurring that the entire Jewish community should be punished for the crimes of specific Jews, Bewley declared:

> Anyone familiar with the criminal courts even in Ireland must be aware that every Jew convicted of a crime can count with confidence on the Chief Rabbi testifying on oath that he knows the man intimately and is convinced that he could not possibly be guilty of the crime of which he has been found guilty by an Irish jury.[46]

---

41 Ibid. 42 He probably inferred this from the falsified Nazi figures of fallen Jews during the Great War. 43 NAI, DFA 202/63, Bewley–Walshe, 9 Dec. 1938. 44 Ibid. 45 His 1938 report is completely inconsistent with that of his own recollected response to the Nazis' purification of the Berlin red-light district in his sanitised post-war memoirs. In these he feigned total contempt for the 'stock Nazi clichés' consisting of crude racism (Bewley, *Memoirs*, p. 118). 46 NAI, DFA 202/63, Bewley–Walshe, 9 Dec. 1938. A few days after filing this report, on 15 December 1938 Bewley took leave but did not return to his post until 8 January 1939 necessitating a rebuke from Dublin because he had exceeded his annual leave quota (NAI, DFA, Berlin letterbooks, Boland–Bewley, 20 Feb. 1939).

Bewley accepted the necessity for 'special measures' against Jews[47] and justified Nazi anti-Semitic measures by reference to papal moves against Jews in medieval Rome,[48] although there were no direct parallels. He condemned negative reactions to Germany's policies from other countries, especially Britain, as judgemental and hypocritical. They denied the existence of a Jewish problem assuming a superior moral attitude towards the German measures.[49] In every state where Jews lived, including states led by Catholic clergy, their hosts perceived them as unwelcome and undesirable foreigners. The lesson he drew was: 'it is impossible to take up with any degree of reason the attitude that they should be treated like ordinary citizens of the country'.[50] Bewley denied any personal knowledge of deliberate cruelty on the part of the German government towards Jews on Kristallnacht.[51]

Bewley, as so often before, criticized Irish foreign policy and portrayals in the Irish press of events in Germany, particularly attacking press dependence on British based agencies for international news, because the Jews controlled the latter.[52] In Bewley's view, Irish foreign policy and public opinion was formed uncritically by 'anonymous agencies ... bitterly opposed both to Irish Nationalism and to the Catholic Church', and which misled the government.[53] He advised the Irish people and press to turn their attentions to persecuted and martyred Christians, especially in Spain. He admonished the Irish press and public opinion for indulging in 'paroxysms of moral indignation at the treatment of the Jews' while remaining oblivious to atrocities perpetrated against Catholics elsewhere in the world.[54]

In January and February of 1939 Bewley submitted four further reports on the attitudes of other countries towards Jewish immigration and Jews in general. His consultation with the Greek, Egyptian, Finnish, Latvian, Albanian and San Domingan ministers invariably revealed restrictive Jewish refugee policies, conveniently affirming Bewley's own attitudes and recommendations to the Irish government.[55] Bewley's anti-Semitism dictated his official relations with Jews and, as a representative of the Irish state, this had an impact on a number of individual cases.[56]

Bewley became highly critical of the relatively autonomous ICCR in early 1939 for allowing what he characterized as 'an influx of common criminals' into the country. The tone Bewley used throughout was sarcastic and insubordinate

---

47 Ibid.   **48** Ibid.   **49** Ibid.   **50** Ibid.   **51** Ibid.   **52** Ibid.   **53** Ibid.   **54** Ibid. **55** NAI, DFA 202/63, Bewley–Walshe, 30 Jan. 1939, 31 Jan. 1939, 8 Feb. 1939, & 9 Feb. 1939.   **56** The evidence to assess the practical impact of Bewley's prejudices on his work is limited by the closure of many refugee application records. The reason is that they reportedly reveal Bewley's 'scurrilous' anti-Semitic attitudes, and would be of considerable embarrassment to both the state and the department of foreign affairs (confidential source). Nonetheless, some individual cases have been released which demonstrate Bewley's unreliable judgement, for example: NAI, DFA 102/642, Bewley–Walshe, 2 Feb. 1939.

and forced John A. Belton of the department of external affairs to issue a detailed rebuttal of Bewley's complaints. The ICCR for its part used its international connections to facilitate the salvation of a few eminent Jewish and German academics,[57] bypassing Bewley and other departmental obstacles.

Despite Bewley's fears, however, Éire accepted only a handful of practising Jews before September 1939 because of the protectionist, and frequently prejudiced, mindset that prevailed in Irish society, even in key government departments. Jews fleeing Nazi persecution encountered a largely religious based Irish indifference to their plight.[58] Lewis-Crosbie, Church of Ireland dean of Christ Church cathedral, was prompted to attack the Irish government publicly as being 'most niggardly' in placing tight restrictions on Jews seeking asylum while praising the work of charitable and non-governmental organisations such as St Vincent de Paul and the ICCR.[59] However, those seeking entry or residence in Éire after 1938 faced stringent vetting, as fears of subversion and espionage grew in proportion to Irish and international fears about the prospect of another Great War. Simultaneously a propaganda war developed between Britain and Germany.

PROPAGANDA WARS

Public statements against past British actions in Ireland were the first indications of an appreciable German policy adjustment on the Irish question after Munich and Kristallnacht. Despite Chamberlain's proclamation of 'peace in our time', Britain and France accelerated their rearmament programmes, while Germany's neighbours in eastern Europe attempted to form a cordon sanitaire around the Reich as a guarantee of their future security.[60] The *Irish Press* editorial of 7 November noted 'the peace of the world stands on a very insecure basis',[61] following Hitler's speech the previous day. Hitler had restated his position that Germany had to negotiate from a position of strength since the pacifist methods of earlier years had failed to achieve Germany's goals. Bewley noted that German newspapers and Nazi leaders' speeches began to express anti-British sentiments highlighting the imperial injustices and excesses of British rule in Palestine, India and Malta. In particular, an emergent theme was the atrocities committed by the Black and Tans and British army during the Irish War of Independence. This was part of a deliberate Nazi effort to distract world opinion from allegations of German abuses, notably against the Jews, within the

57 Keogh, *Jews*, pp 138–44.   58 Ibid., pp 115–52.   59 See MAI, G2/10040B; II, 11 May 1939. Although the Church of Ireland Jews Society did undertake some valuable work, it too was constrained by a religious bias in its attitudes to Jews. It acknowledged the fact that increasing numbers of Jews were converting to Christianity (II, 10 May 1939).   60 Kershaw, *Nemesis*, p. 158.   61 IP, 7 Nov. 1938.

newly enlarged Third Reich.[62] Nonetheless, German newspapers maintained a neutral or noncommittal line on Irish partition and contemporary Anglo-Irish relations.[63]

Negative British newspaper reaction to Kristallnacht and further Nazi anti-Semitic actions accentuated this anti-British trend in Nazi newspapers. It was a reversal of the respectful line previously taken to solicit British acquiescence to Nazi objectives on the continent. To external commentators it could only signify one of two far reaching alternatives: either Hitler supposed he possessed a *carte blanche* because Britain was unwilling to act militarily against Germany, or he was willing to provoke an open conflict with Britain in the near future calculating he had a reasonable chance of victory. In reality, it was the former that Hitler mistakenly believed, supported by the similarly deluded Joachim von Ribbentrop (Nazi foreign minister); at least until he launched the invasion of Poland in September 1939.

Simultaneously, the Nazis found it difficult to attract positive newspaper coverage of Nazi Germany in Éire.[64] The more understanding attitude towards National Socialism in the weeks following the Munich crisis was destroyed by the Nazi reaction to the von Rath murder. Articles sympathetic towards Nazism were limited and in November 1938 Hempel highlighted the importance of the journalism of Arthur H. Rae, and the official Irish correspondent of the Deutsche Nachrichten Büro (German Press Agency or DNB), Lia Clarke, in the *Irish Independent*.[65] Eoin O'Duffy, the now marginalized former Blueshirt leader, set out his views on the international situation in the aftermath of Munich in the *Irish Independent*. It was a diatribe against 'International Jewry', 'International Finances', Comintern, and 'International Masonry' (in fact this indicates an identity of views with Bewley).[66] However, Hempel indicated that even the *Irish Independent*, the paper previously more sympathetic towards Germany than the other two dailies, was adopting a generally negative line towards the Third Reich.[67] By December 1938, Hempel was reporting that those who had previously held a favourable view of Nazi Germany and even harboured a disapproving view of Judaism condemned Kristallnacht. He feared a 'countermovement' against Nazi Germany was developing in many Irish circles.[68]

Nazi Germany had a jaundiced view of protestations by the democracies (UK, US, France, Éire) that freedom of the press and opinion was necessary for the healthy functioning of democratic politics. The Nazi government insisted any indications of anti-German attitudes in the foreign press endangered its relationship with the states concerned. They believed it was the responsibility

62 NAI, DFA 105/1B, Bewley–Walshe, 15 Nov. 1938 & 17 Nov. 1938; Dickel, *Aussenpolitik*, p. 83. **63** Dickel, *Aussenpolitik*, p. 83. **64** Duggan, *Neutral Ireland*, p. 19–21. **65** PA, AA, R122531, Hempel–AA, 12 Nov. 1938; II, 17 Oct. 1938. **66** II, 31 Oct. 1938. **67** PA, AA, R122531, Hempel–AA, 12 Nov. 1938. **68** PA, AA, R102282, 7 Dec. 1938.

of democracies to end anti-Nazi press reporting within their jurisdiction to ensure amicable relations with Germany. When the Irish government requested in early January 1939 that the German press adopt a more anti-partitionist line in their coverage of Irish affairs,[69] Hempel was instructed from Berlin to inform the Irish government that this was impossible as long as the Irish press failed to report German events accurately. The Irish government should influence its press to adopt a more positive attitude towards Nazi Germany.[70] To improve the portrayal of Germany in Éire and to gain more insights into Irish politics, Lia Clarke was replaced as the official correspondent of the DNB in Ireland, a position she had occupied since 1936. A trusted official German DNB representative, Dr Carl Petersen, took over as press attaché to the German legation in Dublin just prior to the outbreak of World War II.[71]

The Irish government, too, was engaged in its own propaganda campaign. Following the Anglo-Irish agreement de Valera argued the only issue preventing amicable relations between Britain and Éire was partition. He informed Chamberlain that in a future European crisis, similar to Munich, Northern Ireland's nationalist minority could 'become a positive danger'.[72] De Valera contended that Fianna Fáil was a moderate nationalist party, which could accommodate British interests, but if his government did not achieve unification through peaceful means, it was likely to be outflanked by radical republicans who would adopt unconventional means. He implicitly used the Nazi threat as a negotiating ploy hinting that unresolved Irish nationalist grievances would create a dissatisfied minority in Ireland prepared to act in concert with Germany against Britain. The IRA might resort to force to end partition, destabilising both Éire and Britain in the process.[73]

For de Valera the border represented a 'dangerous anachronism' but he was careful to indicate that 'no Sudeten analogy' should be applied to Northern Ireland. This was a message to Germany that Nazi analogies were not applicable to the Irish question. De Valera attempted to reassure London that he would adopt neither subversive measures nor conventional military means to end partition. He warned that the continuation of partition represented 'a grave danger to England in the event of that country becoming involved in a European war' since it provoked widespread anti-British discontent in ultra-republican circles. While Éire promised not to provide a base for attacks against Britain, it was unlikely to become a British ally since it was not united with Northern Ireland.[74] De Valera meanwhile possibly knew that his anti-partition campaign would fail but it demonstrated his republican credentials. It was a pacification technique to

---

69 PA, AA R122531, Hempel–Aschmann, 6 Jan. 1939.   **70** Ibid., AA–Hempel, 20 Jan. 1939.   **71** O'Halpin, *MI5*, p. 40; PA, AA R122531, AA–Hempel, 20 Jan. 1939; Dickel, *Aussenpolitik*, p. 83.   **72** PRO, DO 35/893/X.11/247, Chamberlain note of a talk with de Valera, 4 Oct. 1938.   **73** Fisk, *In time of war*, pp 186–9.   **74** *Evening Standard*, 17 Oct. 1938; PA, AAII, R102797.

quell the more anti-British elements of the Éire population who feared de Valera was Anglophile, excessively sensitive to British strategic interests and too pro-British on European matters, when he should have taken advantage of Britain's international difficulties to complete the Irish nationalist project.[75]

THE INTERNAL THREAT

Soon the credibility of neutrality was threatened by what de Valera had foreseen: the IRA began its S-Plan (Sabotage Plan) or bombing campaign against Britain in January 1939. If the campaign persisted and the IRA gained wider support from moderate elements of the nationalist community then the foundations of Irish neutrality would be irreparably damaged. If the IRA proved itself to be a force, uncontrollable by either London or Dublin, it could become a useful collaborator for a power harbouring military intent against any part of the British Isles, undermining the hoped-for British tolerance of Irish neutrality in a European war.

The IRA had been declared an illegal organization by the Fianna Fáil government on 18 June 1936 after de Valera's efforts to assimilate it into the democratic fold had failed. At that stage the IRA was much weakened by internal factional disputes between its socialist or radical left-wing and its militant right-wing. However in late 1938, after Seán Russell became chief-of-staff, the IRA emerged as a more effective force. Simultaneously a deterioration in Anglo-German relations led to a more sustained effort than hitherto by German secret services to build links with anti-British forces in the event of war.[76] This

<hr>

75 In this sense there was a significant commonality of perspective between some sections of the IRA and Bewley in their attitude towards Britain and the utility of Germany in satisfying Irish nationalist objectives. 76 The information available on the extent of pre-1939 IRA–Abwehr collaboration is contradictory and piecemeal. Inter-agency rivalry that was an enduring characteristic of Nazi Germany did lead some cultural and propaganda organizations and individuals to take their own initiative at intelligence gathering. Recent research by Mark Hull corroborates the view that Abwehr failed to establish a high-quality intelligence network in Éire and that IRA–Abwehr collaboration only commenced during 1939. Official German policy not to encroach upon the British sphere of influence and a realization that the IRA was a moribund organization may have constrained Abwehr before 1939. Additionally in the early and mid- 1930s the IRA had viewed Nazism and fascism with complete hostility: B. Hanley, *The IRA, 1926–1936* (Dublin, 2002), p. 174. This does not mean, however, that Abwehr neglected Ireland totally before the end of 1938 since one or two cases of Abwehr probes have been uncovered: M. Hull, *Irish secrets: German espionage in wartime Ireland, 1939–45* (Dublin, 2003), pp 45–50. Seán Russell and Seán McBride played a role in proposing cooperation with Germany in 1936. Russell, then quartermaster general of the IRA, attempted to interest Nazi Germany in collaboration with the IRA in October 1936 (PA, AAII, R 102881, Russell–Luther, 21 Oct. 1936). McBride, who has been noted for his pro-

removed the block to Nazi–IRA collaboration, previously ruled out (at least officially) as dangerous meddling in British affairs.[77]

British non-compliance with an IRA ultimatum (12 January 1939) demanding British withdrawal from Northern Ireland was used to justify Seán Russell's
terrorism.[78] This treasonous declaration of war by the IRA as the self-styled
'Government of the Irish Republic' on Britain affronted de Valera who believed
he had restored the full sovereignty of the 26 counties with the Anglo-Irish
agreement of 1938. It undermined de Valera's promise that Éire would not be a
base for attack on Britain and the fundamental rationale of Irish neutrality, that
Britain respect Ireland's right to pursue military neutrality.[79]

The IRA bombing campaign was the first serious test of de Valera's benevolent neutrality policy as he had to reassure Britain about the solidity of his
'friendly neutrality' and to ensure that Germany did not exploit dissident Irish
republican sentiment. The British and Irish governments feared the IRA was
coordinating with Germany in the bombing of Britain. Although this proved to
be untrue, Dublin feared Germany would overestimate the IRA's strength. By
early 1939, much circumstantial evidence of secret German agents and Nazi
propaganda activity in Éire was emerging as a result of G2's and the Garda
Special Branch's surveillance of citizens of fascist states who were either visiting or resident in Éire.[80]

In particular, the activities of the propagandist and Abwehr agent Oscar K.
Pfaus caused considerable unrest during early 1939. Pfaus, fluent in English
having spent many years in the US, was a representative of the Deutscher
Fichte-Bund, a Nazi propaganda organization based in Hamburg. The Fichte-

German tendencies during World War II, was IRA chief-of-staff at the time. Tom Barry
replaced Seán McBride as chief-of-staff in 1937. According to Barry's testimony, Clann na
Gael, the sister republican organization of the IRA in the USA, suggested the IRA undertake
a bombing campaign in Britain sometime during 1937 or 1938. Barry discovered that Clann
na Gael was acting on behalf of German agents who promised financial aid to the IRA if it
initiated a campaign against British forces in Northern Ireland. Barry deduced that both
Clann na Gael and the Germans were 'only interested in causing as much embarrassment as
possible to England...they had not real interest in the purely Irish aspect of the question'. He
refused to commit the IRA to the proposed campaign during his tenure as chief-of-staff
(MAI, G2/X/0093, Minute by Capt. F. G2 Southern, 23 Nov. 1943.). As far as can be ascer-
tained no official linkage was made between Abwehr and the IRA before the launch of
Russell's S-Plan against the British mainland in 1939. If Barry's testimony is accepted then
he as chief-of-staff prevented the formation of a durable IRA–Abwehr relationship before the
outbreak of war because there was insufficient time to build links between the IRA and
Abwehr during the remainder of 1939. After the commencement of the IRA bombing campaign against Britain in January 1939 linking up with the IRA was viewed as sensible
contingency planning by the Abwehr in case the unthinkable happened: an Anglo-German
war.   **77** Duggan, *Neutral Ireland*, p. 59.   **78** T.P. Coogan, *The IRA* (Glasgow, 1990), p.
157. Copies of the ultimatum were also sent to Hitler and Mussolini.   **79** R. Fanning, '"The
rule of order": Eamon de Valera and the IRA, 1923–1940', in J.P. O'Carroll & J.A. Murphy
(eds), *De Valera and his times* (Cork, 1983), p. 169.   **80** Hull, *Irish secrets*, pp 51-62.

Bund was responsible for disseminating to sympathizers worldwide the Nazi cant glorifying Nazi achievements, anti-Semitism and anti-Communism. Pfaus was loaned by the Fichte-Bund to Abwehr in December 1938 which was in need of an English speaking agent. Once the IRA bombing campaign began Pfaus was briefed and sent to Éire to establish cooperation with the IRA.[81] Following a tip-off from the British authorities when an immigration officer at the port of Harwich grew suspicious of his decidedly contradictory, misleading reasons for travelling to Ireland, G2 arranged close surveillance of this 'queer bird'.[82] It became evident quickly to the Gardaí and G2 that although Pfaus did not appear to establish any contact with the German colony living in Éire, his intentions were sinister as he contacted former high-ranking Blueshirts' Captain Liam D. Walsh and General Eoin O'Duffy. Captain Liam D. Walsh was the first person Pfaus contacted in Dublin because he subscribed to Fichte-Bund propaganda. Informants revealed Pfaus was seeking contact with the IRA through the Blueshirts, indicating serious gaps in the Abwehr's knowledge about Irish politics. Nonetheless, Walsh and O'Duffy put Pfaus in contact with their former sworn enemies through intermediaries. Irish intelligence on Pfaus' mission failed when they concluded he had not made contact with the IRA, although G2 did ascertain from informants that Pfaus was 'to arrange to have a force of Irishmen organised here to assist Germany on the outbreak of war and that it was immaterial to him what the political persuasions of these Irishmen might be'.[83]

In fact Pfaus did meet several key members of the IRA including chief-of-staff Seán Russell. But the IRA only reluctantly accepted him as an official representative of Abwehr.[84] He fled the country the next day on 14 February in a panicky state according to the Gardaí reports,[85] following his manhandling by the IRA. Nonetheless he had succeeded in his mission to contact the IRA although it later transpired the IRA–Abwehr connection was a failure and of little utility to either side.

Irish authorities were also concerned about the activities of Petersen, the DNB representative in Dublin, some members of the German colony and, in particular, the Auslandsorganisation which was under scrutiny by G2 from late 1938. But lacking tangible evidence, no one was detained, arrested or deported.

THE GERMAN 'COLONY'

Joe Walshe had long held deep reservations about the Auslandsorganisation. Although the Austro-German population of Éire was diminutive many occupied

81 Ibid., pp 53-4.　82 MAI, G2/0183, landing form for Pfaus at Harwich, 2 Feb. 1939; ibid., G2–Carroll, 9 Feb. 1939.　83 Ibid., profile of Pfaus, November 1942; ibid., memo on Pfaus, n.d.　84 Hull, *Irish secrets*, p. 56.　85 MAI, G2/0183, memo on Pfaus, Nov. 1942.

influential and powerful positions in the state and semi-state apparatus since the Irish modernization and industrialization drive in the 1920s had drawn on international expertise. The Irish-German trade agreements of the 1930s had facilitated this too. The German policy of not being seen to take advantage of British difficulties in Ireland before 1938 however meant there was little sustained effort at espionage in Éire before then. But some German organizations and individuals were active, gathering information about Irish infrastructure and defence capabilities from public sources in a state which was naïve about security.[86] There was little need for Nazi Germany to use subversive methods to acquire intelligence in such an open society before 1938. Readily available information was later collated and used in German war planning. One specific example illustrates the dangers. Siemens–Schuckert's knowledge of the Ardnacrusha hydroelectric scheme (which at that time had a virtual monopoly to supply the State's electricity needs)[87] as well as their extensive involvement in the growing electricity generation network during the 1930s, could have been used to cripple industry. The security of Éire's electricity supply was therefore highly vulnerable.

Academic and cultural exchanges were also a means to infiltrate Éire during peacetime. Dr Ludwig Mühlhausen, the Nazi Celtic scholar and nemesis of Professor Pokorny at Berlin University, was a regular visitor to the Gaeltachts in western Ireland. There were suspicions that he engaged in espionage. A prolific photographer, many of his photographs of Ireland were eventually used in a 1941 German military handbook, intended as a supplement to the Operation Green invasion plans for Eire.[88] Before the war Irish officials viewed Dr Helmut Clissmann, the Dublin representative of the German Academic Exchange Service (DADD), as a potential spy and DADD as a front for German espionage. Consequently, Clissmann and his acquaintances were subject to intense surveillance during 1938 and 1939.[89] Clissmann was associated with Ireland since 1933 when he attended Trinity College Dublin as an exchange student. He later completed a doctoral thesis on 'The Wild Geese in Germany' for Frankfurt University before returning to Ireland in the late 1930s to lecture in German and become head of DADD.[90]

The Celtic Studies connection provided an ideal opportunity for familiarising a few postgraduate German students with Éire before 1939, a useful camouflage for subversive or clandestine activities. As war grew more likely

86 Duggan, *Neutral Ireland*, pp 57–8.   87 B. Cullen, 'Some notable features of the design and operational history of Ardnacrusha', in A. Bielenberg (ed.), *The Shannon scheme*, pp 141, 154. In 1931 Ardnacrusha accounted for 96 per cent of the total electricity generated in the Saorstát.   88 O'Donoghue, *Hitler's Irish voices*, pp 15–16; MAI, G2/2473.   89 O'Halpin, *Defending*, p. 142; O'Halpin, *MI5*, pp 39–40. In the summer of 1938, an effort by Clissmann to interest Abwehr in collaboration with the IRA was also rejected (Duggan, *Neutral Ireland*, p. 62; Fisk, *In time of war*, p. 88).   90 Duggan, *Neutral Ireland*, p. 62.

some individuals, cultural exchanges and organisations such as the Auslandsorganisation were seen as useful for propaganda and espionage activities. Hans Hartmann, who during the war became involved in German radio's propaganda Irish service Irland–Redaktion, first visited Ireland as a folklore foreign exchange student who undertook doctoral research and then worked for the Irish Manuscripts Commission between 1937 and 1939. G2 and the Garda Special Branch monitored him closely in his last year in Ireland, but he was a dedicated researcher and his activities appeared innocuous.[91] Jupp Hoven, a supposed anthropology student and close associate of Clissmann, spent time in Ireland during the academic year 1938–1939. G2 and Special Branch concluded that he was actively engaged in espionage, particularly after he was observed marching with the IRA at the Wolfe Tone commemoration in 1938. He was closely monitored, as was Clissmann who was known to have contacts in extreme republican circles.[92]

ADOLF MAHR

Adolf Mahr was the most powerful Nazi in Ireland's Austro–German community as head of the Auslandsorganisation and as highest ranking member or Ortsgruppenleiter (local group leader) of the Nazi party in Éire as well.[93] As director of the National Museum he had a detailed knowledge of Irish cartography and geography. The fear Mahr could instil is perhaps indicated by the fact that Professor Pokorny, who was on the run from the Nazis in Germany in early 1939, was afraid Mahr would gain knowledge of his whereabouts from mutual acquaintances in Dublin and inform the Nazis.[94]

Walshe became seriously concerned about Mahr's double life as both director of the National Museum and the highest ranking Nazi in Éire.[95] In November Dan Bryan of G2 advised Walshe: 'I do not suggest any action should be taken with regard to Mahr for the present, and at any rate the evidence available could not be used if Mahr denied he held this appointment in the group.'[96] In late February 1939 Walshe lost patience and advised de Valera: 'The existence of a Nazi organisation in Dublin, having as its chief member and organiser an employee of our State, was not calculated to improve relations between our two Governments.' After frequent complaints to Hempel, on 22 February Walshe bluntly told Henning Thomsen, first secretary of the German legation who was also a member of the SS, that if Mahr's double life was publicly revealed:

91 MAI, G2/0071; O'Donoghue, *Hitler's Irish voices*, pp 9–11. **92** MAI, G2/0239, surveillance report, 27 Mar. 39. **93** O'Donoghue, *Hitler's Irish voices*, p. 20. **94** NLI, Best papers, MS 11003(8), Pokorny–Best, 1939. **95** G2 maintained close surveillance of Mahr. See MAI, G2/0130. **96** MAI, G2/0130, Byran–Walshe, 11 Nov. 1938.

Our Catholic people and clergy would begin to make public protests and the [Irish] Government would be placed in a very awkward situation when the position of Dr. Mahr, Director of the National Museum, as head of the Nazi cell in Dublin, became a matter of public controversy.[97]

O'Donoghue suggests that public exposure of Mahr's high-ranking Nazi status could provoke a damaging British reaction.[98]

On 23 March 1939 Bryan noted that Mahr had attended a department of education conference which had been arranged to discuss alternative secure accommodation for valuables from the National Library, Gallery and Museum, and at which an Air Raid Precaution (ARP) army captain, Lawlor, was present to give advice. During the conference Mahr 'proved troublesome'. In discussing the threat of invasion he 'stated it was unlikely or remote but that if we were invaded it would be only by a highly cultured nation who would value articles of art, culture, etc. as much as we did. Seemingly the assumption might be made that obviously the very cultured people contemplated were, or in fact could only be, the Germans'. In addition, 'Mahr displayed a surprising and detailed knowledge of the geography of the country; knew all about villages in the West that Drs Best, Furlong, etc. knew nothing of'. Mahr was fully familiar with the ARP proposals and revealed knowledge of aircraft and bombs.[99] Dublin academic circles apparently considered it 'rather "funny" that a German (Mahr) should be arranging ARP protection (of the museums, etc.), presumably against possible raids by his own fellow countrymen'.[1]

Increased scrutiny of Mahr led ultimately to his replacement as Ortsgruppenleiter (local group leader) of the Auslandsorganisation in Ireland by Heinz Mecking, chief adviser to the Turf Development Board. The decision appears to have been planned as early as December 1938.[2] Mahr claimed to his superior, the secretary of department of education, that he had resigned from the Nazi party in a formal letter to Berlin in 1938. Walshe and G2 were unclear when Mahr actually stepped down from his position and appeared to believe the news of Mecking's accession was a ruse to deflect criticism.[3] There is considerable reason to believe Mahr did not relinquish control of the Irish branch of the Auslandsorganisation until he finally left Ireland.[4] It has been alleged Mahr may have taken detailed maps of Ireland back with him to Germany when he left

97 Franciscan Library, Dublin, de Valera papers, file no. 953, Walshe–de Valera, 22 Feb. 1939. 98 O'Donoghue, *Hitler's Irish voices*, p. 27. 99 MAI, G2/130, DB (Dan Bryan) Memo: 'Adolph Mahr – Curator National Museum', 23 Mar. 1939. 1 Ibid., note: 'German Nazis in Dublin – Mahr', 9 May 1939. 2 Mahr's superiors thus anticipated the contentiousness of Mahr remaining in post during a time of international tension stemming from Nazi Germany's policies. See also MAI, G2/0143, Heinz Mecking file, 15 Apr. 1939; ibid., profile of Mecking, 9 Apr. 1945. 3 MAI, G2/0130. 4 O'Donoghue, *Hitler's Irish voices*, pp 24–5.

hurriedly on 19 July 1939. These were later allegedly used in Nazi Germany's putative invasion plans for Ireland, Operation Green (or Fall Grün), in mid-1940.[5]

NAZI PROSELYTIZATION

Also of concern to the Irish authorities was the development of an anti-Semitic campaign in Dublin in early 1939, which bore the hallmarks of continental propagandists.[6] There were already indigenous Jew haters in Éire but Nazi propagandists attempted to inflame this sentiment to create support for Nazi Germany. Active anti-Semitism was relatively rare in independent Ireland although many people, including leading personalities in Irish politics and society, expressed anti-Semitic beliefs. Generally, however, anti-Semitic beliefs were camouflaged and there tended to be no overt violence directed against the Jewish community.[7]

However, towards the end of the 1930s an upsurge in virulent and overt anti-Semitism occurred. A Garda report in 1939 noted that 'about two years ago a considerable amount of literature of an anti-Jewish nature was in circulation in Dublin City'. The provenance of the literature was traced to a small anti-Jewish organization lead by a plasterer, James Curran of South Circular Road, Dublin.[8] Then on 20 November 1938, a 1916 Veteran's Association passed a motion protesting against 'the growing menace of alien immigration' and demanding that the government restrict it.[9] Later, in the first week of February 1939, a 'Boycott Jews' slogan was painted at various locations around Dublin city. Simultaneously a number of Dublin Jews received similar intimidating typewritten notes 'warning them to clear out of the country or they would meet the same fate here as the Jews in Germany'. The Gardaí immediately interviewed Curran who denied any involvement and said the anti-Jewish campaign was 'in better hands' of 'big shots' such as Mr P. Belton and J.J. Walsh who were running the anti-Jewish campaign from the Stephen's Green Loan Fund Society. Mr P Belton was possibly Paddy Belton, the anti-Semitic founder of the by now defunct pro-Franco Irish Christian Front. After further investigation, the Gardai concluded that a George Griffin from Crumlin, Dublin, who suffered from 'anti-Jewish mania', was responsible for the anti-Semitic campaign. He ran an organization called the Irish Christian Rights' Association which campaigned against alleged Jewish moneylenders. The Garda investigation uncovered a foreign influence because Griffin, whom they considered as 'not a very intelligent person and in fact is inclined to be slightly abnormal', 'was being used for this

5 Ibid.; Duggan, *Neutral Ireland*, pp 117–8. 6 Keogh, *Jews*, p. 148. 7 Regan, *Counter-revolution*, pp 333–5. 8 MAI, G2/x/0040 Part I, Connell–Archer, 25 May 1939. 9 NAI, DFA 102/568, Ó Braonáin–de Valera, 21 Nov. 1938.

type of work by an organisation known as "The International Fascist Movement" emanating from the Italian legation and sponsored by Captain Liam D. Walsh, who is employed there'.[10] Griffin continued his Christian Rights' Association campaign throughout the first half of 1939.[11]

Liam D. Walsh, subscriber to Fichte-Bund and Pfaus' first contact in Dublin, was a former Irish army captain who had been variously associated with organisations such as the Blueshirts, League of Youth and the Irish Christian Front during the mid-1930s.[12] O'Duffy, the former Blueshirt leader, had secured him a minor position in the Italian legation in 1938 using his connections with the Italian minister there.

This outbreak of anti-Semitic activity also occurred at approximately the same time as Pfaus' visit to Ireland to make contact with the IRA during which he added the names of Nazi sympathizers with radical republican beliefs to the Fichte-Bund's mailing list, providing them with a steady stream of vitriolic anti-Semitic and anti-Bolshevik propaganda. The aim was to convert radical republicans to Nazi ideology and to engage them against Britain in any future Anglo-German conflict. The Irish authorities, however, collated the addressees of the Fichte-Bund literature coming from Pfaus in Hamburg and built up an extensive database of possible security threats for future use.[13]

On 23 February 1939 the *Irish Times* published the contents of an anti-Semitic circular that had been sent to 'a number of prominent Dublin citizens' on behalf of a body called the Irish-Ireland Research Society. The circular was signed by a Mr A.J. Browne. It demanded that in the interests of the Irish nation's racial purity and economic good, Jews should be prevented from settling in Ireland in large numbers. It reproduced the classic Nazi categorization of Jews as a separate race adopting a special code inimical to the interests of gentiles. It argued that anti-Semitism arose wherever there were significant populations of Jews because they were hostile to their hosts. Jews were characterized as capitalists, immoral, criminally inclined, materialist and dominating the world's cinema, press agencies and finance.[14] The accompanying *Irish Times* editorial remarked: 'Although couched in reasonably moderate language, this document represents the crudest form of anti-Semitic propaganda'. It added: 'We would treat this effusion with the contempt which it deserves but for the fact that attempts have been made of late to stir up anti-Jewish feeling in this country' and proceeded to demolish the circular's anti-Semitic arguments.[15]

Petersen, the Nazi DNB correspondent in Dublin, then published an article on the circular in the *Völkischer Beobachter* on 26 February, commenting: 'There have recently been increasing signs in Ireland of a widespread enmity to Jews, which has been caused not least of all by the "refugee" policy of the

---

10 MAI, G2/x/0040 Part I, Connell–Archer, 25 May 1939. 11 See *Evening Herald*, 16 May 1939. See also MAI, G2/x/0040 Part I, memo: Anti-Jewish organisation, n.d. 12 MAI, G2/0183, profile of Liam Walsh, n.d. 13 MAI, G2/0183. 14 IT, 23 Feb. 1939. 15 Ibid.

Government.' He further suggested that the Irish press adopted no particular attitude to the Jews and implied that it failed to draw the attention of the Irish public to Jewish criminal acts. Petersen deliberately misrepresented the *Irish Times* as printing the circular in full 'without comment' in 'an unusually large space' and thus enabling the circular to receive the widest possible circulation.[16] This pleased the Nazis especially since it was a result of their own propaganda efforts.

The Gardaí discovered the Irish-Ireland Research Society, apparently responsible for the production and circulation of the anti-Semitic circular, had never existed and that A.J. Browne was a fictitious name. The circular's origins were traced to the pro-German journalist Lia (or Lisa) Clarke, Petersen's predecessor as the official DNB representative in Éire. Clarke produced about 200 circulars in her home in Dublin with the help of two employees of the *Irish Press* and had them distributed to about 80 individuals in Éire. Further investigations revealed that a sum of money, of source and amount unknown, had been placed at Clarke's disposal for anti-Jewish propaganda purposes.[17]

Next on 10 March 1939 Clissmann, the head of DAAD in Ireland, wrote to the department for education suggesting an alteration in the German prize scheme for secondary schools to encourage the study of German in Ireland: an annual four week travelling scholarship rather than picture and book prizes.[18] The minister for education consulted the minister for external affairs. De Valera felt 'sure that ... in the present position of the Catholic Church in Germany, the government should not take the responsibility of sponsoring a scheme for sending Catholic children to German Youth Camps'. He advised the education minister to reject the offer.[19] The Nazi tactic of using state youth camps to indoctrinate German youth was widely publicized in Ireland. Soon after de Valera's advice to reject the Clissman's travelling scholarship offer the *Irish Press* published an editorial dealing with a remark by the president of the Irish National Teacher's Organization (INTO) that the philosophy of youth movements in other countries was 'Snap the child from his mother's arms and give him a gun.' The editorial criticized the attempt to erode the influence of the family and religion on children in totalitarian societies, where neo-paganism and militarism were cultivated instead through the use of state youth movements. It complained, too, about egotistical nationalism based 'on racial hatred and aggressive militarism' in such totalitarian states as Germany.[20]

Meanwhile Captain Walsh was kept under close surveillance by G2. In May he received a German-made portable typewriter from the headquarters of

16 NAI, DFA 227/24, Warnock–Walshe, 28 Feb. 1939; *Völkischer Beobachter*, 26 Feb. 1939. 17 MAI, G2/x/0040 Part I, Connell–Archer: 'Anti-Jewish propaganda, etc. in Dublin', 25 May 1939. 18 NAI, DFA 238/59, Clissmann-secretary, department of education, 10 Mar. 1939. 19 Ibid., Walshe-secretary, department of education, 2 May 1939. 20 IP, 13 Apr. 1939. See also M.M. Macken, 'Moulding the soul of young Germany', *Studies*, 24 (1937).

CAUR (Committee of Action for the Universality of Rome), considered to be a cover organisation for the Fichte-Bund or another Nazi organisation. In mid-summer G2 intercepted a request from Pfaus to Walsh to go to Hamburg. Pfaus arranged that Walsh's luggage would not be searched by German customs officers on arrival and explicitly instructed him not to contact the German legation in Dublin about the trip. Walsh duly took temporary leave from his position at the Italian legation and left for Germany on 2 July 1939 where he met the director of the Fichte-Bund, Dr Theodor Kessenmeier. G2 believed Kessenmeier discussed how Walsh could use the Celtic Confederation of Occupational Guilds (CCOG) to further German interests in Éire. Walsh had formed the CCOG during 1939 with a Commandant Brennan–Whitmore and attempted to use it to spread the Nazi message in Éire. Later, after World War II started, G2 noted that he received funding from the Fichte-Bund.[21]

BEWLEY'S RECALL

In this context of growing Irish disquiet about Nazism in late 1938 and early 1939, Bewley completely lost the trust of his superiors. He lacked the necessary diplomatic skills to market Irish neutrality successfully to the Germans, particularly given his own clear preference for cultivating Irish-Germany intimacy at the cost of the Anglo-Irish relationship. Bewley's inveterate Anglophobia was an embarrassment, especially since Anglo-Irish relations had improved. In September 1938 the British foreign office received a report that Bewley threatened to resign if de Valera took the side of Britain in a conflict against Germany during the Munich crisis.[22] The report referred to him as 'a professional admirer of Germany'.[23] Earlier the official visit of the king and queen of England to Paris in the summer of 1938 and the retirement of Art O'Brien, the Irish minister at Paris, in October 1938 was the occasion of a serious, perhaps irreparable, breakdown in the relationship between Bewley and his government. O'Brien, like Bewley, was a staunch nationalist who was not regarded as an effective diplomat and had been the source of some dissatisfaction at the department of external affairs on a number of occasions.[24] Bewley was adamant that the British government forced its Irish counterparts into altering an 'old nationalist tradition' of not permitting Irish representatives to attend Commonwealth-only diplomatic functions, and O'Brien's opposition had led to his forced retirement.[25] In November 1938, Bewley was reprimanded by the department for his refusal to attend a dinner-party at the South African legation

21 MAI, G2/0183, profile of Oskar Pfaus, n.d.; ibid., profile of Pfaus, Nov. 1942. 22 Duggan, *Neutral Ireland*, p. 30.   23 Duggan in Bewley, *Memoirs*, p. xi.   24 Patterson, 'Ireland and France', pp 70–6; Bewley, *Memoirs*, pp 170–1; Keogh, *Ireland & Europe*, p. 54; IT, 8 Aug. 1938.   25 NAI, DFA, Paris Embassy files P. 19/7, Walshe–Murphy, 30 Jan. 1939.

in Berlin because the only other diplomat in attendance was the British chargé
d'affaires. Then in January 1939 Bewley, critical of a report that Irish diplomats
could meet Chamberlain during his European tour to promote appeasement and
peace,[26] requested clarification of Irish policy. He recalled bitterly:

> in the end I received a lengthy rebuke from the Secretary. My offence con-
> sisted in laying emphasis on the 'anti-English or non-English character of
> our policy'. Walshe further informed me that it was possible that in the
> future 'our external policy may coincide even more than now with that of
> Great Britain'.[27]

On 30 January 1939 Walshe instructed all Irish legations to refer to Dublin for
advice on receipt of all invitations to attend official functions at which members
of the British colony or members of the Commonwealth were to attend. The
department would issue instructions on whether or not to attend on a case-by-
case basis.[28]

By this stage Bewley's relationship with his superiors had collapsed completely. Bewley alleged that the department boycotted the Berlin legation after
he demanded clarification of the O'Brien situation and rules for attendance at
Commonwealth functions.[29] His conspiratorial view of Irish foreign policy, his
anti-Semitism, his simplification of the true complexity of reality and his
unwillingness to compromise, produced an insolent, insubordinate Irish diplomat categorically opposed to de Valera's foreign policy in public and private. By
early 1939 it was essential Dublin received timely and judicious reports about
central Europe and that its representative accurately represented Dublin's foreign policy. In January 1939 an exasperated Walshe castigated Bewley for not
filing a report since July 1938 and ordered him to do so because de Valera was
concerned about:

> the gravity of the September crisis and the predominant part which is
> being taken by the German Government in a situation which might at any
> moment bring our Government face to face with issues of vital impor-
> tance to the Irish people.[30]

De Valera was disappointed by the reports Bewley filed. In his report of 8
February 1939, Bewley foresaw an ideological war between the authoritarian fascist states and the liberal democratic states (allied with the Soviet Union), failing
to recognize that matters of state security, strategy and even international

26 Duggan in Bewley, *Memoirs*, p. xi.   27 Bewley, *Memoirs*, p. 173.   28 NAI, DFA, Paris
embassy files, P 19/7, Walshe–Murphy, 30 Jan. 1939.   29 Bewley, *Memoirs*, p. 176; NAI,
DFA 229/13, Bewley–Walshe, 6 Feb. 1939.   30 NAI, DFA, CRS 219/4, Bewley–Walshe, 26
Jan. 1939.

justice were involved. He mistakenly believed Germany was unlikely to initiate such a conflict because National Socialism was a form of nationalism and therefore lacked expansionist objectives. To convert other states to German nationalism would be a 'contradiction' in terms according to Bewley.[31] Western liberal democracy was the cause of international tension he argued:

> Liberalism like Communism is in its essence international, and, as has become increasingly evident in the last years, is intolerant of systems of government which do not pay at least lip service to 'democratic' theories. The attitude does appear to constitute a threat to the peace of the world.[32]

He believed an influential elite in liberal democracies wanted 'war for an ideological pretext'. In support of this hypothesis he cited German opinion that, according to him, believed this decadent elite had financial, Semitic, imperialist and communist reasons for seeking war. He portrayed this elite as manipulating the vast majority of peace loving Englishmen, Frenchmen and Americans into war to obtain its own selfish ideological goals. The German press identified Roosevelt and his advisers as members of this elitist liberal democratic club. He alleged these people created 'international tension' and prevented the creation of 'a durable peace'. Bewley's perspective was totally in sympathy with that of the Nazis. He feared the appeasers would be 'overruled' leading to a boycott of fascism and a failure to return the German colonies. This would force Germany and Italy to consider war as the only feasible option. Then, 'Germany and Italy might be the nominal aggressors but the persons really responsible would be those who in the name of democracy denied them the means to live. This is in my opinion undoubtedly the danger'.[33]

Concerns about Bewley led to a departmental review of the Berlin legation's work in early 1939 and, ultimately, to the decision to recall Bewley to Dublin.[34] The secretary of the legation, William Warnock, was to remain in his position. Bewley was informed of de Valera's decision to recall him in a letter on 27 February 1939. He would cease to be head of mission from 1 August.[35] F. H. Boland, the assistant secretary of the department, accounted for this decision in the following way:

> It is the practice of many other countries not to leave their representatives abroad for too long in any one place the Minister considers that it is a sound one ... apart from the question of the length of residence in a particular place there is the question of length of absence from the home country. The effect of prolonged absence will vary in individual cases ... in particular cases it may reach such a point as to render an officer ...

31 Ibid., 8 Feb. 1939. 32 Ibid. 33 Ibid. 34 NAI, DFA, E.86/2/34, Boland–Ó Muimhneacháin, 9 Aug. 1939. 35 Ibid., 29 Aug. 1939.

wholly unsuitable to represent the country abroad, and ... constitutionally incapable of re-adapting himself to the conditions of service in a Home Department. The Minister considers it very important in the interests of the Service ... that, before this point is reached in any individual case, the officer concerned should be recalled home and enabled by means of resi-dence and official service in Dublin to renew his acquaintance with the local environment ... the Minister has reached the conclusion, on the strength of foreign considerations, that Mr. Bewley should return for a period of service in Dublin.[36]

Bewley was no longer capable of representing Ireland abroad. However, there was no equivalent post to that of minister of legation available in Dublin for Bewley and the government did not wish to promote him in light of his evident failings. Instead he was offered the post of principal officer at the department of external affairs which held a status and salary below that of minister of a lega-tion. As concession, it was proposed that Bewley retain his existing higher salary scale and home cost-of-living bonus. On 10 March Bewley replied that he was not prepared to accept a position in Dublin.[37]

MORAVIA AND BOHEMIA

Meanwhile, Hitler also finally proved that he could no longer be trusted when he manufactured a justification to annex the rump Czechoslovakia. In the remaining months of his posting in Berlin Bewley reinforced Walshe's and de Valera's estimation of his poor performance. He defended Hitler's takeover of the rump Czechoslovakian state of Bohemia and Moravia in March 1939. Chamberlain's infamous 'scrap of paper' (the Munich Agreement) was no check on Hitler. Bewley accepted uncritically Hitler's intervention as legal because Monsignor Tiso, the Slovakian national leader, had appealed for help and, even more surprisingly, Dr Hácha, the Czech president, had called for German pro-tection for the Czech nation. Both were pretexts manufactured by Hitler. Hitler personally bullied and threatened Tiso on 13 March 1939 to declare an inde-pendent Slovakian state, and then Dr Hácha on the night of 14/15 March to accept German 'protection'. Hitler had kept in contact with the Slovak nation-alists after the Munich crisis in September 1938 and encouraged them to secede from Czechoslovakia totally undermining that state.

None of this is highlighted in Bewley's reporting. Instead he blamed the appeasers' unwillingness to act in a series of recent crises for undermining inter-national belief in democracy. He concluded his report concerning the German

36 Ibid., 9 Aug. 1939. 37 Ibid., 29 Aug. 1939.

march into Prague by blaming English and French cowardice: 'The events of the last few days will go very far to convince the remaining countries of middle and eastern Europe that democracy as a political system can only lead to weakness and eventually disaster'.[38]

On the other hand de Valera, the Irish government, and the *Irish Press* did not believe that Germany had a legitimate national claim on Czechoslovakia following Hitler's extortion of permission from Dr Hácha to march into Prague on 15 March 1939. Hitler had revealed underlying aggressive intentions and his declarations of peace were unreliable. De Valera agreed with Chamberlain that it was impossible to negotiate with Hitler. He also 'much feared that we should find it impossible to stop Hitler's further advance in eastern Europe ... with the crumbling resistance of the small states who would be so frightened that they would make agreements with Germany ...'[39] Hitler exploited Slovakian and Ruthenian nationalism for his own strategic priorities to use the Czech lands for a future thrust eastwards to achieve *Lebensraum* in Poland and the USSR. The *Irish Press* believed Czechoslovakia, like Ireland, was just another small nation for which there could be 'no ethical or moral justification' of the German takeover: Hitler did not intervene in Czechoslovakia for the benefit of the Slovaks, as Bewley alleged. The Irish government did not extend *de jure* recognition to the new German protectorate of Moravia and Bohemia or the new state of Slovakia.[40] Bewley's failures meant that the Irish government was dependent on other Irish diplomats in Europe to provide more accurate information and a balanced analysis of the developing European situation.

G2, by contrast, was able to provide more reliable and informed reports on the European military and strategic environment than Bewley.[41] Its account of the causes and implications of the Hitler's actions in Czechoslovakia from mid-1938 acted as an antidote to Bewley's jaundiced perspective. They saw the takeover of Czechoslovakia as ample evidence of Hitler's 'aggressive intentions'. Hitler was an opportunist who had utilized the slogan of self-determination to partition Czechoslovakia during the Munich crisis, but discarded it on 16 March 1939 instead citing the need for *Lebensraum* and self-preservation to justify his takeover in Prague. Six days later he used the threat of military force to coerce Lithuania to cede the territory of Memel to the Third Reich. He violated the Munich agreement by such acts of coercion. G2 saw the newly underlined importance of *Lebensraum* and 'self-preservation' to the Third Reich as putting the whole of central and eastern Europe under threat in particular Hungary for agricultural produce, Rumania for its oil supplies, and Danzig and the Polish corridor.[42]

38 NAI, DFA, CRS 219/4, Bewley–Walshe, 15 Mar. 1939. 39 PRO, FO 800/310, Chamberlain note, 27 Mar. 1939. 40 NAI, DFA 227/23. 41 MAI, MIS 28, 1 Oct. 38–31 Dec. 38. 42 MAI, MIS 29, 1 Jan. 1939–31 Mar. 1939; MAI, MIS 30, 1 Apr. 1939–30 June 1939.

Rumania and Poland became the subjects of intensified German propaganda which G2 recognized as the German stratagem used before launching an attack on another country. Irish intelligence officers concluded the next few months would be 'a period of great strain' as Germany engaged in a campaign of intimidation against Poland and other east-central European states. G2 noted recent propaganda in German newspapers, particularly the official *Völkischer Beobachter*, which tried to justify German expansionism because Germans were discriminated against in the territorial holdings of the Great Powers. It argued:

> Forty-seven million Englishmen to-day rule a territory which is 140 times as great as their home country. Forty million Frenchmen rule a territory which is 21 times as great as France. Eight million Dutchmen rule a territory 60 times the size of their own country and eight million Belgians territory 80 times the size of their State.[43]

In April the tone of Bewley's analyses was one-sided, pro-German and bitterly anti-British. He noted 'a definite military superiority on the side of the authoritarian states'. The British and French failure to intervene in either Czechoslovakia or Memel, he argued, was interpreted by Hitler as an indication of their 'complete powerlessness' and a sign that the Third Reich was immune from 'the danger of military defeat'.[44] The evidence of the dictator's military superiority was fourfold: the establishment of a German protectorate in Bohemia and Moravia; the completion of an advantageous commercial treaty between Germany and Moravia; the occupation of Albania by an Italian army; and the 'adhesion' of Franco's Spain to the anti-Comintern pact. To a significant degree this was an accurate assessment. However, he accepted uncritically that Czechoslovakia had been 'hostile' and a strategic 'menace' to Germany. He denied rumours that Germany had served Rumania with an ultimatum to gain an advantageous commercial agreement and blamed the 'Anglo-Jewish news agencies' for propagating lies. He accused Britain of cowardice pointing to its reluctance to re-introduce conscription and added 'she cannot in 1939 find other countries willing to be slaughtered in the British interests as she did in 1914'.[45] He continued airing his grievances against the Irish press arguing that 'it took its news exclusively from Reuters and similar agencies and was consequently very hostile to Germany'.[46]

While it might have been valuable for the Irish government to have an insight into Nazi thought and propaganda during peacetime it was not helpful that Bewley replicated Nazi propaganda without any critical assessment of Nazi policymaking. Bewley, despite his pretensions, appeared to have few if any high-level insights into Nazi foreign policy formulation or government in 1938 and 1939.

43 MAI, MIS 29, 1 Jan. 1939–31 Mar. 1939.   44 NAI, DFA CRS 219/4, Bewley–Walshe, 11 Apr. 1939.   45 Ibid.   46 Ibid.

OBSTACLES TO NEUTRALITY

After Munich, de Valera increasingly advocated neutrality as the only practicable course for Irish foreign policy. For neutrality to work Germany had to be convinced of its sustainability and of the Irish government's commitment. Hempel's role became vital. In the year before September 1939, de Valera and Walshe made repeated efforts to convince him of the Irish government's determination to maintain neutrality.

The Irish government had reason to be satisfied with the measured diplomatic performance of Hempel, unlike their representative in Berlin. As Duggan has established, Hempel remained an exemplar of the 'old school' of German diplomacy which resisted Nazification and pursued cautious professionalism. De Valera and Walshe discovered that his reliable well-balanced approach was a substantial asset because unlike many of the amateur Nazi would-be diplomatists such as Petersen (the DNB representative and soon-to-be German legation's press attaché),[47] Hempel recognized the complex nature of Irish politics and the constraints placed on Irish foreign policy by its proximity to Britain. He was the best informed and most balanced German commentator on Ireland and understood the difficulties of establishing and maintaining neutrality. Hempel generally produced lengthy reports avoiding simplistic and hazardous conclusions. Rather his reports habitually and understandably reflected the uncertainty encountered in Irish foreign policy and political circles about the feasibility of neutrality, Irish defence capabilities, the importance of partition, the role of Irish nationalism and the character of the problematic Anglo-Irish relationship. Hempel's prudent reports to the AA should have acted as an antithesis to the view of the Irish state and foreign policy propagated by Bewley in Berlin.

It would have been extremely destructive, for instance, if Hempel had propounded the view that de Valera was a simple deferential Anglophile and an insincere Irish nationalist, as Bewley repeated *ad nauseam*. He understood the constraints restricting de Valera's freedom of action as he attempted to reconcile Irish republicanism and irredentism with the unavoidable reality of Ireland's geographical proximity to Britain. Worrying too would be a German overestimation of the IRA's capabilities and support. Such misinterpretations, if Hempel had confirmed them to his superiors, had the potential to wreck Irish neutrality.[48] Neutrality, to be successful, had to be viewed as placing Éire equidistant from Germany and Britain at least in overt diplomatic terms. Hempel played a crucial role in presenting an even-handed account of Irish developments and popular support for neutrality, although he doubted whether Éire had the necessary military capabilities to defend neutrality. He successfully

---

47 Dickel, *Aussenpolitik*, p. 86.   48 Ibid., p. 85.

interpreted and communicated the main lines and nuances of Irish foreign policy to Berlin.

On 31 December 1938, Hempel called on de Valera to express his good wishes for the year 1939. He reported de Valera revealed his 'greatest admiration' for German recovery after defeat in the Great War, but cautioned that in a new Anglo-German crisis no repetition of the Munich solution was possible. If war had erupted over Munich, de Valera warned that 'there would have been a great danger that what had been achieved [by Germany] would be annihilated again'. Éire remained 'impartial' in its policy towards Germany. The taoiseach, however, was dissatisfied with the Third Reich's treatment of the Catholic Church, which he suggested 'greatly prejudiced the general feeling toward Germany in Ireland, which formerly had been definitely favourable to Germany'. However, on the Jewish question, de Valera reportedly agreed with Hempel's proposition that Nazi treatment of the Jews was 'primarily ... explained by the behaviour of the Jews after the war'.[49] In line with Irish policy, de Valera was not prepared to alienate the Nazis or endanger Irish neutrality by engaging on a moral crusade on behalf of Jews. Neither was he prepared to go beyond expressing disquiet at the poor condition of church–state relations in Germany.

Throughout the early months of 1939 Hempel closely monitored all public statements and defence developments in Éire to understand its future stance in the event of war. Reporting on the Dáil debate and defence vote of early February 1939 he 'remained unconvinced' that the increase in defence expenditure to £3.2 from the paltry £2 million the preceding year represented a serious defence commitment by the Irish government. By this stage Hempel was informing Berlin that Éire would not initiate hostilities against Britain under any circumstances, except in self-defence, and that Irish neutrality was instead preparing to resist any third power seeking to use Éire as a base for operations against Britain.[50]

He also drew attention to de Valera's milestone statement in the Dáil on 16 February 1939 to the effect that neutrality would be precarious and difficult to maintain. Nonetheless, he reproduced de Valera's challenge 'that no one can hope to attack us, or violate our territory with impunity'. He even highlighted de Valera's statement during the speech that Éire had not made a mutual defence arrangement with Britain, so Éire retained its absolute freedom of choice. However, de Valera argued that if a third power invaded Éire, it was in Britain's automatic interest to eradicate that threat.[51] Implicitly, geography and strategy negated the need for an Anglo-Irish defence agreement..

Nonetheless, both Hempel and the AA remained unsure about the sincerity of de Valera's rhetoric despite his continuous repetition of it throughout the spring of 1939.[52] However, in April 1939 apparent deteriorating relations

49 DGFP, Series D, Vol. 4, Hempel–AA, doc. 285, 3 Jan. 1939. 50 Duggan, *Neutral Ireland*, p. 44. 51 Ibid., p. 45. 52 Dickel, *Aussenpolitik*, p. 87.

between Belfast and Dublin, and between Dublin and London on the issue of partition vividly highlighted to German eyes the insurmountable gulf in Anglo-Irish relations. De Valera had persisted in his high profile anti-partition campaign throughout the winter and spring of 1938–9.

De Valera stubbornly, or perhaps desperately, egged Chamberlain to continue appeasement and counselled against a preventive war. But he was frustrated by his inability to induce Chamberlain to tackle the problem of Irish partition as a means to improve Irish, and by implication British, security in the face of possible further German expansion in central Europe in the immediate aftermath of the Nazi takeover of Moravia and Bohemia.[53] On 26 April, Chamberlain introduced conscription to Britain and Craigavon sought its extension to the six counties, to the anger of northern and southern nationalists. De Valera protested strenuously to the British government that such conscription contradicted the Irish constitution which laid claim to the sovereignty of all 32 counties of the island of Ireland. Extending conscription to Northern Ireland was an 'act of aggression'.[54] Ironically it was the fallout from US President Roosevelt's 'peace appeal' to Hitler that resolved the issue.

ROOSEVELT'S PEACE APPEAL

Roosevelt's appeal on 14 April asked Hitler to desist from invading 30 named countries, including Poland, the Soviet Union, France and Britain. Éire or Ireland was not recognized as an independent state in Roosevelt's list and was coupled with Britain. Compounding Irish government chagrin was that Éire unlike some other states mentioned in Roosevelt's appeal had not been consulted in advance by the US. Other dominions of the Commonwealth had been mentioned explicitly and consulted in advance seemingly indicating they were regarded as separate sovereign entities.[55] Combining Ireland with Britain suggested Éire did not have an independent foreign policy and another self-declared neutral, the US, did not recognize Éire's right to pursue neutrality.

Hitler in response to Roosevelt on 28 April said Germany had approached each of Roosevelt's named countries and discerned that they did not feel threatened. In a sop to anti-imperialists and nationalists everywhere Hitler accused Roosevelt of hypocrisy for including states such as Syria and Palestine, which lacked the freedom to speak since they were militarily controlled by the democratic powers of France and Britain.[56] Hitler added:

---

53 Bowman, *De Valera*, p. 201.   54 Coogan, *De Valera*, p. 534.   55 Dickel, *Aussenpolitik*, p. 87; Duggan, *Neutral Ireland*, p. 46.   56 Kershaw, *Nemesis*, p. 189.

> Now, I have just read a speech by de Valera, the Irish taoiseach, in which, strangely enough, and contrary to Mr. Roosevelt's opinion, he does not charge Germany with oppressing Ireland, but he reproaches England with subjecting Ireland to continuous aggression.[57]

This rhetorical appeal to de Valera's nationalist Ireland in the midst of the conscription–partition crisis won plaudits from aggrieved Irish nationalists.[58] It was also deemed significant in Irish circles that de Valera was referred to by his formal Irish title of 'taoiseach' and this could be, and was, interpreted as signifying Hitler's recognition of Éire's independence to pursue a different foreign policy to Britain. The nationalist furore generated in Northern Ireland, in Éire and in the Irish-American community prevented the extension of conscription to Northern Ireland.

The press section of the AA was 'pleased with the reception' of Hitler's speech in Ireland and, according to Bewley, implied there had been 'a modification of the hostile attitude of the *Irish Press*, which they attribute to pressure from the Irish Government, and which they wish to reciprocate by a friendly attitude towards Ireland'.[59] Hempel also believed Ireland extended greater sympathy to Germany as a result of Hitler's explicit mention of Ireland in his speech on 28 April.[60] Indeed, there was some moderation of Irish press and popular opprobrium towards the Nazi regime as both the Irish public and government realized that neutrality would require a more impartial Irish attitude towards Germany.

Further deterioration in international relations, signalled by Hitler's renunciation of the Anglo-German naval pact and the German-Polish non-aggression pact of 1934 in his landmark 28 April speech, concentrated Irish minds.[61] Nazi sabre rattling on the issue of returning control of Danzig and the Polish corridor to Germany reinforced in Éire, as elsewhere, perceptions of how precarious was the European peace. Europe was in fact hurtling towards war. Hitler had totally misread British and French responses to his annexation Czechoslovakia in March. Anglo-French appeasement of Germany was now abandoned and Chamberlain's guarantee to protect Poland's integrity reinforced Polish resistance to Hitler's requests for the return of Danzig and the Polish corridor. Hitler remained determined to resolve the Danzig question if necessary

57 Shirer, *Rise & fall*, p. 474.   **58** Bewley noted a curious difference between the speech that Hitler actually delivered on 28 April and that printed in German and in international newspapers. Hitler had actually said 'Ireland' in his speech and this was reproduced in German newspapers, but in foreign newspapers the word had been transformed into 'Northern Ireland' (NAI, DFA, CRS 219/4, Bewley–Walshe, 4 May 1939).   **59** NAI, DFA, CRS 219/4, Bewley–Walshe, 4 May 1939. The AA press officials, however, did not expect any such change on the part of the *Irish Times*, whose editor Robert Smyllie was anti-Nazi, antifascist and pro-British.   **60** PA, AA II, R102797, Hempel–AA, 5 May 1939.   **61** Kershaw, *Nemesis*, pp 189–90.

through the use of force. On 3 April he issued a directive to the armed forces to prepare plans for an attack on Poland any time after 1 September. Hitler thought it improbable that Britain would intervene despite the British guarantee, as it had not previously put its threats into operation. Secondly, Hitler considered Poland's central European location within Germany's easy reach, and far from a Britain that preferred naval war to conventional land warfare, would prevent British intervention. Hitler thus sought a rapid, limited, localized campaign against Poland, not a global conflagration. He further attempted to deter British intervention by signing a non-aggression pact with Stalin's Soviet Union on 23 August 1939. A secret protocol to the Nazi–Soviet pact delimited Soviet and German spheres of influence in eastern Europe including a partition of Poland. The Soviet Union, not Britain or France, was seen as the major direct threat to German expansionism. Hitler believed he could isolate Poland to the extent that it would be practically suicidal for Britain to intervene.[62] Meanwhile the Danzig Nazis were activated to destabilize the situation there.

In this atmosphere of apprehension the Irish population and government renounced any moral stance against Nazi Germany as a luxury surplus to the requirement of maintaining vital national interests; it was a state incapable of influencing the outcome of any major European conflict beyond making pro-appeasement noises from the margins of Great Power politics.

HEMPEL AND NEUTRALITY

Hempel had reported in April 1939 that southern Irish opinion was unsettled by continental developments, most notably the assault on Bohemia and Moravia, and Britain's guarantee of 31 March to aid Poland if she was attacked.[63] The mentality of Irish neutrality was developing. In early May Hempel elaborated in a confidential report to the AA how de Valera's government was now more neu-tralist in its intentions.[64]

Hempel, even as he questioned de Valera's commitment to neutrality and cast doubt on de Valera' denial of secret agreements with Britain, said the vast majority of the Irish population wished to stay out of a war if possible. He noted since the Anglo-Irish treaty of 1938, the 'war scare' surrounding Munich and the recent international crises Irish national individualism *vis-à-vis* Britain had increased steadily. He thought the Irish dislike of Britain as a Great Power had also grown more prevalent. Although the Irish public had supported Chamberlain's Munich policy and remained critical of Hitler, disapproval of Britain's warlike stance towards Germany in 1939 was being voiced.

Hempel noted the domestic pressures pushing de Valera to commit to and

62 Ibid., pp 189–97. 63 Dickel, *Aussenpolitik*, p. 86. 64 PA, AA II, R102797, Hempel–AA, 5 May 1939.

define Irish neutrality in the event of a European war involving Britain. On one side stood the IRA and some elements of his own Fianna Fáil party. The former fellow fighters and the IRA would act against Northern Ireland and even Éire if de Valera chose to align with Britain. On the other side were the more Anglophile Irish nationalists in the Fine Gael and Labour parties who nonetheless favoured neutrality. Meanwhile the Anglo-Irish component of Éire's population remained resolutely opposed to Germany, because of their identification with Britain and their commitment to democracy and religious freedom. Hempel considered these competing forces were compelling de Valera to adopt a more unqualified pro-neutralist policy. Éire could join neither Britain nor Germany in a war for fear of domestic radicalization and violence. Hempel predicted that de Valera would be unable to achieve an end to partition because his stance on neutrality meant he had increasingly to differentiate Éire's identity from Britain. And emphasize its innately republican nature as a state, to the anger of the Stormont government. Hempel suggested, too, that de Valera would probably be unwilling, because of the political complexion of Éire, to abandon neutrality and side with Britain to achieve national unification.[65] This was the conclusion that the Irish government at the time wanted the German government to form.

Hempel also had a conversation with Walshe, in which it was reiterated that Éire had to adopt a neutrality policy and remain careful not to damage relations with any Great Power. Walshe added that the proximity of the islands of Ireland and Britain forced Éire to extend some special consideration to Britain if neutrality was to survive. Hempel concluded the Irish government would do everything in its power to avoid open transgressions to neutrality, although political realism required Éire to be agreeable to Britain within the limits of neutrality. He noted that this caution towards Britain was interpreted as a sign of weakness in some circles, including extreme republicans, but the Irish government was now determined to battle for neutrality.[66] Thus by May 1939 Hempel was convinced that Éire was intent on pursuing neutrality but relations with Britain together with the activities of the IRA and German agents posed substantial difficulties. Those two factors in particular weighed heavily on Irish-German diplomacy during the summer of 1939 as the crisis over Danzig and the Polish corridor escalated between Germany and Poland. The first hurdles to neutrality appeared to have been overcome but could de Valera convince the AA and other agencies in Berlin of Irish commitment to neutrality?

65 Ibid.   66 Ibid.

PREPARING FOR THE 'EMERGENCY'

The Irish government and civil service had been preparing to implement neutrality 'in time of war' since late 1938 and were drafting legislation to ensure the state's survival. A detailed Emergency Powers Order was drafted in 1939 in case war broke out. It covered subversion, rationing, official secrets, the functioning of the legal system, policing, price controls, censorship, and safeguarding supplies of food and other essentials. The issue of essential supplies was a particular concern. Could Éire achieve the minimum self-sufficiency necessary to maintain neutrality?

In April 1939 the department of industry and commerce acknowledged the constraints of Irish economic dependence on Britain from which 50 per cent of Irish imports originated and to where Éire exported approximately £18 million-worth (or 90 per cent) of its total export trade of £22.5 million in 1937. Éire would be in considerable difficulty if a war broke out as a 'high proportion' of imports consisted of essential supplies. In addition only 5 per cent of total shipping tonnage entering Irish ports in 1938 was Irish owned while 64 per cent was British owned. Thus the department's report confessed Ireland was 'very largely at the mercy of other countries, and particularly of the United Kingdom, in respect of ... external trade' so Irish economic activities could be 'completely paralysed' 'in time of war'. Export subsidies, industrialization, trade diversification and protectionism had not altered the historic pattern of Irish external trade.[67]

According to those 1937 figures Germany, Ireland's second largest trading partner, provided only 3.2 per cent of total Irish imports and 3.8 per cent Irish exports.[68] Germany had been perceived as a potentially profitable outlet for Irish agricultural produce during the Anglo-Irish Economic War but this had not been realized. Once the Anglo-Irish trading relationship began to return to normal from the mid-1930s and punitive British tariffs on Irish goods were lifted, it quickly became apparent that German prices for Irish produce were lower than those generally offered by British buyers. Transaction costs (primarily transport) and the complexity of the Irish-German annualized bargaining process meant that in 1939, during the eight-month period before the outbreak of war, Irish-German trade stagnated.

However, firms such as the ESB and the Turf Development Board continued to rely on German imported machinery, electrical apparatus, and iron and steel goods. They would experience grave inconvenience if trade with Germany was halted as a result of a British blockade of German or European ports.[69] But Éire's economic well-being 'in time of war' depended far more on a cordial relationship between Éire and Britain than between Éire and Germany. It was

67 NAI, DFA, SOF EA D. 31, memo for government, 18 Apr. 1939. 68 Ibid. 69 NAI, DFA 232/1, Boland–Warnock, 5 Oct. 1939.

deemed necessary, too, to seek alternative sources of supply to Germany.[70] Irish economic survival in time of war depended upon maintaining a working relationship with Britain, even if Britain was a belligerent and Éire was neutral, and Germany had to accept this as the necessary price of Irish neutrality.

Germany meanwhile was concerned that non-neutral members of the British Commonwealth, in particular Britain itself, could register ships under the Irish mercantile flag to safeguard supplies during a war and render ineffective any German blockade against Britain. Hempel advised Walshe on 22 July that if 'British ships were able to transfer wholesale to Irish Registry' and fly the neutral Irish flag during wartime this would create confusion and embarrassment. Walshe instantly assured Hempel that such a British ploy would not be allowed as it would critically injure Irish neutrality.[71]

DISMANTLING THE SUBVERSIVE MENACE

The Irish government was simultaneously seeking to terminate the activities of the IRA and prevent collaboration with Germany. At the outbreak of the IRA's S-Plan bombing campaign, department of justice secretary Stephen Roche advised that at a time of international unrest 'a small country cannot afford to invite attacks from without by a seeming inability to keep order within its own territory. The danger in this case becomes acute when the unlawful organisations extend their activities into other states, while using this country as a base'.[72] Fortunately, for the Irish government, the IRA's S-Plan was 'appallingly ill-conceived'[73] and was destined to be a complete failure.

The IRA and Abwehr had barely initiated worthwhile discussions before the outbreak of war. James O'Donovan, IRA director of chemicals, travelled to Hamburg to meet Abwehr II in late February 1939, late April and August. The Irish authorities had very limited information about O'Donovan's liaison work with Abwehr,[74] but Abwehr–IRA liaisons were stymied during 1939 before they could develop into a serious threat. Serious differences emerged. The Abwehr and the IRA only made contact after Pfaus' visit to Éire and the Abwehr considered the IRA's bombing campaign to be dangerously provocative. The Abwehr wanted the IRA to instead launch military operations against British troops in Northern Ireland if a war broke out between Britain and Germany. The intention was to disguise a future German war effort and give the IRA's terrorism the semi-legitimacy of a struggle for the rights of oppressed minori-

---

70 NAI, DFA, SOF, EA D. 31, dept. of supplies memo, 20 Nov. 1939. 71 NAI, DFA 241/113, Memo, 27 July 1939. 72 DFA, DT S10454B, Justice memo, January 1939. 73 Coogan, *IRA*, p. 157. 74 Neither did MI5, although in July 1939 it learnt that a conference had taken place between Admiral Canaris, Abwehr's head, and 'a responsible member of the IRA'. See O'Halpin, *MI5*, p. 43.

ties, as Nazi Germany had claimed for its actions in the Sudetenland and Danzig. The Germans believed this would also serve as a diversionary tactic in an Anglo-German war, on the model of the Easter Rising 1916, but claimed it would prove more immediately successful this time.

Precious time was wasted in rebuilding trust between O'Donovan and the Abwehr operatives after O'Donovan's third visit to Hamburg in August when a German customs officer confiscated O'Donovan's wife's undeclared cigarettes.[75] Consequently the IRA–Abwehr liaison failed to establish a *modus operandi* for cooperation during war which never progressed beyond the amateurish and comical.

The Abwehr was correct to view the S-Plan as foolhardy. Although the IRA campaign eventually killed 7 people and injured nearly 200 during 1939, such was the threat it posed to Irish security and neutrality that the Irish government crackdown was unparalleled and completed de Valera's break with his previously paternalistic attitude to the IRA. As G2 noted in the immediate aftermath of World War II, the IRA's campaign prompted the British to arrest and imprison members of the IRA units involved, ensuring the organisation lost many experienced operatives and destroying the IRA network in Britain before the outbreak of war.[76]

De Valera's government passed draconian legislation designed to destroy the IRA as an effective force using the rationale that the popular referendum on the 1937 constitution undermined IRA claims to legitimacy. Initially termed the Treason Bill, an indication of the government's attitude, the Offences against the State Bill became law on 14 June 1939. It permitted detention and imprisonment without trial of IRA members and members of other unlawful organisations.[77] The annual IRA Bodenstown commemoration of 25 June was banned.[78] On 22 August the Special Military Court to try individuals under the Offences against the State Act was established. Public opinion and the other democratic parties supported de Valera in his hardened attitude towards the IRA.

Even the suspicion that the IRA–Abwehr connection existed was potentially damaging to de Valera's neutrality stance. Any internal subversive forces which threatened British security had to be dealt with decisively. Stories alleging 'Nazi Gold for the IRA' in British newspapers during the summer of 1939 were problematic.[79] But more perilous for Éire's neutrality was the publication in the *Birmingham Post* on 7 August of rumours that a secret meeting had taken place in July 'in the wilds of Donegal between members of the IRA and certain

75 Hull, *Irish secrets*, p. 62. **76** MAI, G2/X/0093, M.L. Memo: 'Re my talk with ___', 20 Mar. 46. **77** Fanning, 'The rule of order', p. 167. Treason as closely defined by Article 39 of the 1937 Constitution had a new importance: 'Treason shall consist only in levying war against the state or assisting any state or person or inciting or conspiring with any person to levy war against the state...' **78** Lee, *Ireland*, p. 221. **79** *Birmingham Post*, 7 Aug. 1939.

German officials who hold high place in Éire'.[80] The Gardaí and G2 had already heard a more specific rumour a week earlier of a meeting that took place at a hotel in Inver, Co. Donegal whose participants included Hempel, Robert Wenzel (German legation counsellor), two members of the German colony (Dr Mer Stumpf and Franz Winkelmann), members of the headquarters staff of the IRA and General Eoin O'Duffy. Rumours circulated that the meeting took place before Hempel went to Germany on 25 July so he could report it personally to Berlin.[81] Other rumours suggested up to 25 IRA delegates attended[82] and that Theodor Kordt, counsellor at the German embassy in London, had been in Ireland in early July to arrange this IRA–German summit meeting.[83]

A kernel of truth fed these rumours. Kordt visited Éire in early July ostensibly to take a vacation in Killarney with a woman (supposedly Frau Kordt). A German citizen also owned the Drumbeg Hotel at Inver[84] and Winkelmann's children spent two weeks on holiday there in the latter half of July[85] and, both Wenzel and Stumpf were there for a few days that same month.[86] Hempel explicitly denied he had been in Donegal or had any relations with General Eoin O'Duffy.[87] It seems that the arrival of some members of the German colony for holidays in Inver coinciding with the Polish crisis led to speculation and gossip. Such scares were common during the summer of 1939. Neither the Gardaí nor G2 were able to substantiate rumours of a further meeting in August which circulated in the climate of fear gripping Éire and Europe.

HEMPEL'S CONTRIBUTION

It was most improbable that Hempel, an old school diplomat who saw professional diplomacy and espionage as two discrete spheres, would compromise his role to engage so openly with subversive forces in Éire. Hempel maintained no regular contact with the 'physical force' IRA or O'Duffy although he had developed a close personal relationship with some extreme republicans, in particular with ex-IRA member Seán MacBride who disagreed with the Seán Russell's bombing campaign against Britain.[88]

MacBride became a personal and unofficial adviser to Hempel on Irish matters in the later 1930s. Although of a radical republican and nationalist mindset, he favoured neutrality as the best policy for Éire. This 'responsible radical nationalism', as Hempel termed it, viewed Britain as the greatest threat to Irish neutrality and, if Britain invaded, believed the IRA should assist the defence of

80 Ibid. 81 MAI, G2/X/0093, Weekly miscellaneous report – D.M.D. Section "D" – Aliens, week ended 1 Aug. 1939. 82 Ibid., Connell–Archer, 17 Aug. 39. 83 O'Halpin, *MI5*, p. 43. 84 Ibid. 85 MAI, G2/X/0093, Connell–Archer, 17 Aug. 1939. 86 Ibid., two notes by Byran, n.d. (*c.*August 1939). 87 Ibid. 88 Duggan, *Neutral Ireland*, p. 64; Dickel, *Aussenpolitik*, p. 90.

the Irish state, possibly with German aid.[89] Hempel, too, by early summer considered neutrality the best possible option for Germany.[90]

His visit to Berlin between 25 and 29 July 1939[91] (passing through London beforehand to meet Kordt) was to discuss Irish-German policy in case of war and to convince the sceptical AA state secretary, Ernst von Weizsäcker, that Éire was sincere in its determination to maintain neutrality. The AA and Weizsäcker doubted the Irish government could defend itself. Hempel was also aware of the Seekreigsleitung's (German Naval Command) possible objections to Éire's neutrality and wanted to reverse their negative appraisal,[92] based on treating Ireland as an extension of Britain in 'Atlantic war' naval planning scenarios even after the Anglo-Irish agreement of 1938. It assumed the Treaty ports would be made available to Britain in 'a time of war' and that Britain could not permit Irish neutrality. Only after April 1939 did Hempel's conviction about the growing Irish commitment to neutrality begin to impact on the Seekreigsleitung's thinking. It concluded if the Irish ports were denied to Britain and Britain respected the Irish decision then Britain's Atlantic supply routes would be more difficult to defend, although it remained concerned lest Britain could camouflage imports under an Irish neutral flag. Nonetheless, on 4 August the Seekreigsleitung was prepared to accept that on balance Irish neutrality could serve German interests.[93] Hempel also persuaded the German authorities that an additional political dividend, if Germany respected neutrality, would be the gratitude of the large Irish-American population, and this would be an impediment to an Anglo-American alliance.[94]

AGREEING THE RULES OF THE NEUTRALITY GAME

Both the AA and Seekreigsleitung had been converted just in time. Hitler planned to launch his attack on Poland to coincide with the annual Nuremberg rally between 2 and 11 September. Following feigned border incidents German troops invaded Poland on 4.45 a.m. on 1 September. On 3 September Hitler received the British ultimatum demanding a ceasefire and German withdrawal from Poland that morning or the two countries would be at war. In the afternoon the French declared war. World War II had finally begun.

In the final tense days before the German invasion of Poland, the foreign services of Éire and Germany agreed the terms of Irish neutrality. On 26 August, three days after the Nazi–Soviet pact was signed, Walshe lunched with Hempel. Walshe endeavoured to downplay the role of economics while emphasizing the politics and diplomacy of Irish neutrality. He 'stated definitely that

89 Duggan, *Neutral Ireland*, p. 64.   90 Ibid.   91 MAI, G2/X/0093, Weekly miscellaneous report – D.M.D. Section 'D' – Aliens, week ended 1 Aug. 1939.   92 Dickel, *Aussenpolitik*, p. 88.   93 Ibid., p. 89.   94 Ibid., p. 90.

Ireland would remain neutral except in the case of a definite attack' by Germany on Irish territory. Walshe did not think that such a German attack was in the German interest, since 'Irish sympathy – especially in view of the strong, perhaps decisive influence, of the American-Irish against an American-British influence – could not be a matter of indifference to us'. He believed the Irish–American lobby in the US would force Britain to respect neutrality and emphasized, too, that a continuation of 'normal trade' with Britain was 'vital' for Irish survival although Éire would confine its exports to Britain to purely agricultural produce – a disingenuous claim since Éire hardly exported anything except agricultural goods to Britain and was to become Britain's larder during World War II as it had during World War I. The central objective of the conversation with Hempel was to ask for 'a formal declaration ... that Germany has no aggressive aims in Ireland, but on the contrary has sympathy for Ireland and Irish national aims – mentioning, if necessary, Northern Ireland – that she regrets Irish suffering and will attempt to keep this to the unavoidable minimum'.[95]

Three days later on 29 August, German foreign minister, Ribbentrop sent a telegram to Hempel instructing him to make a declaration to de Valera on behalf of Germany clarifying its 'friendly' attitude to Éire in light of the deteriorating international situation. Specifically Hempel was to deliver the German declaration in the most amiable manner possible, emphasising German sympathy for Irish national aspirations and German recognition of the 'difficulties involved in the geographical position of Ireland'. The central element of the declaration was to be that Germany was 'determined to refrain from any hostile action against Irish territory and to respect her integrity, *provided that Ireland, for her part, maintains unimpeachable neutrality towards us in any conflict* [author's emphasis]'. In addition, Germany agreed to minimize the 'unavoidable repercussions' for Irish trade arising from a war.[96]

Hempel duly delivered the statement to de Valera in Walshe's presence on 31 August, on the eve of the German invasion of Poland. De Valera reiterated Éire's desire to remain neutral and maintain friendly relations with Germany in the event of a war, a stance that would have to be ratified by the Dáil. He took issue, however, with Germany's requirement that Éire maintain an unimpeachable or unobjectionable neutrality, because it was easy to find objections. He appealed to Germany to accept the constraints upon Éire, stating bluntly that Irish economic dependence on Britain and Britain's vital interest in ensuring that Éire did not threaten British security necessitated the Irish maintain a certain consideration for Britain. He warned, too, of the dangers to Irish neutrality if either Britain or Germany violated Irish territorial waters, if Germany attempted to exploit anti-British radical nationalism, or if the nationalist population of

---

95 DGFP, Series D, vol. 7, doc. 303, Hempel-AA, 26 Aug. 1939. 96 Ibid., doc. 428.

Northern Ireland was abused. Hempel reported to the AA that de Valera was utterly sincere but his doctrinaire attitude was an attempt to conceal the 'real weakness' of both his and Éire's position in case of war. De Valera's citing of the possible threats to Irish neutrality was a warning against Germany taking unnecessary risks if it considered Irish neutrality as meeting its interests, while simultaneously indicating that the survival of Irish neutrality was also heavily conditional on Britain respecting it.[97] De Valera had indeed effectively encapsulated the main challenges the Irish government would have to overcome in the forthcoming war. On 2 September, one day after the German invasion of Poland, de Valera declared Irish neutrality and the Dáil legislated for a national emergency using its pre-prepared draft legislation.

CONCLUSION

However, there were still some outstanding problems if Irish neutrality was to be a success with Germany. Bewley persisted in his maverick behaviour in Berlin. Although the department had sent notice of his 1 August recall months earlier, he only appears to have informed Weizsäcker at the AA of his imminent move in early July. He used the occasion to violently abuse his own government's policy which he suggested would be anti-German out of fear of Britain.[98] This extremely unprofessional intervention by Bewley could have undermined totally Irish government efforts and Hempel's work to convince the AA that Éire was in earnest.

In a final bout of recalcitrance, Bewley on 2 August wrote a long memorandum to Walshe reiterating his well-rehearsed complaints against Irish foreign policy.[99] He set out to analyse the state of Irish-German relations in 1939 pointedly adding a criticism and a disclaimer:

> While I am aware that reports made by a Minister are never communicated to Ministers accredited in other countries and are frequently not submitted to the Minister of External Affairs, I desire to put on record a short and objective statement of the facts, in order that no suggestion may be made that I myself have any responsibility for the present state of affairs.[1]

Ireland was still regarded in Germany as a British dependency because 'foreign spectators naturally pay less attention to phrases like "Commonwealth of Nations" or "external association" than to the reality of the situation, that is, that Ireland, or the 26 counties, remains a member of the British Empire'.[2] This lack of independence, Bewley theorized, emanated from two sources: the

---

97 Ibid., doc. 484.   98 Dickel, *Aussenpolitik*, p. 89.   99 NAI, DFA, CRS 219/4, Bewley–Walshe, 2 Aug. 1939.   1 Ibid.   2 Ibid.

'inferior complex' of Irish governments and the Irish civil service which modelled themselves on British institutions;[3] and the 'lack of experience and apparent reluctance or incapacity to learn' of officials who failed to instruct their representatives abroad and answer their queries. In a calculated criticism of Walshe, secretary at the department since 1927, Bewley said:

> I desire however to suggest the possibility that the practice of all other countries during their centuries of independent national life is not less important than the views held by officials, whose experience began in the year 1922 and has since then for practical purposes been confined to Dublin.[4]

Bewley's removal left unanswered the question of why the department had allowed him to remain in a post for six years, for which he amply demonstrated his unsuitability. In Bewley's case, contemporaries considered him pro-German even before he got the post. But the saga did not end when he left Berlin. Bewley had not submitted an official letter of resignation and officials learned he had returned to Dublin in August. The department was forced to demand a written explanation for his failure for being absent from duty without leave since 3 August. A letter informed Bewley that if he did not provide a satisfactory answer by 11 September the department would seek his formal dismissal from public service.[5] This prompted Bewley to reply by letter on 11 September reiterating his objections to taking up an inferior position in the department and threatening to resign unless the minister reconsidered his position.[6]

In addition, the department of external affairs had the problem of appointing a successor to Berlin. Warnock, secretary of the Berlin legation, was appointed temporary chargé d'affaires in expectation of the imminent arrival of a replacement for Bewley. De Valera had already decided to appoint Dr T.K. Kiernan, the then acting director of broadcasting, a man deemed trustworthy and with 'considerable diplomatic experience' after spending ten years as secretary to the office of the Irish high commissioner in London, under the supervision of the experienced Dulanty.[7] A leak to the *Irish Press* prematurely disclosed his approaching 'important diplomatic appointment in a European capital' on 31 July[8] generating considerable concern because the department of finance had not yet sanctioned the appointment and, more importantly, the revelation could cause complications with the AA.[9] In the event, the finance department and the AA agreed to accept Kiernan as the new Irish minister to Germany.[10]

However, the declaration of war between Germany and Britain raised an

3 Ibid. 4 Ibid. Before Walshe was appointed the secretary in 1927, he had been acting secretary (since 1922). 5 NAI, DFA, E 86/8/39, Walshe–Bewley, 29 Aug. 1939. 6 Ibid., Bewley–Walshe, 11 Sept. 1939. 7 IP, 31 July 1939. 8 Ibid. 9 NAI, DFA 217/29, Boland–Kiernan, 1 Aug. 1939. 10 Ibid., Warnock–Walshe, 23 Aug. 1939.

insurmountable constitutional hurdle. Éire's Commonwealth status and the theory of the diplomatic unity of the British Commonwealth required that for Kiernan's appointment to Berlin to be official, the British king had to sign a letter addressed to Hitler requesting Kiernan be appointed as Irish minister to Germany. But after 3 September the British Commonwealth had severed all diplomatic ties with Germany.[11] Éire as a neutral was the exception, but an Irish government approach to the British monarch to sign the request for Kiernan's accreditation would create a political and constitutional crisis, which de Valera was anxious to avoid in view of Éire's necessity to have a good working relationship with Britain at this time of international upheaval. Kiernan could not, therefore, be appointed and Warnock had to remain as chargé. Fortunately, Warnock was one of a new wave of professional career Irish diplomats who succeeded the tainted first generation of revolutionary diplomats. He did not share Bewley's views nor did he allow himself to become personally involved in his posting.[12] Hempel, a known and trusted quantity in Irish government circles, remained in Dublin as German minister. As a high calibre professional career diplomat, his deftness in negotiating the hazards of wartime diplomacy in a neutral Ireland was to serve de Valera well. Hempel demonstrated how even in Nazi Germany a professional diplomat could still act as a moderating influence. In a sense the Irish policy of insisting that a non-Nazi should be appointed German minister to Dublin in 1937 worked and de Valera, in light of his appreciation of Hempel as a diplomat, was forever to remain grateful to Hempel personally for facilitating neutrality.

On 11 September another prospective complicating factor was dealt with when 50 members of the small German colony in Ireland, which was a potential fifth column in the view of the Irish and British authorities, were repatriated to Germany via Britain with the support of the British, grateful to facilitate the exodus. Many of those who chose to leave were politically active in the Nazi party or the Auslandsorganisation or of military age and believed it was their patriotic duty to return to Germany. A few other senior members of the colony had already left Ireland in August to attend the Nuremberg rally.[13]

Two weeks later another seven German nationals, one Dutch woman and one Pole were also to leave Éire for Britain. However, their journey was involuntary. They were Jewish refugees who had fled from Britain before and after the outbreak of war but who had now been ordered to leave Ireland by the justice department.[14]

11 Ibid.   12 See Keogh, *Ireland & Europe*, pp 53–4, 105.   13 O'Halpin, 'Intelligence and Security', p. 67; O'Donoghue, *Hitler's Irish voices*, pp 29–31.   14 MAI, G2/X/0093, Weekly miscellaneous report, D.M.D., week ended 15 Sept. 1939.

Conclusion: Secret histories

'a dangerous double game was in play' (J.J. Lee).[1]

Irish-German relations during the inter-war period were characterized by continuity, ambiguity and appeasement. In terms of continuity, Bewley and Walshe were fixtures in the Irish-German inter-war diplomatic relationship. Another element of continuity was German foreign policy indifference to Irish nationalist sensitivities. Under both the Weimar and Nazi regimes, Germany was determined to maintain Anglo-German relations to counteract French revanchism. Irish-German intimacy was a potential threat to Anglo-German friendship. Therefore, Germany, almost inevitably, subordinated Irish-German relations to greater German strategic and diplomatic considerations, although Berlin's official attitudes also reflected an unconcealed empathy with Irish nationalism.

Ambiguity permeated the stance of de Valera and the Irish government towards pre-war Nazi Germany. The government, newspapers and the Catholic Church increasingly deplored the rabid anti-religious, anti-Semitic and totalitarian nature of Nazism as it developed, particularly in the mid-1930s, although sections of Irish society were anti-Communist, anti-Semitic and disillusioned with parliamentary democracy.

De Valera and other decisionmakers and opinion leaders harboured reservations about Nazism's domestic extremes, but were well disposed towards German aspirations to revise the 1919 treaty of Versailles. According to this view, the treaty had unjustly stripped Germany of its national sovereignty, wealth, territories and population. Nationalist empathy with Germany's national degradation was linked to de Valera's and the Irish state's staunch support for the League of Nations and collective security. This led to an Irish appeasement policy. Its rationale was that nationalist slights against Germany should be admitted and corrected by the international community to satisfy Hitler's Germany and avoid a European conflict.

De Valera's disgust at the Nazis' domestic policies did not encompass the Third Reich's revisionist foreign policy until 1939. He was an appeaser. He recognized a parallel between the aspirations for a Grossdeutschland and Irish irredentism. Hence until the establishment of Nazi puppet regimes in

---

1 J.J. Lee, 'Introduction' in O'Donoghue, *Hitler's Irish voices*, p. xiii.

Czechoslovakia in March 1939, de Valera's foreign policy discriminated between the excesses of Hitler's internal rule and the apparent legitimacy of German foreign policy. Thereafter, Hitler's regime was deemed reprehensible in both its internal and external policies in private, though publicly Irish survival required neutrality and hence recognition of Hitler's regime.

Thus as the European situation deteriorated during 1938 the initially inchoate forces and considerations of security, strategy, stability and national interest forced de Valera to weigh the benefits and costs associated with making a difficult decision between belligerence and neutrality. He managed to achieve, during 1938 and 1939, what many had supposed was impossible: to convince the Great Powers that Éire as a nominal dominion would not be a belligerent in a war in which Britain participated. He also succeeded in ensuring Irish neutrality would not lead to a conflict with Britain. How did Éire accomplish this difficult task?

Colonel Dan Bryan of G2 was perhaps the most articulate advocate that Irish neutrality was impossible, although he later played a crucial role in safeguarding it. In 1936 he argued neutrality would prove acceptable to Britain's opponents in a war and would be unacceptable to Britain as it would disrupt British defence and trade. Bryan contended that in a European war Britain would demand extensive cooperation from the Saorstát and that it was therefore very difficult, perhaps impossible to sustain a neutrality policy.[2]

The return of the Treaty ports altered such calculations because Éire could choose, in theory at least, not to act as a base for British operations in a war.[3] The new objective was to convince the British government that Éire would remain neutral in any future conflict but also retain a 'certain consideration' for Britain's legitimate security and strategic interests.

Undoubtedly, Hempel was correct in his assertion that de Valera's government was vulnerable as it attempted to implement disarmed neutrality. Geostrategic reality inevitably twinned the two islands of Ireland and Britain, and Éire was economically dependent on Britain. Although these facts proved highly unpalatable to the militant IRA and to unreconstructed Anglophobic nationalists, such as Bewley, who advocated taking advantage of Britain's difficulties, the reality remained that Éire's fate was to a great degree entwined with Britain's. Despite Irish nationalism's sensitivities, the new Irish state also inherited the British preference for parliamentary democracy which, in addition to its profound Catholic confessionalism, ensured it was, in sentiment, at odds with German Nazism by the latter 1930s.

---

2 MAI, G2/0057, Fundamental factors affecting Irish defence, May 1936.   3 Lee, *Ireland*, p. 214.

A 'SPECIAL CONSIDERATION' OR A 'PHONEY NEUTRALITY'?

The Irish war experience commenced long before the shooting started in Poland in September 1939. As J.J. Lee has indicated, a 'dangerous double game' started between Éire and Germany.[4] But this game had originated much earlier than commonly supposed. It can tentatively be dated to late 1938 or early 1939 when the possibilities of a destructive IRA–German subversive nexus against Britain and/or Northern Ireland developed. Ironically just as German espionage and military strategic services realized Éire's disruptive potential for British planning, thereby reversing their aloof attitude to Éire, de Valera had already acknowledged that Britain had legitimate national security interests in regard to Éire. Two parallel dimensions characterized the emerging Irish-German 'double-game': the covert (intelligence, espionage and counterespionage) and the overt (diplomacy).

De Valera engaged in a dual-track policy of secret cooperation with Britain and formal neutral diplomacy with Nazi Germany. His purpose was to ensure that externally neutrality appeared impartial, while developing a surreptitious and considerate intelligence relationship with Britain. The extension of a 'special consideration' to British security interests was in part an acknowledgement that the survival of neutrality would depend on this. Using partition as justification de Valera retreated from any suggestion of a formal defence agreement after the 1938 Anglo-Irish treaty and most pointedly after the return to Irish control of the Treaty ports. He ensured the territory of Éire would not become a base for attack on Britain and attempted to persuade Britain of Éire's 'goodwill'. His persuasiveness prevailed through reiteration of the argument that an Anglo-Irish defensive alliance would split the Irish people causing violent conflict just as did World War I and the Anglo-Irish Treaty of 1921.

De Valera suggested it was preferable that Ireland was a 'friendly neutral' rather than an unreliable ally internally split between pro- and anti-British elements as had happened between 1916 and 1918. He hinted to the British authorities that he did not want a defence pact with Britain as a sign of good faith in return for later reward, as had happened during the Great War, to then discover that the Irish people no longer supported him. He did, however, sanction the reactivation of G2 as Éire's counterespionage agency and its close relationship with MI5.[5] Meanwhile overt diplomacy continued as the Irish government marketed its neutrality policy as the most mutually beneficial solution for all parties concerned, both internal and external to Éire.

---

4 J.J. Lee, 'Introduction' in O'Donoghue, *Hitler's Irish voices*, p. xiii.   5 This is well documented and well-known. See O'Halpin, *Defending*; O'Halpin, *MI5*, passim for example.

INTELLIGENCE, COUNTERESPIONAGE AND SUBVERSION

Informal Anglo-Irish intelligence cooperation survived during World War II because it was relatively unproblematic for Éire to maintain this link by leaving it in the hands of discreet individuals such as Bryan at G2. Irish and British fears about German espionage and possible German efforts to recruit republican dissidents in the IRA for a war against Britain required a covert liaison between G2 in its counterespionage role and MI5. This exchange of intelligence (e.g., vetting immigrants and suspects, exchanging and collating data on suspects) led to the rapid development of Irish capabilities in postal censorship and telephone tapping in late 1938.

The Munich crisis spurred Irish fears about Nazi espionage and subversion.[6] Only then did the movements and activities of Axis nationals resident or visiting the country come under the close scrutiny of the Irish authorities who pooled information with MI5. The Irish and indeed the British authorities had some cause, as it transpired, to be concerned about German and IRA activities and a possible alliance of convenience between the two.

In deciding whether to pursue, neutrality or belligerence, the Irish government's challenge lay in reconciling conflicting demands. As the likelihood of war between the democracies and fascists grew, Irish policymakers found themselves having to mediate between the British government's demand for Irish support in the event of war (including British use of the Treaty ports) and the German aspiration that Éire should not materially strengthen a British war effort. The implications of Éire's strategic location had to be confronted by the Irish government moving military strategy from the background to centre stage in late 1938.

As long as the concept of collective security prevailed, military strategy had not been important. But in the mid-1930s realpolitik had reduced the League of Nations to a talking shop and a small power such as Éire had to deal with the precariousness of its strategic position in an increasingly hostile environment. Since the breakdown in the efficacy of the League of Nations, de Valera had repeatedly promoted neutrality as the most effective solution to Irish foreign and domestic dilemmas in the event of a European war in which Britain was a belligerent.[7]

The challenge then was to satisfy both Britain and Germany and to ensure both sides respected Éire's position. Integral to meeting this challenge were the answers to questions about Ireland's capabilities and intentions. Did Éire have the political will, military resources and domestic support necessary to pursue its favoured policy? It was in this respect that neutrality was most vulnerable

6 O'Halpin, *Defending*, pp 142–5.   7 Salmon, *Unneutral*, pp 94–8.

because of Ireland's limited defence capability and economic dependence on Britain. No less important was the absolute priority of maintaining a national consensus in a situation where Irish republican extremists (the IRA) threatened to use Éire as a base of attack against Northern Ireland and Britain in event of an Anglo-German conflict and to subvert the Irish state in the event of Éire forming a defensive alliance with Britain against Germany. Related to this was the fear that the IRA and other malcontents were a valuable asset for German espionage and sabotage against Britain. At the other side of the spectrum sections of the Anglo-Irish minority maintained strong pro-British sympathies.

Between these two positions stood the vast majority of moderate Irish nationalist opinion and, despite some variation of opinion and emphasis, the three main democratic parties of Fianna Fáil, Fine Gael and Labour. The three parties began to realize that a certain commonality existed between them and a non-partisan Irish neutrality policy emerged. All retained a distinctive antipathy, to a greater or lesser degree, towards joining an alliance with Britain. This did not, however, imply they were antidemocratic or profascist. Although there had been flirtations with fascist ideas earlier in the early 1930s (particularly within Cumann na nGaedheal), Fianna Fáil was now accepted as a normal democratic player and the Irish party system settled into a democratic consensus. By the late 1930s Nazism had proven itself abhorrent to much of Irish public and political opinion because of its domestic and external policies, use of force, *fait accomplis*, anti-Christianity, persecution of minorities and so on. Thus a more mature national democratic consensus was emerging. But this was still fragile and a widespread and palpable sense of looming international disaster could undermine it. Perhaps for the first time since the foundation of an independent Irish state the possibility of a non-partisan view of the 'national interest' was forming in the face of both external and internal security threats. A realization was also emerging in the government and opposition parties that if Éire was to survive in a hostile international environment a workable national consensus was required.

Unfulfilled expectations remained a potent defining issue. As a youthful nation–state still heavily involved in the processes of nation–state building and whose general population remained quite introverted, Irish government and populist priorities remained strongly informed by the processes of consolidating a sense of a separate Irish national identity. Irish foreign policy and identity were defined to a large extent by reference to Ireland's position in relation to Britain, its erstwhile ruler. An acute sense of nationalist resentment against Britain remained prominent in the typical Irish nationalist psyche and identity, although most vestiges of Irish subordination to Britain had been eliminated. Despite the successful establishment of sovereignty in the 26 counties, stauncher democratic republicans within Fianna Fáil still found the ambiguous link with the Commonwealth problematic. The end of partition and unification was aspired to by the vast majority of democratic nationalist opinion, not only those in Fianna Fáil, the self-styled 'republican' party. The evidence indicates de Valera recognized Éire lacked the means to achieve this. Consequently, partition was transformed into a crucial tool to persuade Nazi Germany that Éire would remain neutral and to provide a means to resist British, French, Commonwealth (and later US) pressure for Éire to join the emerging anti-German alliance after March 1939.

In retrospect, the inevitable consequence of anti-partitionist rhetoric and neutrality was an increased differentiation between Éire and Northern Ireland likely to ensure that unification became a distant aspiration, although an end to partition had never seemed near before 1938 in any case. But in 1938 and 1939 it was impossible for de Valera to square the circle of conflicting priorities, to choose sides in a war, to maintain domestic stability, to recognize Éire's relative defencelessness, to manage the strategic importance placed on Éire by both sets of potential belligerents to the satisfaction of all, to preserve Irish security, and to resolve the last remaining Anglo-Irish dispute concerning partition. Despite his continuous stream of anti-partitionist propaganda in the winter of 1938 to 1939, he may have recognized that claims to end partition were about to be irretrievably damaged in the short- to medium-term by opting for neutrality. Perhaps his anti-partitionism was purely for public consumption and diplomatic leverage? Maybe he contemplated the growing gap between North and South was one of the acceptable costs of non-participation in a war? Or possibly not.

These calculations and dynamics had to be considered in the framing of an Irish foreign policy as war grew more likely after the end of 1938. Neutrality materialized as the most likely direction for Irish policy during 1939. It is against this background of uncertainty concerning the Irish position in a potential conflict that Irish-German relations must be viewed in the final period of inter-war peace. From the German perspective de Valera's neutralist intentions had to be repeatedly questioned and probed: was de Valera seriously committed to neutrality? Was Irish neutrality feasible in view of the island's proximity to Britain? Could Éire maintain a credible neutrality policy throughout a war and resist British pressure and/or enticements? Would minimum German requirements for Irish military neutrality be met if Éire displayed a 'certain consideration' for Britain in food and manpower supplies but still managed to prevent use of the 26 counties as a base by Britain or her allies?

The Irish government and diplomatic service, despite the hampering of Bewley, repeatedly assured Germany that neutrality was the most feasible policy for Éire and best suited Germany's interests. A similar persuasive effort was required with Britain and its prospective allies. The process of persuading all domestic and international parties that Irish neutrality was the best policy was already unconsciously underway in 1938, long before the outbreak of war which both de Valera and Chamberlain (and in fact Hitler) had hoped to avoid. That process of cajoling, persuading, convincing, and resisting pressures from the soon–to-be belligerents to establish and maintain credible neutrality was unending. The Irish diplomatic war of defending neutrality began long before the formal outbreak of European hostilities.

De Valera's neutralist foreign policy required patient and reliable Irish diplomats in Berlin, Paris, London and Washington DC who would adhere strictly to the government line. Bewley's removal from Berlin during 1939 was essential. By the late 1930s a new generation of young Irish professional diplomats was emerging which would replace many of the 'revolutionary diplomats' (inherited from the War of Independence). Many of the latter were either leaving the diplomatic service for reasons of age and ill-health or were being replaced as a result of Dublin's dissatisfaction with their performance. The removal of Bewley proved to be exceptional in light of the rancour it created. The controversy generated was a major irritation to the Irish government during this precarious period and had serious repercussions for Irish representation in Berlin when war broke out.

FINAL THOUGHTS

During WW2, De Valera maintained neutrality for national self-preservation motives and demonstrative effect. It was not a display of common cause with Germany. On the contrary, it was a 'benevolent neutrality' towards Britain. Meanwhile, Bewley pursued an eccentric course and returned to Axis Europe once war started, to follow his chosen path as a 'Wild Goose' and remain a barb in the side of Irish diplomatic considerations during World War II. Binchy, antithetically, pursued his academic interests becoming a Fellow of an Oxford College. He was then seconded to the press section of the British foreign office for war service. He was appointed to report on Italian affairs because 'The Foreign Office felt that he was too biased to be asked to report on the Germans'.[8] Concurrently tens of thousands of Irish men and women from diverse backgrounds took the personal decision to emigrate to Britain and in the process made a substantial contribution to the British war effort.[9] Most perceived little difficulty at the time in reconciling their Irish identity with fighting in the British armed forces or contributing on the equally vital home front against Nazism. Therefore the first two Irish ministers to Berlin and many Irish people found themselves on opposite sides of the conflict while de Valera tried to maintain the 'middle way' symbolising the dilemmas which many Irish citizens faced. There are numerous complex histories of the Irish role in the

8 Duggan, *Neutral*, p. 34.   9 R. Doherty, *Irish volunteers in the Second World War* (Dublin, 2002); R. Doherty, *Irish men and women in the Second World War* (Dublin, 1999); Aidan McElwaine, 'The oral history of the volunteers' in B. Girvin & G. Roberts (eds), *Ireland and the Second World War* (Dublin, 2000), pp 107-20.

Second World War.[10] Complexity, difference and confusion characterised Ireland's war (as it did its inter-war experience).

De Valera's government and administration was forced to persist in its 'dangerous double game' with Germany and with the Allies, too. Even as Nazi Germany maintained diplomatic recognition of Irish neutrality understanding that de Valera's denial of the treaty ports to Britain complicated British naval defence, it made efforts to recruit ultra-republicans and the IRA for its own purposes and even produced its own Operation Green (Fall Grün) for an invasion of Éire. Abwehr's ineptness in comprehending the Irish situation tended to minimize the danger from this quarter. Nazi Germany developed its own largely ineffective radio service for Éire during wartime (Irland–Redaktion) dedicated to pro-Nazi propaganda which aimed to reinforce the Irish popular will to maintain neutrality and heighten the Irish sense of nationalist grievance against Britain.

As the war progressed, and it became apparent after 1940 that Britain would not fall to German invasion, the Allied camp's growing strategic initiative strengthened the Irish government's special considerations to Britain and by extension to the Allies. Releasing Allied internees en masse across the border (while keeping Axis internees within the jurisdiction), aiding British codebreaking, passing on meteorological information, and turning a blind eye to hundreds of plain clothed Allied top brass flying through Foynes Airport in unmarked flying boats (or clippers) on their transatlantic trips, all became part of the day-to-day business of neutrality. Pragmatism was the order of the day at the time when Churchill and de Valera publicly exchanged insults about German espionage and the Treaty ports, feeding British resolve and Irish nationalism respectively but also ironically serving to sustain the myth that Éire was a pro-German neutral. De Valera compounded this mythology by making the serious error of offering his condolences to Hempel on the death of Hitler in 1945 out of a determination to adhere to strict diplomatic protocol and also arising out of de Valera's personal sense of gratification to Hempel for having conducted German diplomacy in such a professional matter during the many difficult days before and during the war that had actually been vital to sustaining Irish neutrality. The Irish government was, therefore, ironically better served by the German representative to Éire between 1937 and 1945 than its own problematical minister in Berlin between 1933 and 1939. It might be more appropriate to term Charles Bewley Hitler's diplomat and Hempel de Valera's representative in light of their respective contributions to the accurate representation of Irish foreign policy during this period of Irish, European and global turmoil.

---

10 G. Roberts, 'Three narratives of neutrality: historians and Ireland's war', in B. Girvin & G. Roberts, *Ireland and the Second World War*, pp 165-80.

Select bibliography

UNPUBLISHED SOURCES

Dublin Archdiocesan Archives
    Edward Byrne papers
Franciscan Archives, Killiney
    De Valera papers (now in UCDA)
Military Archives of Ireland (MAI)
    General Files
    Irish Military Intelligence (G2) files
National Archives of Ireland (NAI)
    Department of Foreign Affairs (DFA)
        Early Papers Series, 1919–24
        Confidential Reports – Berlin, Paris, League of Nations, and Rome
        Legation Files – Berlin
        Main Departmental Registry Files
        Secretary's Office Files – A and P files
    Department of Finance (DFIN)
    Department of Justice (DJ)
    Department of An Taoiseach (DT)
    Department of Trade and Commerce (DIC)
National Library of Ireland, Dublin (NLI)
    Art O'Brien papers
    Richard Irvine Best papers
Political Archives, Berlin (PA)
    Auswärtiges Amt (AA)
Public Records Office, London (PRO)
    Dominions Office (DO)
    Foreign Office (FO)
    Cabinet Office (CAB)
Trinity College Dublin, Manuscripts Collection
    Eleanor Knott papers
University College Dublin, Archives Department (UCDA)
    De Valera papers
    Ernest Blythe papers
    Dan Bryan papers
    George Gavan Duffy papers
    Patrick McGilligan papers

PUBLISHED PRIMARY SOURCES

Dáil Éireann Debates
Documents on British Foreign Policy, 1919–1939 (HMSO, London)
Documents on German Foreign Policy, 1918–1945 (HMSO, London)
Documents on Irish Foreign Policy, 1919–1945 (Royal Irish Academy, Dublin)

Newspapers

Berliner Tageblatt	*Irish Independent*
Birmingham Post	*Irish Press*
Cork Examiner	*Irish Times*
Daily Express	*Kölnische Zeitung*
Daily Telegraph	*Sunday Press*
Evening Herald	*Völkischer Beobachter*

SECONDARY SOURCES

Ahmann, R., A.M. Birke & M. Howard (eds), *The quest for stability: problems of west European security, 1918–1957* (Oxford, 1995)

Barcroft, S.A., 'The international civil servant: the League of Nations career of Sean Lester, 1929–1942' (unpublished PhD, TCD, 1972)

—— 'Irish foreign policy at the League of Nations, 1929–1936', ISIA, 1:1 (1979)

Bell, P.M.H., *The origins of the Second World War in Europe* (Harlow, 1997, 2nd ed.)

Bergen, D.L., 'Catholics, Protestants, and Christian anti-Semitism in Nazi Germany', *Contemporary European History*, 27: 3 (1994)

Bewley, C., *Hermann Göring and the Third Reich* (New York, USA, 1962)

—— *Memoirs of a wild goose* (Dublin, 1989)

Berghahn, V.R., *Modern Germany: society and politics in the twentieth century* (Cambridge, 1987, 2nd ed.)

Bielenberg, A. (ed.), *The Shannon scheme and the electrification of the Irish Free State: an inspirational milestone* (Dublin, 2002)

Binchy, D.A., 'Heinrich Brüning', *Studies*, 21 (Sept. 1932)

—— 'Adolf Hitler', *Studies*, 22 (Mar. 1933)

—— 'Paul von Hindenburg', *Studies*, 26 (June 1937)

Bowman, J., *De Valera and the Ulster question, 1917–1973* (Oxford, 1982)

Bracher, K.D., *The German dictatorship: the origins, structure and consequences of National Socialism* (London, 1985)

Brandon, P., *The dark valley: a panorama of the 1930s* (London, 2000)

Briscoe, R. (with Alden Hatch), *For the life of me* (Boston and Toronto, 1958)

Buchanan, T. & M. Conway (eds), *Political Catholicism in Europe, 1918–1965* (Oxford, 1996)

Bullock, A., *Hitler: a study in tyranny* (London, 1968, revised ed.)

Burke, B.V., *Ambassador Frederic Sackett and the collapse of the Weimar Republic, 1930–1933* (Cambridge, 1994)

Burleigh, M., *The Third Reich: a new history* (London, 2000)

Butler, H., *Independent spirit* (New York, 1996)

Canning, P., *British policy towards Ireland, 1921–1941* (Oxford, 1985)

—— 'Yet another failure for appeasement? The case of the Irish ports' *International historical review*, 4: 3 (1982)

Carr, W., *A history of Germany, 1815–1945* (London, 1969)

—— *Arms, autarky and aggression: a study in German foreign policy, 1933–1939* (London, 1981)

Carroll, J.M., 'Owen D. Young and German reparations: the diplomacy of an enlightened businessman', in K.P. Jones et al. (eds) *U.S. diplomats in Europe, 1919–1941* (Oxford, 1981)

Carroll, J.P., *Ireland in the war years, 1939–1945* (Newton Abbot, 1975)

Carter, C.J., *The shamrock and the swastika* (California, 1977)

Clark, E., *Corps diplomatique* (London, 1973)

Coogan, T.P., *The IRA* (London, 1980)

Coppa, F.J. 'The Vatican and the dictators between diplomacy and morality', in Wolff & Hoensch, *Catholics, the state, and the European radical right* (Boulder, 1987)

Cornwell, J., *Hitler's pope: the secret history of Pius XII* (London, 1999)

Craig, G.A. & F. Gilbert (eds), *The diplomats, 1919–1939* (New York, 1972)

Cronin, A., *Samuel Beckett: the last modernist* (London, 1996)

Cronin, M., *The Blueshirts and Irish politics* (Dublin, 1997)

—— & J.M. Regan (eds), *Ireland: the politics of independence, 1922–49* (London, 2000)

Daly, M.E., *Industrial development and Irish national identity, 1922–1939* (New York, 1992)

Dickel, H., *Die deutsche Aussenpolitik und die Irische Frage von 1932 bis 1944* (Wiesbaden, 1983)

Dodd, M., *My years in Germany* (London, 1939)

Dodd, W.E. Jr. & M. Dodd, *Ambassador Dodd's diary* (New York, 1941)

Doerr, P.W., *British foreign policy, 1919–1939* (Manchester, 1998)

Doherty, R., *Irish men and women in the Second World War* (Dublin, 1999)

—— *Irish volunteers in the Second World War* (Dublin, 2002)

Duggan, J.P., *Neutral Ireland and the third Reich* (Dublin, 1989)

—— *A history of the Irish army* (Dublin, 1991)

Elsasser, M., *Germany and Ireland: 1000 years of shared history* (Dublin, 1997)

Emsley, C., A. Marwick & W. Simpson (eds), *War, peace and social change in twentieth century Europe* (Milton Keynes, 1989).

Fanning, R., *Independent Ireland* (Dublin, 1983)

—— '"The rule of order": Eamon de Valera and the IRA, 1923–40' in J.P. O'Carroll et al., *De Valera and his times* (Cork, 1983)

Fest, J.C., *Hitler* (London, 1974)

Fischer, J. & J. Dillon (eds), *The correspondence of Myles Dillon, 1922–1925: Irish–German relations and Celtic Studies* (Dublin, 1998)

Fisk, R., *In time of war: Ireland, Ulster and the price of neutrality, 1939–45* (London, 1983)

François-Poncet, A., *Souvenirs d'une ambassade à Berlin* (Paris, 1946)

Friedländer, S., *Nazi Germany & the Jews*, vol. 1, *The years of persecution, 1933–1939* (London, 1997)

Fromm, B., *Blood and banquets: a Berlin social diary* (Glasgow, 1943),

Gageby, D. *The last secretary general: Sean Lester and the League of Nations* (Dublin, 1999)

Gellately, R., *Backing Hitler: consent and coercion in Nazi Germany* (Oxford, 2001)

Germanus, 'The present position of Catholics in Germany', *Studies*, 34 (June 1935)

Gilbert, M., *Sir Horace Rumbold: portrait of a diplomat, 1869–1941* (London, 1973)

—— *Britain and Germany between the wars* (London, 1976, 2nd ed.)

Girvin, B. & G. Roberts (eds), *Ireland and the Second World War* (Dublin, 2000)

Goldstone, K., ' "Benevolent helpfulness"? Ireland and the international reaction to Jewish refugees, 1933–9', in Skelly & Kennedy, *Irish foreign policy* (Dublin, 2000)

Griffiths, R., *Fellow travellers of the right: British enthusiasts for Nazi Germany* (London, 1980)

Hale, O.J., *The captive press in the Third Reich* (Princeton, 1973)

Henderson, N., *Failure of a mission: Berlin, 1937–1939* (London, 1940)

Hiden, J., *Germany and Europe, 1919–1939* (London, 1977)

—— *The Weimar Republic* (London, 1996)

Hitler, A., *Mein Kampf* (translated by R. Manheim, introduced by D.C. Watt, London, 2001)

Hovi, K., 'Security before disarmament, or hegemony? The French alliance policy, 1917–1927', in Ahmann et al. (eds), *The quest for stability* (Oxford, 1993)

Hull, M., 'German military intelligence operations in Ireland', 1939–1945 (PhD thesis, UCC, 2000)

—— *Irish secrets: German espionage in wartime Ireland, 1939–1945* (Dublin, 2002)

Johnson, P., *A history of the Jews* (London, 1995)

Jones, K.P. & A. DeConde (eds), *U.S. diplomats in Europe, 1919–1941* (Oxford, 1981)

Keatinge, P., *The formulation of Irish foreign policy* (Dublin, 1973)

Kennedy, K.A., T. Giblin & D. McHugh, *The economic development of Ireland in the twentieth century* (London, 1988)

Kennedy, M., *Ireland and the League of Nations, 1919–1946: international relations, diplomacy and politics* (Dublin, 1996)
—— 'Chicanery and candour: the Irish Free State and the Geneva Protocol, 1924–5', IHS, 29: 115 (1995)
—— 'The Irish Free State and the League of Nations, 1922–1932' (PhD thesis, UCD, 1993)
—— 'The Irish Free State and the League of Nations, 1922–32: the wider implications', ISIA 3:4 (1997)
—— 'Prologue to peacekeeping: Ireland and the Saar, 1934–5', IHS, 30:119 (May 1997)
—— 'Civil servants cannot be politicians: the professionalisation of the Irish foreign service, 1919–22', ISIA, 8 (1997)
—— 'Our men in Berlin: some thoughts on Irish diplomats in Germany, 1929–1939', ISIA,10 (1999)
Kennedy, M. & J. Skelly (eds), *Irish foreign policy, 1919–1966: from independence to internationalism* (Dublin, 2000)
Keogh, D., 'Origins of Irish diplomacy in Europe, 1919–1921', *Études Irlandaises*, 7 – Nouvelle Serie (Dec. 1982)
—— 'De Valera, the bishops and the red scare' in J.P. O'Carroll, et al. (eds), *De Valera and his times* (Cork, 1983)
—— 'The Irish constitutional revolution: an analysis of the making of the constitution'; *Administration*, 35: 4 (1988)
—— 'Eamon de Valera and Hitler: an analysis of international reaction to the visit to the German minister, May 1945', ISIA, 3: 1 (1989)
—— 'Profile of Joseph Walshe, secretary, department of foreign affairs, 1922–46', ISIA, 3: 2 (1990)
—— *Ireland & Europe, 1919–1989: a diplomatic and political history* (Cork/Dublin, 1990)
—— *Twentieth-century Ireland: nation and state* (Dublin, 1994)
—— *Ireland and the Vatican: the politics and diplomacy of church–state relations, 1922–1960* (Cork, 1995)
—— *Jews in twentieth century Ireland: refugees, anti-Semitism and the Holocaust* (Cork, 1998)
Kershaw, I., *The Nazi dictatorship: problems and perspectives of interpretation* (London, 1988)
—— *Hitler, 1889–1936: hubris* (London, 1998)
—— *Hitler, 1936–1945: nemesis* (London, 2000)
Kirkpatrick, I., *The inner circle: Memoirs* (London, 1959)
Klemperer, V., *The Klemperer diaries, 1933–1945* (London, 2000)
Knowlson, J., *Damned to fame: the life of Samuel Beckett* (London, 1996)
Kolk, E. (translated by P.S. Falla), *The Weimar Republic* (London,1988)
Krausnick, H. & Broszat, M., *Anatomy of the SS state* (London, 1982)
Laffan, M. (ed.), *The burden of German history, 1919–1945* (London, 1988)
Lamb, R., *Mussolini and the British* (London, 1997)
Lee, J.J., 'Policy and performance in the German economy, 1925–35: a comment on the Borchardt thesis', in M. Laffan, *The burden of German history* (London, 1988), pp. 131–50
—— *Ireland, 1912–1985: politics and society* (Cambridge, 1989)
Leitz, C. (ed.), *The Third Reich: the essential readings* (Oxford, 1999)
—— 'The German Roman Catholic hierarchy and the Saar plebiscite of 1935', *Political science quarterly*, 79: 2 (1964)
Lewy, G. *The Catholic Church and Nazi Germany* (New York, 2001)
Longford, Earl & T.P. O'Neill, *Eamon de Valera* (London, 1971)
Lowry, D., 'New Ireland, old empire and the outside world, 1922–49: the strange evolution of a "Dictionary Republic"', in M. Cronin & J.M. Regan (eds), *Ireland: the politics of independence, 1922–49* (London, 2000)
MacManus, F. (ed.), *The years of the great test, 1926–39* (Cork/Dublin, 1967)

Maier, C.S., *Recasting bourgeois Europe: stabilization in France, Germany and Italy in the decade after World War I* (Princeton, NJ, 1975)

Maier, C.S, 'Recasting Bourgeois Europe', in C. Emsley et al., *War, peace and social change in twentieth century Europe* (Princeton, 1989)

Manning, M., *The Blueshirts* (Dublin, 1970)

Mansergh, N., 'Ireland: external relations, 1926–1939', in F. MacManus, *The years of the great test* (Cork, 1978)

McDonough, F., *Neville Chamberlain, appeasement and the British road to war* (Manchester, 1998)

McGarry, F., *Irish politics and the Spanish Civil War* (Cork, 1999)

McMahon, D., *Republicans and imperialists: Anglo-Irish relations in the 1930s* (New Haven and London, 1984)

—— 'Ireland, the dominions and the Munich crisis', ISIA, 1: 1 (1979)

—— '"A transient apparition": British policy towards the de Valera government, 1932–5', IHS, 22: 88 (1981)

Meenan, J., 'From free trade to self-sufficiency', in F. MacManus (ed.), *The years of the great test* (Cork, 1978)

Mendes-Flohr, P., *German Jews: a dual identity* (London, 1999)

Molohan, C., *Germany and Ireland, 1945–1955: two nations' friendship* (Dublin, 1999)

Mommsen, W.J. & L. Kettenbacker, L. (eds), *The fascist challenge and the policy of appeasement* (London, 1983)

—— 'The breakthrough of the National Socialists as a mass movement in the late Weimar Republic', in M. Laffan (ed.), *The burden of German history* (London, 1988)

—— 'The failure of the Weimar Republic and the rise of Hitler', in M. Laffan (ed.), *The burden of German history* (1988)

Moynihan, M. (ed.), *Speeches and statements by Eamon de Valera, 1917–73* (Dublin, 1980)

Munting, R. & B.A. Holderness, *Crisis, recovery and war: an economic history of continental Europe, 1918–1945* (London, 1991)

Murphy, B.P., *John Chartres: mystery man of the treaty* (Dublin, 1995)

Nicholls, A. & E. Matthias (eds), *German democracy and the triumph of Hitler: essays in recent German history* (London, 1971)

Nicholls, A.J., *Weimar and the rise of Hitler* (London, 1974)

Nolan, A. 'Joseph Walshe and the management of Irish foreign policy, 1922–1946: a study in diplomatic and administrative history' (unpublished PhD, UCC, 1997)

O'Beirne, G & M. O'Connor, 'Siemens-Schuckert and the electrification of the Irish Free State', in A. Bielenberg (ed.), *The Shannon scheme and the electrification of the Irish Free State* (Dublin, 2002)

O'Brien, C.C., *Passion and cunning: essays on nationalism, terrorism and revolution* (New York, 1988)

O'Carroll, J.P. & J. A. Murphy (eds), *De Valera and his times* (Cork, 1983)

O'Connor, P.B, 'France and the Free State: Franco-Irish diplomacy, 1922–31' (unpublished MA, Maynooth, 1991)

O'Donoghue, D., *Hitler's Irish voices: the story of German radio's wartime Irish service* (Belfast, 1998)

Ó Drisceoil, D., *Peadar O'Donnell* (Cork, 2001)

O'Driscoll, M., 'Irish–German relations, 1929–32: Irish reaction to Nazis', *Cambridge review of international affairs*, 11: 1 (1997)

—— 'Irish–German Commerce, 1932–39: Irish foreign trade policy, the Economic War and the Anglo-Irish-German diplomatic triangle', ISIA, 10 (1999)

—— 'Inter-war Irish–German diplomacy: continuity, ambiguity and appeasement in Irish foreign policy', in Michael Kennedy & Joseph Skelly (eds), *Irish foreign policy, 1919–1969: from independence to internationalism* (Dublin, 2000)

—— '"To bring light unto the Germans": Irish recognition-seeking, the Weimar Republic and the British commonwealth, 1930–2', *European history quarterly*, 33: 1 (2003)

O'Halpin, E., 'Intelligence and security in Ireland, 1922–45', *Intelligence and national security*, 5: 1 (1990)

—— *Defending Ireland: the Irish State and its enemies since 1922* (Oxford, 1999)

Ó Lúing, S., *Celtic Studies in Europe and other essays* (Dublin, 2000)

O'Malley, P.F., *The origins of Irish neutrality in World War II, 1932–1938* (Ann Arbor, Michigan, 1980)

O'Neill, M., *From Parnell to de Valera: a biography of Jennie Wyse Power 1858–1941* (Dublin, 1991)

Oppen, B.R., 'Nazis and Christians', *World politics*, 21: 3 (1969)

Orlow, D., *The history of the Nazi party*, 1, *1919–1933* (Newton Abbot, 1971).

Overy, R.J., *Goering: the 'Iron Man'* (London, 1984)

Parker, R.A.C., *Chamberlain and appeasement: British policy and the coming of the Second World War* (London, 1993)

Patterson, R., 'Ireland and France: an analysis of diplomatic relations, 1929–1950' (unpublished MA, UCC, 1993)

Peukert, D.J.K., *The Weimar Republic: the crisis of classic modernity* (London, 1991).

Pokorny, J., *A history of Ireland* (London, 1933)

Raymond, R.J., 'The economics of neutrality: the United States, Great Britain and Ireland's war economy, 1937–1945' (PhD, University of Kansas, 1980)

Regan, J.M., *The Irish counter-revolution, 1921–1936* (Dublin, 1999)

Rhodes, A., *The Vatican in the age of dictators, 1922–1945* (London, 1973)

Ritchie, A., *Faust's metropolis: a history of Berlin* (London, 1998)

Ross, G., *The great powers and the decline of the European states system* (London, 1983)

Roth, A., *Mr Bewley in Berlin: aspects of the career of an Irish diplomat, 1933–1939* (Dublin, 2000)

—— 'Gun running from Germany to Ireland in the early 1920s', *Irish Sword*, 22: 88 (2000)

Salmon, T., *Unneutral Ireland: an ambivalent and unique security policy* (Oxford, 1989)

Shirer, W.L., *Berlin diary: the journal of a foreign correspondent, 1934–1941* (London, 1941)

—— *The rise and fall of the Third Reich* (London, 1998)

Sloan, G.R., *The geopolitics of Anglo–Irish relations in the 20th century* (London, 1997)

Steiner, Z., 'The League of Nations and the quest for security', in Ahmann et al. (eds), *The quest for stability* (Oxford, 1993)

Stephen, E., *Spies in Ireland* (London, 1965)

Stewart, G., *Burying Caesar: Churchill, Chamberlain and the battle for the Tory party* (London, 1999)

Toland, J., *Adolf Hitler* (New York, 1976)

Towle, P., 'British security and disarmament policy in Europe in the 1920s', in Ahmann et al. (eds), *The quest for stability* (Oxford, 1993)

Vaïsse, M., 'Security and disarmament: problems in the development of the disarmament debates, 1919–1934', in Ahmann et al. (eds), *The quest for stability* (Oxford, 1993)

Vital, D., *A people apart: a political history of the Jews in Europe, 1789–1939* (Oxford, 2001)

Weinberg, G.L., *The foreign policy of Hitler's Germany: diplomatic revolution in Europe, 1933–36* (Chicago, 1970)

Weitz, John, *Hitler's diplomat: Joachim von Ribbentrop* (London, 1997)

Whyte, J.H., *Church and state in modern Ireland, 1923–1979* (Dublin, 1980, 2nd ed.)

Williams, T.D., 'De Valera in power' in F. MacManus (ed.), *The years of the great test* (Cork, 1978)

Williamson, D.G., *The Third Reich* (Harlow, Essex, 1990)

Wilson, H.R., *A career diplomat. The third chapter: the Third Reich* (Westport, Conn, 1960)

Wolff, R.J. & J.K. Hoensch (eds), *Catholics, the state, and the European radical right, 1919–1945* (Boulder, 1987)

Addendum to the Bibliography

Aan de Wiel, J., *The Irish factor, 1899–1919: Ireland's strategic and diplomatic importance for foreign powers* (Dublin, 2008)

—— *East German intelligence and Ireland, 1949–90: espionage, diplomacy and terrorism* (Manchester, 2015)

Bourke, E. (ed., trans.), *Poor green Erin: German travel writers' narratives on Ireland from before the 1798 Rising to after the Great Famine* (Oxford, 2012)

Cunningham, J. & R. Fleischmann, *Aloys Fleischmann (1880–1964): immigrant musician in Ireland* (Cork, 2010)

Doerries, R.R., *Prelude to the Easter Rising: Sir Roger Casement in imperial Germany* (London, 2001)

Egger, S. (ed.), *Cultural/literary translators: selected Irish-German biographies II* (Trier, 2015)

Elvert, Jürgen, *Vom Freistaat zur Republik: der außenpolitische Faktor im irischen Unabhängigkeitsstreben zwischen 1921 und 1948* (Bochum, 1989)

Fischer, J., *Das Deutschlandbild der Iren 1890–1939: Geschichte – Form – Funktion* (Heidelberg, 2000)

—— & G. Holfter, *Irish-German studies: creative influences – selected Irish-German biographies* (Trier, 2009)

Garvin, T., *The lives of Daniel Binchy: Irish scholar, diplomat, public intellectual* (Dublin, 2016)

Hamilton, H., *The speckled people* (London, 2003)

Holfter, G., *Erlebnis Irland – Deutsche Reiseberichte über Irland im zwanzigsten Jahrhundert* (Trier, 1996)

—— *German-speaking exiles in Ireland, 1933–1945* (Amsterdam, 2006)

—— *Heinrich Böll and Ireland* (Newcastle upon Tyne, 2011)

—— *The Irish context of Kristallnacht: refugees and helpers* (Trier, 2014)

—— & H. Dickel, *An Irish sanctuary: German-speaking refugees in Ireland, 1933–1945* (Berlin, 2017)

—— & H. Rasche (eds), *John Hennig's exile in Ireland* (Galway, 2004)

Keogh, N., *Con Cremin: Ireland's wartime diplomat* (Cork, 2006)

Keown, G., *First of the small nations: the beginnings of Irish foreign policy in the inter-war years, 1919–32* (Oxford, 2015)

Kluge, H., *Irland in der deutschen Geschichtswissenschaft, Politik und Propaganda vor 1914 und im Ersten Weltkrieg* (Frankfurt, 1985)

Leach, D., *Fugitive Ireland: European minority nationalists and Irish political asylum, 1937–2008* (Dublin, 2009)

Lenehan, F., *Intellectuals and Europe: imagining a Europe of the regions in twentieth-century Germany, Britain and Ireland* (Trier, 2014)

—— *Stereotypes, ideology and foreign correspondents: German media representations of Ireland, 1946–2010* (Oxford, 2016)

Lerchenmüller, J., *Keltischer Sprengstoff: eine wissenschaftsgeschichtliche Studie über die deutsche Keltologie von 1900 bis 1945* (Tübingen, 1997)

McCarthy, K, 'Éamon de Valera's relationship with Robert Briscoe: a reappraisal', *Irish Studies in International Affairs*, 25 (2014)

—— *Robert Briscoe: Sinn Féin revolutionary, Fianna Fáil nationalist and revisionist Zionist* (Oxford, 2016)

Mc Cormack, W.J., *Blood kindred: W.B. Yeats: the life, the death, the politics* (London, 2005)

Mullins, G., *Dublin Nazi no. 1: the life of Adolf Mahr* (Dublin, 2007)

O'Connor, Siobhan, '"Alien family": the impact of the Aliens Act 1935 and subsequent orders on the family in Ireland', *History of the Family,* 13:4 (2008)

Ó Dochartaigh, P., *Julius Pokorny, 1887–1970* (Dublin, 2004)

O'Donoghue, D., *The devil's deal: the IRA, Nazi Germany and the double life of Jim O'Donovan* (Dublin, 2010)

O'Driscoll, M., D. Keogh & J. Aan de Wiel (eds), *Ireland through European eyes: Western Europe, the EEC and Ireland, 1945–1973* (Cork, 2013)

O'Halpin, E., *Spying on Ireland: British intelligence and Irish neutrality during the Second World War* (Oxford, 2008)

O'Reilly, C. & V. O'Regan (eds), *Ireland and the Irish in Germany – reception and perception* (Baden-Baden, 2014)

Remmel, H., *From Cologne to Ballinlough: a German and Irish boyhood in World War II and post-war years, 1946–49* (Aubane, 2009)

Sagarra, E., *Kevin O'Shiel: Tyrone nationalist and Irish state-builder* (Dublin, 2013)

Sterzenbach, Christopher, *Die deutsch-irischen Beziehungen während der Weimarer Republik, 1918–33: Politik – Wirtschaft – Kultur* (Berlin, 2009)

Index